Trade Union Handbook

Trade Union Handbook

A guide and directory to the structure,
membership, policy and personnel
of the British trade unions

Second Edition

ARTHUR MARSH
*Senior Research Fellow in Industrial Relations
at St Edmund Hall, Oxford*

Gower

Published by

Gower Publishing Company Limited,
Westmead, Farnborough, Hants, England

First edition 1979
Second edition 1980

Marsh, Arthur Ivor
   Trade union handbook. – 2nd ed.
   1. Trade-unions – Great Britain
   I. Title
   331.88′0941   HD6664

ISBN 0-566-02208-7

Printed in Great Britain by Biddles Limited, Guildford, Surrey

Contents

Foreword

J.E. MORTIMER
Chairman of ACAS

I am pleased to learn of the publication of a new edition of the Trade Union Handbook. It has already established itself in the literature of industrial relations. The Handbook is a helpful source of reference. Trade unions play an important part in modern industrial and commercial life and it is essential that all who participate in collective bargaining or have other dealings with trade unions should have information about them readily available.

A lot of work has gone into compiling this Handbook. It is not an easy task to provide a concise and accurate account of so many different organisations. Fortunately the author and his team already have an established reputation for the quality of their work.

Preface

In 1861 there appeared, under the imprint of Thomas Jones, of 19 Great Chapel Street Soho, and the auspices of the London Trades Council, the *First Annual Trades' Union Directory* for the United Kingdom. Regrettably there is no record of the continuation of the Council's initiative and the first Directory appears to have been the last. Since that time, although to this day some excellent local directories exist, there has been a gap in the national provision of information about trade unions. For many years the Department of Employment and the departments of state which preceded it have produced, and regularly updated, a *Directory of Employers' Associations, Trade Unions, Joint Organisations etc.*,* and the Statistical Statement submitted to annual Trades Union Congresses has contained a list of affiliated unions and their addresses. Neither source has given information about unions other than at head office level.

This Handbook, in addition to providing details of head office addresses and national office bearers, also gives information about district and branch organisation where this is appropriate and available, together with a brief sketch of each union's background, coverage, method of operation and, where the union would wish it, of its current policies. The details given have been supplied by the unions themselves, subject only to editorial adaptation in order to obtain a degree of consistency of treatment between one entry and another. In a very few cases it may be the policy of a union not to make available information giving the names and addresses of full-time or lay officials. Where unions failed to respond to our inquiries, and there have been very few of these, we have provided such names and addresses as are already publicly available from other sources, particularly the Department of Employment's *Directory*.

A glance through the list of contents on page v will show that the Handbook does more than provide useful details about individual unions. In particular it also attempts to give a commentary on the legal status, structure, finance, and organisation of the trade union movement and on some of the issues in which it is currently involved. This, and the commentary on the work of federations and of the Trades Union Congress are, with the exception of information from

---

*HMSO; compiled by the Department of Employment, Statistics Division D2, Orphanage Road, Watford, Herts. WD1 1PJ.

sources noted and acknowledged*, entirely the responsibility of the author. Any views expressed are his alone and should not be attributed to any of the organisations, unions, or individuals who have contributed to much of this compilation.

This, the second edition of the Handbook, has been expanded and updated. The success of the first edition was obvious from the enthusiastic response which greeted its publication. Our thanks are due to the unions which have so readily responded to our enquiries and commented on how useful they themselves find the book.

The Handbook would not have been possible without the kindly and understanding encouragement of Ken Graham, Head of the Organisation and Industrial Relations Department of the TUC, nor without the patient application in Oxford of John Fray of St Peter's College and Jenni Atkinson, whose skill in disentangling and ordering complex information remains to me a matter for astonishment and admiration.

Special thanks are due to Mr Mel Doyle of the Workers' Educational Association for permission to reproduce his bibliography of official trade union histories, originally published by the WEA in their series *Bibliographies in Trade Union Studies*.

St Edmund Hall,   ARTHUR MARSH
Oxford
February 1980

---

*In particular of George Bain and Robert Price and of the Editor of the *British Journal of Industrial Relations* for permission to use the invaluable data on trade union membership, density and growth contained in Part I.

Part 1
The Trade Union Movement in the United Kingdom

Background and recent developments
The Trades Union Congress and regional TUCs

Background and recent developments

Legal status

The British trade union movement is unquestionably the oldest in the world. A few current trade unions can claim a continuous existence from the end of the seventeenth century and many more from the eighteenth. It was not, however, until the Trade Union Act 1871 that they acquired the basis of a legal identity which, after many vicissitudes, has persisted to the present time. This puts little in the way of any group seeking to operate for trade union purposes. Any organisation in Great Britain or Northern Ireland[1] may lawfully do so if it consists wholly or partly of workers and if among its principal purposes is that of bargaining, or even consulting, with an employer or employers about terms and conditions of work, or if it has been established, as in the case of a trade union federation, to regulate relationships between trade unions themselves.[2] Trade unions cannot be companies registered under the Companies Act 1948, registered friendly societies *per se*, or, with exceptions, other types of corporate bodies whose *principal* purpose does not fall within the statutory definition of a trade union.[3] After the first year of their existence they are statutorily required to keep proper accounts and to submit an annual return to the Certification Officer for Trade Unions and Employers' Associations in London, or in the case of Scottish unions to an Assistant Certification Officer in Edinburgh and in Northern Ireland to the Registrar of Friendly Societies in Belfast. All but a handful of known trade unions do so. At the end of 1977 there were about 570 such organisations known to these officers in the UK, including 24 with head offices in Scotland and 12 in Northern Ireland. This figure can give a false impression of numbers. Some of those organisations formally identified as trade unions are, in practice, area or local constituents of national organisations. The National Union of Mineworkers is an example of this. When such technical 'double-counting' is eliminated, the total number of unions operating in the UK at that time was not 570, but nearer to 480. The total membership of these unions was about 12.8 millions (13.1 millions at the end of 1978).[4] Of these, 112, with a total membership of 11.8 millions, were affiliated to the Trades Union Congress based in London (at the end of 1978 the figures were 112 unions and 12.1 million members). Those TUC unions with membership in Wales were also affiliated to the Wales Trade Union Council in Cardiff and those with membership in

3

Scotland, with the addition of purely Scottish unions, to the Scottish Trades Union Congress based in Glasgow.

All but about seventy of the organisations known to the Certification Officers are 'listed'. *Listing* is a formality provided that the organisation concerned is a trade union within the definition laid down in the Trade Union and Labour Relations Act 1974. It is also voluntary so far as individual unions are concerned. But it does have some advantages which are not easily disregarded. Unlisted unions enjoy no tax relief on provident or friendly benefits; nor can they make effective applications for *certificates of independence* under s.8 of the Employment Protection Act 1975. Since the possession of such a certificate is necessary to enable a union to take advantage of some of the provisions of that Act such a status is not lightly to be ignored. Without it no union can use the procedure statutorily laid down for obtaining recognition for collective bargaining purposes where this is denied by an employer (ss.11–16, EPA) or claim that recognised terms and conditions of work should be applied to its members (Schedule 11, EPA); nor can it assert a statutory right to information for collective bargaining under the Act (ss.17–21, EPA), to protection for its members as trade unionists (ss.53–56, EPA) or to time off work for them for trade union activities (ss.57–62, EPA). By the end of 1978, 70 per cent of listed trade unions had applied for certificates of independence and 56 per cent obtained them, including substantially all those affiliated to the Trades Union Congress. The decision whether a trade union should receive a certificate of independence rests, except after appeal on a matter of fact or of law, with the Certification Officer (Employment Protection (Consolidation) Act 1978 s.136(3)), who has quite simply to be satisfied that the union concerned (s.30(1) TULRA) is not under the domination or control of an employer or group of employers or liable to such interference from such an employer or bodies as will tend to such control.

All trade unions falling within s.28 of the Trade Union and Labour Relations Act, whether listed or not, and whether certificated or not, may operate lawfully; they also enjoy such protection as the law affords. Two legal considerations are of particular importance. The first is that collective agreements between trade unions and employers are not legally enforceable unless they are in writing and contain a provision to that effect (s.18, TULRA); the second arises out of the immunity which trade unions enjoy against actions for torts or civil conspiracy when acting 'in contemplation or furtherance of a trade dispute' (s.13, TULRA).

The absence of legally enforceable collective agreements in the United Kingdom ensures the wholly 'voluntary' nature of its industrial relations. Neither trade unions nor employers can sue each other for failures to abide by the agreements they have made with each other; they are 'gentlemen's agreements' honoured for themselves and not because legal consequences might follow if they are not. Each party is left to exercise control over itself and over its

4

own members. They usually succeed in doing so, though there are exceptions. It remains true, however, that if a trade union makes an agreement which is not acceptable to its members, that agreement is unlikely to stick no matter what pressure the union puts upon them to honour it. It can, in the final resort, do no more than persuade. Discipline laid down in trade union rules can be applied to those who dissent if they are few in number. It can rarely be applied to the many. For his part the employer can rarely, even if he wishes, persuade a trade union to accept a legally enforceable collective agreement. But most employers are themselves sceptical about the practical authority of the courts to enforce such things and would prefer to pursue agreement rather than fruitless litigation.

Even more important is the protection which the law affords to trade unions in pursuing their bargaining functions to the extreme of taking industrial action. There is, as Lord Denning, Master of the Rolls, has frequently assured us, no 'right to strike' in the United Kingdom. Workers who strike *after giving proper notice* are, in effect, terminating their contracts of employment, not suspending them;[5] workers who strike *without notice* are individually breaking their contracts and no employer would be wrong in assuming that in such circumstances those contracts were at an end. No employer faced by a strike has any obligation to take the strikers back, though, as the law now stands, he must take none or all. He can replace his whole labour force or none of it; he cannot discriminate between those strikers whom he would be prepared to accept back to work and those he would not (EPA (CA) s.62). The effectiveness of this on the employer's side can be seen in the Grunwick dispute of 1976–77 in which no amount of union pressure could force the employer to take back the striking part of his work force. On the other hand, in other circumstances the provision serves to protect the union. Well organised labour forces are difficult to replace in a country where workers' solidarity is great and where the organisation of 'scab' labour has rarely been in evidence in recent years.

The protection of trade unions against actions for torts while engaged in actions 'in contemplation or furtherance of a trade dispute' is of particular significance. Neither trade unions nor their members enjoy any *general* immunity from legal action being taken against them. As unincorporated associations trade unions can be sued in the courts in respect of acts of negligence, nuisance, breach of duty resulting in personal injury and breach of duty connected with the ownership or control of property (TULRA s.14(2)), while their members are liable for whatever criminal acts they commit, and for some as especially relating to trade disputes – using violence, intimidating others, or injuring property, persistently following other persons from place to place, hiding tools or clothes, 'watching and besetting'.[6] But a trade union can at present pursue its bargaining with employers under the certain assurance that, however this affects the employers concerned, or other employers, or their customers, the union cannot be sued for civil wrongs arising – for conspiring to induce its members to breach their contracts of employment or to induce, either directly or indirectly, breaches of commercial contracts, e.g. those to purchase or deliver goods.

The trade union movement in the United Kingdom is probably the least hedged around by legal restrictions of any trade union movement in the world and possibly the movement most encouraged by government in the past. These characteristics are mainly the result of history and tradition. The period preceding the Trade Union Act 1871 reflected the high noon of Victorian *laissez-faire*. Having liberated itself from the shackles of pre-nineteenth century government control and witnessed the failure of repressive legislation to prevent trade union growth, it seemed by the 1870s simple common sense to industry that it should be allowed to make its own arrangements with organised labour free of interference from the courts. If this could only be done by ensuring that the courts were unable to intervene in trade union affairs, so be it. This hardly seemed to be conferring 'immunities' upon the unions themselves, for industry was sceptical of the capability of the law to achieve anything useful and convinced of its own capacity to handle the problem.

Had the UK industrial revolution taken place a century later it may be that a different view would have emerged. In the years before 1970 it became the view of influential members of the Conservative Party that it was not too late to turn back the tide of history and to follow the example of the United States of America in establishing a positive (rather than the currently negative) framework of law in which trade unions, employers and their associations could operate. The advice of the Donovan Commission was overruled. In the Industrial Relations Act 1971 the Heath government was intent on going much further than merely patching up the voluntary system.[7] The Act represented a wholly new approach. Trade unions were, in effect, to be licensed on good behaviour. Collective agreements were to be legally enforceable unless otherwise determined by their signatories and the whole edifice of industrial relations was to be presided over by a National Industrial Relations Court which would act both as ultimate judge and as maker of new industrial relations law.

The 1971 Act did not work. Trade unions refused for the most part to co-operate and employers to depart from the principles of voluntarism. Its provisions were, with some exceptions on matters guaranteeing the rights of individuals at work, a dead letter and disowned by the government itself before it left office in 1974. The current Trade Union and Labour Relations Act 1974 buttressed by the Employment Protection Act of the following year restored the legal position to its pre-1971 condition on terms marginally more favourable to the unions. In particular the EPA emphasised the importance of the activities of a new body, the Advisory, Conciliation and Arbitration Service, in encouraging the extension of collective bargaining, particularly through the operation of a new statutory procedure for obtaining trade union recognition for independent trade unions where employers were reluctant to concede this.[8] It also ruled that ACAS should provide for industry codes of practice as guidance in such matters as the disclosure of information for collective bargaining purposes and on time off for trade union activities.

Such a tendency of government to favour the growth of trade unionism was, as already noted, not new. The Act of 1871 and the legislation which followed could be so interpreted. In 1906 and in 1964, Parliament thought fit to fend off actions by the courts which might hamper trade union operation and growth. The Whitley Committee of 1917-19 took the view that trade union involvement and recognition were desirable in the interests of industrial peace and 'self-government' and this led, among other things, to the unionisation of the Civil Service with government approval. Trade unionism has been similarly encouraged in the statutes establishing new public corporations from those in civil aviation to iron and steel, and by the Fair Wages Resolutions of the House of Commons. Trade unions have, nevertheless, seldom thought of themselves as asking for governmental support, still less governmental preference. In this sense the 1974 and 1975 Acts represent a departure from tradition. They were blatantly based upon demands made by the unions in return for their co-operation in a 'Social Contract' designed to bring a Labour government back to power in succession to the Conservative government of Mr Heath. It remains to be seen whether this more overt type of approach towards trade union protection and growth will become a permanent part of the trade union movement's attitude to government when Labour is in power, and whether the trade union movement will repeat its resistance to Mr Heath in also actively seeking to negative the legislative reforms promised by the 1979 Thatcher government and begun in the Employment Bill of December of that year.

A note of three further aspects of the law relating to trade unions completes this brief survey of the situation. These relate to the 'check-off' and the closed shop, to picketing and to political funds. Where the first of these is concerned, no statutory provisions exist which make it lawful for employers to deduct trade union dues from the wages and salaries of their employees. Many deductions are unlawful under the Truck Acts. At common law check-off deductions are not among them provided that there is an agreement to deduct, either with the individual or with the union concerned. Nor, where the latter applies, can the individual unilaterally cancel his deduction.[9] Check-off practice, which does much to stabilise trade union membership, has evolved uncontroversially within the law until somewhat more than 50 per cent of trade unionists have their dues collected by this method.

The closed shop has, by contrast, been subject to the bitterest argument. Before 1971 it broke no law, though the courts frequently awarded in favour of plaintiffs who claimed that they had been wronged by closed shop agreements or arrangements. The 1971 Act, following and building upon federal labour statutes in the United States, made pre-entry closed shops[10] illegal and made it an unfair industrial practice to discriminate against non-union members unless an agency shop had been set up making it possible for him to be a 'dues to charity' or a 'contributing non-member' or unless a legally constituted 'approved closed shop' existed. These provisions caused great difficulty and were, as in the United States, substantially ineffective in outlawing closed shops maintained by informal, but effective, pressures by trade union members. Legislation replacing the Industrial Relations Act 1971, restored the closed shop as an entirely legal object of trade union activity and, where a 'union membership agreement' (or arrangement) exists, made it fair for the employer to dismiss any person who refused to join on grounds other than genuine religious belief (EPA(CA) s.58(3)), a term since construed by the courts to take into account individual convictions as well as the tenets of any particular sect.[11]

The law on picketing, a practice almost unknown in the two decades following the end of the Second World War but now not uncommon, has changed very little since 1906. It is a criminal offence to use violence or intimidation (see above) and the right to picket is confined to peaceful persuasion only (s.15, TULRA). No right exists to stop vehicles. Of long standing also is the Trade Union Act 1913 which authorises trade unions, on the adoption of rules approved by the Certification Officer, to maintain political funds and to do so by a 'contracting out' process, i.e. by allowing those not wishing to pay the levy to contract out of so doing. (In Northern Ireland 'contracting in' still applies.) Political funds, and those only, may be used by trade unions for the support of political objects.

Trade union structure and finance

Trade unions have always been numerous in industrial Britain. In the nineteenth century, when the foundations of so much of the trade union movement was laid, this was principally the result of the desire of groups of craftsmen in widely spaced centres to establish such control as they could over wages in their localities, to assist members tramping in search of work and in many cases to provide sick, accident, burial and other benefits in addition. The first Trade Union Directory, compiled in 1861, lists branches of numerous craft societies in no fewer than 405 towns in the UK, many of them relating to national organisations such as the famous Amalgamated Society of Engineers, founded in 1851 and the predecessor of the present-day Amalgamated Union of Engineering Workers, the Amalgamated Society of Tobacco Manufacturers and the United Operative Stone Masons of Scotland, but others of more purely local importance, such as the Edge-tool Hardeners and the Fork-grinders of Sheffield and the Framework-knitters of Nottingham.

Unions for labourers without specific skills to sell on the labour market were more difficult to establish and are reckoned to have played but a small part in trade union development until the Great Dock Strike of 1889. Will Thorne's Gasworkers' and Ben Tillett's Dockers' Union, both set up in that year, came to be seen as the origins of those general worker amalgamations dominant from the early 1920s, the present General and Municipal Workers' Union and the Transport and General Workers' Union. 'General unionism', depending on numerical strength rather than scarcity value, and upon bargaining rather than 'craft control', thus became established alongside societies of skilled workers.

At much the same time other organisations of workers began to arise determined to aspire to 'industrial unionism', in part as a revolutionary creed, and in part as a system of trade union organisation. For a time this affected existing unions such as the Electricians and the Foundryworkers, adding to the *pot pourri* of trade union types and objectives. Today, in practice, trade unions are more uniform in their approach and in their preference for collective bargaining with employers, though they still differ significantly according to their origins, and new 'types' of union have appeared to cater for different groups of employees, especially those catering for non-manual workers. A few 'white collar' unions originated in the 1850s and 1860s but it is more accurate to think of non-manual organisations as a child of the 1890s. They rapidly became established in some sectors of the civil service and later in the public sector generally as a result of the Whitley Committee recommendations of 1917–19, but failed to make significant inroads into private industry until the late 1960s. Today they are a significant force in the trade union movement.

Numbers of trade unions in the United Kingdom have steadily declined over a long period. In the 1930s there were rather more than 1,000. By the time the Second World War ended, this number had fallen by about one-quarter and, by the 1970s, by about one-half. Many unions have disappeared; many have amalgamated to form larger unions. As collective bargaining institutions have become established and as existing unions have found means of defending their positions, it has become increasingly difficult for new organisations to become established. Overall, membership has grown to levels undreamed of by the founding fathers of the last century. The 1.6 millions of 1892 have become the 13.1 millions of 1978 (Figure 1).

Overall growth has not been achieved easily or without setbacks. The First World War, which, so long as its influence lasted, emphasised and protected trade unionism, served to produce by 1920 a national trade union membership of over 8 millions. The economic depressions of the 1920s and 1930s cut this figure almost by half.

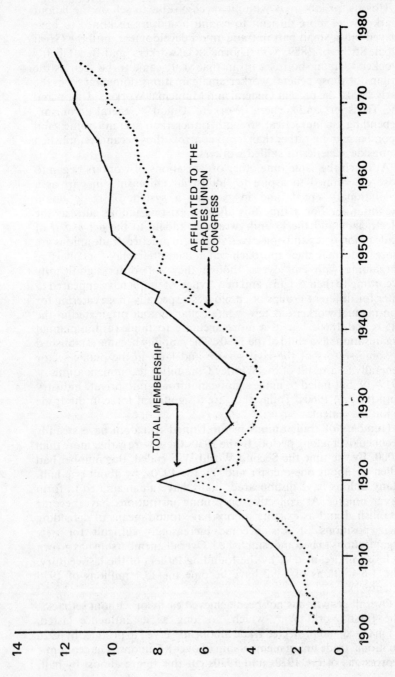

Figure 1 Membership of trade unions 1900–78

AFFILIATED TO THE TRADES UNION CONGRESS

TOTAL MEMBERSHIP

Table 1
Total trade union membership and density in the United Kingdom: selected years, 1892–1978

Year	Labour force '000	Annual change in labour force %	Total union membership '000	Annual change in union membership %	Density of union membership %
1892	14,126	–	1,576	–	11.2
1901	16,101	–	2,025	–	12.6
1911	17,762	–	3,139	–	17.7
1913	17,920	–	4,135	–	23.1
1917	18,234	–	5,499	–	30.2
1920	18,469	–	8,348	–	45.2
1923	17,965	–	5,429	–	30.2
1933	19,422	–	4,392	–	22.6
1938	19,829	–	6,053	–	30.5
1945	20,400	–	7,875	–	38.6
1948	20,732	–	9,362	–	45.2
1949	20,782	+0.2	9,318	– 0.5	44.8
1950	21,055	+1.3	9,289	– 0.3	44.1
1951	21,177	+0.6	9,535	+2.6	45.0
1952	21,252	+0.4	9,588	+0.6	45.1
1953	21,352	+0.5	9,527	– 0.6	44.6
1954	21,658	+1.4	9,566	+0.4	44.2
1955	21,913	+1.2	9,741	+1.8	44.5
1956	22,180	+1.2	9,778	+0.4	44.1
1957	22,334	+0.7	9,829	+0.5	44.0
1958	22,290	– 0.2	9,639	– 1.9	43.2
1959	22,429	+0.6	9,623	– 0.2	42.9
1960	22,917	+1.7	9,835	+2.2	43.1
1961	23,112	+1.3	9,916	+0.8	42.9
1962	23,432	+1.4	10,014	+1.0	42.7
1963	23,558	+0.5	10,067	+0.5	42.7
1964	23,706	+0.6	10,218	+1.5	43.1
1965	23,920	+0.9	10,325	+1.0	43.2
1966	24,065	+0.6	10,259	– 0.4	42.6
1967	23,809	– 1.1	10,188	– 0.7	42.8
1968	23,667	– 0.6	10,200	+0.1	43.1
1969	23,603	– 0.3	10,479	+2.7	44.4
1970	23,446	– 0.7	11,187	+6.8	47.7
1971	23,231	– 0.9	11,135	– 0.5	47.9
1972	23,303 (22,959)	+0.3	11,359	+2.0	48.7 (49.4)
1973	23,592 (23,244)	+1.2	11,456	+0.9	48.5 (49.2)
1974	23,689 (23,339)	+0.4	11,764	+2.7	49.6 (50.4)
1975	23,522 (23,172)	– 0.7	12,193	+3.6	51.8 (52.6)
1976	23,538 (22,539)	+0.1	12,386	+1.5	52.6 (54.9)
1977	24,074 (22,619) *	+1.0	12,846	+3.7	53.3 (56.0)
1978	24,000 (22,700)*	–	13,112	+2.1	54.6 (57.0)

Source: Robert Price and George Sayers Bain, 'Union Growth Revisited', *British Journal of Industrial Relations*, Vol. XIV, No. 3, revised and updated.
From 1972 the labour force data are derived from Annual Censuses of Employment (in brackets), with numbers of unemployed added.

*Estimated

Economic recovery and the outbreak of the conflict of 1939–45 restored the position but did not lead to further notable growth. In the 1950s and early 1960s, the proportion of the labour force organised in trade unions actually fell (see Table 1), a fall which was not convincingly arrested until about 1970. Five years later, for the first time in British trade union history, more than one-half of the total labour force was in trade union membership. Despite rising unemployment, that proportion is still modestly increasing. In 1980 there are almost 3 million more members than there were in the 1960s, with apparently more to come.

Price and wage movements have throughout the twentieth century been influential in determining ebb and flow in trade union growth. Rapid downward pressures tend to discourage it as they did in the 1920s and 1930s; rapid upward pressures, like those of the inflationary 1970s, may well have had the opposite effect, encouraging employees to join unions in the hope that collective action would defend their living standards against the threat posed by soaring consumer prices.[12] But this is not the whole story. Institutional changes and structural movements over the past decade have altered the character of trade unionism so much as to make comparison with the stagnant 1950s and 1960s partially invalid and generalisations about the reasons for growth correspondingly difficult to formulate.

These changes have owed relatively little to the Donovan Commission or to the attempts of governments to reform industrial relations law. On the one hand they relate to the increasing importance of workplace organisation in British industrial relations, on the other to the decline of traditional areas of trade union strength and their replacement by membership in hitherto lightly organised areas of white collar workers and among women.

British trade unionism in the nineteenth century arose from the grass roots – from the spontaneous desire of workers to protect their trade interests as Victorian industry expanded and diversified. It was the trade unionism of the workshop, built around small groups of craftsmen associating where necessary into district committees and, for limited purposes only, into national organisations. Some industries developed machinery for settling grievances and resolving problems at national level but it was for the most part not until the First World War that national bargaining began to appear. The interwar depressions reinforced such bargaining and the authority of national officials of unions by making trade union activity in the workplace so vulnerable to action by employers that few shop stewards or other workplace representatives survived to operate on their members' behalf.

And so it remained until shortly before the Second World War when, as rearmament gathered pace, workshop bargaining began to revive. The war and the success of governments in avoiding a subsequent economic collapse like the one which had destroyed trade union membership after 1918 ensured that such bargaining, though affected by the closing of wartime factories and the consequent disbanding of shop steward organisations within them, did not on this occasion disappear. Instead, particularly after the middle 1950s, it began to expand apace, rapidly overtaking in importance to trade union members the national agreements which provided only for minimum wages and conditions which, in circumstances of high employment, could readily be improved on by activity at the workplace.

In the 1950s and 1960s British workers learned the lesson that, if they were to better their wages and conditions, they had to become organised within their factories and offices and to seek to improve their lot by their own efforts rather than relying upon paid officials to do the work on their behalf. Here was a recipe for increased membership within the trade union movement and means were at hand to ensure that such membership, once acquired, did not readily slip away. Shops became '100 per cent' as soon as numbers and strength were sufficient to cut off supplies of non-unionists, and from the later 1960s the check-off became a convenient device, short of a closed shop, which could be used to stabilise membership. From small beginnings at least 2 million trade unionists were having their trade union dues collected by their employers as payroll deductions by 1966; today the proportion is much higher, some unions having 90 per cent or more of their subscription income collected in this way, reliably, without fear of defalcations and, above all, in circumstances sufficiently painless to make continuing membership easy for the individual and decisions to discontinue membership relatively difficult (in the sense that the employer and/or the union have to be informed of a decision to have check-off facilities individually withdrawn).

Table 2
TUC industrial groups with large membership
declines 1959–78

	Industrial group	Membership '000				
		1959	1969	1971	1977	1978
1	Mining and quarrying	679	322	299	295	291
2	Railways	477	290	278	280	277
8	Iron, steel and minor metal trades	210	152	149	146	142
9	Building, woodworking, furnishing	537	381	354	390	410
11	Textiles	216	148	141	125	121
14	Agriculture	135	115	90	85	85
	All above groups	2,254	1,408	1,311	1,321	1,326

13

While these developments were taking place, part of the traditional heartland of British trade unionism was numerically slipping away. So much can be seen from an examination of some of those industrial groups of the Trades Union Congress which have historically featured among the most reliable core of its membership (Table 2). This result has, of course, principally been produced by the decline of the industries concerned – of textiles, of the coal industry, of railways and of iron and steel. But other factors have also been involved – increasing mechanisation and improved techniques, for example. In building the development of 'the lump', of sub-contracting to gangs of workers for labour only rather than employing such workers on a regular basis, has also played its part.

Since there has been an overall rise in trade union membership over the period; this has mainly been attributable to other sections of the movement, and particularly to those covered by general worker unions and by those catering for non-manual employees. Various aspects of this shift can be seen from Tables 3 to 8.

Table 3 shows the ten unions with highest membership in the trade union movement, in rank order, between 1945 and 1978. The Transport and General Workers, the General and Municipal Workers and the Amalgamated Engineers, themselves for organisation purposes a general engineering union, continue to dominate in numbers. The National Union of Mineworkers, like the Railwaymen, has fallen out of the 'top ten' altogether; also the Tailors and Garment Workers and the Post Office Workers, while the Woodworkers, now amalgamated with the Bricklayers into UCATT, have barely kept their place. By contrast the Electricians have grown in comparison with other large unions; most significant of all, there now feature in the 'top ten' the National Union of Public Employees, a general worker organisation in the public sector, and three completely 'white collar' unions, the National and Local Government Officers, the Association of Scientific, Technical and Managerial Staffs and the National Union of Teachers.

Most remarkable of all development, as Table 4 shows, has been the vast increase in membership which has taken place in the last decade among white collar workers in the *private* sector of the economy.

In the last decade, in a recruitment area traditionally regarded as among the most difficult in British industry, membership of these four unions has more than trebled, and in this growth and that elsewhere in the economy, an increasing female trade union membership has also played its part. Tables 5 to 8 summarise the resultant position.

Overall, between 1948 and 1974 (the most recent years for which estimates have been calculated), membership of manual worker unions in the United Kingdom, given internal shifts in declining industries and increases in general worker and other unions, remained about the same. During the same period, white collar

14

Table 3
The ten trade unions with largest membership

1945 Union	M'ship '000	1956 Union	M'ship '000	1966 Union	M'ship '000	1977 Union	M'ship '000	1978 Union	M'ship '000
TGWU	984.8	TGWU	1,263.8	TGWU	1,428.0	TGWU	2,022.7	TGWU	2,072.8
AEU	704.3	AEU	860.5	AEU	1,054.6	AUEW	1,155.4	AUEW	1,199.5
NUGMW	605.0	NUGMW	799.2	NUGMW	793.0	NUGMW	945.3	NUGMW	964.8
NUM	533.4	NUM	673.6	NUM	412.9	NALGO	709.3	NALGO	729.4
NUR	409.8	NUR	369.4	NALGO	360.7	NUPE	693.1	NUPE	712.4
USDAW	274.6	USDAW	348.8	USDAW	366.3	USDAW	441.5	ASTMS	471.0
ASW	176.0	ETU	228.1	ETU	293.2	ASTMS	441.0	USDAW	462.2
UPW	145.3	NUPE	198.0	NUPE	250.1	EETPU	420.0	EETPU	420.0
ETU	133.0	NUR	163.3	NUR	227.8	NUT	288.8	NUT	291.2
T&GWU	118.7	CSCA	148.8	ASW	188.1	NUM	258.7	NUM	254.9

Table 4
Membership of four private sector
white collar unions in 1966, 1971 and 1978

Union	Membership '000		
	1966	1971	1978
Association of Scientific, Technical and Managerial Staff (ASTMS)	72	250	471
Association of Professional, Executive, Clerical and Computer Staff (APEX)	76	118	151
Amalgamated Union of Engineering Workers (Technical and Scientific Staff Section) (TASS)	73	101	201
Banking, Insurance and Finance Union	58	93	126
Four-union total	279	562	949
1966 = 100	100	210	340

Table 5
Growth of white collar and manual trade union
membership in the United Kingdom 1948–74

	Union membership '000				Increase %	
	1948	1964	1970	1974	1948–74	1970–74
White collar	1,964	2,684	3,592	4,263	+117.1	+18.7
Manual	7,398	7,534	7,587	7,491	+ 0.1	- 1.3
	Union density %				Increase	
White collar	30.2	29.6	35.2	39.4	+ 9.2	+ 4.2
Manual	50.7	52.9	56.0	57.9	+ 7.2	+ 1.9

Source: Price and Bain, op. cit.

Table 6

Unionisation by sex and major occupational group in the United Kingdom, 1948–74

Union membership '000

	Male				% Increase		Female				% Increase	
	1948	1964	1970	1974	1948–74	1970–4	1948	1964	1970	1974	1948–74	1970–4
White collar	1,267	1,681	2,143	2,593	+104.7	+21.0	697	1,003	1,447	1,629	+133.7	+12.6
Manual	6,410	6,329	6,123	5,972	–6.8	–2.5	988	1,206	1,364	1,561	+58.0	+14.4
Total	7,677	8,010	8,266	8,565	+11.6	+3.6	1,685	2,209	2,811	3,190	+89.3	+13.5

Union density %

	Male				Increase		Female				Increase	
	1948	1964	1970	1974	1948–74	1970–4	1948	1964	1970	1974	1948–74	1970–4
White collar	33.8	33.4	40.0	44.5	+10.7	+4.5	25.4	24.9	30.7	32.6	+7.2	+1.9
Manual	59.5	60.0	63.3	64.7	+5.2	+1.4	26.0	32.6	35.2	42.1	+16.1	+6.9
Total	52.9	51.4	55.0	56.9	+4.0	+1.9	25.7	28.6	32.7	36.7	+11.0	+4.0

Source: Price and Bain, op. cit.

Table 7

Union membership and density by sector
in the United Kingdom, 1974

Sector	Labour force ('000)	Union membership ('000)	Density (%)
Public sector	6,112.6	5,079.4	83.1
Manufacturing	7,778.9	4,836.4	62.2
Manual	5,678.6	4,164.2	73.3
White collar	2,100.3	672.2	32.0
Agriculture, forestry, and fishing	427.7	99.7	23.3
Private sector services	6,689.3	810.0	12.1

Source: Price and Bain, op. cit.

membership increased by almost one-fifth. In 1974, because of an overall fall in manual employment, almost 58 per cent of manual employees were organised into trade unions compared with 51 per cent in 1948; in circumstances in which the non-manual labour force has been increasing, almost 40 per cent of white collar employees belonged to unions in 1974 compared with about 30 per cent in 1948.

The female membership position in trade unions can be seen from Table 6. Female densities of membership are still low compared with those for males, but the gap has narrowed substantially where manual workers are concerned. Among white collar workers female membership had increased faster over the period 1948–74 than male. While more than keeping pace with increasing numbers of women in the white collar labour force, this has been insufficient to narrow the gap between female and male densities – indeed, the gap has widened.

Table 7 shows that, despite advances in the private sector, the Civil Service, local government and nationalised industries remain the most highly organised part of the UK economy. Variations, industry by industry, are shown in Table 8.

Shifts in the distribution of trade union membership in the past decade have involved the Disputes Committee of the General Council of the Trades Union Congress in increasing activity. The rules under which the Committee operates originated in 1924 and were confirmed at the Bridlington Congress in 1939 – hence their popular title 'Bridlington Agreement'. Their intention was to regulate transfers of membership between affiliated unions and to deter poaching. Many recent cases have dealt with instances of competition between unions for white collar recruits, competition increased by the fact that, following the example of the Transport and General Workers' Union, most organisations traditionally concerned with manual workers have, since the 1960s, set up staff sections for white collar employees. Intense development of non-TUC staff associations recruiting similar employees, usually, but not

Table 8
Union membership and density by industry
in the United Kingdom, 1974

Industry	Labour force ('000)	Union membership ('000)	Density (%)
Agriculture and forestry	415.5	92.3	22.2
Fishing	12.2	7.4	60.5
Coal mining	314.0	302.1	96.2
Other mining	50.6	26.2	51.8
Food and drink Tobacco	783.9	401.1	51.2
Chemicals	483.6	247.4	51.2
Metals and engineering	4.118.0	2,862.7	69.4
Cotton and man-made fibres Other textiles	596.7	243.8	40.9
Leather	44.0	20.5	46.6
Clothing	345.8	207.7	60.0
Footwear	87.1	68.8	79.0
Bricks and building materials	171.9	69.4	40.4
Pottery	60.5	56.8	93.8
Glass	74.5	58.5	78.5
Wood and furniture	289.6	102.0	35.2
Paper, printing, and publishing	596.1	426.6	71.6
Rubber	127.2	71.1	55.9
Construction	1,428.8	388.1	27.2
Gas, electricity, and water	352.3	324.0	92.0
Railways	224.0	217.0	96.9
Road transport	468.3	445.4	95.1
Sea transport	90.6	90.3	99.6
Port and inland water transport	81.5	77.2	94.7
Air transport	79.8	74.7	93.6
Post office and telecommunications	509.7	448.1	87.9
Distribution	2,810.1	321.8	11.4
Insurance, banking, and finance	680.5	305.1	44.8
Entertainment and media services	189.6	123.0	64.9
Health	1,175.2	715.8	60.9
Hotels and catering	824.2	42.5	5.2
Other professional services	470.2	17.6	3.7
Education and local government	2,752.4	2,356.0	85.6
National government	623.7	564.5	90.5

Source: Price and Bain, op. cit.

invariably, on a company by company basis, has even more complicated the situation in this membership area. Since such organisations are, in TUC terms, not *bona fide* trade unions, they enjoy no protection against poaching by affiliated unions. The TUC may have supposed that, in issuing Certificates of Independence, the Certification Officer would, having accepted TUC unions as independent of employer control or influence, also take a TUC view of the standards to be applied to non-affiliated organisations. Following strictly the terms provided in s.8 of the Employment Protection Act, the Certification Officer has issued certificates (as the list of unions in Part 3 of this book shows) to numbers of non-TUC organisations.

It is, nevertheless, true that for the past forty years the existence of the 'Bridlington Agreement' has both restricted certain aspects of union competition and discouraged the rise of new unions.[13] It is also widely believed to have favoured large unions against small ones. If so, this has tended to work, however fortuitously, in the direction favoured by Congress on a number of occasions, but particularly since the early 1960s, of simplifying trade union structure by encouraging amalgamations. This policy, assisted by the Trade Union (Amalgamations) Act 1964, which made the conditions of merger easier, has largely been responsible for the steady decline in numbers of trade unions in the United Kingdom in recent years. Table 9 gives the relevant Department of Employment data for the years 1966 to 1977.

In the past few years a new trend has appeared in the merger with TUC affiliated unions of non-TUC staff associations, the TUC unions principally concerned being the Association of Scientific, Technical and Managerial Staffs (particularly in relation to insurance and banking), the Transport and General Workers' Union (Kodak Staff Association), the Association of Professional, Executive,

Table 9
Changes in trade union numbers and membership
1966–78

| Year | Number of unions at end of year | Membership at end year (to nearest thousand) | | | Percentage change in membership since previous year |
		Males ('000)	Females ('000)	Total ('000)	
1966	622	8,003	2,256	10,259	−0.6
1967	606	7,908	2,286	10,194	−0.6
1968	586	7,836	2,364	10,200	+0.1
1969	565	7,972	2,507	10,479	+2.7
1970	543	8,444	2,743	11,187	+6.8
1971	525	8,382	2,753	11,135	−0.5
1972	507	8,452	2,907	11,359	+2.0
1973	519	8,450	3,006	11,456	+0.9
1974	507	8,586	3,178	11,764	+2.7
1975	501	8,729	3,464	12,193	+3.6
1975*	470	8,600	3,427	12,026	–
1976	473	8,825	3,561	12,387	+3.0
1977	481	9,071	3,775	12,846	+3.7
1978	462	9,322	3,789	13,112	+2.1

+These notional figures exclude 31 organisations previously regarded as trade unions.
Source: *Department of Employment Gazette*, December 1979, p. 1242.

Table 10
Number of trade unions analysed
by size of union

	1945		1956		1966		1976		1977		1978	
	No.	%	No.	%	No.	%	No.	%	No.	%	No.	%
Under 100 members	182	23.8	121	18.7	126	20.3	69	14.7	74	15.4	72	15.6
100–499	205	26.8	171	26.4	147	23.6	142	29.2	144	30.0	135	29.2
500–999	90	11.8	62	9.6	68	10.9	47	10.2	45	9.4	48	10.4
1,000–2,499	100	13.1	103	15.9	89	14.3	60	13.0	66	13.7	62	13.4
2,500–4,999	60	7.8	62	9.6	65	10.5	45	9.5	41	8.5	37	8.0
5,000–9,999	49	6.4	36	5.6	30	4.8	30	6.3	28	5.8	26	5.6
10,000–14,999	19	2.5	20	3.1	22	3.6	8	1.8	10	2.1	9	1.9
15,000–24,999	17	2.2	23	3.5	18	2.9	15	3.2	13	2.8	14	3.0
25,000–49,999	18	2.3	14	2.2	19	3.0	17	3.7	18	3.8	19	4.1
50,000–99,999	10	1.3	18	2.8	20	3.3	14	3.0	15	3.1	14	3.0
100,000–249,999					9	1.4	14	3.0	15	3.1	15	3.2
250,000 and more	15	2.0	17	2.6	9	1.4	11	2.4	11	2.3	11	2.4
Number of unions at end of year	765	100.0	647	100.0	622	100.0	472	100.0	480	100.0	462	100.0

Clerical and Computer Staff (Staff Association General Accident and AA Staff Association) and Engineers' and Managers' Association (formed in 1977 by amalgamation between the TUC affiliated Electrical Power Engineers' Association and the non-TUC Association of Supervisory and Executive Engineers).

Table 10 shows that in 1978 there were 54 fewer unions with under 100 members than there had been in 1966, and smaller, though substantial, falls in numbers of all medium-size unions in the same period, while the 'giants', with over 100,000 members, had increased in number from 18 to 26.

The average size of a trade union in the United Kingdom (Table 11) has increased from 10,000 in 1945 to 28,000 in 1978. Over 80 per cent of trade union membership is now in unions with over 100,000 members, compared with 64 per cent in 1945. The bulk of that shift has taken place in the past ten years.

Trade union amalgamations are not always durable. Small unions are readily assimilated by large ones. For unions of more equal size or status, or with unlike forms of government and administration, merger may on occasion prove to be temporary. An example is the amalgamation which in 1966 produced the Society of Graphical and

Table 11
Membership of trade unions analysed
by size of union

	1945		1956		1966		1978	
	No. ('000)	%	No. ('000)	%	No. ('000)	%	No. ('000)	%
Under 100 members	9	0.1	6	0.1	6	0.1	4	0.0
100–499	51	0.7	44	0.5	37	0.4	34	0.3
500–999	64	0.8	44	0.5	48	0.5	34	0.3
1,000–2,499	162	2.1	168	1.7	146	1.4	103	0.8
2,500–4,999	214	2.7	216	2.2	227	2.2	134	1.0
5,000–9,999	342	4.4	241	2.5	206	2.0	169	1.3
10,000–14,999	236	3.0	246	2.5	274	2.7	112	0.9
15,000–24,999	332	4.3	438	4.5	332	3.2	267	2.0
25,000–49,999	625	8.0	510	5.3	666	6.5	711	5.4
50,000–99,999	790	10.1	1,266	13.0	1,379	13.4	947	7.2
100,000–249,999	4,978	63.8	6,521	67.2	1,477	14.4	2,263	17.2
250,000 and more					5,461	53.2	8,335	63.6
Total at end of year	7,803	100.0	9,700	100.0	10,259	100.0	13,112	100.0
Males	6,206	79.5	7,817	80.6	8,003	78.0	9,323	
Females	1,597	20.5	1,883	19.4	2,256	22.0	3,789	
Average member- ship per union	10		15		16		28	

Table 12
Trade union income and expenditure
1970–77

	1970	1972	1974	1976	1977
Membership covered ('000)	9,277	8,115	9,204	11,360	11,600
Income per member					
Contributions	£4.72	£6.10	£6.99	£10.10	£11.56
Investment	77	42	74	81	1.09
Other sources	14	30	45	40	23
Total income	£5.63	£6.82	£8.18	£11.31	£12.88
Expenditure per member					
Administration	£3.26	£4.91	£4.98	7.72	8.66
Dispute	39	69	39		
Unemployment	6	9	4		
Accident and Sickness	42	31	34	Benefits	Benefits
Superannuation/Retirement	30	28	31		
Death/Funeral/Benevolence	15	11	16	97	1.51
Total of above expenditure	£4.58	£6.39	£6.22	£8.69	£10.17
Excess income over expenditure	£1.05	43p	£1.96	£2.62	£2.71

Source: TUC, *Sixth Annual Survey of Union Income and Expenditure*, General Council Report.

Allied Trades and, four years later, broke up again into its two component parts. It has often been reported that another amalgamation subject to strain is the Amalgamated Union of Engineering Workers, a loose composite of the former Amalgamated Engineering Union, Amalgamated Union of Foundry Workers, Constructional Engineering Union and Draughtsmen and Allied Technicians' Association for which it has proved impossible to agree a common rule book.

Major, or well-established, unions rarely amalgamate until a break in national leadership occurs which makes it possible for them to do so without major clashes of dominant personalities. The prime motive for merger may be numerical, tactical or financial. 'Membership', it has been said, 'is to a trade union leader what profits are to a businessman.' But a merger may also consolidate the hold of a particular union on a particular industry. The amalgamation of the National Union of Vehicle Builders into the Transport and General Workers' Union in 1972 is a case in point, since this consolidated the hold of the former on the automotive industry. It may also become pressing for economic reasons. Contrary to popular opinion, the trade union movement is not rich. Some unions may be encouraged by financial difficulties to consider amalgamation; few are likely to ignore the fact that an increase in membership will probably spread costs.

The general financial situation of unions is illustrated in Tables 12 to 14.

Table 13 Income, expenditure and funds of trade unions 1976

Union	Number of members (1) '000	INCOME (a) From members (2) £'000	INCOME (b) From investments (3) £'000	INCOME (c) Total income (4) £'000	EXPENDITURE (d) Unemployment benefit (5) £'000	EXPENDITURE (d) Dispute benefit (6) £'000	EXPENDITURE (d) Total benefits to members (7) £'000	EXPENDITURE Administration expenses and other outgoings (8) £'000	EXPENDITURE (e) Total expenditure (9) £'000	TOTAL FUNDS Beginning of the year (10) £'000	TOTAL FUNDS End of the year (11) £'000	ASSETS Fixed assets (12) £'000	ASSETS Investments (13) £'000	ASSETS Gross assets (14) £'000	Political fund income (inc. in cols (2), (3) & (4)) (15)	Political fund expenditure (inc. in cols (8) & (9)) (16)
Unions each with 100,000 members or more:																
Transport and General Workers Union	1,929,834	16,809	1,972	18,804	—	343	3,211	11,471	15,493	(10)26,515	31,826	8,386	22,428	32,676	530	425
Amalgamated Union of Engineering Workers																
Engineering Section	1,168,990	12,496	663	13,272	14	3,643	6,117	10,439	11,738	14,571	884	5,960	6,020	884	530	272
Constructional Section	34,056	484	58	543	129	61	406	482	823	1,062	246	544	884	16	10	4
Foundry Section		665	152	2,686	10	146	479	652	1,096	884	8,386	73	918	1,129	21	22
Technical, Administrative and Supervisory Section	161,607	1,933	99	1,078	144	278	1,459	2,942	1,734	1,738	932	832	2,008	39	272	—
National Union of General and Municipal Workers	916,438	9,620	1,078	10,710	106	489	3,958	6,939	5,887	16,015	3,914	5,046	16,063	306	249	
National and Local Government Officers Association (h)	683,011	8,418	316	9,807	77	489	3,958	6,039	5,887	16,015	4,474	4,832	10,684	249		
National Union of Public Employees	650,530	4,607	373	5,435	50	278	3,160	3,734	3,501	5,202	1,461	4,524	6,749	350	315	
Electrical Electronic Telecommunication and Plumbing Union	428,636	3,579	274	3,933	46	349	2,554	3,114	4,940	5,759	1,708	3,870	5,915	89	105	
Union of Shop Distributive and Allied Workers	412,627	3,071	287	3,606	10	246	2,564	3,262	3,319	3,663	369	2,239	3,681	103	105	
Association of Scientific, Technical and Managerial Staffs	396,000	3,395	15	3,830	17	224	3,399	3,830	1,348	1,201	1,125	94	2,033	54	37	
National Union of Mineworkers (i)	370,541	3,216	102	3,363	112	955	3,956	5,475	(015,013)	16,519	738	12,290	19,597	256	131	
Union of Construction Allied Trades and Technicians	297,264	2,064	319	3,063	20	633	3,286	2,242	1,904	2,197	1,114	1,371	2,528	48	46	
National Union of Teachers	294,081	2,782	183	2,506	2	63	1,554	1,930	1,363	1,064	932	4,722	2,528			
Civil and Public Services Association	230,905	3,327	59	3,062	132	234	1,495	2,145	2,059	2,976	709	2,324	3,329			
Union of Post Office Workers	201,699	1,681	17	3,973		163	2,029	1,679	2,909	1,108	1,157	2,909				
Confederation of Health Service Employees	200,689	1,943	67	1,734	8	63	1,120	1,240	645	1,139	657	300	1,222	24	59	
Society of Graphical and Allied Trades 1975	195,107		401	2,542	7	401	2,268	2,749	2,565	1,725	440	2,762	21	13		
National Union of Railwaymen	177,548	2,910	996	3,917		642	2,042	2,249	12,155	13,261	502	12,022	13,368	21	89	
Association of Professional, Executive, Clerical and Computer Staff	141,766	1,646	32	1,831	56	59	1,114	1,351	1,677	2,157	544	1,036	2,385	56	44	
Amalgamated Society of Boilermakers, Shipwrights, Blacksmiths and Structural Workers	128,403	1,357	222	2,395	21	152	1,041	2,665	2,989	484	1,716	3,037	66	22		
Post Office Engineering Union	124,535	1,936	35	2,395		220	1,501	1,879	2,235	2,751	1,898	474	3,005	53	55	
Iron and Steel Trades Confederation	117,411	1,255	695	1,954	11	508	1,185	1,775	9,195	9,374	385	9,069	9,763	49	39	
National Union of Tailors and Garment Workers	112,783	764	265	1,031	88	739	879	2,954	3,106	464	2,542	3,158	20	19		
National Union of Bank Employees	111,609	780	11	795		676	653	676	258	118	88	371				
National Graphical Association	107,723	2,277	683	2,512	463	1,093	1,176	2,395	9,399	9,516	306	8,368	9,550			
Society of Civil and Public Servants	102,097	683	33	2,149	72	34	1,328	1,406	713	835	102	1,918			8	
Institution of Professional Civil Servants	100,233	40	40	1,949			1,389	1,408	1,456	981	163	611	1,090			
Total of above unions each with 100,000 members or more	9,854,813	102,093	10,770	116,804	735	15,689	70,219	94,599	148,049	170,254	40,844	110,022	183,294	2,687	2,081	
Total of 339 other listed unions with less than 100,000 members	2,254,619	28,009	2,967	34,384	263	2,558	23,704	30,102	41,256	45,538	9,597	27,993	48,682	254	197	
Total of 379 listed unions	12,109,434	130,102	141	151,188	998	18,247	93,923	124,701	189,305	215,792	50,441	138,015	231,976	2,278		
Total of 47 unlisted unions which have submitted returns	23,339	141	47	313	1	(g)	300	654	667	74	548	660	(e)			
TOTAL of all unions for 1976	12,132,773	130,243	13,184	151,501	999	18,254	94,194	125,001	189,959	216,459	50,515	138,563	232,636	2,942	2,278	
TOTAL of all unions for 1975	11,656,414	100,800	12,075	127,716	831	16,059	79,449	105,728	174,243	190,251	43,648	135,714	205,366	2,335	1,893	

NOTES:

(a) By far the largest part of the Income from members is derived from regular contributions but a very small part (probably less than 1%) is derived from such items as sale of diaries.

(b) Investment income is net of certain items such as outgoings on property held as an investment but for most unions tax paid on investment income has not been deducted.

(c) Total income and Total expenditure include all items which increased or decreased a union's total funds during the year and are not confined to normal revenue income and expenditure. Tax recoveries and provisions no longer required are therefore included in total income.

(d) For most unions the figure for Total benefits to members will be comprised of sums, such as Sickness benefit and Dispute benefit, paid direct to individual members; for some unions however expenditure on more general items of benefit, for instance group insurance policies or convalescent homes is included.

(e) These figures include debtors without making allowance for creditors.

(f) Less than £500.

(g) These figures have been adjusted to take account of later information.

(h) These figures include branch transactions for the first time.

(i) These figures include those of the 29 areas and other constituents of the union which submit separate returns.

Source: Certification Officer for Trade Unions and Employers' Associations, Annual Report, 1977.

Table 14 Income, expenditure and funds of trade unions 1977

Union	Number of members (1)	INCOME: From members £'000 (a) (2)	From investments £'000 (b) (3)	Total income £'000 (c) (4)	EXPENDITURE: Unemployment benefit (5)	Dispute benefit £'000 (6)	Total benefits to members £'000 (7)	Administration and other expenses and outgoings £'000 (8)	Total expenditure £'000 (9)	TOTAL FUNDS: Beginning of the year £'000 (10)	End of the year £'000 (11)	ASSETS: Fixed assets £'000 (12)	Investments £'000 (13)	Gross assets £'000 (14)
Unions each with 100,000 members or more:														
Transport and General Workers Union	2,022,738	19,371	2,273	21,673	—	765	3,736	13,580	18,132	(f)32,194	35,735	10,239	23,362	37,126
Amalgamated Union of Engineering Workers				28	—	—	—	18	23	18	23	(g)		31
Constructional Section	33,689	541	62	671	125	6	74	464	554	884	1,001	246	674	1,001
Engineering Section	1,173,000	12,784	855	13,963	7	1,284	4,290	6,243	11,294	14,571	17,240	6,149	8,186	20,219
Foundry Section	58,888	628	106	734	—	36	162	487	679	1,096	1,151	80	929	1,181
Technical, Administrative and Supervisory Section	183,492	2,192	86	2,303	—	120	247	1,877	2,200	(f)1,778	1,881	1,053	729	2,050
National Union of General and Municipal Workers	945,324	10,748	1,139	11,982	8	159	1,663	8,702	10,847	16,015	17,150	4,726	5,228	17,184
National and Local Government Officers Association	709,331	9,376	976	11,279	9	141	666	4,699	8,612	8,755	11,422	5,212	5,312	13,590
National Union of Public Employees	693,097	6,416	669	7,504	—	30	377	4,264	4,968	5,202	7,738	1,790	6,879	9,113
Union of Shop Distributive and Allied Workers	441,539	3,966	371	4,578	—	284	284	3,130	3,800	3,663	4,441	442	2,759	4,487
Association of Scientific, Technical and Managerial Staffs	441,000	5,560	11	5,881	—	168	291	3,990	4,662	(f)1,253	2,472	1,480	101	3,138
Electrical Electronic Telecommunication and Plumbing Union	432,628	3,786	360	4,271	(g)	199	531	2,669	4,037	5,759	5,993	1,901	4,087	6,302
National Union of Mineworkers (h)	370,194	6,204	1,365	7,619	23	—	852	5,001	6,079	16,396	17,936	890	13,451	18,858
Union of Construction Allied Trades and Technicians	305,727	3,399	109	3,551	—	—	680	2,616	3,425	2,197	2,323	1,224	1,357	2,638
National Union of Teachers	296,092	2,479	367	3,009	—	—	91	1,820	2,303	5,372	6,078	513	5,440	6,224
Civil and Public Services Association	226,495	3,776	236	4,065	—	642	939	1,977	3,214	2,976	3,827	778	2,921	3,933
Confederation of Health Service Employees	211,636	1,983	45	2,115	—	—	68	1,372	1,527	1,139	1,727	736	938	1,789
Society of Graphical and Allied Trades 1975	198,182	2,564	78	3,166	56	—	407	2,398	2,877	2,564	2,853	1,730	205	2,929
Union of Post Office Workers	197,247	3,849	108	3,978	(g)	26	276	2,522	3,232	2,909	3,655	1,111	1,900	3,655
National Union of Railwaymen	171,825	3,334	2,655	5,274	(g)	(g)	596	2,227	3,065	13,261	15,470	526	14,541	15,677
Association of Professional, Executive, Clerical and Computer Staff	146,385	1,836	120	2,102	—	121	193	1,309	1,658	2,157	2,601	590	1,331	2,854
Amalgamated Society of Boilermakers, Shipwrights, Blacksmiths and Structural Workers	129,956	1,483	252	1,772	—	36	176	1,195	1,596	2,989	3,165	516	2,424	3,413
National Association of Schoolmasters/Union of Women Teachers	127,056	1,087	77	1,251	—	—	49	914	1,072	1,108	1,287	243	246	1,418
Post Office Engineering Union	122,564	2,113	25	2,178	(g)	—	243	1,704	2,132	2,647	2,693	1,899	490	2,983
National Union of Tailors and Garment Workers	117,840	840	300	1,146	(g)	(g)	99	839	1,000	3,106	3,252	440	2,654	3,337
Iron and Steel Trades Confederation	117,401	1,542	728	2,277	210	103	478	1,341	1,900	9,374	9,751	448	9,396	10,230
National Union of Bank Employees	116,739	965	71	982	—	—	54	480	911	257	335	169	82	417
National Graphical Association	109,438	1,990	706	2,786	(g)	—	889	1,390	2,327	9,516	9,975	339	8,450	10,040
Society of Civil and Public Servants	105,320	2,381	40	2,513	—	—	18	1,559	1,662	1,456	2,307	1,091	636	2,732
Royal College of Nursing	101,210	774	—	774	—	—	5	756	774	—	—	—	—	927
Total of above unions each with 100,000 members or more	10,306,033	117,967	13,566	135,434	438	3,857	18,434	82,143	110,565	170,613	189,482	46,561	126,080	209,276
Total of 356 other listed unions with less than 100,000 members	2,405,006	31,422	3,298	39,094	185	420	3,208	28,315	34,126	43,651	48,619	10,171	30,520	53,048
Total of listed unions	12,711,039	149,389	16,864	174,528	623	4,277	21,642	110,458	144,691	214,264	244,101	56,732	156,600	262,324
Trades Union Congress	—	2,017	59	2,151	—	(g)	265	1,072	1,992	740	899	35	633	1,233
Total of 20 other unlisted unions which have submitted returns	7,872	231	12	252	1	(g)	5	204	226	188	214	54	125	244
TOTAL of all unions for 1977	12,718,911	151,637	16,935	176,931	624	4,277	21,912	111,734	146,909	215,192	245,214	56,821	157,358	263,801
TOTAL of all unions for 1976	12,532,773	130,243	13,184	151,501	909	2,039	18,254	94,194	125,007	189,959	216,459	50,515	138,563	232,636

NOTES:

(a) By far the largest part of the Income from members is derived from regular contributions but a very small part (probably less than 1%) is derived from such items as sale of diaries.

(b) Investment income is net of certain items such as outgoings on property held as an investment but for some unions tax paid on investment income has not been deducted.

(c) Total income and Total expenditure include all items which increased or decreased a union's total funds during the year and are not confined to normal revenue income and expenditure. Tax recoveries and provision no longer required are therefore included in total income.

(d) For most unions the figure for Total benefits to members will be comprised of sums, such as Sickness benefit and Dispute benefit, paid direct to individual members; for some unions however expenditure on more general items of benefit, for instance group insurance policies or convalescent homes is included.

(e) The figures include debtors without making allowances for creditors.

(f) These figures have been adjusted to take account of later information.

(g) Less than £500.

(h) These figures include those of the 29 areas and other constituents of the union which submit separate returns.

(i) These figures include branch transactions for the first time.

Source: Certification Officer for Trade Unions and Employers' Associations. Annual Report, 1978.

Low contributions compared with those of trade unions in other countries are a feature of the UK situation. The Certification Officer's data for 1977 show an average weekly payment per member for all unions of almost 23p; the TUC Survey, covering 10 millions out of the 11.8 million members of affiliated organisations in the same year, gives almost the same figure, 22p. Contributions make up about 86 per cent of total income. In some years since the war these and other minor sources have hardly been enough to cover current expenditure. Reluctance to raise contributions for fear of losing membership is less evident than it once was. On average, the TUC Survey indicates, contributions were on average, almost 150 per cent higher in 1977 than in 1970. Reserves, however, remain generally low. Most unions were prevented by rule or by principle from profiting in the postwar boom in equities and have not invested heavily elsewhere. The 30 largest organisations with over 80 per cent of total membership have no more than £126 million invested and had an investment income in 1977 of little more than £13.5 million. Such resources could not easily be turned into liquid assets at short notice. More important for practical purposes are the sums which unions maintain permanently in this condition in case of strikes and other emergencies. In 1977 this amounted to some £230 million, a little over £18 per member. This, like other general trade union statistics, conceals considerable variations between unions. Few except the largest could finance substantial industrial action for long without borrowing from other organisations, though there always remains, in the last resort, the expedient of levying members to finance extraordinary expenditure or to recoup losses. This has not been widely resorted to since the periods of chronic membership loss and depression after the First World War. It remains true that any sustained aggressive action on a wide front is likely to bring a union to the edge of financial problems (the Draughtsmen, for example, in the 1960s) and that many small unions are chronically underfinanced. Mergers tend to spread risks, but even size is no guarantee of financial stability during a period of sharp inflation. At least one large union was widely considered to be in financial difficulties in 1978.

An underlying problem in trade union finance is that of rapidly rising administrative costs. These have persistently exceeded contribution increases for many years and form the highest single item of expenditure – three-quarters or more of all money spent. British unions are, in terms of paid officials and back-up resources such as research and education, commonly believed to be underprovided, though there have been evident improvements in the past few years. There has also been some revival of interest in friendly benefits. These, before the advent of National Insurance and other aspects of the Welfare State, formed a substantial part of trade union activity and have traditionally enjoyed tax relief, as they still do today where unions are listed. The evidence suggests, however, that the real value of benefits to members is still, overall, on the decline. Only 28

Table 15 Political Funds of Trade Unions

Unions each with a political fund of £10,000 or more	Total union membership (a) (1)	Number of members contributing to the political fund (2)	% of total membership contributing to political fund (3)	POLITICAL FUND			
				Income £000s (4)	Expenditure £000s (5)	Fund at beginning of year £000s (6)	Fund at end of year £000s (7)
Transport and General Workers Union	2,022,738	1,962,615	97	572	356	660	876
National Union of Mineworkers	370,194	250,293	68	320	176	652	796
National Union of Mineworkers (Durham Area)	44,102	17,661	40	35	35	225	225
Amalgamated Union of Engineering Workers							
Constructional Section	33,689	24,533	73	10	4	9	15
Engineering Section	1,173,000	875,314	75	368	266	206	308
Foundry Section	53,888	42,000	71	21	22	20	19
Technical Administrative and Supervisory Section	183,492	85,736	47	50	28	34	56
National Union of General and Municipal Workers	945,324	926,110	98	327	255	243	315
National Union of Public Employees	693,097	682,817	98	476	378	217	315
National Union of Railwaymen	171,825	164,059	95	109	93	178	194
Union of Shop Distributive and Allied Workers	441,539	402,223	91	147	115	140	172
Association of Professional Executive Clerical and Computer Staff	146,385	108,794	74	68	48	104	124
Amalgamated Society of Boilermakers Shipwrights Blacksmiths and Structural Workers	129,956	81,710	63	66	24	51	93
Society of Graphical and Allied Trades 1975	198,182	49,203	25	27	17	61	71
National Union of Sheet Metal Workers Coppersmiths Heating and Domestic Engineers	74,004	60,157	81	31	6	46	71
Association of Scientific Technical and Managerial Staffs	441,000	147,000	33	60	45	42	57
Post Office Engineering Union	122,564	88,642	72	78	71	45	52
Union of Construction Allied Trades and Technicians	305,727	200,000	65	64	56	21	29
Iron and Steel Trades Confederation	117,401	101,102	86	49	36	14	27
Associated Society of Locomotive Engineers and Firemen	27,681	26,388	95	20	13	17	24
Amalgamated Textile Workers Union	41,624	36,653	88	11	11	24	24
National Union of Dyers Bleachers and Textile Workers	61,416	61,247	100	23	14	14	23
Furniture Timber and Allied Trades Union	84,304	51,425	61	18	12	17	23
National Graphical Association	109,438	43,724	45	11	11	20	20
National Society of Metal Mechanics	50,255	40,896	81	14	4	9	19
Union of Post Office Workers	197,247	186,683	95	84	67	1	18
National Union of the Footwear Leather and Allied Trades	68,149	61,252	90	21	18	15	18
Electrical Electronic Telecommunication and Plumbing Union	432,628	364,881	84	80	74	8	14
Confederation of Health Service Employees	211,636	193,622	91	39	37	10	12
Liverpool Victoria Section of the National Union of Insurance Workers	3,241	315	10	(b)	(b)	11	11
Bakers Food and Allied Workers Union	57,321	38,720	68	16	10	4	10
Total of above unions	9,018,047	7,374,845	82	3,215	2,302	3,118	4,031
Total of 42 other unions with political funds	697,181	539,749	77	177	158	58	77
TOTAL of unions with political funds for 1977	9,715,228	7,914,594	81	3,392	2,460	3,176	4,108

NOTES:

(a) Some members included in these figures (e.g. retired members) may be exempt from paying union contributions.

(b) Represents less than £500.

unions now have members' superannuation schemes. The additional examination of such schemes required by TULRA 1974 appears to have provided an added discouragement to their retention.

Political funds form the last element of trade union finance. An agreement exists between trade unions and the Labour Party on the extent to which trade union finance may be used to sponsor and maintain Members of Parliament. Unions commonly accumulate reserves which can be made available for General Elections. In such years the Political fund income and expenditure account shows a deficit – as it does in the Certification Officer's figures reproduced from those of the Chief Registrar for 1974. More up-to-date information is provided in Table 15 for 1977, a year in which unions were accumulating political fund balances.

It is interesting to note that TULRA 1974 sets out accounting standards for trade union returns to the Certification Officer which are appreciably stricter than those required by pre-1971 legislation and apply to all organisations, whether listed or not. In 1979 a Working Party set up by the accountancy bodies published a guidance statement which covers the accounting and auditing responsibilities of trade unions, auditors' rights and responsibilities, and deals with special features of trade union auditing. While it is unusual for a union to find itself in conflict with the Certification Officer, it may be that a number are not at the present time complying with the provisions of TULRA and that changes will be required in their accounting and auditing arrangements to bring them up to standard.

Trade union organisation

For the most part trade unions in the United Kingdom follow a similar pattern of organisation. Where differences exist, these are principally the result of history and origin or of industrial circumstances.

Overall policy making usually lies in the hands of a delegate conference, in most cases held annually. Conferences vary in the attention which they pay to the performance of their officials in the previous year, but all do so to some extent; they also discuss resolutions about future policy remitted from branches and other levels in the organisation, and commonly appoint an Executive Council or Committee to conduct business between Conferences. This is not invariably so. In some unions, particularly those of a traditionally craft character, Executive Councilmen and most, if not all, executive officials are directly elected by the membership. Such is the case, for example, in the Engineering Section of the Amalgamated Union of Engineering Workers. Here, the Delegate Conference takes the form of a small National Committee of 52 delegates rather than a larger and more widely based arrangement. Against this the Executive is to some extent counterpoised since its members owe their seats to postal ballots of the membership held at different times, part of a system of checks and balances in the constitution of the union not unlike that incorporated by the Founding Fathers into the Constitution of the United States of America.

In most unions the General Secretary is the chief executive and representative. He may be appointed by the Executive or, as in the case of the Transport and General Workers' Union, by ballot of the membership (the only official in that union to be appointed in this way). General Secretaries normally appointed until retirement or, like Her Majesty's judges, *quamdiu se bene gesserint*, as long as they behave themselves. Like judges, they are seldom removed before their period of office expires. Presidents of unions are commonly lay officials, elected or appointed annually. In some cases, however, they outrank their General Secretaries. This is the case in the Engineering Section of the Amalgamated Union of Engineering Workers; here the General Secretary is less the chief representative of the union and its principal negotiator than its principal, and highly influential, chief administrative officer, his functions clearly separated in rule from those of the President. In this union also, as in some others, President and General Secretary are, like other executive officials, subject to re-election after limited periods until they can be confirmed in office without further re-election until retirement. Unions of this kind offer the most obvious evidence of the existence within them of 'government' and 'opposition' organisation of a more-or-less overtly political character. In general, trade unions dislike the notion that 'party' rather than 'purpose' influences their actions. Where it does appear to do so the situation rarely reflects with any precision the pattern of political activity in the community in general. Most informed observers tend to treat with caution the labelling of trade union candidates for office entirely upon lines familiar to the commonplaces of current politics.

The periodic election of executive officials produces, however, a substantially different climate than where such officials are appointed or, as in the case of minor officials of the General and Municipal Workers' Union, elected after experience on the job as appointees. This is less a matter of turnover of officials (since officials, once elected, stand a good chance of re-election) than of attitude. The appointed official may well feel freer to act in the interests of his members as he sees them rather than at their behest, though no official of any kind can, in a British trade union, be expected for long to pursue courses of action out of sympathy with the rank and file. The distinction is to some extent one of tradition. Craft-based membership is inclined to think of officials as an extension of itself – as *taking on* or forwarding, rather than *taking over*, issues which have arisen in the workplace. It is not inclined to regard officials, outside this context, as possessing special status or competence by virtue of their office. Non-craft membership and that of white collar unions has traditionally thought otherwise, neither feeling competent to pursue workplace issues so completely on its own behalf. Today, as a consequence of the extended development of workplace bargaining among these two latter groups also, differences in attitude appear to be narrowing. Employees generally are approximating more and more to traditional craft behaviour. Undoubtedly this change has been encouraged by recent pay policies which, for the time being at least, have diminished the independent negotiating role of the outside official.

The same developments have latterly given a prominence previously unfamiliar in many industrial situations to the workplace representative. In most unions it has been customary to think of the trade union branch or, in craft organisations, the district committee as the lowest level of negotiating competence and the focus of local representative activity. In some circumstances, this arrangement still holds good. Where branches are based upon factories or companies, or where district committees hold predominant representation in a particular labour market, these continue to dominate the situation. In general, however, shop stewards or their equivalents in function, if not in title (including staff representatives for non-manual workers) have, since the middle 1950s, assumed more and more of the active face of trade unionism. Where this has happened branch life, as in traditional craft unions, has increasingly become preoccupied with union administration, while district committees deal with a small proportion only of the negotiating work which goes on in their areas.

Trade unions, while changing their rule books but little, have not for the most part sought to prevent or discourage developments of this kind. The assistance of a large army of volunteers, either unpaid or operating at no cost to the union because of the willingness of their employers to provide payment for lost time on relevant trade union work, has been welcome in handling the huge volume of representative activity generated during the past two decades. Trade unions could scarcely have maintained the low levels of financial contributions from members had the situation been otherwise, and much time of full-time officials has been taken over by other responsibilities which unions are now expected to assume – representation of members in industrial tribunal cases, committee work with national and local government and with other public institutions and the like. Workplace developments have, however, greatly complicated relations between unions.

The existence of many unions does not necessarily imply 'multi-unionism'. 'Many unions' can be so distributed as to ensure one union per industry in some cases, one union per factory or establishment in others, or simply a situation in which unions in a given situation 'co-exist' but do not compete. The Teston Independent Society of Cricket Ball Makers creates no 'multi-union' problem because it organises such workers in one firm in Kent, nor the Card Setting Machine Tenters Society by catering for all the factories in which that kind of work goes on; nor is there anything organisationally unsound in organising unions on the 'layer-cake principle' in the Civil Service. 'Many unions' only begin to raise problems of 'multi-unionism' when the spheres of influence or representation between those unions in the workplace are so ill-defined that competition between them becomes endemic or representation so fragmented in any particular industry or establishment that decisions which ought to be taken in common cannot be so determined. Two or three unions can be as difficult as ten or twenty, e.g. in British Rail. Ultimately, the situation depends on how well the unions concerned get on together.

At industry level British employers learned long ago how to deal with most 'multi-union' problems by means of Joint Councils or Committees, which usually function adequately. It is often otherwise where no such tradition exists, or where relationships at plant or establishment level are the core of the regulative arrangements of the industry, as in engineering. Today there are some nineteen unions catering for manual and staff workers in the industry; twenty years ago, there were over forty, such has the effect of amalgamation been since that time. This does not necessarily mean excessive numbers of unions in any one establishment. In 1969, the year in which the data in Tables 16 and 17 were collected from 432 establishments in

Table 16
Engineering industry – number of unions
per establishment, 1969

Number of unions with members at the establishments	Number of establishments with this number of unions	Percentage of the whole sample of 432 establishments
none	4	0.9
1	60	13.9
2	78	18.0
3	72	16.7
4	62	14.4
5	44	10.2
6	30	6.9
7	25	5.8
8	25	5.8
9	15	3.5
10	7	1.6
11	6	1.4
12	4	0.9
Total	432	100.0

Source: Marsh, Evans and Garcia, *Workplace Industrial Relations in Engineering*, Engineering Employers' Federation, 1971, Table 73.

engineering employing 588,000 manual workers, there were twenty-three manual unions with national negotiating rights in the industry. Table 16 shows that 15 per cent of these establishments had no union or only one manual union, almost one-third had no more than two, one-half no more than three and almost two-thirds no more than four. In many of these establishments some of the unions concerned had so few members that they made no attempt to represent them and numbers of unions and shop stewards per union were, as Table 17 illustrates, largely a question of size of establishment as defined by numbers employed.

Table 17

Engineering industry – average number of unions with members in establishments by employment size, 1969

Size by number of manual workers employed	Average number of unions	Average number of shop stewards per union
1– 99	1.7	1.1
100–249	2.7	1.4
250–499	3.5	2.7
500–999	4.0	2.7
Over 1000	5.1	9.5
All establishments	4.1	5.8

Source: Marsh, Evans and Garcia, op. cit. Table 74.

Staff workers in engineering were, at the same time, represented by five unions with national recognition. Taken across whole industries, the situation can appear to be extremely complex, as Tables 18, 19 and 20, taken from another set of industry surveys relating to Engineering, Chemicals, and Printing and Publishing show, each table in this case showing numbers and names of unions with members within particular departmental functions and including both manual and staff organisations. Establishment by establishment, the complexity of trade union organisation is likely to be no greater than that reflected for engineering in 1969.

Exaggerated as the multi-union situation may be in popular belief, it still provides problems of co-ordination at company and workplace or establishment level between unions which are essentially independent one of the other, and which may, on occasion, have overriding policies which it is difficult to reconcile. In some industries, such as engineering, Joint Shop Stewards Committees have been authorised for many years, but these have never been designed to include staff unions; in other industries, no formal framework of co-operation may be laid down, but unofficial joint committees may be common. At company level, where in any case

32

Table 18
Management categories by unions represented in
areas managed – engineering industry

Function	No. of unions	Names of unions
Research and development	6	AUEW, AUEW(TASS), ASTMS, TGWU, NUSMWCH and DE, UKAPE
Professional engineers, etc.	7	AUEW, AUEW(TASS), ASTMS, APEX, EEPTU, TGWU, ACTSS
Technician	8	AUEW, AUEW(TASS), ASTMS, APEX, TGWU, GMWU, MATSA, ACTSS
Administrative	7	AUEW, AUEW(TASS), ASTMS, APEX, TGWU, MATSA, ACTSS
Finance	7	AUEW, AUEW(TASS), ASTMS, APEX, TGWU, NUSMWCH and DE, ACTSS
Marketing	2	ASTMS, APEX
Sales	5	AUEW, AUEW(TASS), ASTMS, APEX, TGWU, ACTSS
Production	14	AUEW, AUEW(TASS), ASTMS, APEX, EEPTU, TGWU, GMWU, NSMM, MATSA, UCATT, ASBSB and SW, NUSMWCH and DE, ASWM, ACTSS
Maintenance	8	AUEW, AUEW(TASS), ASTMS, APEX, EEPTU, TGWU, GMWU, UCATT
All categories	15	

One of the above organisations, UKAPE, is not affiliated to the Confederation of Shipbuilding and Engineering Unions.
MATSA = Managerial, Administrative, Technical and Supervisory Association (staff section of GMWU).
ACTSS = Association of Clerical, Technical and Supervisory Staffs (staff section of TGWU).
ASWM = Amalgamated Society of Woodcutting Machinists.
All other unions as in Part 3.
Source: Marsh and Gillies, *The Training of Managers in Industrial Relations*, St Edmund Hall, 1976.

management–union negotiating arrangements are still relatively rarely to be found, almost all joint meetings between workplace representatives of unions are not only unauthorised, but officially frowned upon, and formal meetings of officials rarely take place. Individual unions themselves have only within recent years begun to evolve machinery for co-ordinating their efforts at this level and this may be especially difficult where companies span different areas or districts of unions and where these areas and districts fall within different intra-union jurisdictions. Companies which are content to

Table 19
Management categories by unions represented in
areas managed – chemical industry

Function	No. of unions	Names of unions
Research and development	3	ASTMS, TGWU, APST
Professional engineers, etc.	6	AUEW, AUEW(TASS), ASTMS, EEPTU TGWU, APST
Technician	3	ASTMS, TGWU, APST
Administrative	5	ASTMS, TGWU, GMWU, USDAW, APST
Finance	3	ASTMS, EEPTU, APST
Marketing	–	–
Sales	–	–
Production	8	AUEW, ASTMS, EEPTU, TGWU, GMWU, ASBSB and SW, USDAW, APST
Maintenance	10	AUEW, AUEW(TASS), EEPTU, TGWU, GMWU, UCATT, ASBSB and SW, USDAW, NUSMWCH, EESA
All categories	12	

(EEPTU now = EETPU – EESA is the staff side of the EEPTU.)
Source as for Table 18.

bargain establishment by establishment have at least the advantage of avoiding the complexities of ensuring co-operation between unions at levels at which those unions are not organisationally equipped to provide it. The situation is no easier for the unions than it is for the employer.

Trade union federations

Traditionally, trade unions have attempted to resolve difficulties of joint working between themselves as independent organisations by means of federal machinery. Generally speaking, federations have been of two types, those seeking to develop common services between organisations and/or to furnish opportunities for general policy making in relations with the outside world, and those principally aimed at bringing unions together for negotiating purposes. The former type of federal organisation is readily identifiable in the form of the Trades Union Congress, the Scottish Trades Union Congress, the Wales Trade Union Council and the General Federation of Trade Unions, all of which are described later in this book. Other examples of it may be less well known – the National Federation of Professional Workers, for example, or the general federations of staff associations,

Table 20
Management categories by unions represented in areas managed – printing and publishing industry

Function	No. of unions	Names of unions
Research and development	7	AUEW, APEX, EEPTU, NATSOPA, SOGAT, NGA, SLADE
Professional engineers, etc.	5	APEX, TGWU, NATSOPA, SOGAT, NUJ
Technician	9	AUEW, AUEW(TASS), ASTMS, EEPTU, NATSOPA, SOGAT, NGA, SLADE, NUS
Administrative	8	AUEW, ASTMS, APEX, TGWU, NATSOPA SOGAT, NGA, NUJ
Finance	4	ASTMS, APEX, NATSOPA, SOGAT
Marketing	2	ASTMS, NATSOPA
Sales	3	APEX, NATSOPA, SOGAT
Production	10	AUEW, ASTMS, EEPTU, TGWU, UCATT, NATSOPA, SOGAT, NGA, SLADE, NUJ
Maintenance	7	AUEW, AUEW(TASS), ASTMS, EEPTU, TGWU, GMWU, SOGAT
All categories	13	

Source as for Table 18.

e.g. the Confederation of Bank Staff Associations and the Managerial, Professional and Staff Liaison Group.

Major federations of trade unions on an industry-wide scale for the purposes of representation or negotiation with employers are now uncommon. The National Federation of Building Trades Operatives and the Printing and Kindred Trades Federation, both in their day powers in the land so far as their respective industries were concerned, have, for example, now disappeared as union amalgamations have made their co-ordinating work unnecessary, or as such functions have been taken over by TUC Industry Committees (see p. 55). The largest federation of this kind which remains is the Confederation of Shipbuilding and Engineering Unions. This brings together at national level and in 48 district committees the 23 principal trade union organisations which have negotiating relationships with the Engineering Employers' Federation and its constituent organisations. The CSEU meets annually in conference to debate lines of policy and serves as a medium of communication with government on certain issues, particularly in engineering and shipbuilding. It also provides servicing facilities for unions concerned in the Sector Working Parties of the National Economic Development Council. Principal negotiations with the Engineering Employers for manual workers are conducted by a subcommittee chaired and led by the President of the Amalgamated Union of Engineering Workers; other committees deal with shipyard negotiations, with pay and conditions of railway workshop staff and with aerospace problems. Machinery also exists for liaison between staff worker unions, though this is not at present active.

In addition to the TUC, the STUC and the Wales TU Council, the Department of Employment lists a total of 44 federations operating in the United Kingdom. Some of these, such as the General Union of Loom Overlookers, have a title suggesting that they are unitary organisations though they consist in practice of autonomous organisations; others perform similar functions to those of the CSEU, albeit in smaller industries and on a smaller scale; a few are joint bodies of craft unions in particular sectors of the economy, e.g. in the steel industry or in papermaking and boardmaking. No fewer than nine federations are to be found in the textile industries, where problems of amalgamation of local and sectional associations have been particularly difficult. Table 21 lists all the federations known to the Department of Employment at the end of 1978. However, there have been changes since then and these are noted where known.

Table 21
Federations of trade unions 1979

Trades union congresses
Trades Union Congress
Scottish Trades Union Congress
Wales Trades Union Council

Federations listed by the Department of Employment as at end 1978
Banking Staff Council (ceased 1978)
British Aerospace Federation of Employee Associations
British Federation of Textile Technicians
British Hospital Doctors Federation
British Seafarers Joint Council
Central Committee of ICI Foreman's and Supervisors Associations
Confederation of Employee Organisations (ceased 1979)
Confederation of Entertainment Unions
Confederation of Insurance Trade Unions
Confederation of Professional and Executive Associations (ceased 1978)
Confederation of Shipbuilding and Engineering Unions
Confederation of Bank Staff Associations
Council of Bank Technical and Services Staff Associations
Council of Post Office Unions
Federal Council of Teachers in Northern Ireland
Federation of British Trawler Officers
Federation of Broadcasting Unions
Federation of Cadbury Schweppes Representatives Associations
Federation of Film Unions
Federation of Professional Officers Associations
Federation of Theatre Unions
General Federation of Trade Unions

General Union of Associations of Loom Overlookers*
Joint Committee of Light Metal Trades Unions
Joint Committee of the Four Secondary Associations (ceased end 1978)
National Affiliation of Carpet Trade Unions
National Association of Unions in the Textile Trade
National Craftsmen's Co-ordinating Committee for the Iron and Steel Industry
National Craftsmen's Negotiating Committee for the Papermaking and Boardmaking
   Industry
National Federation of Carding Engineers
National Federation of Continuative Teacher Associations
National Federation of Furniture Trade Unions
National Federation of Professional Workers
National Union of Insurance Workers*
Northern Counties Textile Trades Federation
Northern Ireland Public Service Alliance
Nottingham and District Federation of Club Stewards
Officers (Merchant Navy) Federation Ltd
Pen Workers Federation (ceased March 1979)
Post Office Senior Staffs Negotiating Council
Scottish Council of Textile Trade Unions
Technical and Services Banking Staff Council
Textile Manufacturing Trades Federation of Bolton and Surrounding Districts
Yorkshire Association of Power Loom Overlookers*

*TUC affiliated union

In January 1978 the Managerial, Professional and Staff Liaison
Group was formed.

Current issues

The closed shop
In 1978 rather more than 5.2 million employees in British industry
(about one-in-four) have been reckoned to be in closed shops, five out
of six of these in post-entry situations, i.e. they had been expected to
join *after* accepting employment, when approached by the union or
within a given period of the time of hiring. The current legal position
of the closed shop, defined as a 'union membership agreement or
arrangement', has already been discussed (p. 7). Until 1971 closed
shops were perfectly legal but the attitude of unions towards the
practice was guarded. The trade union movement was well aware that
compulsory membership was controversial and that undue pressure
to extend it was likely to bring unfavourable publicity. On the other
hand it also believed that the object of '100 per cent trade unionism'
was legitimate and desirable and that, both to enforce it and where
trade union principles were at stake, it was reasonable for members to
refuse to work with 'nons'. The 'pre-entry closed shop', i.e. one in
which the possession of a card is necessary *before* a job can be
obtained, it tended to regard, except in such industries as docks and
merchant shipping, with some caution as being too exclusive to be
reconcilable with British trade union traditions. Of the three and
three-quarter million workers (or 16 per cent of the labour force)

reckoned at the beginning of the 1960s to be in closed shops, three out of every four were, therefore, in post-entry closed shop situations.

Post-entry closed shops were clearly on the increase before the 1971 Act[14]. In private industry they rarely involved formal agreement with employers that trade union membership was a condition of employment and were seldom pressed until a very high proportion of any shop or department had been voluntarily recruited. Since they were not in themselves unlawful, complaints about their administration in individual cases depended on the willingness of aggrieved individuals to make these known. Where this happened trade union officials frequently found themselves in the role of conciliators where non-membership of particular individuals appeared to pose no threat to union security. A few instances in which trade union attitudes seemed to lead to unacceptable pressures found their way into the courts. More than a few employers took the view that post-entry closed shops were a small price to pay in circumstances in which they cleared up problems of 'free-riders' who could create resentment by benefiting from trade union agreements without paying contributions, of poaching of members by one union or another or of individuals whose attitudes were not acceptable to their fellow workers as a whole.

The legal effect of the Industrial Relations Act, except in those rare cases in which a joint claim for an 'approved closed shop' from both a registered union and an employer could be justified, was to outlaw the practice but to allow for 'agency shops' by union-employer agreement in which those who were not full trade union members could be contributing non-members, or if they conscientiously objected to paying such contributions, pay equivalent amounts to charity. In addition, the law guaranteed the right of individual employees to join or not to join a trade union.

The practical effect of these provisions on the extent of the closed shop was slight. Though formal closed shop agreements were for the most part 'written out', unions saw no reason to abandon their '100 per cent' practices. Their managements found ways of ensuring that this could be tolerated without serious objection from employees, including increased use of check-off. Very few cases arose in which such employees sought to end closed shops by appealing to the legal machinery provided. The Trade Union Congress policy of non-registration by affiliated organisations had the effect of making 'agency shops' a non-runner for almost all trade unionists, since only registered unions could take advantage of the Act's provisions. Most significant of all, the law providing that workers had the right *not* to be members of trade unions proved in practice to be unenforcable. Non-unionists could not be guaranteed their jobs where their organised colleagues were determined that this should not be so.

The evident failure of the Act where closed shops were concerned did nothing to reassure those who believed that such practices were an intolerable curtailment of the liberty of the subject. Its immediate effect was to ensure that, on the return of a Labour government to office in February 1974 all traces of the 1971 Act considered adverse to trade unionism were removed and all those favourable to them retained. References to the rights of workers *not* to be members of trade unions, to the illegality of closed shops and to agency and approved closed shops were removed by Trade Union and Labour Relations Acts 1974 and 1976. The statutory right to *be* trade union members remained. Had the changes provided for by the Acts gone no further than this it could have been claimed that all that the government intended so far as closed shops were concerned was a return to the pre-1971 situation. In the event the Acts went further as they were almost certainly bound to do because of the continued existence of provisions protecting employees generally against unfair dismissal. If the law made it automatically unfair to dismiss an employee on grounds of trade union membership and if any dismissal without sufficient reason was also unfair, what was it to do about those dismissed for refusing to join a closed shop? The Labour government's answer was that it should be automatically *fair* for an employer to dismiss in such a situation, provided that there was in existence at the time a 'union membership agreement or arrangement' (i.e. a closed shop device of some kind) *unless* the employee concerned 'genuinely objects on grounds of religious belief to being a member of any trade union whatsoever'.

Satisfactory as this situation seemed to be to trade unions generally, it was never to the taste of everyone as the Conservative opposition made clear during the passage of the Acts. The law could be read extremely restrictively. 'Genuine religious belief' might suggest that only those sects with written requirements of non-membership of unions might be included, or only those which subscribed as part of their credo to specific biblical texts. What of those who might hold non-membership as a *personal* religious belief? And those who might simply have strong personal convictions, albeit of a non-religious nature, against union membership? And why should successful objection be limited to those who object to trade unionism altogether? Would it not also be desirable to exempt those who objected, not to trade unionism in its entirety, but only to the particular union they were being compelled to join?

After 1974 the Trades Union Congress did its best to reassure those who thought that justice might not always be done by setting up its own Independent Review Committee to act as an appeal body in cases of alleged hardship arising within its own affiliated organisations. A number of bodies with formal union membership agreements (like the Post Office) followed suit in instituting appeal machinery accessible to individuals likely to be dismissed for reasons of non-membership. A Conservative policy statement in October 1977 made it certain that, when the party was next returned to office, it would take steps to amend the position. Having been successful in the General Election of May 1979, the Secretary of State for Employment issued a working paper in the summer of that year and an amending Employment Bill in December. This is expected to complete its parliamentary stages and receive royal assent by the summer of 1980.

The Bill, as at present drafted, does nothing to make closed shops illegal. Rather, it seeks to do four things. First, union membership agreements made after the date of the passing of the Bill will have no validity in law unless approved by a secret ballot in which *not less than 80 per cent* of those entitled to vote are in favour of its application. Second, the grounds on which an employee may successfully claim that he has been unfairly dismissed under a union membership agreement are enlarged in three respects. He may now object *'on grounds of conscience or other deeply held personal conviction* to being a member of any trade union whatsoever'; on similar grounds he may also object to being a member 'of a particular trade union'. He may also object that he was not a trade union member at the time when the union membership agreement came into force and cannot now be dismissed for refusing to join. Thirdly, appeal against an action taken against an individual in respect of a refusal to join a union or any particular union on grounds of conscience etc., is no longer to be confined to dismissal but extended to any 'action short of dismissal'. Fourthly, the Bill seeks to deal with those situations in which pressure for dismissal of an individual or individuals in a closed shop or other situation involves a strike or threat of a strike or other industrial action by a trade union. Here the employer may require the trade union or person who he claims exercised the pressure to be 'joined' with him in the action so that an industrial tribunal may order that party to pay a contribution to the employer in respect of any compensation awarded.

It remains to be seen what amendments, if any, will be made to the Bill during its passage through Parliament. What will happen as a result of the passage into law of those clauses already drafted is by no means certain. It is clearly the government's intention to make union membership agreements more difficult to achieve in future. We shall, when the Bill becomes law, clearly have seen the end of the 'union membership *arrangement*' in a formal sense, though in practice, as we have come to understand, many ways can be found of continuing the informal maintenance of closed shops. It is not easy to predict whether it will be possible easily to uphold non-membership 'on grounds of conscience or other deeply held personal conviction'. The courts have already held that the narrower term 'religious belief' should be interpreted to take account both of the religious sect to which a complainant belongs and his own personal belief. Will it now be possible to argue successfully on the basis of 'convictions' which are not religious at all – political convictions, for example? If that is so there may be little basis for acceptable application among active trade unionists and difficulties may also arise in relation to a legal provision which takes into account individual objections *to particular unions*. 'Joined' actions are also unknown territory. Though actual amounts extracted from union funds are likely to be small, resentment caused may be out of all proportion to the sums of money involved. A final issue relates not to the UK situation itself, but to our membership of the European Community and involvement with the European Convention on Human Rights. At the time of writing the findings of the European Commission on Human Rights on the appeal of three railwaymen against their exclusion from employment under the British Rail union membership agreement are not known. If their plea that the 'freedom of association' provision of the Convention implies also the right *not* to join a trade union it may or may not be that the provisions of the Employment Bill will meet its terms. If not, it seems certain that the UK would take the matter to the European Court on Human Rights for a final and binding ruling.

Trade union recognition
Industry in the United Kingdom has been singularly free from aggravated disputes about trade union recognition. Since the First World War it has gradually become incumbent upon all *public* authorities to consult and in practice to negotiate with organisations representative of their employees. In the *private* sector few employers of any size have adamantly resisted acknowledging the existence of unions, but there have been many concerns, particularly smaller ones, in which unions have been able to make very little headway with recruitment and even less with claims to be recognised. Until 1969 cases of this kind, in which unions claimed that they had unreasonably been denied the possibility of representing their members, were usually handled by conciliation officers of the Ministry of Labour or of its successor the Department of Employment. In 1966 30 per cent of the conciliation cases handled were of this kind.

In the face of resistance from the employer, conciliation officers could do little for the unions concerned and some of them may well have considered that greater powers would have enabled them to deal with recognition cases more adequately. In the event the matter was tackled differently. In its 1968 Report, the Donovan Commission recommended that, in order to secure an extension of the collective bargaining arrangements which it considered to be the best means of regulating relationships between employers and employed in the country, a Commission on Industrial Relations should be set up which would *inter alia* investigate and make recommendations in recognition cases. The CIR dealt with 13 such cases before it became incorporated, in the Industrial Relations Act 1971, in an involved statutory procedure with a similar aim in view. Under this it handled a further 32 cases until the Industrial Relations Act was repealed and new provisions were made under the Employment Protection Act 1975. Under s.11 of this Act, an independent trade union may refer to the Advisory, Conciliation and Arbitration Service issues in which it claims that recognition is being denied to it. ACAS is then required to

41

examine the issue, consult all affected parties to make inquiries and conciliate the matter if possible. Before making a final report recommending full or partial recognition or otherwise it is required to ascertain 'the opinion of workers to whom the issue relates by any means it thinks fit [and may under provisions laid down] determine to take a formal ballot of those workers or any description of such workers' (s.14). An employer who fails to comply with an ACAS recommendation may, on complaint by the trade union concerned, eventually be referred to the Central Arbitration Committee, which may require him to observe the terms and conditions specified by the trade union.

Between 1 February 1976, when the s. 11 recognition activities of ACAS began, and the end of 1978, 1,316 claims to recognition were made by trade unions. 734 (about 56 per cent) of these claims were withdrawn before the statutory procedure had run its full course, 411 (31 per cent) were still within the procedure, and 171 (13 per cent) had been reported on. It is hardly surprising that unions have complained that the procedure is slow and that the membership recruited in a company may well fall away as the proceedings drag on, in some cases, into their first and second years. This may in part be the explanation of falling numbers of s. 11 references after the first flush of trade union enthusiasm had died away in 1976 and 1977. In those two years, the annual average rate of claims was 540; in 1978 it fell to 279 and in the first five months of 1979 to no more than 99. It may also be that trade unions have been disappointed by the results of ACAS recommendations themselves. About one-half of the final reports have recommended recognition. Their total effect to 31 December 1978 was, in the words of the ACAS Chairman himself, to extend collective bargaining to only a little more than 10,000 employees[15], less than 1/10th of 1 per cent of current trade union membership in the United Kingdom.

At the same time trade unions have, since s. 11 came into force, made good use of their right to use the Section to involve employers in recognition discussions and to withdraw from these discussions at a later date, having already reached some understanding about representational or negotiating rights with the employers concerned or in the anticipation of doing so. The 734 cases of withdrawal already noted led to full recognition in 250 cases and to at least partial recognition in 96 others, covering a total of 40,000 employees[15]. Many unions may therefore believe that s. 11 has in this respect been of greater use to the movement and would favour its continuation at least in this form.

It is possible that some members of ACAS Council share this view, including the Chairman himself and would believe that the present procedure might well be replaced by some kind of 'compulsory arbitration' arrangement under which trade unions would, on recognition issues, be legally entitled to institute 'proceedings' against an employer whether he was willing or not. No doubt the CBI representatives on Council would dissent from this view, since s. 11 has not been popular with employers. Indeed, it has encountered a number of problems, not the least of which has been the lack of agreement on ACAS Council itself on how recognition procedures ought to be operated under the Act. For the Employment Protection Act gives considerable discretion to Council in carrying out its duties in regard to recognition under the broad requirement that the Advisory, Conciliation and Arbitration Service is to promote the improvement of industrial relations and to encourage the extension of collective bargaining[16]. The assumption appears to be that such discretion will not be interfered with, that the methods to be used by the Service in encouraging the extension of collective bargaining by trade union recognition will command general assent and that both are compatible with the obligation to promote better industrial relations. In practice, in three years of operation, persistent problems have arisen in each of these three respects. Courts of law, particularly in the Grunwick case, and that of UKAPE/W.H. Allen, have produced interpretations of the wording of the Act which have, in the view of ACAS, frequently made its job impossible[17]. Secondly, it has often proved to be impracticable to secure recognition by the procedures laid down without the danger of exacerbating, rather than improving, industrial relationships. Thirdly, employers, far from accepting ACAS methods of inquiry and procedure as fair and reasonable, have often considered them to be at best intrusive and at worst biased in the trade union direction – a direction imposed on the Service by the terms of the Act itself.

While it would not be true to say that in 1979 *all* support for the operation of the recognition provisions of the Employment Protection Act was seen to disappear, it did become evident that unless Parliament was willing either to redefine the powers of ACAS or to make provision for some form of unilateral union access to conciliation and arbitration on recognition questions in a form widely acceptable to trade unions and employers, there would be little prospect for their effective operation. In September 1979 it became clear what the attitude of the present government was likely to be. Pointing out that ACAS itself had reported that between February 1976 and the end of May 1979 more than 50 per cent more cases involving recognition had been processed through ordinary voluntary conciliation procedures[18] than through those specially provided under s. 11 it questioned whether the EPA's provisions might not simply be ended. The Employment Bill published on 6 December 1979 provides that ss. 11–16 shall be repealed.

Industrial democracy
The Labour government of 1974, as a third part of its legislative programme on industrial relations under the Social Contract between the Labour Party and the Trades Union Congress, [19] undertook to sponsor a statute on industrial democracy. The statute

did not appear before the government fell in spring 1979. One reason for this was its dependence during 1977/8 on Liberal Party support; another was the difficulty of drafting a Bill which would command general assent within the Labour movement.

The interest of trade unions in the idea of industrial democracy dates back at least to the nineteenth century, but began to take notably modern forms from about 1910. The Syndicalists and Guild Socialists of the period had notably little practical effect and their influence disappeared in the economic collapse of the early 1920s. Nevertheless, the movement left some trace behind. The Whitley Committee, which had concerned itself with the postwar reconstruction of industrial relations, had evolved by 1917 a scheme of 'self-government in industry' based upon Joint Industrial Councils, which was a milder form of approach, but owed something to the background of anticipation which more dogmatic socialists had created. Whitley idealism proved unjustified in the event, but the spirit of industrial democracy survived in the objects of the Trades Union Congress with their reference to 'adequate participation of the workers in the control and management of public services and industries', in interwar resolutions on trade union participation in industry and in the 'workers' control' rules of a number of leading trade unions.

These aspirations brought few tangible results. It came to be the understanding in the Labour movement that, when industries were nationalised, their Boards would carry no direct union representation, trade unionists being asked to stand down from their union commitments on appointment. The device which emerged from the Second World War was not 'participation' but 'consultation'. The Joint Production, Consultative and Advisory Committees established in the wartime engineering industry became a general model for adoption, workers' representatives being asked to sit on joint committees on matters of common interest between employees and management such as productivity and safety, but eschewing the use of negotiation and avoiding the discussion of individual grievances and bargaining about wages and conditions of work.

Joint Consultation has proved to be an extremely difficult animal to kill, though its imminent demise has been continually predicted. Committees have died and been reformed and died again, only to reproduce themselves elsewhere. Nevertheless it has found itself few confident friends. Consultative Committees carry little weight and tend to rely heavily on management enthusiasm for survival, while unions can often do better for their members by negotiation. Interest in industrial democracy seemed to be low until two new arrivals appeared upon the scene. The first was the reaffirmation by the TUC in its evidence to the Donovan Commission of its belief in the importance of industrial democracy with the rider that this ought to be extended to a change in company law to allow, at least in a discretionary form, the *direct* representation of trade unions on company boards; the second was the production of draft Directives on the subject by the European Economic Commission after the accession of the UK to that Community.

The EEC draft Directives on Company Law and on the European Company proved to be initially unacceptable to both sides of industry in this country since they followed the lines of the German and Dutch participative systems, making provision for a two-tier board arrangement of management and supervisory boards with union nominees in membership of the latter, and for a system of non-union works councils. Nevertheless they made inevitable some fundamental discussion of the questions involved and in 1973 the TUC elaborated on its evidence to the Donovan Commission, cautiously accepting the two-tier board provided that one-half of the supervisory board could be directly appointed by workpeople through trade union machinery, but rejecting the notion of Works Councils; these conclusions were later also adopted by the Labour Party.

By this time, a Labour government was in office and it seems to have been assumed that the principle of board representation by trade unionists was firmly accepted. All that remained was to obtain further advice on the wisdom or otherwise of adopting the amended EEC plan. The terms of reference of the Committee set up under Lord Bullock were not whether board participation was desirable, but how this might best be achieved. The Committee reported in January 1977 recommending a unitary board arrangement with equal numbers of directly elected worker representatives and shareholder representatives together with an odd number, more than one, of co-opted directors, the so-called '2x + y' formula. By this time divisions had appeared between those affiliated unions who subscribed to the notion of direct trade union involvement in, and therefore responsibility for, managerial decisions and those who preferred the more traditional approach of avoiding direct trade union involvement in such matters. Nationalised industries were one thing; private industry was another. Meanwhile, the Labour government was also modifying its position, moving towards a preference for a two-tier board structure, with phased movements towards parity of membership and a statutory framework of employee representation, and the TUC re-affirmed its own earlier position. The government was also, by the beginning of 1978, showing signs of acknowledging the need to compromise with employer as well as trade union opinion.

The result of these realignments became evident in the White Paper *Industrial Democracy* issued in May 1978[20] proposing that private employers employing more than 500 workers should be obliged, through a Joint Representative Committee representing trade unions, to discuss all major proposals affecting investment and organisation according to the new Code of Practice and subject to an

Industrial Democracy Commission, with employees able to retain the right to board level representation with two-tier board structure introduced into company law as an option to the present unitary board situation. Whether the broad consensus claimed in the White Paper to be the Labour government's new aim in industrial democracy 'was not ultimately tested before its defeat in the General Election of May 1979. The present Conservative government, unlike its counterpart between 1970 and 1974 under Mr. Heath, shows no apparent desire to move into a field which it prefers to call 'employee participation'. 'Each management and workforce must agree', in the words of the Secretary of State for Employment, 'that greater participation is to their mutual benefit and then hammer out a system that suits them best'.[21].

Strikes and picketing
Early in 1979 a number of calls were made from the Confederation of British Industry, the British Institute of Management and other bodies representing employers for a review of the law on strikes and picketing. These calls had a number of origins. Concern was expressed about the possibility that supplementary benefits paid to strikers' families might have a major effect in longer strikes which involved a real test of strength between employers and unions; the disruption caused by secondary picketing during the road haulage dispute in the winter of 1978–79 brought suggestions that changes should be made in a legal situation substantially unchanged since 1906; the tactics used by the Slade Art Union in extending membership in art and design firms had raised much criticism.

The Conservative government's Employment Bill published on 6 December 1979 deals with some of these matters. One clause seeks to provide protection against SLADE type recruitment tactics by providing that protection in a trade dispute against legal action for tort shall not apply where a person induces an employee of one employer to break his contract of employment in order to compel workers of another employer to join a particular trade union unless they are working in the same place. Principally, however, the Bill attempts to redefine the position of pickets. The proposal is that peaceful picketing 'in contemplation or furtherance of a trade dispute' shall only be protected when carried out by a person *attending at or near his own place of work* or by a trade union official accompanying him.

Notes

[1] Law on industrial relations passed by the Westminster parliament does not normally apply to Northern Ireland which has its own, usually similar, legislation.
[2] Trade Union and Labour Relations Act 1974, s.28.
[3] Certain corporate bodies, mostly professional associations, registered as trade unions under the now repealed Industrial Relations Act 1971, were allowed to

retain trade union status if registered under the Act before 16 September 1974, despite the fact that their *principal* purposes were not those of trade unions.

[4] *Department of Employment Gazette* December 1979. Comparable figures appear each year in the *Gazette*.

[5] The 'suspension' doctrine was incorporated into the Industrial Relations Act 1971 (now repealed); it does not appear in current legislation, though some leading cases have appeared to uphold it.

[6] Conspiracy and Protection of Property Act 1875, s.7. It is interesting also to note that in the course of trade disputes trade unions are at least assured that no special criminal offences can arise out of the collective nature of their actions. In the words of CPPA, s.3, 'an agreement or combination by two or more persons to do or procure the doing of any act in contemplation or furtherance of a trade dispute between employers and workmen shall not be indictable as a conspiracy is such a crime committed by one person would be punishable as a crime'.

[7] The Donovan Royal Commission on Trade Unions and Employers' Associations reported in 1968. Its recommendations, broadly construed, approved the voluntary system as the only practical approach to industry relations in Britain, while suggesting that the system would operate better if there was a development of more formal plant and company agreements and setting up a Commission on Industrial Relations to improve procedural and other devices. The Conservative Party's policy statement *Fair Deal at Work*, on which the 1971 Act was based, preceded the Donovan Report and had almost nothing in common with it.

[8] The so-called 'Section 11 procedure': see p. 42.

[9] The relevant cases are those of Hewlett *v.* Allen (1894) and Williams *v.* Butlers Ltd (1975).

[10] i.e. the form of closed shop in which employees are required to hold a trade union card *before* they can be considered for a job in contrast with a *post entry closed shop* in which the employee is required to join the union *after* hiring, perhaps within a specified period of time.

[11] Saggers *v.* British Railways Board (1977).

[12] An argument persuasively advanced by Robert Price and George Bain and supported by an econometric study published by the latter in conjunction with Farouk Elsheik as *Union Growth and the Business Cycle*, Basil Blackwell, 1976.

[13] It has also tended to prevent the access of existing and new unions alike to negotiating arrangements with which they have not previously been associated (see 'Trade union recognition' in this chapter).

[14] John Gerrard, Stephen Dunn & Michael Wright. 'The extent of closed shop arrangements in British Industry'. *Department of Employment Gazette*. January 1980.

[15] Published letter from the Chairman of the Council of the Advisory, Conciliation and Arbitration Service to the Secretary of State for Employment, 29 June 1979.

[16] Employment Protection Act s.1(2).

[17] The Grunwick case [1978 ICR 231 HL] established that ACAS had a mandatory duty to ascertain the opinions of workers to whom a recognition issue relates, whether or not unions and employers co-operate with it on a voluntary basis, a condition which in the Grunwick circumstances left the Service with a duty it could not perform. In the UKAPE case [UKAPE *v.* ACAS, 1979 IRLR 68 CA] in which ACAS recommended *against* the recognition of the United Kingdom Association of Professional Engineers by the engineering firm W.H. Allen of Bedford on the grounds that such recognition would be opposed by the Engineering Employers' Federation and the Confederation of Shipbuilding and Engineering Unions representing respectively the vast majority of employers and employees in that industry and would lead to industrial strife incompatible with its duty to promote 'good industrial relations', the Court of Appeal found that its findings were inadequate as to content, and that it had failed to perform its obligation under EPA s.1(2) to examine fully and fairly the case for the extension of collective bargaining.

[18] *Working Paper on the Trade Union Recognition Provisions of the Employment*

— *Protection Act 1975.* Department of Employment, September 1979, para. 6.

[19] The first and second parts were covered by the Trade Union and Labour Relations Act 1974 and the Employment Protection Act 1975.

[20] Cmnd. 7231, May 1978.

[21] James Prior, address to Industrial Society conference, London, 18 June 1979.

The Trades Union Congress and regional TUCs

TRADES UNION CONGRESS
Congress House, Great Russell Street, London WC1B 3LS
Tel: 01–636 4030

The TUC celebrated its centenary in 1968. Its role as a forum for British trade union opinion is unrivalled. Constitutionally it is a federation of autonomous organisations. While it enjoys a prestige which sets the seal of respectability in the Labour Movement upon any trade union which is accepted into its ranks, its power over affiliated organisations is more moral than formal.

Despite this limitation, it is widely held that the authority of the TUC has increased substantially during the past decade. With the support of the main affiliated unions it has enforced important TUC decisions such as those over pay policy between 1974 and 1977, even when these have not been universally popular. Its initiatives have become bolder and the interventions of its officials in disputes and other matters more assured. Whether or not this trend will continue remains to be seen. Reflecting the traditional attitudes of trade unions, the TUC is conservative by nature. Its long-established position has been that of moving with caution in an environment in which affiliated unions have been willing to vest in it only such functions and resources as would supplement their effectiveness but provide no challenge to their independence. It is still too early to say whether the TUC will truly develop into the 'General Staff of Labour' which its more enthusiastic supporters have often claimed it to be.

TUC organisation

The TUC consists of an annual Congress and a General Council with its attendant subcommittees, serviced by a permanent establishment of officials – a General Secretary, Assistant General Secretary, heads of Departments and their staff. For the year 1979–80, the personalities, committees and departments involved are as follows:

GENERAL COUNCIL 1979–80
Chairman
T. Pavry   Fire Brigades Union

A.L. Sapper	The Association of Cinematograph, Television and Allied Technicians
W. Sirs	Iron and Steel Trades Confederation
J.H. Slater, CBE	National Union of Seamen
A.R. Smith	National Union of Tailors and Garment Workers
E.A.G. Spanswick	Confederation of Health Service Employees
K.R. Thomas	Civil and Public Services Association
C.H. Urwin	Transport and General Workers' Union
S. Weighell	National Union of Railwaymen
W.H.P. Whatley	Union of Shop, Distributive and Allied Workers
L. Wood	Union of Construction, Allied Trades and Technicians

OFFICIALS
General Secretary: Rt. Hon. Lionel Murray, P.C., OBE
Deputy General Secretary: N.D. Willis
Assistant General Secretaries: D.E. Lea, OBE
                                                    K. Graham, OBE
Economic: W. Callaghan
Education: R.A. Jackson
Finance: C. Page
International: J.A. Hargreaves
Organisation and Industrial Relations: J. Monks
Press and Information: B.P. Barber
Social Insurance and Industrial Welfare: P. Jacques

COMMITTEES
Standing Committees

Finance and General Purposes	Employment Policy and Organisation
International	Economic
Education	Equal Rights
Social Insurance and Industrial Welfare	

Industry Committees

Construction Industry Committee	Steel Industry Trade Union Consultative Committee
Fuel and Power Industries Committee	
Health Services Committee	Textile, Clothing and Footwear Industries Committee
Hotel and Catering Industry Committee	
Local Government Committee	Transport Industries Committee
Printing Industries Committee	

Joint Committees

Women's Advisory Committee	Public Services Committee
Race Relations Advisory Committee	Nationalised Industry Committee
Trades Councils' Joint Consultative Committee	
National Economic Development Council	

JOINT BODIES
National Council of Labour TUC/CBI Joint Standing Committee
Joint BMA/TUC Committee
TUC Centenary Institute of Occupational Health Standing Committee
TUC Educational Trust

TUC REGIONAL COUNCILS: SECRETARIES

Northern
J.W. Harper
Archbold House,
Archbold Terrace,
Newcastle upon Tyne 2
Tel: Newcastle upon Tyne
(0632) 814355

North West
C. Barnett
222 Stamford Street,
Ashton-under-Lyne,
Lancashire OL6 7YZ
Tel: 061–330 6652
or 061–330 7073

East Midlands
J.M. Hardy
13 Delaware Road,
Leicester LE5 6LJ
Tel: Leicester (0533) 415437

South East
J. Dromey
13 Plympton Road,
London NW6
Tel: 01–328 7598

Wales TUC
~~George Wright~~ D. JENKINS
Transport House,
1 Cathedral Road,
Cardiff,
South Glamorgan
Tel: (0222) 394521

Yorkshire and Humberside
Mrs B. Huffinley
Leeds Trades Council Club,
Savile Mount,
Leeds 7
Tel: Leeds (0532) 620629

West Midlands
Sir David Perris
191 Corporation Street,
Birmingham B4 6RU
Tel: 021–236 1240

East Anglia
I.A.H. Jordan
119 Newmarket Road,
Cambridge CB5 8HA
Tel: Cambridge (0223) 67691

South West
B. Bailey
16 The Crescent,
Taunton,
Somerset
Tel: Taunton (0823) 88031

Table 22
The Trades Union Congress – Trade Groups,
General Council representation, delegates,
membership and affiliation fees, 1979

	Trade Group	Number of			Membership '000	Affiliation fees £'000
		Seats	Unions	Delegates		
1	Mining and quarrying	2	3	59	291.3	58.3
2	Railways	2	3	42	277.2	55.4
3	Transport (excl. r'lys)	6	6	109	2,190.1	438.0
4	Shipbuilding	1	1	12	131.1	26.2
5	Engineering, founding, vehicle building	4	10	78	1,434.2	286.8
6	Technical engineering and scientific	2	4	57	728.6	145.7
7	Electricity	1	1	32	420.0	84.0
8	Iron, steel and minor metal trades	1	9	31	141.8	28.4
9	Building, wood-working and furnishing	2	4	43	409.7	82.0
10	Printing and paper	1	6	80	426.3	85.3
11	Textiles	1	15	29	121.0	24.0
12	Clothing, leather and boot and shoe	1	6	42	261.9	52.4
13	Glass, ceramics, chemicals, food, drink, tobacco, brushmaking and distribution	2	9	75	616.8	123.3
14	Agriculture	1	1	15	85.0	17.0
15	Public employees	6	11	207	2,259.2	451.8
16	Civil Servants and Post Office	3	12	147	947.4	189.5
17	Professional, clerical and entertainment	2	10	68	421.7	84.3
18	General workers	3	1	74	964.8	193.0
		41	112	1,200	12,128.1	2,425.4

Today the TUC is probably more widely representative of the interests of British labour than it has ever been in its eleven decades of existence. For a substantial part of its life it was almost wholly concerned with manual worker organisations. Civil Service associations were debarred from membership by the Trade Disputes and Trade Union Act 1927 until that statute was repealed by the first postwar Labour government in 1946. Thereafter the non-manual interests of the TUC began to develop as such unions affiliated, followed by the Local and Government Officers in 1964, the National Union of Teachers in 1970, the Association of University Teachers in 1976 and the First Division Association, which caters for the highest ranks of the Civil Service, in 1977 and, in 1979, by the Hospital

Consultants and Specialists Association. At the same time an increase in membership of private sector white collar unions took place, as noted in Table 4, from the late 1960s. While the assumption continues that it is the senior officials of manual unions who take the lead in TUC policy making, the balance is gradually being redressed in favour of white collar workers as membership proportions change.

It is unquestionable also that the TUC's work load has increased. It is now expected to play an important role in relation to new institutions such as the National Economic Development Council, the Manpower Services Commission, the Health and Safety Commission, the Equal Opportunities Commission and the Council of the Advisory, Conciliation and Arbitration Service, as well as maintaining its customary relations with national government. More activity arises from Britain's membership of the European Economic Community. There is more educational work to be done and the committee structure of the TUC develops almost year by year. Congress, General Council and permanent establishment have all come under pressure, a pressure increased by the growing demands of affiliated unions for closer consultation and involvement in day-to-day decision making between annual Congresses.

Congress itself, with its 1,100 and more delegates, has, since 1900, met on the first Monday in September each year and lasts for five days. Its functions are to consider the work of the General Council over the previous twelve months, to discuss and take decisions on motions submitted by affiliated unions and to elect the General Council for the following year.

It also has the task of electing the TUC General Secretary, though it is rarely called upon to do so, since the TUC has had only five General Secretaries since 1926, three of whom are still alive.[1] Congress has become a major event in the industrial calendar, attended by fraternal delegates from other trade union movements and by innumerable guests and visitors who find attendance advantageous as a means of taking the trade union temperature or of making contact with the most representative group of trade union leaders, great and small, to be found in one place at any time during the year. So important has the platform for trade unionism represented by Congress become that the Confederation of British Industry thought fit to redress the balance so far as it could by beginning its own annual conference in 1977.

The *General Council*, now with 41 members, has existed in its present form since 1921, when it replaced the former Parliamentary Committee. Between Congresses, unless it wishes to consult more widely by calling a Special Congress, Conference of Executives or similar, it is the authentic voice of the TUC, charged with pursuing the aims of Congress, encouraging common action between affiliates, giving assistance with organisation, managing and investing TUC funds and adjusting differences between member unions. Some thirty of the 112 affiliated unions are represented on it, and almost all the biggest names in the trade union hierarchy. Since all unions at

Congress vote in the elections for each of the eighteen Trade Groups (see Table 22) and for the two women's seats, election to the General Council is out of the question without the support of one or more of the TUC membership giants. Seats, once obtained, are rarely lost. Most General Council members remain until the Congress following their retirement from their own union and seniority is important in determining the Council Chairmanship and that of major committees.

Nevertheless voting for the General Council on union size alone would produce a situation much less favourable to smaller unions than at present where seats are concerned. Similarly, small TUC Trade Groups, such as Agriculture, Textiles, Shipbuilding and Iron and Steel, tend to be over-represented on the General Council compared with the largest such as Public Employees, Transport and the Civil Servants (see Figure 2 and Table 22). In partial compensation these last three were given an extra seat in 1977–78, but the problem of achieving both an arithmetically accurate and technically acceptable balance is probably insoluble, especially at a time when dramatic changes in numbers have been taking place between Groups. In 1919 the largest Groups were General Workers, (Group 17), Mining and Quarrying (Group 1), followed by Engineering (Group 5) and Railways (Group 2); Groups for Electricity (the present Group 7) and Technical Engineering and Scientific (the present Group 6) did not exist, while Textiles were then sufficiently large to merit two Groups, one for Cotton and the other for Wool etc., while Clothing was also separated from Boots and Shoes etc. The situation is very different today as Table 22 shows. It is hardly surprising that, given the difficulties and the problems of balancing the interests of affiliated unions, the General Council has so far been unable to recommend to Congress any radical reform of its composition which would secure general assent.

Adaptation of the General Council's Committee arrangements to meet demands for greater consultation with affiliated organisation has presented a simpler problem. Advisory Committees which involve union representatives drawn from outside the General Council's ranks have existed for many years for Women, for Trades Councils and for Non-Manual Workers. In view of the changed composition of both Congress and Council where non-manual workers are concerned, the last named was recently abolished, but a Race Relations Advisory Committee was added. Of more radical importance has been the establishment of Industry Committees. This began when it was agreed in the middle 1960s that the sixteen unions concerned in the Labour government's second nationalisation of the iron and steel industry should be co-ordinated in their relationships with the nascent British Steel Corporation under the umbrella of the TUC. The resultant Steel Industry Trade Union Consultative Committee still continues. To it, since a major decision of Congress in favour of industrial committees in 1970, a further eight have been added. In some cases these take the place of federations which have disappeared in the course of trade

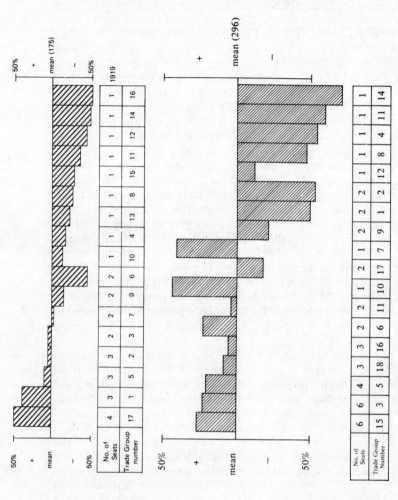

No. of Seats	4	3	3	2	2	2	1	1	1	1	1	1	1	1			1919
Trade Group number	17	1	5	3	7	9	6	10	4	13	8	15	11	12	14	16

No. of Seats	6	6	4	3	3	2	2	2	2	2	2	1	1	1	1	1
Trade Group Number	15	3	5	18	16	6	11	10	17	7	9	1	12	8	4	11	14

Figure 2 Average members per Parliamentary Committee (1919) and per General Council (1979) seat by Trade Group — % from the Mean

The figure shows the mean number of members per Parliamentary Committee seat for 1919 (175) and per General Council seat in 1979 (296) and the percentage deviation of each Trade Group from this mean. Trade Groups being arranged in descending order of size from left to right.

union amalgamations – the Construction and Printing Industry Committees are cases in point. These, and others, may have been set up in the first place for particular purposes, e.g. originally in the case of the Construction Committee to consider 'the lump' and in the case of the Health Services Committee to look into problems of trade union organisation. Only the Steel Committee has negotiating functions, acting rather like the trade unions side of a Joint Industrial Council.

The role of the General Council in inter-union disputes has already been discussed (p. 18). Other Committees of interest are those relating to outside bodies. After the Second World War, the two principal committees linking the TUC with government were the National Joint Advisory Council and the National Production Consultative and Advisory Committee on Industry. These have not met for many years, their functions having been taken over by the National Economic Development Council. The Council has also been used as a link with employers at a national level when government–TUC–Confederation of British Industry relations have been strained. A joint committee with the CBI also formally exists, but no meetings have been held for some time.

The TUC's Liaison Committee with the Labour Party has been more active. Contrary to popular opinion, the TUC itself has no direct political affiliations, nor does it require individual unions to affiliate to the Labour Party as a condition of membership. Not all TUC unions are Labour Party affiliates, nor do all of them maintain political funds under the Trade Union Act 1913 (see pp. 27 and 28). Historically the TUC, the Labour Party and the Co-operative Movement have regarded themselves as sectors or wings of a larger Labour Movement, acting for the most part autonomously in their respective industrial, political and distributive and production fields, but sharing many common objectives and uniting on important issues – hence the National Council of Labour, the oldest, and irregularly convened, national forum for the three socialist interests.[2] So far as trade unions were concerned, this concept of separate roles could hardly survive intact the development of incomes policies in which the independence of collective bargaining was threatened. Hence the deterioration of relationships between unions and the Labour Party under the Labour government of 1964 to 1970, which developed an interventionist policy through the Department of Employment and the National Board for Prices and Incomes. The dislike which this stimulated from trade unions was only outdone by the even more determined opposition of trade unions, led by the TUC, to the Conservative Heath government's Industrial Relations Act 1971. It was only resolved by the development of the 'Social Contract' between the TUC and the Labour Party. For some time the TUC's Liaison Committee with the Labour Party performed an active function in discussing Labour government proposals in implementation of the 'Contract' and in attempting, not always successfully, to bridge any gap between the aspirations of trade unionism and those of political reality as seen by the Party.

Recent developments

General Council attitudes are often supposed to be affected by the personalities and policies of major affiliated organisations. The immediate postwar period, for example, until the middle 1950s, is often recalled as a period of moderation under the influence of Arthur Deakin of the Transport and General Workers' Union, Tom Williamson of the General and Municipal Workers and Will Lawther of the Mineworkers – an era immediately followed by the more radical militancy of Frank Cousins. It may simply be that the leaders of large unions on their election to office and almost automatic translation to the General Council of the TUC closely reflect the views and aspirations of the members who elected them. The past decade has, for many purposes, been seen as the period of Jack Jones of the TGWU and Hugh Scanlon of the Engineers, first in terms of active support for shop stewards and workplace bargaining and then, from about the time of the fall of the Heath government in 1974, of close co-operation with the Wilson–Callaghan administration on pay and prices policy under the 'Social Contract' in return for acceptably socialist policies, favourable legislation on industrial relations and moves towards industrial democracy.

In 1978 the retirements of both Jack Jones and Hugh (now Lord) Scanlon brought changes in the leadership of both the Transport Workers and the Engineers. Already the advantages gained by the unions in the Employment Protection Act seemed, in some respects, to be less evident than formerly. Not only had the 'Social Contract' run its course; bright hopes for an extension of collective bargaining through statutory recognition procedures, for a radical move in the direction of industrial democracy, for participation agreements under the Industry Act and for a deepening of collective regulation through disclosure of information by companies, had also become dim.

The fall of the Callaghan government in the spring of 1979 was no more, in the trade union sense, than a farewell to an administration that seemed to have already run its natural span of life. The TUC Congress at Blackpool in the previous September had been less than enthusiastic about its performance. Unemployment demanded stronger action to stimulate demand and growth, the European Economic Community was imposing unfair burdens, the General Agreement on Tariffs and Trade ought to be amended to permit the introduction of import controls, a Wealth Tax ought to be introduced and the House of Lords reformed. These items formed part of a new package called *The Next Three Years and into the Eighties*. Solidarity with the Labour Government appeared to be tempered not only by the expectation of a General Election in the not too distant future, but also by the need to make it evident to any future Labour government that radical socialist measures were expected. Congress suspected that the rights newly won in the Employment Protection Act were being eroded by the courts. This had to be put right. A major effort had to be made to reach Planning Agreements with at least 100 major companies. The benefits of North Sea oil ought to be used to regenerate British industry and to set new goals in the creation of a compassionate society. Above all, there was to be no government control over wages. Collective bargaining was to be free.

After the election of May 1979 the TUC found itself faced, not by a sympathetic Labour administration but by a government led by Margaret Thatcher pledged to monetarist non-interventionism in economic affairs and to moderate but nevertheless recognisably Conservative attitudes towards the further reform of industrial relations. The Congress of 1979 was outspoken in its opposition to both aspects of policy. In practice, the General Council had already set out to be cautious. The loss of its most prominent personalities had lessened its impact on the Labour movement as a whole and it has so far not sought the confrontation it encouraged in 1971. Before Congress it had already decided that it would not embark upon a militant campaign against the new Conservative administration. Rather it would aim to convince public and trade union opinion that Conservative policies were against the interests of working people and ultimately doomed to failure. This view was reflected in Congress itself, where Council tabled for debate a motion headed *Campaign for Economic and Social Advance*, which called for a balanced growth of employment and output in both public and private sectors of the economy, the planned development of technical change, a national consensus on the distribution of income and wealth, and the recognition of the indispensable part which pensions, child benefits, education, health and other public services play in the 'social wage'. The publication of the government's proposals for industrial relations reform in the Employment Bill of December 1979 served to raise the temperature but has not set the trade union movement alight. At the time of writing (January 1980) the Bill, the evident desire of the government to enforce even greater economies in public expenditure and the effect of its enforcement of cash limits in producing a crisis of labour-management relationships in the steel industry threaten, but have not yet produced, a confrontation. The stance of the government, with its reliance on market forces rather than direct intervention, has been remote and conciliatory rather than involved and aggressive; the attitude of the TUC has been one of disbelief rather than militancy. It remains to be seen whether either government or the General Council will be able to retain these positions.

SCOTTISH TRADES UNION CONGRESS
Middleton House, 16 Woodlands Terrace, Glasgow G3 6DF
Tel: 041-332 4946/7/8

The Scottish TUC was established in 1897 and is the national co-ordinating body for the trade union movement in Scotland. Its formation resulted from a meeting of Scottish trades councils following a decision of the Trades Union Congress in 1895 to exclude trades councils from direct TUC representation. Since the 1920s it has been generally agreed between the TUC and the STUC that the latter should look after Scottish issues and make appropriate representation to the British government on such matters. Trade unions with membership both in Scotland and elsewhere in the United Kingdom commonly affiliate both to the STUC and to the TUC; a few unions wholly confined to Scotland are affiliated to the STUC only. At the first Congress in 1897, 55 trade unions with a total membership of 41,090 were present; at the 1979 Congress the number of unions affiliated was 80 and the number of trades councils 42. Total affiliated membership was 1,053,908.

Congress meets annually in April and comprises delegates from each affiliated union elected on the basis of one for every 500 members affiliated, with the addition of three delegates from each affiliated trades council. Each affiliated organisation has the right to submit three motions for inclusion in the agenda and three amendments to motions appearing on the preliminary agenda. Affiliated unions are divided into eleven industrial sections:

Section 1 – Fuel and power
Section 2 – Transport and docks
Section 3 – Shipbuilding, engineering, founding, iron and steel, vehicle and minor metal trades
Section 4 – Building, woodworkers and furnishing
Section 5 – Printing and paper
Section 6 – Clothing, boot and shoe, leather, textile and pottery
Section 7 – Food, drink, tobacco and distributive
Section 8 – Non-manual workers
Section 9 – Civil and public servants
Section 10 – Local government employees
Section 11 – Education
Section 12 – Trades councils

Congress elects annually a General Council comprising 21 members, one of whom is elected from nominations made by trades councils. Organisations with over 100,000 membership are entitled to nominate two persons for membership; all other organisations are entitled to nominate one person only. The General Council is responsible for implementing annual Congress decisions and for deciding on issues on which no policy has been made.

Congress is specifically concerned with matters relating to the employment of its affiliated membership and to the services provided for them by both national and local government. It has specifically campaigned on issues of regional economic policy and is represented on a multiplicity of committees attached to and appointed by the Scottish Office. It is also much taken up with education, health, housing and other social provisions, many aspects of which are covered by separate and distinct Scottish legislation.

The General Council appoints from its membership an Economic Committee, a General Purposes Committee (responsible for Health, Housing, political issues and relations between unions) and an Education Committee. Subcommittees of these three main committees cover local government – Employment and Service, Health Services – Employment and Service; Transport and Entertainment; and the Arts. Congress is responsible for the organisation of a Youth Advisory Committee Conference from which the Youth Advisory Committee is elected and a Women's Advisory Committee Conference from which a Women's Advisory Committee is elected.

OFFICERS OF CONGRESS 1979
Chairman: W. Dougan,
District Delegate,
Amalgamated Society of Boilermakers, Shipwrights, Blacksmiths and
Structural Workers,
6 Lansdowne Crescent,
Glasgow G29 6NQ

Vice-Chairman: J. Morrell,
Scottish Secretary,
General and Municipal Workers' Union,
4 Park Gate,
Glasgow G3 6BD

Treasurer: A. Kitson,
Executive Officer,
Transport and General Workers' Union,
308 Albert Drive,
Glasgow G41 5RR

FULL-TIME OFFICIALS
General Secretary: J. Milne
Deputy General Secretary: J. Henry
Assistant Secretary Research: D. Harrison
Assistant Secretary: W. Speirs
Administrative Officer: Mrs R. McDonald

WALES TRADE UNION COUNCIL Cyngor Undebau Llanfur Cymru
1 Cathedral Road, Cardiff
Tel: (Cardiff) 0222 371495

The Wales TUC represents trade unionists in Wales on economic, social and political matters of interest to their work and conditions of employment in the Principality; it also keeps the Trades Union Congress informed of such matters and is responsible for giving effect to TUC policies in Wales. It is formally regarded by the TUC as part of its regional structure, together with eight Regional Councils in England.

The Wales TUC is a relative newcomer on the trade union scene. Executive decisions by the Transport and General Workers' Union and the National Union of Mineworkers formed a basis for the establishment of a working party and the calling of a meeting of unions in Wales to consider its proposals in December 1972. A Trades Union Congress decision in September 1973 to reorganise its regional arrangements and to incorporate within them the Wales TUC made possible a first annual conference in 1974. Conference takes place each year on the first Friday in May and the Saturday and Sunday which follow. In 1979 75 TUC affiliated unions with membership in Wales were represented, together with 48 trades councils and 8 County Associations of Trades Councils. The total affiliated membership at the end of 1978 was 656,000.

The General Council of the Wales TUC consists of 45 members, 30 representing affiliated unions in 16 Trade Groups and 15 representing County Associations of Trades Councils. The Secretary is subject to annual election by Council.

OFFICIALS 1978–79
Secretary: G.H. Wright, MBE
Research and Administrative Officer: D.J. Jenkins

1979/80 GENERAL COUNCIL
Chairman: Mrs. S.J. Jones, Mid Glamorgan CATC
Vice-Chairman: J.M. Griffiths, TGWU
Treasurer: C.L. Paul, IRSF

Mining (2)
G. Rees, NUM,
Sardis Road,
Pontypridd,
Mid Glamorgan

E. Williams, NUM,
Sardis Road,
Pontypridd,
Mid Glamorgan

Railways (1)
A. Kirkwood, NUR,
10 Padarn Close,
Lakeside,
Cardiff

Transport
D. Driscoll,
3a Bryncelyn Road,
Corseinon,
Swansea

A. North, T&GWU,
Dockers Hall,
Coronation Street,
Barry Dock

C.B. Pitson,
346 Llangyfelach Road,
Brynhyfryd,
Swansea

J.L. McLaren,
78 Manod Road,
Blaenau Ffestiniog,
Gwynedd

Engineering Founding (4)
W.A. Cooper, AUEW(F),
1/3 Fitzalan Place,
Cardiff

T.D. King, AUEW(C),
25 Victoria Gardens,
Neath,
W. Glamorgan

T.J. Lloyd, AUEW(E),
1/3 Fitzalan Place,
Cardiff

D.S. Gough, AUEW(E),
AUEW House,
46/48 Mount Pleasant,
Liverpool L3 5SE

Technical Engineering, Scientific (1)
N. Hufton, ASTMS

Electricity (1)
R.D. Jones, EETPU

Iron, steel, metal trades (2)
J. Foley, ISTC,

I.C. Wigley, ASBSBSW,
14 Park Street,
Bridgend,
Mid Glamorgan

Building, woodworking, furniture (1)
R. Bowen, UCATT,
61 Cowbridge Road East,
Cardiff

Printing and paper (1)
N. Chinnock,
5 Eustace Drive,
Tyn-y-Coed,
Bryncethin,
Bridgend

Textiles, clothing, footwear (1)
A.J. Hawkins, NUTGW,
57 Churchill Way,
Cardiff

*Agriculture, food, drink, tobacco
distribution, ceramics* (2)
B. Davies, NUAAW,
Derwendeg,
36 Hall Drive,
North Cornelly,
Bridgend,
Mid Glamorgan

W.J. Jones, USDAW,
2nd Floor, Caerwys House,
1 Windsor Lane,
Cardiff

Public employees (3)
W.J. Davies, NALGO,
17 Cwmamman Road,
Glanamman,
Ammanford,
Dyfed SA18 1DQ

G.J. Phillips, NALGO,
58 Bryn Catwg,
Cadoxton,
Neath

D. Gregory, NUPE

Civil servants Post Office
J.D. Stevens, UPW,
26 Alexandra Road,
Canton,
Cardiff

Professional, clerical, entertainment (1)
O.G. Saunders, APEX,
57/59 St Mary Street,
Cardiff

General workers (2)
I. Dunn, GMWU,
17 Newport Road,
Cardiff

H. Harris, GMWU,
17 Newport Road,
Cardiff

CATC Section

Clwyd
B. Scragg,
4 Llwyni Drive,
Connahs Quay,
Deeside,
Clwyd

J.O. Morris,
65 Regent Street,
Wrexham,
Clwyd

Gwynedd
C. Hughes,
'Koholeth',
131, London Road,
Holyhead,
Gwynedd

Dyfed
D.H. Williams,
16 Christopher Street,
Llanelli

T.G. Thomas, ASLEF,
63 Llewellyn Street,
Llanelli

Powys
B. Wilson,

Gwent
H.R. Monday,
12 Melfort Road,
Newport,
Gwent

G.R. Morgan, T&GWU,
32 Berkeley Crescent,
Sebastopol,
Pontypool,
Gwent

West Glamorgan
B. John, T&GWU,
18 Park Crescent,
Lonlas,
Skewen,
W. Glamorgan

J.F. Ryan

Mid Glamorgan
D.I. Davies,
66 Merthyr Mawr Road,
Bridgend CF31 3NR

D. Evans,
58 Garfield Avenue,
Bridgend

South Glamorgan
W.J. Ball, IRSF,
130 Caerau Lane,
Ely,
Cardiff

[1] Walter (now Lord) Citrine, Sir Vincent Tewson, George Woodcock, Victor Feather and Lionel Murray. Victor Feather died in 1976 and George Woodcock in 1979.
[2] The National Council of Labour has met several times during the past few years at the request of the Co-operative Union to discuss such subjects as counter-inflation policies, workers' co-operatives, consumer protection and other matters of common interest.

Part 2
Trade Union
Organisations

International organisations
Trade union confederations
Trade union federations
Trades Councils

International organisations

EUROPEAN TRADE UNION CONFEDERATION (ETUC)
37 rue Montagne-aux-Herbes-Potageres, 1000 Brussels, Belgium
Tel: Brussels 217.91.41 and 217.91.42

Founded in 1958 as the European Trade Union Secretariat of ICFTU. In 1969 new statutes were adopted and the name was changed to the European Confederation of Free Trade Unions in the Community. The present title was adopted in 1973, the year the United Kingdom became a member of the European Economic Community. The aims of the ETUC are to represent and uphold the social, cultural and economic interests of workers in Europe.

Members are to be found in 30 national trade union confederations, in 17 countries, and in 1976 totalled approximately 37 million.

Secretary General: Theo Rasschert

INTERNATIONAL CONFEDERATION OF FREE TRADE UNIONS (ICFTU)
37–41 rue Montagne-aux-Herbes-Potageres, 1000 Brussels, Belgium
Tel: Brussels 217.80.85

Formed in London in December 1949 by non-communist countries formerly in membership of the World Federation of Trade Unions (see below), but now consisting of both these and underdeveloped countries, 88 in all in 1975 with a total membership of more than 53 million.

Africa:	Ethiopia, Gambia, Guinea Bissau, Guyana, Liberia, Madagascar, Malawi, Mauritius, Nigeria, St Helena, Sierra Leone, Tunisia, Upper Volta
America:	Argentina, Barbados, Belize, Bermuda, Bolivia, Brazil, Canada, Chile, Colombia, Costa Rica, Curacao, Dominica, Dominican Republic, Ecuador, El Salvador, Falkland, Grenada, Guatemala, Honduras, Jamaica, Mexico, Nicaragua, Panama, Paraguay, Peru, Puerto Rico, St Kitts/Nevis, St Lucia, St Vincent, Surinam, Trinidad/Tobago, USA, Uruguay, Venezuela
Asia:	Bangladesh, China, Hong Kong, India, Indonesia, Israel, Japan, South Korea, Lebanon, Malaysia, Nepal,

	Pakistan, Philippines, Singapore, Sri Lanka
Australasia:	Australia, Fiji, New Zealand, Papua/New Guinea
Europe:	Austria, Basque Country, Belgium, Cyprus, Denmark, Estonia, Finland, France, Germany, Greece, Iceland, Italy, Luxembourg, Malta, Netherlands, Norway, San Marino, Spain, Sweden, Switzerland, Turkey, United Kingdom

Secretary General: Otto Kersten

Publications: *Free Labour World* (monthly), *International Trade Union News* (fortnightly), *Economic and Social Bulletin* (every 2 months); handbook, congress reports.

INTERNATIONAL LABOUR ORGANISATION (ILO)
International Labour Office (BIT), 4 route des Morillons, CH1211 Geneva 22, Switzerland
Tel: Geneva 98.52.11

Established in June 1919 as a result of the Treaty of Versailles and associated in 1946 with the United Nations as a specialised agency. Its objects are to raise living and working standards throughout the world and to eliminate social injustices and the causes of unrest which constitute a cause of war. The Declaration of Philadelphia of 1944 obliged nations to pursue programmes to achieve full employment and the raising of living standards, to employ workers in jobs for which they were best fitted, to provide facilities for the training and transfer of workers and to secure the effective recognition of the right to collective bargaining and the rights of management and labour to protect the workers' life and health.

The ILO is a tripartite body of government, workers' and employers' representatives. The International Labour Conference (normally once a year) adopts standards embodied in international labour conventions and recommendations by two-thirds of delegates present. Conventions require ratification by member countries; recommendations are not subject to ratification but serve as a guide on various labour matters.

The USA gave notice to leave the ILO in 1975 and this has not been revoked. The decision was taken on the grounds that the ILO applied unequal standards to its various members, it made irresponsible charges against countries without proper evidence and debated extraneous political matters and that many countries had no independent labour or employer organisations.

OFFICIALS
Director General: Francis Blanchard
Deputy Directors General: Bortil Bolin, S. Jain, J. McDonald
Assistant Directors General: S. Bugan, X. Caballero Tmayo, P Astapenko, N. Tkahashi

States members of the ILO on 2 May 1978 (135)

Afghanistan	Iran
Algeria	Iraq
Angola	Ireland
Argentina	Israel
Australia	Italy
Austria	Ivory Coast
Bahamas	Jamaica
Bahrain	Japan
Bangladesh	Jordan
Barbados	Democratic Kampuchea
Belgium	Kenya
Benin	Kuwait
Bolivia	Lao Republic
Botswana	Lebanon
Brazil	Liberia
Bulgaria	Libyan Arab Jamahiriya
Burma	Luxembourg
Burundi	Madagascar
Byelorussian Soviet	Malawi
Socialist Republic	Malaysia
United Republic of Cameroon	Mali
Canada	Malta
Central African Empire	Mauritania
Chad	Mauritius
Chile	Mexico
China	Mongolia
Colombia	Morocco
Congo	Mozambique
Costa Rica	Nepal
Cuba	Netherlands
Cyprus	New Zealand
Czechoslovakia	Nicaragua
Democratic Yemen	Niger
Denmark	Nigeria
Dominican Republic	Norway
Ecuador	Pakistan
Egypt	Panama
El Salvador	Papua New Guinea
Ethiopia	Paraguay
Fiji	Peru
Finland	Philippines
France	Poland
Gabon	Portugal
German Democratic Republic	Qatar
Germany, Federal Republic of	Romania
Ghana	Rwanda
Greece	Saudi Arabia
Guatemala	Senegal
Guinea	Seychelles
Guinea Bissau	Sierra Leone
Guyana	Singapore
Haïti	Somalia
Honduras	Spain
Hungary	Sri Lanka
Iceland	Sudan
India	Surinam
Indonesia	Swaziland

Sweden	Union of Soviet Socialist
Switzerland	Republics
Syrian Arab Republic	United Arab Emirates
Tanzania	United Kingdom
Thailand	Upper Volta
Togo	Uruguay
Trinidad and Tobago	Venezuela
Tunisia	Viet Nam
Turkey	Yemen
Uganda	Yugoslavia
Ukrainian Soviet Socialist	Zaire
Republic	Zambia

Publications: International studies, surveys, works of practical guidance or reference on questions of social policy, manpower, industrial relations, working conditions, social security, training, management development, etc. (English, French, Spanish unless otherwise stated.) *International Labour Review* (monthly): special articles, notes on current developments and bibliography. *Official Bulletin* (quarterly): information and documents relating to ILO activities. *Legislative Series* (bi-monthly): selected labour and social security laws and regulations. *Bulletin of Labour Statistics* (quarterly). *Year Book of Labour Statistics. CIRF Abstracts* (in English and French): a service providing digests of articles, laws, reports dealing with vocational training (annual subscription). *CIRF monographs* : reports for the annual sessions of the International Labour Conference (English, French, German, Russian, Spanish). Minutes of the Governing Body of the ILO. *ILO-Information* (6 a year): a bulletin issued in Arabic, Danish, English, Finnish, French, German, Hindi, Italian, Japanese, Norwegian, Russian, Spanish, Swedish and Urdu.

INTERNATIONAL TRADE SECRETARIATS (ITS)

International trade union organisations based upon federal structure of national trade unions in particular trades and industries, associated with the International Confederation of Free Trade Unions.

INTERNATIONAL FEDERATION OF BUILDING AND WOODWORKERS (IFBWW)
27–29 rue de la Coulouvreniere, 1204 Geneva, Switzerland
Tel: Geneva 21.16.11

Founded in August 1891 in Brussels and adopting its present title in 1934. Membership in 1976 totalled 3 million members in 110 national trade unions based in 50 countries.

Secretary General: John Löfblad

Publication: *IFBWW Bulletin* (quarterly)

INTERNATIONAL FEDERATION OF CHEMICAL AND GENERAL WORKERS UNIONS (ICF)
58 rue de Moillebeau, 1211 Geneva 19, Switzerland
Tel: Geneva 33.77.60

Until 1964 this federation was known as the International Federation of General Factory Workers, originally founded in Stuttgart in 1947. Membership is to be found in cement, ceramic, rubber, glass, chemical, paper-making, atomic energy and other industries. In 1972 it spread throughout 60 countries with some 3 million members from 90 trade unions.

Secretary General: Ch. Levinson

Publications: *Bulletin* (8 a year), News sheets, conference reports

INTERNATIONAL FEDERATION OF COMMERCIAL, CLERICAL AND TECHNICAL EMPLOYEES (FIET)
15 ave de Balexert, CH1210 Chatelaine-Geneva, Switzerland
Tel: Geneva 96.27.34

Founded at an international congress of non-manual workers in Vienna in 1921, but with origins dating from 1904, when an International Information Bureau had been set up. Members are to be found among clerical and administrative staff, technicians and foremen from industry, banking, insurance and commerce. Membership numbered nearly 6 million in 1976 from 146 unions spread throughout 73 countries.

Secretary General: Héribert Maier

Publications: *The Non-Manual Worker* (monthly), *Interamerican Bulletin* (monthly)

INTERNATIONAL FEDERATION OF FREE TEACHERS UNIONS (IFFTU)
Ave G. Bergmenn 111, 1050 Brussels, Belgium
Tel: Brussels 648.68.73

Founded in Paris in 1951, as one of its activities has since established a special European Teachers Trade Union Committee for the Common Market Countries. Membership in 1976 totalled 2,200,000, these to be found in 49 national unions from 47 countries.

Secretary General: A. Braconier

Publications: *Information Bulletin, News Flashes*

INTERNATIONAL FEDERATION OF PETROLEUM AND CHEMICAL WORKERS (IFPCW)

Madison Plaza, Suite 215, 90 Madison Street, Denver, Colorado 80206, USA
Tel: Denver 388-9237

Founded in Paris in 1954. Membership in 1976 totalled more than 2 million from 74 countries.

General Secretary: Curtis J. Hogan

Publications: *Petro* (monthly), *Union Builder* (monthly), *Petrogram* (weekly)

INTERNATIONAL FEDERATION OF PLANTATION, AGRICULTURAL AND ALLIED WORKERS (IFPAAW)

17 rue Necker, 1201 Geneva, Switzerland
Tel: Geneva 31.31.05

Founded in Brussels in 1959 by the Plantation Workers International Federation and the International Landworkers Federation. Membership in 1975 was spread throughout 47 countries and covered 3,500,000 members.

General Secretary: Tom S. Bavin

Publications: *IFPAAW Snips* (monthly), *IFPAAW Journal*

INTERNATIONAL GRAPHICAL FEDERATION (IGF)

Monbijoustrasse 73, CH3007 Berne, Switzerland
Tel: Berne (031) 45.99.20

Founded by a joint meeting of the International Federation of Bookbinders and Kindred Trades, Process Workers and Kindred Trades, International Federation of Lithographers and the International Typographers Secretariat with eight graphical trade unions of the United Kingdom in 1949. Membership in 1976 was to be found in 25 countries and totalled upwards of 830,000.

Secretary General: Heinz Goke

Publications: *Communications of the IGF* (2 a year), *Technical Progress and the Future Policies of the Graphical Unions* (Paper)

INTERNATIONAL METALWORKERS FEDERATION (IMF)

54 bis route des Acacias, 1227 Geneva, Switzerland
Tel: Geneva 43.61.50

Founded as a federation in 1904, but with origins dating back to 1893 as an information bureau. Membership totalled 13 million from 66 countries in 1976.

Secretary General: Herman Rebhan

Publications: *IMF News* (fortnightly), special issues Facts Sheets and IMF Studies

INTERNATIONAL SECRETARIAT OF ENTERTAINMENT TRADE UNIONS (ISETU)
2nd Floor, Kings Court, 2 Goodge Street, London W1P 2AE

Founded in March 1965 at the International Conference of the ICFTU in Brussels. Membership was over 470,000 from 53 trade unions in 28 countries in 1973.

Publications: Reports of Congresses, Bi-monthly Newsletter

INTERNATIONAL TEXTILE, GARMENT AND LEATHER WORKERS FEDERATION (ITGLWF)
8 rue Joseph Stevens, 1000 Brussels, Belgium

Founded in 1970 by the International Garment Workers Federation and the International Shoe and Leather Workers Federation, but with origins from 1960. Membership in 1976 was 5 million and could be found in 60 countries and 93 trade unions.

Secretary General: Charles Ford

Publications: *Bulletin* (quarterly) and other reports

INTERNATIONAL TRANSPORT WORKERS FEDERATION (ITF)
Maritime House, Old Town, Clapham, London SW4 0JR
Tel: 01–622 5501–3

Founded in 1896 as the International Federational of Ship, Dock and River Workers, and adopted its present title in 1898. Membership in 1976 totalled around $6\frac{1}{2}$ million from 351 trade unions in 82 countries.

Secretary General: C.H. Blyth

Publications: *History and Activities* (1952), *Transport* (bi-monthly), *ITF news letter* (monthly), *ITF Brochure*

INTERNATIONAL UNION OF FOOD AND ALLIED
WORKERS ASSOCIATIONS (IUF)
Rampe du Pont-Rouge 8, CH1213 Petit-Lancy, Switzerland
Tel: Petit-Lancy 93.22.33 and 92.22.37

Founded in 1920 in Zurich by a merger of brewery, bakery and meat
workers' international secretariats. In 1958 a merger took place with
the International Federation of Tobacco Workers, with a further
merger in 1961 with the International Union of Hotel, Restaurant and
Bar Workers. Membership in 1976 was nearly 2,200,000 and spread
throughout 57 countries.

Publications: *News Bulletin* (monthly), *Asian Food Worker* (bi-
monthly), *IUF News* (monthly)

MINERS INTERNATIONAL FEDERATION (MIF)
75–76 Blackfriars Road, London SE1 8HE
Tel: 01–928 2262 and 2263

Founded in Belgium in 1890 by a conference of miners from Belgium,
Bohemia, France, Germany and the United Kingdom. In 1976
membership was to be found in 33 national trade unions throughout 30
countries and totalled over 1 million.

Secretary General: Dennis Edwards

Publications: *Newsletter* (bi-monthly), *Report on the conditions in the
mining industry* (quarterly)

POSTAL, TELEGRAPH AND TELEPHONE
INTERNATIONAL (PTTI)
36 avenue du Lignon, CH1209 Geneva, Switzerland
Tel: Geneva 96.83.11

Founded in 1920. Members can be found in 165 trade unions from 83
countries and total nearly 3,300,000.

Secretary General: Stefan Nedzynski

Publications: *Unity* (Inter-American Bulletin, monthly), *PTTI Inter-
American Bulletin* (monthly), *PTTI Studies* (quarterly)

PUBLIC SERVICES INTERNATIONAL (PSI)
26–30 Holborn Viaduct, London EC1
Tel: 01–583 1841

Founded in 1935 by the International Federation of Civil Servants and
the International Federational of Employees in Public Service.

Members are to be found in trade unions and professional associations, 160 in all, these being spread through 64 countries. The membership in 1972 was around 3,700,000.

Secretary General: C.W. Franken

Publications: *Bulletin* (quarterly), *Newsletter* (monthly)

UNIVERSAL ALLIANCE OF DIAMOND WORKERS (UADW)
66–68 Plantin-en-Moretuslei, 2000 Antwerp, Belgium
Tel: Antwerp (031) 32.91.51 and (031) 32.48.60

This Alliance was formed in 1905 to act as an information centre on industrial and social matters and for research. Members can be found in trade unions in Africa, Israel, Belgium, France, Netherlands and the United Kingdom.

Secretary: Albrecht Buelens

Publication: *Bulletin* (irregular)

WORLD FEDERATION OF TRADE UNIONS (WFTU)
Namesti Curieovych 1, 11688 Prague 1, Czechoslovakia
Tel: Prague 67856

Established in October 1945 by the World Trade Union Congress. In 1949 the non-communist countries broke away to form the International Confederation of Free Trade Unions (see above). Membership now consists of about 155 million members affiliated in 62 countries originally communist but now also in underdeveloped countries as follows:

Africa:	Benin, Congo, Ethiopia, Gambia, Madagascar, Mauritius, Réunion, Somalia, South Africa, Sudan, Upper Volta, Zimbabwe
America:	Argentina, Colombia, Costa Rica, Cuba, Dominican Republic, Ecuador, French Guyana, Guadeloupe, Guatemala, Guyana, Martinique, Mexico, Panama, Peru, El Salvador, Venezuela
Asia:	China, Fiji, India, Indonesia, Iran, Iraq, Jordan, Kuwait, North Korea, Laos, Lebanon, Mongolia, Pakistan, Palestine, Philippines, Sri Lanka, Syria, North Vietnam, South Vietnam, Yemen DR, Yemen Republic
Australasia:	New Caledonia
Europe:	Albania, Austria, Bulgaria, Cyprus, Czechoslovakia, France, German Democratic Republic, Hungary, Poland, Romania, San Marino, USSR

It consists of a number of Trade Union Internationals.

Secretary General: Pierre Gensous

Publications: *World Trade Union Movement* (monthly), *Flashes* (weekly), WFTU reports of activity between the Congresses

Trade union confederations

CONFEDERATION OF EMPLOYEE ORGANISATIONS

A confederation formed on 5 June 1973 to meet a demand from non-TUC unions, staff and professional associations for a voice with government on such matters as labour legislation, pay and prices policy and industrial democracy and to assist them in their negotiations with employers. The CEO was disbanded on 30 September 1979.

Members of the CEO based their actions on three main principles – constructive rather than militant relationships with employers; powerful but responsible representation of the interests of employees by collective bargaining; and political and financial independence in representing the interests of employees to government and internationally. Each member organisation retained its autonomy within the CEO. They were all closely identified with single enterprises, with professions or with geographical locations. Total affiliated membership was about 75,000.

MEMBER ASSOCIATIONS JANUARY 1978
Aerospace
Association of HSD (Hatfield) Employees
British Aerospace Staffs Association
HSD (Stevenage) Staff Association

Banking
Barclays Group Staff Association

Education
Association of Cambridge University Assistants

Insurance
Australian Mutual Provident Staff Association
Britannic Assurance Chief Office Staff Association
Clerical, Medical and General Staff Association
Commercial Union Group Staff Association
Eagle Star Staff Association
Legal & General Staff Association
Lloyd's Staff Association
Phoenix Staff Union
Sun Alliance & London Staff Association
Sun Life Staff Association
United Friendly Head Office Management Association

L

Managers
Cadbury Schweppes Senior Managers Association
EMI Electronics Limited (Feltham) Junior & Middle Management Staff Association
Rolls Royce (1971) Ltd. Management Association
Star Aluminium Managerial Staff Association

Representatives
Burton's Biscuits Field Sales Staff Association
Federation of Cadbury Schweppes Representatives Associations:
    Cadbury Limited Representatives Association
    Cadbury Typhoo Representatives Association
    Schweppes Limited Representatives Association
    Jeyes Representatives Association
Rowntree Mackintosh Sales Staff Association
Schering Chemicals Representatives Association
Trebor Sharps Salesmen's Association

Others
A. Monk & Co. Staff Association
Construction Industry Training Board Staff Association
Corporation of London Staff Association
Dean Clough Staff Association
Halcrow Staff Association
Johnson Matthey Chemicals Royston Staff Society
Johnson Matthey Headquarters Staff Society
Laurence, Scott & Electromotors Foremen's Association
Professional Flight Instructors Association
Whatman Reeve-Angel Staff Association

Associates

Insurance
Friends Provident Line Managers Association

Others
Colman Association of Staff
Institution of Mechanical Engineers Staff Association
Lloyd's Register (UK) Staff Association

CONFEDERATION OF PROFESSIONAL AND EXECUTIVE ASSOCIATIONS

A confederation of:
COSESA
M.L. Richards, 2 High Street, Coventry CV1 5RE
Tel: Coventry (0203) 20274

United Kingdom Association of Professional Engineers
J.D. Sampson, MA, CEng, FIMechE, FIMarE, 32 High Street, Bookham, Leatherhead, Surrey KT23 4AG

Executives' and Managers' Association of Great Britain and Ireland
I. Gayus, FICM, 337 Gray's Inn Road, London WC1X 8PX
Tel: 01–837 6789

Association of Professional Scientists and Technologists
M. Gillibrand, PhD, FRIC, MBIM, Hinchley House, 14 Harley Street, London W1N 2BE
Tel: 01–636 7021 and 1243

National Union of Labour Organisers
A.V. Clare, 59 Bethel Street, Norwich NR2 1NL
Tel: Norwich (0603) 22107

The Confederation was wound up in 1978.

MANAGERIAL, PROFESSIONAL AND STAFF LIAISON GROUP
BMA House, Tavistock Square, London WC1H 9JP
Tel: 01–387 4499

The Managerial, Professional and Staff Liaison Group was formed in January 1978 as an alliance of non-TUC unions and staff associations in order to establish for managerial, professional and staff employees the following rights:

(a)   the right to belong to a trade union of their choice, or to no trade union, and to be free to resign from a union without attracting any sanction other than loss of entitlement from that union;
(b)   the right to free and independent expression of opinion within the context of employment;
(c)   the right of employees to maintain their own ethical standards and to be protected against attempts to modify these standards adversely;
(d)   the right to be treated by government on their merits and not to be discriminated against on grounds that they are not affiliated to any specified federation of unions.

OFFICIALS
Chairman: M.I. Gillibrand
Secretary: J.D. Havard
Treasurer: W. Aspinall

PARTICIPANTS
Association of Career Teachers
Association of Management and Professional Staffs
Association of Optical Practitioners
Association of Polytechnic Teachers
Association of Public Service Professional Engineers
British Aircraft Corporation Senior Staffs Association
British Dental Association
British Medical Association
British Transport Officers Guild
Cadbury Schweppes Senior Managers Association

Confederation of Bank Staff Associations
Federation of Industrial Managerial and Professional Associations
National Unilever Managers Association
Professional Association of Teachers
Rolls Royce Management Association
Society of Public Analysts
United Kingdom Association of Professional Engineers

Observers
Assistant Masters' and Mistresses Association
Association of Clinical Biochemists
Association of Education Officers
British Orthoptic Society
Chartered Society of Physiotherapy
Federation of Building Society Staff Associations
Federation of Professional Officers Associations
Institute of Journalists
Royal College of Midwives
Royal College of Nursing
Secondary Heads Association
Society of Metropolitan and Country Chief Librarians
Steel Industry Management Association

These organisations have a total membership of 500,000.

Trade union federations

In this section * indicates a TUC affiliated union, appearing in Part 3, and † indicates a federation listed elsewhere in this section.

BANKING STAFF COUNCIL

The Banking Staff Council was formed in 1968 and comprised representatives from the National Union of Bank Employees* and from staff associations of the Clearing Banks, namely the Council of Bank Staff Associations†. In March 1978 the formal 6 months' notice was given by NUBE and an agreement followed signed by the CBSA which enabled the Banking Staff Council to cease in September 1978.

BRITISH AEROSPACE FEDERATION OF EMPLOYEE ASSOCIATIONS
68 Joiners Lane, Chalfont St Peter, Buckinghamshire

OFFICIAL
Secretary: B. Minett

BRITISH FEDERATION OF TEXTILE TECHNICIANS
First Floor, 3 Manchester Road, Bury BL9 0DR
Tel: 061–764 4244

A federation of three unions, the General Union of Associations of Loom Overlookers*, the Scottish Union of Power Loom Overlookers* and the Yorkshire Association of Power Loom Overlookers*, established in 1971. Because of the decline of the British textile industry the unions concerned recognised an amalgamation as desirable but were unable to achieve this because of the complexities in the organisation of the GUALO. The officials noted below are also full-time officials of the affiliated unions.

OFFICIALS
President: E.D. Sleeman,
Textile Hall,
Westgate,
Bradford BD1 2RG
Tel: Bradford (0274) 27966

Secretary: H. Brown,
First Floor, 3 Manchester Road,
Bury BL9 0DR
Tel: 061–764 4244

Asst. Secretary/Treasurer: J.A. Bradshaw,
14 George Street,
Denton,
Manchester M34 3DJ

BRITISH HOSPITAL DOCTORS' FEDERATION
Old Court House, London Road, Ascot, Berkshire SL5 7EN

OFFICIAL
Secretary: J. Paisley

BRITISH SEAFARERS JOINT COUNCIL
Merchant Navy and Airline Officers' Association,
'Oceanair House', 750–760 High Road, Leytonstone, E11 3BB
Tel: 01–989 6677
and
National Union of Seamen,
Maritime House, Old Town, Clapham, London SW4 0PJ
Tel: 01–622 5581

A joint council consisting of the:
Amalgamated Society of Boilermakers, Shipwrights, Blacksmiths
    and Structural Workers*
Amalgamated Union of Engineering Workers – Engineering
    Section*
Mercantile Marine Service Association
Captain W.W.P. Lucas, Nautilus House, Mariners' Park, Wallasey,
Merseyside L45 7PH
Tel: 051–639 6139/40
Merchant Navy and Airline Officers' Association*
National Union of Seamen*
Radio and Electronic Officers' Union*

Joint Secretaries:
C.L. Bulford, Merchant Navy and Airline Officers' Association
J. Kinahan, National Union of Seamen

CENTRAL COMMITTEE OF ICI FOREMEN'S AND
SUPERVISORS' ASSOCIATION
Engineering Works Construction, ICI Mond Division, Westonpoint,
P.O. Box 18, Runcorn, Cheshire
Tel: Runcorn 73434

OFFICIAL
Secretary: W. Harrison

CONFEDERATION OF BANK STAFF ASSOCIATIONS
25 John Street, London WC1
Tel: 01–242 5127/8

A confederation consisting of the:
Barclays Group Staff Association
W.E. Gale, Oathall House, Oathall Road, Haywards Heath, West Sussex
RH16 3EN
Tel: Haywards Heath (0444) 52223

Lloyds Bank Group Staff Association
S.H. Bealey, 6 Dean Park Crescent, Bournemouth BH1 1HG
Tel: Bournemouth (0202) 28926

National Westminster Staff Association
C. Carthy, 8–10 Dean Park Crescent, Bournemouth, Dorset BH1 1HH
Tel: Bournemouth (0202) 293616

Acting General Secretary: W.E. Gale

CONFEDERATION OF ENTERTAINMENT UNIONS
c/o Musicians' Union, 60/62 Clapham Road, London SW9
Tel: 01–582 5566

A confederation consisting of the:
Association of Broadcasting and Allied Staffs*
Association of Cinematograph, Television and Allied
    Technicians*
British Actors' Equity Association*
Electrical, Electronic, Telecommunication and Plumbing Union*
Film Artistes' Association*
Musicians' Union*
National Association of Theatrical, Television and Kine
    Employees*
National Union of Journalists*
Writers' Guild of Great Britain*
The confederation has three constituent Federations:
    the Federation of Broadcasting Unions,
    the Federation of Theatre Unions, and
    the Federation of Film Unions

Secretary: John Morton (General Secretary, Musicians' Union)

CONFEDERATION OF INSURANCE TRADE UNIONS
Transport House, Smith Square, London SW1P 3JB
Tel: 01–828 7788

A confederation consisting of the:
National Union of Insurance Workers*
Transport and General Workers Union (Insurance Section)*
Association of Scientific, Technical and Managerial Staffs
    (Insurance Section)*
Union of Shop, Distributive and Allied Workers (Insurance
    Section)*
National Union of Co-operative Insurance Society Employees

Secretary: G. Low

CONFEDERATION OF SHIPBUILDING AND ENGINEERING UNIONS
140–142 Walworth Road, London SE17
Tel: 01–703 2215

The Confederation of Shipbuilding and Engineering Unions provides a basis for common action for both manual and staff unions in those industries at national and district level. In its present form it was constituted in 1936 but it had its origins in the Federation of Engineering and Shipbuilding Trades established in 1891. In 1979 23 organisations were affiliated, four of these being Sections of the Amalgamated Union of Engineering Workers, three of them Groups or subsidiaries of the Transport and General Workers' Union, two of them relating to the General and Municipal Workers' Union and two to the Electrical, Electronic, Telecommunication and Plumbing Union. Total affiliated membership was over 2.6 millions. For technical reasons this underestimates the engineering and ship-building membership of the unions concerned.

Historically the Confederation has provided a means of securing a unified approach to the making of national agreements for manual workers in the engineering and shipbuilding industry through the Annual Meeting and through subcommittees which have allowed the predominant union in each industry to take the negotiating lead. This is now less important in the former than was once the case, though the manual workers' national procedure agreement is now held by the CSEU. Agreements covering staff workers in engineering are in practice dealt with by their respective unions, though CSEU co-ordinating machinery is formally in existence.

In the past two decades the Confederation has acted as a bridge with government on matters concerned with shipbuilding and engineering and has taken an active part in servicing affiliated organisations with representatives concerned in relevant activities of the National Economic Development Council.

Amalgamated Society of Boilermakers, Shipwrights, Blacksmiths and Structural Workers	120,000
Association of Clerical, Technical and Supervisory Staffs	50,000
Union of Construction, Allied Trades and Technicians	37,000
National Union of Domestic Appliance and General Metal Workers	8,000
Electrical, Electronic, Telecommunications Union and Plumbing Union	200,000
Electrical, Electronic, Telecommunication and Plumbing Union (Electrical and Engineering Staff Association)	10,000
Amalgamated Union of Engineering Workers (Constructional Section)	20,000
Amalgamated Union of Engineering Workers (Engineering Section)	770,000
Amalgamated Union of Engineering Workers (Foundry Section)	54,000
Amalgamated Union of Engineering Workers (Technical and Supervisory Section)	201,000
Furniture, Timber and Allied Trades Union	8,000
General and Municipal Workers Union	180,000
Managerial Administrative, Technical and Supervisory Association	10,000
National Society of Metal Mechanics	41,000
Associated Metalworkers Society	8,000
Association of Patternmakers and Allied Craftsmen	8,000
Association of Professional, Executive, Clerical and Computer Staff	80,000
Screw, Nut, Bolt and Rivet Trade Society	8,000
National Union of Scalemakers	8,000
National Union of Sheet Metal Workers, Coppersmiths, Heating and Domestic Engineers	75,000
Association of Scientific, Technical and Managerial Staffs	171,000
Transport and General Workers Union (Power Group)	300,000
Transport and General Workers Union (Vehicle Building Automotive Group)	150,000
Female Affiliation included in the above	168,313
	2,685,313

OFFICIALS 1979–80
President: F.A. Baker
Executive Council
F.A. Baker: General and Municipal Workers' Union
Sir J.M. Boyd, CBE: Amalgamated Union of Engineering Workers
J. Chalmers: Amalgamated Society of Boilermakers, Shipwrights,
    Blacksmiths and Structural Workers
T.J. Crispin: Transport and General Workers' Union
G. Hawley: Transport and General Workers' Union
F. McGuffie: Electrical, Electronic, Telecommunications and Plumbing
    Trades Union
T. Duffy: Amalgamated Union of Engineering Workers
R. Garland: Amalgamated Union of Engineering Workers (Foundry
    Section)
K. Brett: Amalgamated Society of Boilermakers, Shipwrights, Blacksmiths
    and Structural Workers.

J. Baldwin: Amalgamated Union of Engineering Workers
(Constructional Section)
G. Eastwood: Association of Patternmakers and Allied Workers
G.H. Laird: Amalgamated Union of Engineering Workers
R. McCusker: Association of Scientific, Technical and Managerial Staffs
J.H. Wood: National Society of Metal Mechanics
K. Cure: Amalgamated Union of Engineering Workers (Engineering
Section)
G. Howieson: Amalgamated Union of Engineering Workers (Foundry
Section)
L.G. Guy: National Union of Sheet Metal Workers, Coppersmiths,
Heating and Domestic Engineers
R.D. Preston: National Union of Domestic Appliance and General Metal
Workers
J. Whyman: Amalgamated Union of Engineering Workers (Engineering
Section)
J.G. Murray: Amalgamated Society of Boilermakers, Shipwrights,
Blacksmiths and Structural Workers
J.G. Russell: Amalgamated Union of Engineering Workers
Mrs P. Turner: General and Municipal Workers' Union
R.A. Grantham: Association of Professional Executive Clerical and
Computer Staff
E. Tullock: Associated Metalworkers Union
J. Hardman: Union of Construction Allied Trades and Technicians
K. Gill: Amalgamated Union of Engineering Workers (TASS)
T.A. Breakell: Electrical, Electronic, Telecommunications and Plumbing
Trades Union
Mrs M. Paterson, OBE: Transport & General Workers' Union
H. Robson: Amalgamated Union of Engineering Workers (Engineering
Section)
E.M. Scrivens: Amalgamated Union of Engineering Workers
(Engineering Section)
A.C. Sullivan: Association of Clerical, Technical and Supervisory Staffs

General Secretary: A. Ferry, MBE

District Secretaries

1	*Falmouth*	4	*Yeovil*
	V.C. Evans,		P. Smith,
	52 Stuart Road,		21 Christopher Close,
	Plymouth,		Yeovil,
	Devon		Somerset BA20 2EH
2	*Devonport*	5	*Southampton*
	R.A. Webber,		C.A. Croucher,
	65 Bretonside,		EETU/PTU Offices,
	Plymouth,		81a Bedford Place,
	Devon		Southampton SO1 2DF
3	*South Devon*	5a	*Isle of Wight*
	R. Wadlan,		H. Sims,
	41 Lancaster Drive,		4 Magdallens Crescent,
	Churston Heights,		King James Estate,
	Paignton,		Cowes, IOW
	Devon		

5b	Portsmouth C.E. Arrowsmith, 49 Kenyon Road, North End, Portsmouth, Hampshire PO2 0RG	13	Gloucester S.P. Rowlands, Rear 29–35 Lowesmoor, Worcester
6	Brighton W.A. Rowlatt, 20 Church Road, Hove 3, BN3 2FN	14	Coventry G. Butler, 61 Corporation Street, Coventry CV1 1GO
7	Rochester J. Jenkins, AUEW, 39 Belmont Road, Erith, Kent	15	Bedford D.F.G. Stopp, 396–198 Dunstable Road, Luton, Bedfordshire
8	London Mr. Gibbard, 28 Denmark Street, London WC2	16	Colchester E.T. Brown, AUEW Office, 7 Magdalen Street, St Botolph's Colchester, Essex
9	Reading G.H. Hardy, 65 Woodbridge Road, Guildford, Surrey	17	East Anglia E.T. Brown, AUEW Office, 7 Magdalen Street, St Botolph's, Colchester, Essex
9a	Swindon L.A. Thompson, AUEW House, Fleming Way, Swindon, Wiltshire	18	Cambridge R. Shaw, AEU House, 49 Lincoln Road, Peterborough
10	Bristol V.A. Ryan, 162 Gloucester Road, Bristol BS7 8NT	19	Leicester G. Bromley, TGWU, Horsefair Street, Leicester
11	Swansea F. C. Evans, AUEW, 25 Victoria Gardens, Neath, West Glamorgan	20	Birmingham S. Robinson, TGWU, 211 Broad Street, Birmingham 15
12	Cardiff S.N. Howe, 199 Newport Road, Roath, Cardiff	21	North Wales R. Bull, 17 Ash Grove, Shotton, Deeside CH5 1AF

22 *Mersey*
D.S. Gough,
46–48 Mount Pleasant,
Liverpool L3 5SE

23 *Crewe*
H.W.J. Ollier,
St Paul's Street,
Crewe,
Cheshire

24 *Derby*
W.B. Morgan,
AEU,
210 Osmaston Road,
Derby

25 *Nottingham*
S.H. Hallam,
59a Derby Road,
Nottingham

26 *Lincoln*
D. Gossop,
238 Nettleham Road,
Lincoln

27 *Humber*
J. Mulgrove,
'Carron House',
78 Beverley Road,
Hull

27a *Grimsby*
A.E. Salmon,
22 Dudley Street,
Grimsby,
South Humberside

28 *Sheffield*
W. Owen, JP,
Transport House,
Hartshead,
Sheffield 1

29 *Manchester*
J.W. Tocher,
AEU House,
43 Crescent,
Salford M5 4PE

29a *Bolton*
K. Abbott,
AEF Offices,
Spinners' Hall,
St George's Road,
Bolton,
Lancashire

30 *Preston*
R. Crook,
9–10 Cross Street,
Preston PR1 3LT

31 *Barrow*
G. Allewell,
92 Greengate Street,
Barrow-in-Furness LA14 1EZ

32 *Leeds*
H. Swain,
AEU House,
Bridge Street,
Leeds LS2 7RA

32a *Bradford*
K. Handy,
42 New North Road,
Huddersfield,
Yorks HD1 5LL

33 *Tees and Hartlepools*
G.D. Dixon,
6 Longlands Road,
Middlesbrough,
Cleveland TS4 2JL

34 *Wear*
H. Wilkinson,
AUEW House,
189 Roker Avenue,
Sunderland SR6 0BS

35 *Carlisle*
H. Banks, JP,
9–10 Cross Street,
Preston,
Lancashire PR1 3LT

36 *Tyne and Blyth*
A. Scott,
34 Claypath
Durham DH1 1TU

37 *Clyde*
A. McAlpine,
420 Sauchiehall Street.
Glasgow G2

38 *Falkirk*
J. Hamilton,
11 Graham's Road,
Falkirk

88

39	*Forth*	41	*Aberdeen*
	E. Leslie,		J. McConnachie,
	145 Morrison Street,		24 Adelphin,
	Edinburgh EH3 8AL		Aberdeen

40	*Dundee*	43	*Belfast*
	H. McLevy.		J. Graham,
	26 South Ward Road,		AEU House,
	Dundee DD1 1TR		26–34 Antrim Road,
			Belfast 15

COUNCIL OF BANK TECHNICAL AND SERVICES STAFF ASSOCIATION
Flat 1, 31b Western Road, Hove, Sussex BN3 1AD
Tel: 01–626 1500 Ext. 3122

Formed in the early 1940s for the purpose of informal meetings between the secretaries and chairmen of non-clerical staff associations to discuss and exchange information. The Bank Staff Associations involved are the National Westminster Technical and Services Committee and the Barclays Bank Technical and Services Committee.

Secretary: vacant

COUNCIL OF POST OFFICE UNIONS
11–12 Maiden Lane, London WC2 7NE
Tel: 01–379 6662

Formed in 1969 as a grouping of the unions in the Post Office to co-ordinate their views on matters of common concern such as conditions of service, operational issues, planning and the financial programme of the Post Office. The unions forming COPOU represent approximately 98 per cent of staff. Six of them form the 'constituent' members of the Council, viz:
  Union of Post Office Workers*
  Post Office Engineering Union*
  Society of Post Office Executives*
  Post Office Management Staffs Association*
  Civil and Public Services Association* (Post Office Group)
  National Federation of Sub-postmasters
Two further unions are 'associate' members of the Council, viz:
  Society of Civil and Public Servants*
  (Post Office Executive Group)
  Telephone Contract Officers' Association
The Council operates on a 'consensus' rule in which only 'constituent' members participate. 'Associate' members are expected to transfer their representative interest within a definite period of

time. It functions at national level and also at 21 regional and 300 area levels. Thus it operates at National Joint Council level, and also through Regional and Area Joint Committees. A joint two-year experiment in industrial democracy which started in January 1978 was being evaluated at the end of 1979.

OFFICIALS
The Council employs four full-time officials:
Secretary General: A. Carter
Assistant Secretaries: R.K. Worth, K.S.C. Good, A.R. Chamberlain

CRAFTSMEN'S NATIONAL NEGOTIATING COMMITTEE (PAPERMAKING AND BOARDMAKING INDUSTRY)
110 Peckham Road, London SE15 5EL
Tel: 01–703 4231

This committee is comprised of the following:
Amalgamated Union of Engineering Workers*
Union of Construction, Allied Trades and Technicians*
Association of Patternmakers and Allied Craftsmen*
Electrical, Electronic, Telecommunication and Plumbing Union*
Transport and General Workers Union*

Convenor: E.M. Scrivens

FEDERAL COUNCIL OF TEACHERS IN NORTHERN IRELAND
344 Ballynahinch Road, Hillsborough, County Down
Tel: 023 863 272

A joint council consisting of the:
Northern Ireland Women Teachers Association
Mrs G. Douglas, 25 Tweskard Park, Belfast BT4 3JS

Ulster Teachers' Union
D. Allen, 94 Malone Road, Belfast BT9 5HP
Tel: 0232 662216

Secretary: T.W. Lilburn, BSc(Econ)

FEDERATION OF ASSOCIATIONS OF COLLEGE LECTURERS IN SCOTLAND
111 Union Street, Glasgow GS1 3SS
Tel: 041–221 0118

The Federation was formed on 1 January 1978 by the three

constituent associations: the Scottish Further Education Association (SFEA), the Association of Lecturers in Colleges of Education in Scotland (ALCES) and the Association of Lecturers in Scottish Central Institutions (ALSCI).

The Federation has responsibility in all areas of policy which are the subject of common negotiations, and has standing committees dealing with Salaries and with Conditions of Service. The scope of Federation activity is expected to expand greatly when the common negotiating machinery recommended by the Houghton Report, 1974, is established for the whole of the Tertiary Education sector in Scotland.

The Federation co-ordinates the educational policies of the member unions, holding a major Tertiary Education Conference annually. Member unions may receive assistance in administration and in furthering their own policies in areas outwith the Federation's responsibility. All member unions are affiliated to the STUC.

The Federation represents the majority of lecturers in the Scottish sector of Tertiary Education.

OFFICIALS:
General Secretary: D. Bleiman, MA

OFFICERS:
President: A.D. Blues, Motherwell Technical College (SFEA)
Senior Vice-President: Dr R. Lobban, Moray House College of Education (ALCES)
Vice-President: K. Donaldson, Paisley College (ALSCI)

FEDERATION OF BRITISH FIRE ORGANISATIONS
County Fire Brigade Headquarters, The Godlands, Tovil, Maidstone ME15 6XB
Tel: Maidstone (0622) 54311

A technical and conferencing organisation, the founder members of which were the British Fire Services Association, Chief Fire Officers' Association, Commonwealth and Overseas Fire Services Association, Fire Brigades Union*, Institution of Fire Engineers, Industrial Fire Protection Association of Great Britain and the National Association of Fire Officers.

Hon. Secretary/Treasurer: R.H. Doyle, FI Fire E

FEDERATION OF BRITISH TRAWLER OFFICERS
River Chambers, Saint Andrew's Dock, Hull HU5 4PQ
Tel: Hull (0482) 24403

A federation of the following:

Grimsby Trawler Officers' Guild
Aberdeen Trawler Officers' Guild
Hull Trawler Officers' Guild
As a result of the growing influence of the Common Market upon the fishing industry in this country, membership of these guilds is rapidly declining. The Grimsby Trawler Officers' Guild has since amalgamated with the Merchant Navy and Airline Officers Association*.

Secretary: T. Nielson

FEDERATION OF BROADCASTING UNIONS
Third Floor, King's Court, 2–16 Goodge Street, London W1P 2AE
Tel: 01–637 1261

A federation consisting of the following:
Association of Broadcasting Staff*
British Actors' Equity Association*
Musicians' Union*
Writers' Guild of Great Britain*
National Association of Theatrical, Television and Kine Employees*
Association of Cinematograph, Television and Allied Technicians*

Secretary: D.A. Hearn

FEDERATION OF CADBURY SCHWEPPES REPRESENTATIVES ASSOCIATIONS
30 Leyfields Crescent, Warwick CV34 6BA
Tel: 0926 41724

A federation comprising of the following:

Cadbury Limited Representatives' Association	A.J.Peck. Parkside Sales Office, Franklin Road. Bournville, Birmingham B30 2HL Tel: 021–458 5351
Cadbury Typhoo Representatives' Association	J.M. Smith, 36 Markfield, Courtwood Lane, Forestdale, Croydon, Surrey CR0 9HH Tel: 01–657 7415

Jeyes Representatives'	J. Fountain,
Association	6 Stradbroke House,
	High Street,
	Lowestoft,
	Suffolk

Schweppes Ltd. Representa-	C. Wexler,
tives' Association	26 Whitegate Drive
	Bolton,
	Lancashire BL1 8SE
	Tel: 0204 55266

OFFICIAL
Secretary: C. Burton

FEDERATION OF FILM UNIONS
2 Soho Square, London W1V 6DD
Tel: 01-437 8506

This federation consists of the following:
Association of Cinematograph, Television and Allied
Technicians*
British Actors' Equity Association*
Film Artistes' Association*
Musicians' Union*
National Association of Theatrical, Television and Kine
Employees*
Writers' Guild of Great Britain*
Electrical, Electronic, Telecommunication and Plumbing Union*

Secretary: A. Sapper

FEDERATION OF PROFESSIONAL
OFFICERS' ASSOCIATIONS
c/o Apspe Offices, Wimbledon Hill Road,
London SW19 7PF

FEDERATION OF THEATRE UNIONS
8 Harley Street, London W1N 2AB
Tel: 01-636 6367

A federation comprising the:
British Actors' Equity Association*
Musicians' Union*
National Association of Theatrical, Television and Kine
Employees*
Writers' Guild of Great Britain*

Secretary: P. Plouviez

GENERAL FEDERATION OF TRADE UNIONS
Central House, Upper Woburn Place, London WC1H 0HY
Tel: 01-387 2578 and 01-388 0852

A federation of trade unions established in 1899, whose principal function in recent times has been to provide services for small trade unions, including those which are also affiliated to the Trades Union Congress. The GFTU provides a dispute benefit, research and educational facilities for its members and makes representations to government departments and specialised agencies on matters of importance to them. It also provides a pension scheme open to affiliated unions with full-time staff. In the year ended 31 December 1978 42 unions were affiliated, with a gross membership of 474,684.

AFFILIATED UNIONS

Asphalt Workers' Amalgamated Union	H.M. Wareham, Jenkin House, 173a Queens Road, Peckham, SE15 2NF Tel: 01-639 1669
Lancashire Box Packing Case and General Woodworkers' Society	A. Smith, 50 Burton Road, Withington, Manchester M20 9EB Tel: 061-434 6650
Nottingham and District Dyers' and Bleachers' Association	L. Skinner, 59 Bannerman Road, Bulwell, Nottingham Tel: Nottingham (0602) 273007
Boot, Shoe and Slipper Operatives Rossendale Union	T. Whittaker, 7 Tenterfield Street, Waterfoot, Rossendale BB4 7BA Tel: Rossendale (070 62) 5657
Beamers, Twisters and Drawers, Amalgamated Association	F. Sumner, 27 Every Street, Nelson, Lancashire BB9 7NE Tel: Nelson (0282) 64181
National Society of Brushmakers and General Workers	A.W. Godfrey, 20 The Parade, Watford, Hertfordshire WD1 2AA Tel: 01-922 1950
Northern Carpet Trades' Union	L.R. Smith, 22 Clare Road, Halifax HX1 2HX Tel: Halifax (0422) 60492

Power Loom Carpet Weavers' and Textile Workers' Association	D.T. Carter, Callows Lane, Kidderminster, Worcestershire DY10 2JC Tel: Kidderminster (0562) 3192
Card Setting Machine Tenters' Society	G. Priestley, 36 Greenton Avenue, Scholes, Cleckheaton Yorkshire BD19 6DT Tel: Cleckheaton (0274) 670022
Caretakers' Association, Manchester and District (NUPE)	J. Hay, School House, Wendover Road, Wythenshaw, Manchester 23
Tobacco Mechanics' Association	W.D. Brunt, 9 Wootton Crescent, St Anne's Park, Bristol BS4 4AN Tel: Bristol (0272) 73848
Cloth Pressers' Society	G. Kaye, 34 Southgate, Honley, Huddersfield HD7 2NT
Dyers' and Auxiliary Association, Hinckley	L.F. Ellis, JP, 67 Station Road, Hinckley, Leicestershire LE10 1AP Tel: Hinckley (0455) 38592
SLADE (Wallpaper and Textile Section)	D. Hill, 'SLADE' House, 297–9 Chapel Street, Salford, Lancashire M3 5JT Tel: 061–832 3674
Amalgamated Society of Textile Workers and Kindred Trades	H. Lisle, OBE, JP, 'Foxlowe', Market Place, Leek, Staffs ST13 6AD Tel: Leek (0538) 382068
Furniture, Timber and Allied Trades Union	B. Rubner, 'Fairfields', Roe Green, Kingsbury NW9 0PT Tel: 01–204 0273
Amalgamated Textile Workers' Union	J. Brown, JP, Textile Union Centre, 5 Caton Street, Rochdale, Lancashire OL16 1QT Tel: Rochdale (0706) 59551/58367

95

Glassmakers' Society, Pressed	A. De Vere, 11 Oakfield Road, Lobley Hill, Gateshead, Co. Durham NE11 0AA Tel: Gateshead (0632) 605099
National Union of Hosiery and Knitwear Workers	D.A.C. Lambert, 55 New Walk, Leicester LE1 7EB Tel: Leicester (0533) 556703
Hatters, Amalgamated Society of Journeymen Felt	H. Walker, 14 Walker Street, Denton, Manchester M34 3LH Tel: 061-336 2450
Hat Trimmers and Wool Formers' Association, Amalgamated Felt	H. Walker, 14 Walker Street, Denton, Manchester M34 3LH Tel: 061-336 2450
Healders and Twisters Trade and Friendly Society, Huddersfield	G. Booth, 20 Uppergate, Hepworth, Huddersfield HD7 1TG
National Union of Lock and Metal Workers	J. Martin, JP, Bellamy House, Wilkes Street, Willenhall, Staffordshire WV13 2BS Tel: Willenhall (0902) 66651
National Assocation of Licensed House Managers	H. Shindler, 9 Coombe Lane, London SW20 8NE Tel: 01-947 3080
Associated Metalworkers' Union	E. Tullock, 92 Deansgate, Manchester M3 2QG Tel: 061-834 6891
The National Society of Metal Mechanics	J.H. Wood, 70 Lionel Street, Birmingham B3 1JG Tel: 021-236 0726
Jewel Case and Jewellery Display Makers' Union, London	C.G. Evans, 3 Montague House, Whitmore Road, London N1 5QE Tel: 01-739 8164

Union of Jute, Flax and Kindred Textile Operatives	Mrs M. Fenwick, MBE, JP, 93 Nethergate, Dundee DD1 4DH Tel: Dundee (0382) 22273
Loom Overlookers, General Union of Associations of	H. Brown, 6 St Mary's Place, Bury BL9 0DZ Tel: 061–764 4244
National Union of Wallcovering, Decorative and Allied Trades	R.W. Tomlins, 'Huntroyd', 223 Bury New Road, Whitefield, Manchester M25 6GW Tel: 061–766 3645
Power Loom Overlookers, Scottish Union	J. Reilly, 857 Turnberry Avenue, Dundee Tel: Dundee (0382) 86489
Power Loom Overlookers, Yorks Association of	K. Hattersley, Textile Hall, Westgate, Bradford, Yorkshire BD1 2RG Tel: Bradford (0274) 27966
Ceramic and Allied Trades Union	L.R. Sillitoe, OBE, JP, 5 Hillcrest Street, Hanley, Stoke-on-Trent ST1 2AB Tel: Stoke-on-Trent (0782) 24201
Screw, Nut, Bolt and Rivet Trade Union	H. Cater, 368 Dudley Road, Birmingham B18 4HH Tel: 021–558 2001
Shuttlemakers, Society of	E.V. Littlewood, 21 Buchan Towers, Manchester Road, Bradford BD5 0QS
National Union of Tailors and Garment Workers	A.R. Smith, Radlett House, West Hill, Aspley Guise, Milton Keynes MK17 8DT Tel: Milton Keynes (0908) 583099
Lancashire Amalgamated Tape Sizers' Association	H. Howorth, 238 Manchester Road, Nelson, Lancashire BB9 7DE Tel: Nelson (0282) 64613

Textile Craftsmen, Yorkshire Society of	F. Towers, JP. Textile Hall, Westgate, Bradford, Yorkshire BD1 2RG Tel: Bradford (0274) 27965
Textile Workers' Union, Scottish Lace and	J. McChristie, The Cross, Newmilns, Ayrshire KA16 9DE Tel: 0560 21228
Nelson & Dist. Association of Preparatory Workers	H. Phillips, 2a New Brown Street, Nelson, Lancashire Tel: Nelson (0282) 64055
National Woolsorters' Society	G. Armitage, 40 Little Horton Lane, Bradford BD5 0AL Tel: Bradford (0274) 20392
Wool-Comb, Hackle and Gill Makers Amalgamated Society	H. Haigh, 87 Mandale Road, Horton Bank Top, Bradford BD6 3JS Tel: Bradford (0274) 671080

OFFICIALS

Chairman: J. Martin
Vice-Chairman: H.M. Wareham
General Secretary: P. Potts
Research and Education Officers: N. Knowles, J.R. Smith, R. Sutton
Management Committee:

J.K.W. Arnold	J.J. Quinn
H. Brown	L.R. Smith
D. T. Carter	Mrs A. Spencer
D.R. Coates	E. Tullock
D. Hill	T. Whittaker
H.L. Gibson, MBE, JP	J.H. Wood

GENERAL UNION OF ASSOCIATIONS OF LOOM OVERLOOKERS*

See LOOM OVERLOOKERS, GENERAL UNION OF ASSOCIATIONS OF, in Part 3

It consists of the following:
Accrington and District Power Loom Overlookers' Society
Blackburn and District Power Loom Overlookers' Association
Bolton and District Power Loom Overlookers' Association
Church and Oswaldtwistle Power Loom Overlookers' Society

Colne and District Power Loom Overlookers' Association
Derby Power Loom Overlookers' Association
Haslingden and District Power Loom Overlookers' Society
Heywood and District Power Loom Overlookers' Association
Hyde and District Loom Overlookers' Association
National Association of Power Loom Overlookers
Nelson and District Power Loom Overlookers' Society
Oldham Association of Loom Overlookers
Preston and Districts Power Loom Overlookers' Association
Skipton and District Power Loom Overlookers' Association
United Association of Power Loom Overlookers

JOINT COMMITTEE OF LIGHT METAL TRADES UNIONS
Stove Grate Offices, Imperial Buildings, High Street, Rotherham,
South Yorkshire S60 1PB
Tel: Rotherham (0709) 2820

A joint committee consisting of the:
Amalgamated Society of Boilermakers, Shipwrights, Blacksmiths
   and Structural Workers*
Association of Patternmakers and Allied Craftsmen*
Association of Professional, Executive, Clerical and Computer
   Staff*
National Union of Domestic Appliance and General Metal
   Workers*
National Union of General and Municipal Workers*
National Union of Sheet Metal Workers, Coppersmiths and
   Heating and Domestic Engineers*
Transport and General Workers Union*
Amalgamated Union of Engineering Workers (Foundry Section)*
Amalgamated Union of Engineering Workers (TASS)*

Secretary: J. Higham, MBE

JOINT COMMITTEE OF THE FOUR SECONDARY
ASSOCIATIONS
Gordon House, 29 Gordon Square, London WC1H 0PP
Tel: 01-387 7512

This committee ceased to exist at the end of 1978.

LANCASHIRE AMALGAMATED TAPE SIZERS'
ASSOCIATION

See
entry in Part 3

NATIONAL AFFILIATION OF CARPET TRADE UNIONS
Carpet Weavers Hall, Callows Lane, Kidderminster, Worcester
DY10 2JG
Tel: Kidderminster (0562) 3192

The NACTU operates as a loose affiliation and was formed in
November 1917. The objective of the Affiliation is primarily to
determine national collective bargaining in the carpet industry.
It is comprised of the following:
National Union of Dyers, Bleachers and Textile Workers*
Northern Carpet Trades Union*
Power Loom Carpet Weavers' and Textile Workers Association*
Scottish Carpet Workers' Union
J. Deighan, 83 Carlton Place, Glasgow G5 9TU
Tel: 041–429 5199
General and Municipal Workers' Union*

Secretary: D.T. Carter

NATIONAL ASSOCIATION OF UNIONS IN THE TEXTILE TRADE
National House, Sunbridge Road, Bradford, West Yorkshire
BD1 2QB
Tel: Bradford (0274) 25642

An association consisting of the following:
Scottish Council of Textile Trade Unions†
Huddersfield Healders and Twisters' Trade and Friendly Society*
National Wool Sorters Society*
Pattern Weavers Society*
Cloth Pressers Society*
National Union of Dyers, Bleachers and Textile Workers*

Secretary: W.H. Maddocks

NATIONAL CRAFTSMEN'S CO-ORDINATING COMMITTEE (IRON AND STEEL INDUSTRY)
Hayes Court, West Common Road, Bromley, Kent

A committee comprised of the following:
Amalgamated Union of Engineering Workers*
Association of Patternmakers and Allied Craftsmen*
Electrical, Electronic, Telecommunication and Plumbing Union*
Amalgamated Society of Boilermakers, Shipwrights, Blacksmiths
    and Structural Workers*
National Union of Sheet Metal Workers, Coppersmiths, Heating
    and Domestic Engineers*

Union of Construction, Allied Trades and Technicians*
British Roll Turners Trade Society

Chairman: L. Hancock
Vice-Chairman: G.H. Laird
Convener: E. Linton

NATIONAL FEDERATION OF CARDING ENGINEERS' ASSOCIATIONS

A federation consisting of the:
Airedale and Wharfedale Carding Engineers' Association
R. Waller, 10 Salisbury Street, Calverley, Pudsey, West Yorkshire LS28 5PY
Huddersfield and District Carding Engineers' Association
K. Green, 77 Prospect Road, Longwood, Huddersfield HD3 4UY
Tel: Huddersfield (0484) 655899

The Federation has been dissolved as such; however, the two associations involved still continue to function with the same officers, and keep a liaison with each other.

NATIONAL FEDERATION OF CONTINUATIVE TEACHERS' ASSOCIATIONS
5 Naseby Close, Fairfax Road, London NW6 4EY
Tel: 01–328 7430

A federation including the:
London Continuative Teachers' Association
Mrs C.E. Kay, 33 Limpsfield Avenue, Thornton Heath, Surrey CR4 6BG
Tel: 01–684 1583

Secretary: Miss D. Whitehead, LRAM, HND, Dip Ad Ed

NATIONAL FEDERATION OF FURNITURE TRADE UNIONS
'Fairfields', Roe Green, Kingsbury, London NW9 0PT
Tel: 01–204 0273

A federation consisting of the:
Furniture, Timber and Allied Trades Union*
National Union of General and Municipal Workers*
Transport and General Workers' Union*
Union of Construction, Allied Trades and Technicians*

Secretary: B. Rubner

NATIONAL FEDERATION OF PROFESSIONAL WORKERS
30a Station Road, Harpenden, Hertfordshire AL5 4SE
Tel: Harpenden 3692

The Federation was established in 1920 on the initiative of G.D.H. Cole, who was in the Chair at its inaugural meeting. Its function has remained as it was then to be that of encouraging the growth of trade unionism in the non-manual field; to serve as a link between non-manual unions and the TUC; to act as a representative body on issues particularly relating to the non-manual field; to assist affiliated unions in research into mainly white-collar problems, and to represent the collective views of the affiliated unions on non-manual issues to Government Departments, the TUC, etc. It is the Federation's policy to recommend all affiliated unions to be members of the TUC, but there are a few of the smaller organisations which, for one reason or another, remain outside the TUC, though many unions have joined the TUC, partly as a result of their connection with the NFPW.

The Federation holds an annual one-day conference in London and monthly meetings of the Executive Committee upon which each union has one representative, or two for the very large unions.
Membership approximately: 2,000,000

The Officers of the Federation are as follows:
President: D.G. Perryman (NATFHE)
Vice-President: L. Christie (SCPS)
Hon. Treasurer: J. Mills (TSSA)
General Secretary: J.H. Fryd

Affiliated organisations:
Amalgamated Union of Engineering Workers (TASS)*
Association of Scientific, Technical and Managerial Staffs*
National Union of Journalists*
Transport Salaried Staffs Association*
National Association of Schoolmasters and Union of Women
    Teachers*
Civil and Public Services Association*
Association of Government Supervisors and Radio Officers*
Inland Revenue Staff Federation*
National and Local Government Officers Association*
Association of Post Office Management Staffs*
Society of Post Office Executives*
Northern Ireland Public Service Alliance
Thames Water Authority Staff Association
Society of Civil and Public Servants*
National Association of Teachers in Further and Higher
    Education*

Corporation of London Staff Association

Guild of Professional Teachers of Dancing
C. Wellock, 3 Braemar Avenue, Urmston, Manchester M31 3HP
Tel: 061–748 6140
Association of National Health Service Officers
L.J. Abbiss, 130 Regent Road, Leicester LE1 7PE
Tel: Leicester (0533) 28524
English Chiropodists Association
A. Edwards, LCh, MEChA, 13 Whitefriars, Chester CH1 1QB
Tel: Chester (0244) 312115
National Union of Labour Organisers and Election Agents
A.V. Clare, 59 Bethel Street, Norwich NR2 1NL
Tel: Norwich (0603) 22107
National Association of Executives, Managers and Staffs
Institution of Professional Civil Servants*
Greater London Council Staff Association*
Telephone Contract Officers Association
D.L. Edwards, 15 Cranford Road, Tonbridge, Kent TN10 4HL
Tel: Tonbridge (0732) 351368
and in respect of the professional, technical, clerical and admini-
strative sections of the following:
Association of Broadcasting Staff*
Civil Service Union*
Confederation of Health Service Employees*
Electrical, Electronic and Telecommunication Union – Plumbing
TU*
Fire Brigades' Union* (Officers Section)
National Association of Theatrical & Kine Employees*
National Federation of Sub-Postmasters
National Union of Public Employees*
National Union of Railwaymen*
Transport and General Workers' Union – Association of Clerical,
  Technical & Supervisory Staffs*
Union of Post Office Workers*
Union of Shop, Distributive and Allied Workers*

NATIONAL UNION OF INSURANCE WORKERS*
See INSURANCE WORKERS, NATIONAL UNION OF, in
Part 3

It includes:
Liverpool Victoria Section
J.P. Brown, JP, 22 Worple Road, Wimbledon, London SW19 4DD
Tel: 01–947 6333
Prudential Section
E. Lorenz, 91–93 Gray's Inn Road, London WC1X 8TX
Tel: 01–405 1083 and 6798

Royal Liver and Composite Section
J. Flunder, 73a Nuxley Road, Belvedere, Kent DA6 7JT
Tel: 01-304 0311
Royal London Section
F.H.P. Jarvis, 185 Woodhouse Road, North Finchley, London N12 9BA
Tel: 01-368 1098

NORTHERN COUNTIES TEXTILE TRADES FEDERATION
Textile Union Centre, 5 Caton Street, Rochdale, Lancashire
OL16 1QJ
Tel: Rochdale (0706) 58367/59551

The Federation was formed in 1906 by the unions in the Manu-
facturing Section in the Textile Industry in order to effect closer unity
in each section of the industry and to render mutual aid in various
ways.
The Federation comprises:
Amalgamated Textile Workers' Union* (40,000)
General Union of Associations of Loom Overlookers* (3,000)
Amalgamated Textile Warehousemen's Association (3,000)
N. Wareing, 80 St George's Road, Bolton, Lancashire
Amalgamated Association of Beamers, Twisters & Drawers* (1,230)
Lancashire Amalgamated Tape Sizers' Association (400)
H. Howorth, 238 Manchester Road, Nelson, Lancashire BB9 7DE
Amalgamated Tape Sizers' Friendly Protection Society (50)
A. Cottrell, 15 Grey Street, Stalybridge, Cheshire
Nelson & District Association of Preparatory Workers (100)
H. Phillips, 2a New Brown Street, Nelson, Lancashire
Guild of Textile Supervisors (500)
D. Hollingworth, 191 Sandy Lane, Rochdale, Lancashire

OFFICIALS
President: F. Sumner
Secretary: P.G. Walker

NORTHERN IRELAND PUBLIC SERVICE ALLIANCE
Harkin House, 54 Wellington Park, Belfast BT9 6DZ
Tel: Belfast (0232) 661831

The Northern Ireland Public Service Alliance is the largest white
collar trade union in Northern Ireland and with a present
membership in excess of 30,000 it also stands as the second largest
union in the Province.
NIPSA is divided into four constituent organisations. These are the
Northern Ireland Civil Service Association (NICSA), the Civil
Service Professional Officers' Association (CSPOA), the Public
Officers Division (POD) and the Health & Social Services Boards
Division (H&SSBD).

The NICSA has a membership of approximately 15,000 which is divided into more than 140 branches. It caters for, clerical, executive, administrative, typing, messengerial, machine grades, etc, within the NI Civil Service.

The CSPOA which looks after professional, scientific and technical civil servants, has a membership of over 5,000. These are divided between approximately 40 branches.

The POD has some 6,000 members. They are employees of the Area Boards for Education and Libraries, the Northern Ireland Housing Executive, the District Councils together with a number of other statutory bodies. The POD has more than 40 branches.

The H&SSBD is made up of employees of the Area Boards for Health & Social Services. It is the smallest of the four constituent bodies of NIPSA with a membership in excess of 3,000. The H&SSBD has about 30 branches.

ELECTED OFFICERS 1979–80
President: M. Fitzpatrick
Vice-President: J. Martin
Hon. Treasurer: T. Jones

Secretariat
General Secretary: J. McCusker
Deputy General Secretary: S. McDowell
Assistant General Secretaries: Miss M.E. Irwin, G. Pepper
Assistant Secretaries:
    Civil Service: J. Henry, J. Cooper
    Public Officers: Vacant
    H&SS Boards: L. Pimley
Administration Officer: K.R. Hood
Executive Officers: G. Bell, J. Donaghy, A. Heasley, P. McCollum, J. Mackell, A. May

The main objectives of NIPSA are:
(a) to negotiate and control relations with employers on matters of interest to members of NIPSA for the purpose of furthering and protecting their interests; and
(b) to co-ordinate the activities of the constituent bodies of NIPSA.

NOTTINGHAM AND DISTRICT FEDERATION OF CLUB STEWARDS
Labour Club, West Hill Drive, Mansfield, Nottingham

OFFICIAL:
Secretary: J. Hughes

OFFICERS' (MERCHANT NAVY) FEDERATION LIMITED
'Oceanair House', 750–760 High Road, Leytonstone, E11 3BB
Tel: 01–989 6677

This federation consists of the:

Mercantile Marine Service Association

General Secretary: Captain W.W.P. Lucas
Nautilus House, Mariner's Park, Wallasey, Merseyside L45 7PH
Tel: 051–639 6139/40

Merchant Navy and Airline Officers' Association*

General Secretary: Eric Nevin

Radio and Electronic Officers' Union*

General Secretary: K. Murphy, CEng,
4/6 Branfill Road, Upminster, Essex
together with the following overseas organisations of merchant
service officers:

The Canadian Merchant Service Guild
The Merchant Service Guild of Australia
The New Zealand Merchant Service Guild
The Merchant Navy Officers Guild, Hong Kong
The Australian Institute of Marine & Power Engineers
The New Zealand Institute of Marine & Power Engineers
The Maritime Union of India
The Pakistan Merchant Navy Officers Association
The Ghana Merchant Navy Officers Association

OFFICIALS:
Present Chairman: John C. Roberts, Master Mariner, Serving Chief Officer,
British Rail Cross Channel Ships
Vice-Chairmen: Captain J.B. Wright, OBE, RNR Rtd, Mr Henry Allen,
Serving Radio Officer at sea

Secretary: A.R. Begg, TEng(CEI)

PEARL UNIONS FEDERATION

This federation was formed in 1926 from the Pearl Federation and the
Pearl Section, both of which represent agents in insurance. In 1970
the Pearl Combine (clerical workers) joined. The Federation merged
with the Association of Scientific, Technical & Managerial Staffs* in
the Autumn of 1978.

PEN WORKERS' FEDERATION

10 Thornwood Close, Langley, Oldbury, Birmingham

OFFICIAL:
Secretary: N. L. Ovendon

This Federation had ceased by March 1979.

POST OFFICE SENIOR STAFF NEGOTIATING COUNCIL
Society of Civil Servants, 124–126 Southwark Street, London
SE1 0TU
Tel: 01–928 9671

A council consisting of the:
Society of Post Office Executives*
Society of Civil and Public Servants*
in respect of their post office membership.

Chairman: T. Deegan

SCOTTISH COUNCIL OF TEXTILE TRADE UNIONS
Room 11, 13 Bath Street, Glasgow G2 1HY
Tel: 041–332 1281

A council consisting of the:
Amalgamated Society of Textile Workers and Kindred Trades*
Scottish Union of Power Loom Overlookers*
Scottish Lace and Textile Workers Unions
R. Connell, 62 Main Street, The Cross, New Milns, Ayrshire KA16 9DE
Tel: Darvel (0560) 21228
Scottish Carpet Workers Union
J. Deighan, 83 Carlton Place, Glasgow G5 9TU
Tel: 041–429 5199
National Union of Dyers, Bleachers and Textile Workers*

Secretary: R. Gray

TECHNICAL AND SERVICES BANKING STAFF COUNCIL
National Union of Bank Employees, 35 Copthall Avenue, London
EC2R 7BP
Tel: 01–628 0227

A council to which the Banking Insurance and Finance Union*
affiliates.

Secretary: A. Piper

TEXTILE MANUFACTURING TRADES FEDERATION OF BOLTON AND SURROUNDING DISTRICTS
77 St George's Road, Bolton
Tel: Bolton (0204) 22726

This federation consists of the following:
Bolton and District Power Loom Overlookers' Association
J. Ratcliffe, ATI, 80 St George's Road, Bolton BL1 2DD
Tel: Bolton (0204) 32787
Bolton and District Tape Sizers' Protective Society
J. Hill, 172 Paulhan Street, Bolton BL3 3DX
Tel: Bolton (0204) 62154
Amalgamated Textile Warehousemen
Mrs J. Steggles, 80 St George's Road, Bolton
Tel: Bolton (0204) 25398
Bolton and District Power Loom Weavers', Winders', Warpers', Loom Sweepers' and Ancillary Workers' Association

Secretary: E. Garlick, JP

YORKSHIRE ASSOCIATION OF POWER LOOM OVERLOOKERS*
See POWER LOOM OVERLOOKERS, YORKSHIRE
ASSOCIATION OF, in Part 3

An association comprising the:
Bradford and District Power Loom Overlookers' Society
Halifax and District Power Loom Overlookers' Society
Huddersfield and Dewsbury Power Loom Overlookers' Society
Keighley and District Power Loom Overlookers' Society
Leeds and District Power Loom Overlookers' Society

Character Count 15,931

Trades Councils

Trades Councils exist in most major cities, towns and districts of the United Kingdom and consist of representatives of local trades union branches or lodges. Most of them meet monthly. Their function is to provide a local forum for trade union discussion, to provide a common service on industrial, civic and education matters as required, to assist in improving trade union organisation and to nominate representatives of the trade union viewpoint to committees, tribunals etc. Representatives from particular unions remain subject to the rules and policies of those unions. Councils are not regarded by the trade union movement as independent bodies competent to make local decisions which may conflict with those of national or regional trade union organisation. In Scotland they are directly represented at annual meetings of the Scottish TUC and in Wales on the Wales Trade Union Council. In England, the TUC has debarred them from representation at annual Congress since 1895 and allows only a fraternal representative to attend. It nevertheless asks its affiliated organisations to encourage their local branches to affiliate to Trades Councils and recognises those which function in accordance with its requirements on a year-by-year basis. In July 1979 around 440 such Councils were recognised in England and Wales. The TUC considers these Councils to be responsible for making known the national policies of Congress in their localities. Its Trade Councils' Joint Consultative Committee, consisting of nine members of the General Council and an equal number of representatives from the Councils themselves, is responsible for giving advice on their operation. The TUC also provides for 53 County Associations of Trades Councils and since 1925 for an Annual Conference of Trades Councils in May each year. Very few unions, however, make it mandatory for their local branches to affiliate to Trades Councils and, depending on the local situation, some do not.

The TUC is frequently engaged in investigating problems arising in the operation of particular Councils and in attempting to obtain changes which make their registration acceptable. In some cases registration may be withdrawn, a significant sanction in view of the difficulties of Trades Council operation without TUC support. Affiliation fees to Trades Council are small and are normally derived from the general funds of unions. Under the Trade Union Act 1913 they may not, therefore, be used for political purposes.

It is a condition of the recognition of Trades Councils that a model rule on proscribed organisation shall be included in their rule book and that this rule shall be operated. The rule provides that in no circumstances shall Trades Councils co-operate with or subscribe to the funds of any organisation whose policies or activities are contrary to those of Congress nor to any political party other than those of the local Labour Party.

Some Councils find it easier than others to reconcile their primarily 'agency', co-ordinating and nominating role with the inclinations of the delegates who attend them. Where trade union branches may be in disagreement with their own organisations or with their local Constituency Labour Party there is a tendency for such discontents to be expressed in Trades Council resolutions. Nevertheless Trades Councils are deeply embedded in the history of the British trade union movement and preceded the TUC itself in providing common ground for activity between trade unions. The TUC, it has been claimed, needs them as a means of establishing direct contact with the rank and file of the movement and in order to obtain reactions to policy and information on problems.[1] It has the difficulty that in accepting such a role as necessary it may find that Trades Councils present to it embarrassing evidence of local dissent and political manoeuvering within the labour movement and that national unions may tend to regard any strengthening of trades council machinery as creating rivals to their own authority. The problem appears to be less acute today than it was in the 1930s and in the period immediately after the Second World War. Nevertheless, the TUC has proceeded with caution in involving Councils more directly in its activities, taking no significant step in this direction until 1973, when Congress approved a new regional organisation for the TUC in England and Wales, partly in response to the Local Government Act 1972 which altered the structure of local authorities in those countries from April 1974. In May 1974 the ten Regional Advisory Committees of officials which had existed since 1940 were redefined in terms of the central government's eight planning regions.[2] At the same time the former Federations of Trades Councils were realigned as County Associations of Trades Councils to conform to the new local government structure and given the authority to elect within each Region 25 per cent of the membership of each Advisory Committee, or, in the case of Wales, to be represented at the annual meeting of the Wales Trade Union Council and to have one-third of the members on its Executive Council.[3]

In view of the large number of Trades Councils involved in England and Wales and the frequency of change of Secretaries, details of County Associations of Trades Councils only are given below (details as at June 1979).

Notes

[1]   Allan Flanders, *Trade Unions*, Hutchinson 1968 ed. p. 69.
[2]   Northern, North West, Yorkshire and Humberside, West Midlands, East Midlands, East Anglia, South East, South.
[3]   See *TUC Report 1973*. pp. 356–69 and for the Wales TUC. pp. 62–64. above.

A booklet, *Running a Trades Council*, giving advice to Secretaries, Chairmen and Treasurers of Trades Councils about their duties, is available from the TUC, price 20p, plus 10p postage.

COUNTY ASSOCIATIONS OF TRADES COUNCILS
SECRETARIES' ADDRESSES – JUNE 1979

01 *Avon*
D.V. Cook,
SW Regional
Health Authority,
38 Victoria Street,
Bristol BS1 6BD

02 *Bedfordshire*
W.A. Carr,
51 Grove Road,
Houghton Regis,
Bedfordshire
Tel: *H* Dunstable (0582) 65809

03 *Berkshire*
J.E. Still,
31 Dawlish Road,
Reading,
Berkshire
Tel: *H* Reading (0734) 81809

04 *Buckinghamshire*
A.J. Tanner,
28 Terryfield Road,
High Wycombe,
Buckinghamshire
Tel: *H* High Wycombe (0494) 29014
     W High Wycombe (0494) 33321

05 *Cambridgeshire*
W.T. Browning,
19 Montague Road,
Peterborough PE4 6EE
Tel: *H* Peterborough (0733) 71677
     W Peterborough (0733) 60430
         Ext 40

06 *Cheshire*
W.T. Hughson,
14 Daleside,
Springfield,
Buckley,
Clwyd CH7 2PP
Tel: *H* Buckley (024 454) 6496
     W 051–350 4586

07 *Cleveland*
M.A. Garbett,
3 Cleveland Street,
Redcar,
Cleveland TS10 1VA
Tel: *H* Redcar (064 93) 74885
     W Eston Grange (064 95) 4144
         Ext Nylon 298

08 *Cornwall*
Ms M.D. Riley,
18 Hillcrest,
Shortlanesend,
Truro,
Cornwall TR4 9DS
Tel: *H* Truro (0872) 77748
     W Truro (0872) 77635

Cumbria
J.R. Bell,
3 South View Terrace,
Carlisle
Tel: *H* Carlisle (0228) 29350
     W Carlisle (0228) 31081
         Ext 317

10 *Derbyshire*
R. Frisby,
52 Thomas Street,
Chesterfield,
Derbyshire S40 3AH
Tel: *H* Chesterfield (0246) 36810
     W Clowne (0246) 810332

11 *Devon*
A. Bennett,
107 Cotehele Avenue,
Keyham,
Plymouth
Tel: *H* Plymouth (0752) 51574
     W Plymouth (0752) 53740
         Ext 2328

111

12 *Dorset*
A.P. Collins,
109 Haverstock Road,
Winton,
Bournemouth,
Dorset BH9 3HJ
Tel: *H* Bournemouth (0202) 521906
    W Northbourne (02016) 3201

13 *Durham*
Ms N. Nicholson,
128 Westmorland Rise,
Peterlee,
Co Durham

14 *Essex*
S. Telford,
37 Cambridge Road,
Southend-on-Sea,
Essex SS1 1ET
Tel: *H* Southend (0702) 40948

15 *Gloucestershire*
W.J. Jenkins,
47 India Road,
Gloucester GL1 4DL
Tel: *H* Gloucester (0452) 29764
    W Gloucester (0452) 21121
      Ext 2156

16 *Hampshire*
W.H. Tooes,
43 Cornwall Road,
Portsmouth PO1 5AR
Tel: *H* Portsmouth (0705) 21886

17 *Hereford & Worcester*
J. Wardle,
'Hertford House',
Fairfield,
Wolverley,
Kidderminster,
Worcestershire
Tel: *H* Kidderminster (0562) 850355

18 *Hertfordshire*
A.G. Duncan,
49 Pear Tree Lane,
Welwyn Garden City,
Hertfordshire AL7 3UA
Tel: *H* Welwyn Garden City
    (96) 30279

19 *Humberside*
W.L. Wright,
15 Franklin Road,
Scotter,
Gainsborough,
Lincolnshire
Tel: *H* Scunthorpe (0724) 762702

20 *Isle of Wight*
E.J. Maxted,
117 Pelham Road,
Cowes,
Isle of Wight
Tel: *H* Cowes (098 382) 6170

21 *Kent*
F. Baker,
97 Kings Drive,
Gravesend,
Kent DA12 5BQ
Tel: *H* Gravesend (0474) 61802

22 *Lancashire*
B. Howard,
9 Avondale Drive,
Lostock Hall,
Preston PR5 8BQ
Tel: *H* Preston (0772) 35059
    (daytime)
    W Preston Telephone
    Exchange (evenings)

23 *Leicestershire*
P.F. Mulligan,
41 Hereford Close,
Barwell,
Leicestershire

24 *Lincolnshire*
A. Hall,
1 Blankney Crescent,
Lincoln
Tel: *H* Lincoln (0522) 34779
    W Lincoln (0522) 25212
      Ext 332

25 *Greater London*
F. Stiller,
44 Selwyn Road,
New Malden,
Surrey KT3 5AT
Tel: *H* 01-942 6467
    W 01-452 3333
      Ext 6135 or 6223

26 *Greater Manchester*
G. Lange,
10a Kilburn Road,
Radcliffe,
Manchester M26 0NW
Tel: *H* 061–723 3535
    W Rochdale (0706) 39403

27 *Merseyside*
A.B. Williams,
70 Victoria Street,
Liverpool L1 6DB
Tel: *H* 051–428 3702
    W 051–647 7798

28 *West Midlands*
W. Timmington,
'Uplands',
149 Barrs Road,
Cradley Heath,
Warley,
Worcestershire
Tel: *H* Cradley Heath (0384) 69300
    W Dudley (0384) 53585

29 *Norfolk*
M. J. Ayres,
32 Herons Close,
Oulton Broad,
Lowestoft,
Suffolk

30 *Northamptonshire*
R.F. Jones,
58 Osprey Lane,
Wellingborough,
Northamptonshire
Tel: *H* Swanspool 4487
    W Wellingborough
       (0933) 224073

31 *Northumberland*
R. Storey,
30 Melrose Terrace,
Newbiggen-by-the-Sea,
Northumberland NE64 6XN
Tel: *H* Ashington (0670) 816970
    W Lynemouth (067 086) 341
       Ext Storehouse

32 *Nottinghamshire*
T.P. Maddock,
1 Eastwood Avenue,
Warsop,
Mansfield,
Nottinghamshire
Tel: *H* Mansfield (0623) 27191
    W Warsop (062 384) 3272

33 *Oxfordshire*
W. Bloy,
Swinbrook,
Burford,
Oxfordshire

34 *Shropshire*
P.R. Kelly,
4 Claverley Crescent,
Shrewsbury,
Shropshire SY1 4QY
Tel: *H* Shrewsbury (0743) 56712

35 *Somerset*
K. Murphy,
62 St Augustine Street,
Taunton,
Somerset TA1 1QH
Tel: *H* Taunton (0823) 89991

36 *Staffordshire*
A.E. Johnson,
28 West Avenue,
Penkhull,
Stoke-on-Trent ST4 7EU
Tel: *H* Stoke-on-Trent (0782) 44401

37 *Suffolk*
J. Page,
39 Northgate,
Lowestoft,
Suffolk NR32 2RL
Tel: *H* Lowestoft (0502) 61766

38 *Surrey*
G. Peters,
94 Earlswood Road,
Redhill,
Surrey
Tel: *H* Redhill (0737) 67696

39 *Sussex (East and West)*
40
T. Riddington,
155 Northbourns Road,
Eastbourne,
Sussex BN22 RU8

41 *Tyne and Wear*
Mr Allen,
211 Roche Court,
Glebe Village,
Washington,
Tyne and Wear
Tel: *H* Washington (0632) 468520

42 *Warwickshire*
M.F. Eversfield,
41 Queensferry Close,
Rugby,
Warwickshire CV22 7LH
Tel: *H* Rugby (0788) 810974
    W Rugby (0788) 2100
        Ext 464 or 588

43 *Wiltshire*
J. Scott,
59 Cloche Way,
Upper Stratton,
Swindon,
Wiltshire
Tel: *H* Stratton St Margaret
        (079 382) 3632
    W Swindon (0793) 36281
        Ext 230

44 *North Yorkshire*
A. Colbert,
66 Lowther Street,
Groves,
York YO3 7LR
Tel: *H* York (0904) 51442
    W York (0904) 25314

45 *South Yorkshire*
G.H. Ensor,
7 Ashley House,
St Anns,
Rotherham

46 *West Yorkshire*
G.R. Gutheridge,
1 Friar Place,
Bradley,
Huddersfield,
Yorkshire
Tel: *H* Huddersfield (0484) 29716
    W Huddersfield (0484) 850361

47 *Clwyd*
M. Hughes,
4 Caernarvon Terrace,
Clarke Street,
Ponclau,
Wrexham, Clwyd

48 *Dyfed*
T.G. Evans,
28 Raby Street,
Llanelli,
Dyfed SA15 3EY
Tel: *H* Llanelli (055 42) 4448
    W Llanelli (055 42) 2260

49 *Mid Glamorgan*
D.I. Davies,
66 Merthymawr Road,
Bridgend,
Mid Glamorgan CF31 3NR
Tel: *H* Bridgend (0656) 61807

50 *South Glamorgan*
W.J. Ball,
130 Caerau Lane,
Ely,
Cardiff CF5 5HS
Tel: *H* Cardiff (0222) 591505
    W Cardiff (0222) 753271

51 *West Glamorgan*
B.W. John,
18 Park Crescent,
Lanlas Skewen,
Neath,
West Glamorgan
Tel: *H* Skewen (0792) 812968

52 *Gwent*
D.A. Prosser,
10 Mount Pleasant,
Ynysddu,
Newport,
Gwent
Tel: *H* Ynysddu (049 526) 370

53 *Gwynedd*
C. Hughes,
'Koheleth',
131 London Road,
Holyhead,
Anglesey,
Gwynedd LL65 2NY
Tel: *H* Holyhead (0407) 2254

54 *Powys*
K. Griffiths,
3 Plasgwynn,
Temple Street,
Llandrindod Wells
Powys
Tel: *H* Llandrindod Wells (0597) 2986

Part 3
Directory of
Trade Unions

Index of abbreviated titles
Directory
List of registered unions

Index of abbreviated titles

ABS	Broadcasting Staff, Association of
ACTT	Cinematograph, Television and Allied Technicians, The Association of
AGSRO	Government Supervisors and Radio Officers, Association of
APAC	Patternmakers and Allied Craftsmen, Association of
APEX	Professional, Executive, Clerical and Computer Staff, Association of
AMPS	Management and Professional Staffs, Association of
AMU	Metal Workers Union, Associated
ASB	Boilermakers, Shipwrights, Blacksmiths and Structural Workers, The Amalgamated Society of
ASLEF	Locomotive Engineers and Firemen, Associated Society of
ASTMS	Scientific, Technical and Managerial Staffs, Association of
ASTWKT	Textile Workers and Kindred Trades, Amalgamated Society of
AUAW	Asphalt Workers, The Amalgamated Union of
AUEW	Engineering Workers, Amalgamated Union of
AUEW–TASS	Engineering Workers, Amalgamated Union of, Technical, Administrative and Supervisory Section
AUT	University Teachers, Association of
BACM	Colliery Management, The British Association of
BALPA	British Airline Pilots Association
BIFU	Banking, Insurance and Finance Union
BMA	British Medical Association
BRTTS	Roll Turners Trade Society, British
BU	Bakers, Food and Allied Workers' Union
CATU	Ceramic and Allied Trades Union
COHSE	Health Service Employees, Confederation of
CPSA	Civil and Public Services Association
CSU	Civil Service Union

EETPU	Electrical, Electronic, Telecommunication and Plumbing Union
EIS	Educational Institute of Scotland
EMA	Engineers and Managers Association
'Equity'	Actors' Equity Association, British
FAA	Film Artistes Association
FBU	Fire Brigades Union
FDA	First Division Civil Servants, Association of
FTAT	Furniture, Timber and Allied Trades Union
GLCSA	Greater London Council Staff Association
GMWU	General and Municipal Workers Union
HVA	Health Visitors Association
IPCS	Professional Civil Servants, Institution of
IRSF	Inland Revenue Staff Federation
ISTC	Iron and Steel Trades Confederation
MNAOA	Merchant Navy and Airline Officers' Association
MU	Musicians' Union
NACODS	Colliery Overmen, Deputies and Shotfirers, National Association of
NALGO	National and Local Government Officers Association
NALHM	Licensed House Managers, National Association of
NAPO	Probation Officers, National Association of
NAS/UWT	Schoolmasters and Union of Women Teachers, National Association of
NATFHE	Teachers in Further and Higher Education, National Association of
NATSOPA	Printers, Graphical and Media Personnel, National Society of Operative
NATTKE	Theatrical, Television and Kine Employees, National Association of
NGA	Graphical Association, National
NSBGW	Brushmakers and General Workers, National Society of
NSMM	Metal Mechanics, National Society of
NUAAW	Agricultural and Allied Workers, National Union of

NUB	Blastfurnacemen, Oreminers, Coke Workers and Kindred Trades, National Union of
NUDAGMW	Domestic Appliance and General Metal Workers, National Union of
NUDBTW	Dyers, Bleachers and Textile Workers, National Union of
NUFLAT	Footwear, Leather and Allied Trades, National Union of
NUFSO	Funeral Service Operatives, National Union of
NUGSAT	Gold, Silver and Allied Trades, National Union of
NUIW	Insurance Workers, National Union of
NUJ	Journalists, National Union of
NULMW	Lock and Metal Workers, National Union of
NUM	Mineworkers, National Union of
NUMIM	Musical Instrument Makers, National Union of
NUPE	Public Employees, National Union of
NUR	Railwaymen, National Union of
NUS	Scalemakers, National Union of
NUS	Seamen, National Union of
NUSMWC, H and DE	Sheet Metal Workers, Coppersmiths, Heating and Domestic Engineers, National Union of
NUT	Teachers, National Union of
NUT and GW	Tailors and Garment Workers, National Union of
PFA	Professional Footballers Association
POA	Prison Officers Association
POEU	Post Office Engineering Union
POMSA	Post Office Management Staffs, Association of
REOU	Radio and Electronic Officers' Union
SCPS	Civil and Public Servants, Society of
SFEA	Scottish Further Education Association
SLADE	Lithographic Artists, Designers, Engravers and Process Workers, Society of
SOGAT	Graphical and Allied Trades, Society of
SPOE	Post Office Executives, Society of
STAMP	Construction, Allied Trades and Technicians, Union of, Supervisory, Technical, Administrative, Managerial and Professional Section

TGWU	Transport and General Workers Union
TSSA	Transport Salaried Staffs' Association of Great Britain and Ireland
TWU	Tobacco Workers' Union
UCATT	Construction, Allied Trades and Technicians, Union of
UJFKTO	Jute, Flax and Kindred Textile Operatives, Union of
UPW	Post Office Workers, Union of
URTU	Transport Union, The United Road
USDAW	Shop, Distributive and Allied Workers, Union of
WGGB	Writers' Guild of Great Britain

Directory

In this section we have been very dependent on the information supplied by the individual unions. We have tried to include information as follows:

Name of union and abbreviated title

A symbol indicating affiliation: * TUC affiliated union
          † STUC affiliated union
          ‡ GFTU affiliated union

Address and telephone number of its head office

A brief description of the union

Membership ('Current membership' represents figures offered by the union itself or from the latest TUC Statistical Statement, in this case the September 1979 Statement. This statement contains the latest complete figures available and represents the membership in respect of the year ended 31 December 1978. Where the figures are from the trade union itself, particularly in the case of non-affiliated unions, the date may differ)

Details of officials and officers

Publications of the union

Policy

Where this information is not included, the union concerned did not supply it.

ACTORS' EQUITY ASSOCIATION, BRITISH ('Equity')*|
8 Harley Street, London W1N 2AB
Tel: 01-637 9311

Formed in 1929 following the collapse of two other unions, the
Actors' Association and the Stage Guild. The union incorporated the
Variety Artistes' Federation in 1966. Equity policy is based on the
Equity Closed Shop Clause and the Casting Agreement, the first
requiring that 'the Artist shall be required to work only with members
of the British Actors' Equity Association', and the second designed to
establish control over newcomers to the profession.
Current membership: 27,052.

OFFICIALS
President: J. Barron
Vice-Presidents: N. Davenport, H. Manning
Hon Treasurer: M. Johns
General Secretary: P. Plouviez

Periodical: *Equity Journal* (quarterly)

AGRICULTURAL AND ALLIED WORKERS, NATIONAL UNION
OF (NUAAW)*
Headland House, 308 Gray's Inn Road, London WC1X 8DS
Tel: 01-278 7801

Formed in 1906 as the National Union of Agricultural Workers. In
early 1960s the union began to take into membership a number of
workers in industries allied to agriculture such as chicken processing,
mushroom packing, apple sorting, and changed its name to the
National Union of Agricultural and Allied Workers. The union
supported entry into the EEC and pay policy after 1974, but in 1977
presented a wage claim well in excess of the government's norm.
Current membership: 85,000

OFFICIALS
General Secretary: J.R. Boddy, MBE, JP
Head of Organising Department: A. Leary, JP
Head of Wages and Movements Department: R. Pierson
Head of Education and Administration Department: A. Hock
Head of Publicity and Information Department: F. Beckett
Head of Legal Department: J. Watts
Head of Finance Department: J. Tye

Executive Committee 1978
President:
J.H. Hose,
11 Sandringham Road,
Sneinton Dale,
Nottingham NG2 4HA
Tel: Nottingham (0602) 50494

S. Aston,
'Strattons',
Sellars Road,
Hardwicke,
Gloucester GL2 6QD
Tel: Hardwicke (Glos.) (045 272) 569

J. Brocklebank, CBE, JP,
Rose Cottage,
Dishforth,
Thirsk,
Yorkshire YO7 3JU
Tel: Topcliffe (08457) 217

W.H. Wright
'Ashlea',
78 Eastfield Road,
Louth,
Lincolnshire LN11 7AR
Tel: Louth (0507) 604683

A.E. Calver, MBE, JP
8 Cattledyke,
Gorefield,
Wisbech,
Cambridgeshire PE13 4NP
Tel: Newton (094 584) 312

R. Neville,
29 Hooky Lane,
Redhill,
Surrey RH1 6DQ
Tel: Redhill (0737) 69828

J. Rayner,
5 Trinity Guild,
Lavenham,
Sudbury,
Suffolk
Tel: Lavenham (0787) 247586

W.R. Page,
14 Harbord Road,
Overstrand,
Cromer,
Norfolk NR27 0PN
Tel: Overstrand (026 378) 271

J. Paget,
8 Council House,
Rhoon Road,
Terrington St. Clements,
King's Lynn,
Norfolk PE34 4HY

E. Trolley,
8 Hargate Close,
Fleet,
Spalding,
Lincolnshire PE12 8NA
Contact:
Mrs Ashton,
Fleet,
Spalding,
Lincolnshire
Tel: Holbeach (0406) 22151

P. Woodland,
6 Bicton Drive,
East Budleigh,
Budleigh Salterton,
Devon EX9 7BH
Tel: Colaton Raleigh (0395) 68810

General Secretary:
J.R. Boddy, MBE, JP,
36 Station Street,
Swaffham,
Norfolk
Tel: Swaffham (0760) 29916

DISTRICT ORGANISERS
P. Allenson,
NUAAW Office,
47 High Street,
Sutton,
Ely,
Cambs
Tel: Ely (0353) 778247

Part Cambs
Part Suffolk

D. Bareham,
30 Reaper Road,
Prettygate Estate,
Lexden,
Colchester,
Essex CO3 4SH
Tel: Colchester (0206) 77933

Essex

123

G. Barnard   North Norfolk
NUAAW Office,
76 Norwich Street,
Dereham,
Norfolk
Tel: Dereham (0362) 2770

G. Beer,   Part Berkshire and Oxfordshire
NUAAW Office,
Kendrick House,
Wharf Street,
Newbury,
Berkshire
Tel: Newbury (0635) 42255

J. Boddy,   West Norfolk
NUAAW Office,
76 Norwich Street,
Dereham,
Norfolk
Tel: Dereham (0362) 2770

G. Curtis,   Part Lincolnshire
23 Estate Avenue,   Part Humberside
Broughton Brigg,
Lincolnshire DN20 0JY
Tel: Brigg (0652) 53457

T.J. Daniel,   Hampshire
NUAAW Office,   Isle of Wight
40–44 Stockbridge Road,   Part Dorset
Winchester,
Hampshire
Tel: Winchester (0962) 3502

B. Davies   Part Gloucestershire
'Derwendeg',   Part Herefordshire and
36 Hall Drive,   Worcestershire
North Cornelly,   Part Powys, Dyfed, Gwent
Pyle,   West, Mid and South Glamorgan
Bridgend,
Glamorgan
Tel: Bridgend (0656) 740426

C.J. Down,   Part Devon
'Rosina',
Coombesend Road,
Kingsteignton,
Newton Abbot,
Devon TQ12 3DY
Tel: Newton Abbot (0626) 3167

A. Fooks,   Part Cornwall
'Penreath' Bridges,
Luxulyan,
Bodmin,
Cornwall PL30 5EF
Tel: Stenalees (0726) 850294

R.B. Garwell, NUAAW Office, 43 Tamworth Road, Long Eaton, Nottinghamshire NG10 1AX Tel: Long Eaton (060 76) 5918	Nottinghamshire, Derby and Part Leicestershire
A. Gould, NUAAW Office, 31 Albion Place, Maidstone, Kent ME14 5DZ Tel: Maidstone (0622) 55074	Kent
E.E. Hackney, NUAAW Office, Cattle Market, Northfield Avenue, Kettering, Northamptonshire Tel: Kettering (0536) 516145	Northamptonshire and Part Cambridgeshire Part Leicestershire
J. Hardy, NUAAW Office, Wrekin House, Market Street, Wellington, Telford, Shropshire TF1 1DT Tel: Telford (0952) 48249	Shropshire and Gwynedd Part Clwyd
T. Hammond, 17 Ladywell Way, Ponteland, Newcastle upon Tyne, Northumberland NE20 9TE Tel: Ponteland (0661) 23755	Durham and Northumberland Part Cleveland Tyne and Wear
C. Hands, NUAAW Office, 57 Micklegate, Yorkshire YO1 1LG Tel: York (0904) 28206	South Yorkshire West Yorkshire Part North Yorkshire Part Humberside
F.G. Humphreys, 65 Whitefield Road, Penwortham, Preston, Lancashire PR1 0QQ Tel: Preston (0772) 43199	Lancashire and Cumbria Part North Yorkshire Part West Yorkshire Part Greater Manchester Merseyside
S. King NUAAW Office, 16 Northgate, Sleaford, Lincolnshire Tel: Sleaford (0529) 302533	Part Lincolnshire

B. Leathwood,   Somerset
NUAAW Office,   Part Avon
Unity House,
Dampiet Street,
Bridgwater,
Somerset
Tel: Bridgwater (0278) 56378

P. Medhurst,   Suffolk
NUAAW Office,
31 Lower Brook Street,
Ipswich,
Suffolk IP2 8NT
Tel: Ipswich (0473) 54244

A. Mister,   Bedfordshire, Buckinghamshire and
'Lansbury',   Hertfordshire
Potton Road,   Part Berkshire
Wrestlingworth,
Sandy,
Bedfordshire
Tel: Wrestlingworth (076 723) 310

B. Moss,   Surrey and
NUAAW Office,   Sussex
1a High Street,
Dormansland,
Lingfield,
Surrey
Tel: Lingfield (0342) 834068

G. Neish,   Staffordshire
NUAAW Office,   Cheshire
6 Sandford Street,   Part Clwyd
Lichfield,   Part West Midlands
Staffordshire WS13 7NJ   Part Merseyside
Tel: Lichfield (054 32) 23754   Part Greater Manchester

L.V. Pike,   Part Gloucestershire
NUAAW Office,   Part Worcestershire
Labour Hall,   and Herefordshire
115 Barton Street,   Warwickshire
Gloucester   Part West Midlands
Tel: Gloucester (0452) 35332   Part Avon

L.T. Prance,   South Norfolk
NUAAW Office,
76 Norwich Street,
Dereham,
Norfolk NR19 1AD
Tel: Dereham (0362) 2770

D.A. Russell,   Part Lincolnshire
NUAAW Office,   Part Humberside
20 Eastgate,
Louth,
Lincolnshire
Tel: Louth (0507) 4157

J.G. Scally,	Scotland
232 Den Walk,	
Methil,	
Fife KY8 3DN	
Tel: Leven (Fife) (0333) 24867	

J.D. Stuttard,	Wiltshire
Norwich Union House,	
618 Station Road,	
Chippenham,	
Wiltshire	
Tel: Chippenham (0249) 51445	

P. Venn	Dorset
NUAAW Office,	
2 West Walks,	
Dorchester,	
Dorset DT1 1RE	

A.W. Warren,	Part Devon
2 Winkleigh View,	Part Cornwall
Iddesleigh,	
Winkleigh,	
Devon EX19 8DQ	
Tel: Hatherleigh (083 781) 467	

A. Witherington,	Part Lincolnshire
NUAAW Office,	
24 Winsover Road,	
Spalding,	
Lincolnshire PE11 1EJ	
Tel: Spalding (0775) 2921	

C. Young	Part Cleveland
7 De Bruce Road,	Part North Yorkshire
Brompton,	
Northallerton,	
Yorkshire	
Tel: Northallerton (0609) 4679	

Periodical: *Landworker* (monthly)

AMALGAMATED ASSOCIATION OF BEAMERS, TWISTERS AND DRAWERS (HAND AND MACHINE)

See BEAMERS, TWISTERS AND DRAWERS (HAND AND MACHINE), AMALGAMATED ASSOCIATION OF

AMALGAMATED ASSOCIATION OF FELT HAT TRIMMERS AND WOOL FORMERS

See FELT HAT TRIMMERS AND WOOL FORMERS, AMALGAMATED ASSOCIATION OF

AMALGAMATED SOCIETY OF BOILERMAKERS, SHIPWRIGHTS, BLACKSMITHS AND STRUCTURAL WORKERS

See BOILERMAKERS, SHIPWRIGHTS, BLACKSMITHS AND STRUCTURAL WORKERS, AMALGAMATED SOCIETY OF

AMALGAMATED SOCIETY OF JOURNEYMEN FELT HATTERS AND ALLIED WORKERS

See FELT HATTERS AND ALLIED WORKERS, AMALGAMATED SOCIETY OF JOURNEYMEN

AMALGAMATED SOCIETY OF TEXTILE WORKERS AND KINDRED TRADES

See TEXTILE WORKERS AND KINDRED TRADES, AMALGAMATED SOCIETY OF

AMALGAMATED SOCIETY OF WIRE DRAWERS AND KINDRED WORKERS

See WIRE DRAWERS AND KINDRED WORKERS, AMALGAMATED SOCIETY OF

AMALGAMATED TEXTILE WORKERS' UNION

See TEXTILE WORKERS' UNION, AMALGAMATED

AMALGAMATED UNION OF ASPHALT WORKERS

See ASPHALT WORKERS, AMALGAMATED UNION OF

AMALGAMATED UNION OF ENGINEERING WORKERS

See ENGINEERING WORKERS, AMALGAMATED UNION OF

ASPHALT WORKERS, THE AMALGAMATED UNION OF (AUAW)*†‡
Jenkin House, 173a Queens Road, Peckham, London SE15 2NF
Tel: 01–639 1669

Formed in 1938 by an amalgamation between the National Asphalt Workers Union based in London and the Northern Asphalt Workers Union based in Manchester. Organises mainly workers in the manufacture and application of mastic asphalt.
Current membership: 3,012

OFFICIALS
General Secretary: H.M. Wareham
Assistant General Secretary: D.A. McCann
Regional Full-time Officials:

E. Firth,	S. Fullard,
8 Snowdon Close,	29 Atherton House,
Raynville Estate,	Sutton Estate,
Leeds 13	Benwell.
	Newcastle upon Tyne NE4 7UB

ASSOCIATED METALWORKERS' UNION

See METALWORKERS' UNION, ASSOCIATED

ASSOCIATED SOCIETY OF LOCOMOTIVE ENGINEERS AND FIREMEN

See LOCOMOTIVE ENGINEERS AND FIREMEN, ASSOCIATED SOCIETY OF

ASSOCIATION OF BROADCASTING STAFF

See BROADCASTING STAFF, ASSOCIATION OF

ASSOCIATION OF CINEMATOGRAPH, TELEVISION AND ALLIED TECHNICIANS

See CINEMATOGRAPH, TELEVISION AND ALLIED TECHNICIANS, ASSOCIATION OF

ASSOCIATION OF FIRST DIVISION CIVIL SERVANTS

See FIRST DIVISION CIVIL SERVANTS, ASSOCIATION OF

ASSOCIATION OF GOVERNMENT SUPERVISORS AND RADIO OFFICERS

See GOVERNMENT SUPERVISORS AND RADIO OFFICERS, ASSOCIATION OF

ASSOCIATION OF LECTURERS IN COLLEGES OF EDUCATION IN SCOTLAND

ASSOCIATION OF LOCAL AUTHORITY CHIEF EXECUTIVES

See LOCAL AUTHORITY OF CHIEF EXECUTIVES, ASSOCIATION OF

ASSOCIATION OF MANAGEMENT AND PROFESSIONAL STAFF
See MANAGEMENT AND PROFESSIONAL STAFF, ASSOCIATION OF

ASSOCIATION OF OFFICIAL ARCHITECTS

See OFFICIAL ARCHITECTS, ASSOCIATION OF

ASSOCIATION OF PATTERNMAKERS AND ALLIED CRAFTSMEN

See PATTERNMAKERS AND ALLIED CRAFTSMEN, ASSOCIATION OF

ASSOCIATION OF POLYTECHNIC TEACHERS

See POLYTECHNIC TEACHERS, ASSOCIATION OF

ASSOCIATION OF POST OFFICE MANAGEMENT STAFFS

See POST OFFICE MANAGEMENT STAFFS, ASSOCIATION OF

ASSOCIATION OF PROFESSIONAL, EXECUTIVE, CLERICAL AND COMPUTER STAFF

See PROFESSIONAL, EXECUTIVE, CLERICAL AND COMPUTER STAFF, ASSOCIATION OF

ASSOCIATION OF PROFESSIONAL SCIENTISTS AND TECHNOLOGISTS

See PROFESSIONAL SCIENTISTS AND TECHNOLOGISTS, ASSOCIATION OF

ASSOCIATION OF PUBLIC SERVICE FINANCE OFFICERS

See PUBLIC SERVICE FINANCE OFFICERS, ASSOCIATION OF

ASSOCIATION OF SCIENTIFIC, TECHNICAL AND MANAGERIAL STAFFS

See SCIENTIFIC, TECHNICAL AND MANAGERIAL STAFFS, ASSOCIATION OF

ASSOCIATION OF UNIVERSITY TEACHERS

See UNIVERSITY TEACHERS, ASSOCIATION OF

BAKERS AND ALLIED WORKERS, SCOTTISH UNION OF*
127 Fergus Drive, Glasgow G20 6AU
Tel: 041–946 4213

A union originally formed in 1888 for the Scottish Bakery Industry and from 1926 including women as well as men. Falling membership as a result of bakery closures and rationalisation led to rising costs and in 1977 a recommendation was made by the Executive Council of amalgamation by transfer of engagements to the Union of Shop Distributive and Allied Workers. This took place in January 1978. The union is now the Scottish Bakers' Section of USDAW.
1977 membership: 8,693

NATIONAL OFFICIALS
President: A. Douglas
Vice-President: A. Smith
General Secretary: A.H. Mackie
Executive Council:

C. Still	G.N. Currie
C. Strachan	G. Seaton
D. Robertson	T. Scott
A.D. Kelly	J. McIntyre
W. Garvie	J. Glass

National Organisers: T.N. Craig, S. Fyfe, JP, W. Buller, JP

BAKERS, FOOD AND ALLIED WORKERS' UNION (BU)*
Stanborough House, Great North Road, Stanborough, Welwyn
Garden City, Hertfordshire AL8 7TA
Tel: Hatfield (070 72) 60150

Founded in 1849 for bakery workers in Manchester. In 1861 it
became part of the Amalgamated Union of Operative Bakers of
England which then became the Amalgamated Union of Operative
Bakers, Confectioners and Allied Workers. The title was changed to
Bakers' Union in 1964 but later expanded to the present title as the
interests of the union widened.
Current membership: 54,912
    Males: 33,533
    Females: 21,379

OFFICIAL
General Secretary: J. Marino

Periodical: *Food Worker* (monthly)

BANKING, INSURANCE AND FINANCE UNION (BIFU)*
Sheffield House, Portsmouth Road, Esher, Surrey
Tel: Esher (0372) 66624

Officially formed in 1918, following preparatory meetings in 1917, by
a combination of bank clerks in Sheffield. In October of 1919 the
headquarters were transferred to London, and the National Bank
Officers Guild was born. The Bank Officers Guild (BOG) was the
first organisation with the purpose of unionising the English and
Welsh banking and finance industry. By 1925 membership had grown
to 25,000.

In 1919 the Scottish Bankers Association (SBA) was formed. In
1939–40 both the SBA and the BOG affiliated to the TUC and the
STUC. Amalgamation of the SBA and BOG in 1946 led to the
formation of the National Union of Bank Employees (NUBE) now
the Banking, Insurance and Finance Union, which covers employees
of all grades in England, Scotland and Wales.

It is the largest TUC affiliated union in the banking industry.
Recruitment spans the English and Scottish Clearing Banks, Trustee
Savings Banks, Co-operative Banks, Foreign and Commonwealth
Banks, British Overseas Banks, Finance Houses and Credit Card
Companies, Building Societies, Insurance Companies, Bank of
England and the Stock Exchange.

Since BIFU is an industrial union there are many categories of
employees within membership ranging from white collar categories,
such as bank clerks/managers, accountants, computer staff, to blue
collar technical and services employees.

BIFU participates in the activities of FIET (International
Federation of Commercial, Clerical and Technical Employees).

Within FIET there is a specific section concerned with banking issues.
Current membership: 126,343
   Males: 66,200
   Females: 60,143

OFFICIALS
General Secretary: L.A. Mills
Executive Committee 1978/79
Hon. President: W.J. Martin
Hon. Vice-President: J.R. Robinson
Hon. General Treasurer: H. Goodrich

Manchester Area: K.H. Pooler, Mrs C. Harvey
Yorkshire Area: P. Clements, T. Ashford
South Wales Area: G. Cousins
East Midlands Area: P.G. Woodhead
West Midlands Area: Miss P. W. Hart, K. Anderson
East Anglia Area: T.S. Richards
North Wales Area: W.T. Williams
South East Area: R. Smale
South & West Region: G.M.J. Young, Miss A. Legge
North West Area: W.C. Morgan
Merseyside Area: G. Davies
Scottish Area: A. Cruickshank, J.H. Elliot
London Area: M. Mehlin, Mrs P.M. Lynch, I. Khan, A. Meadows
Guardian Royal Exchange: W. Remfry

FULL-TIME OFFICIALS:
General Secretary
L.A. Mills
BIFU Headquarters,   31 Station Road,
Sheffield House,   West Byfleet,
Portsmouth Road,   Surrey
Esher,
Surrey
Tel: Esher 66624   Tel: Byfleet 42829

Personal Assistant to General Secretary
P. Jennings
BIFU Headquarters   34c Marlborough Road,
Tel: Esher 66624   Richmond,
                    Tel: 01–948 3161

Deputy General Secretary:
D. Paterson
BIFU Glasgow Office   32 Crummock Street,
79 West Regent Street,   Beith,
Glasgow G2 2AW   Ayrshire KA15 2BD
Tel: 041–332 0660/8334   Tel: Beith 2762

Assistant Secretary:
P. Allison
BIFU Glasgow Office   9 Larchfield Gardens,
                    Wishaw,
                    Lanarkshire
Tel: 041–332 0660/8334   Tel: Wishaw 72427

Finance and Administration Officer:
S.R. Lewis
BIFU Headquarters

Tel: Esher 66624

51 Arnold Crescent,
Isleworth,
Middlesex
Tel: 01–898 5512

Personal Assistant to Finance & Admin. Officer:
Mrs. J.J. Bogner,
BIFU Headquarters

Tel: Esher 66624

458 Upper Richmond Road West,
Richmond,
Surrey
Tel: 01–878 1863

Assistant Secretaries:
T.A. Molloy
BIFU Headquarters

Tel: Esher 66624

13 Wendela Close,
White Rose Lane,
Woking,
Surrey
Tel: 04862 67417

D.W. Dines
BIFU Headquarters

Tel: Esher 66624

10 Mulholland Close,
Mitcham,
Surrey CR4 1SW
Tel: 01–640 3833

W.W. Whiteman
BIFU Headquarters

Tel: Esher 66624

49 Beckford Road,
Croydon
Tel: 01–654 0421

S. Gamble
BIFU Headquarters

Tel: Esher 66624

99 The Avenue,
Greenacres,
Aylesford,
Maidstone,
Kent
Tel: 0622 78576

I. Cameron
BIFU Headquarters

Tel: Esher 66624

62a Braemar Avenue,
Wood Green,
London N22
Tel: 01–889 8792

A. Piper
BIFU Headquarters

Tel: Esher 66624

Wardens Flat,
Duchess of Kent Court,
Aylesford,
Maidstone,
Kent
Tel: 0622 77206

134

J. Hargraves
BIFU Headquarters

26 Pinkneys Road,
Maidenhead,
Berkshire
Tel: Esher 66624

Tel: 0628 24819

H.H. Woods
BIFU Headquarters

62a Braemer Avenue,
Wood Green,
London N22
Tel: Esher 66624

Tel: 01–889 8792

K. Jones
BIFU
4th Floor,
6/7 Queen Street,
London EC4
Tel: 01–248 7921

'Solana',
Surrey Gardens,
Effingham Junction,
Surrey
Tel: East Horsley 4591

Negotiating Officer:
J. Camfield
BIFU Headquarters

36 The Springs,
Turnford,
Broxbourne,
Herts
Tel: Esher 66624

Tel: Hoddesdon 42291

Assistant Secretary (Research)
J. Robinson
BIFU Headquarters

25 Dunsmore Road,
Walton-on-Thames,
Middlesex
Tel: Esher 66624

Tel: Walton 22197

Assistant Secretary (Publicity):
W. Vose
BIFU Headquarters

2 Egerton Road,
New Malden,
Surrey
Tel: Esher 66624

Tel: 01–942 3581

National Organiser:
L.J. James
BIFU
2nd Floor,
102 Bute Street,
Cardiff
Tel: 0222 23797/24483

5 Romilly Avenue,
Romilly Park,
Barry,
Glamorgan
Tel: 4462 79246

Negotiating Officers:
E. Hutchinson
BIFU,
Oakland House,
Netherfield Road,
Ravensthorpe,
 Dewsbury,
West Yorkshire
Tel: Dewsbury 469528/9

5 Hall Cliff Road,
Horbury,
Wakefield,
Yorks

Tel: 0924 274341

E. Sweeney
BIFU Headquarters

33 Burleigh Road,
Addlestone,
Surrey

Tel: Esher 66624

Tel: Weybridge 52008

REGIONAL ORGANISERS:
North East/North West Areas:
D. Sharples
BIFU,
1st Floor,
Barclays Bank Ltd,
77 Shudehill,
Manchester
Tel: 061–834 7825/6

2 Ennerdale Road,
Longridge,
Preston,
Lancs

Tel: 0774 785198

Manchester Area:
D. Swindells,
BIFU Manchester Office

109 Meadway,
Bramhall, Cheshire

Tel: 061–834 7825/6

Tel: 061–439 7392

Yorkshire Area:
C. Moore,
BIFU,
Oakland House,
Netherfield Road,
Ravensthorpe,
Dewsbury,
W. Yorkshire
Tel: Dewsbury 469528/9

38 Holmdene Drive,
Mirfield,
W. Yorkshire

Tel: Mirfield 498384

North/South Wales Area:
Miss J. Cole,
BIFU,
2nd Floor,
102 Bute Street,
The Docks,
Cardiff.
Tel: 0222 23797

At present, no
permanent
accommodation.

East Midlands Area:
M. McKeown,
BIFU,
Prudential Buildings,
5 St. Philips Place,
Colmore Row,
Birmingham 3
Tel: 021–236 1419

46 West Way,
Cotsgrave,
Nottingham

No Tel. Number

East Anglia Area:
Rick Humphreys,
BIFU,
25a Hills Road,
Cambridge
Tel: 0223 60121

Tel: Ramsey (0487) 840970

South East Area:
Mrs V. Mason,
BIFU,
5 North Street,
Worthing,
Sussex
Tel: 0903 35051

27 Alexandra Road,
Worthing,
West Sussex BN11 2DU

Southern & West Country Area:
D. Bates,
BIFU,
6a Castle Street,
Salisbury,
Wiltshire
Tel: Salisbury 25140

Miss R. Thomas
BIFU Salisbury Office

Tel: Salisbury 25140

3 Fowlers Hill,
Salisbury,
Wiltshire
Tel: Salisbury 22200

Scottish Area:
Mrs B. Hanlon,
BIFU,
79 West Regent Street,
Glasgow G2 2AW
Tel: 041-332 0660/8334

32 Dargavel Avenue,
Bishopton,
Renfrewshire
Tel: Bishopton 2237

Merseyside Area:
A. Lee,
BIFU,
1st Floor,
Barclays Bank Ltd,
77 Shudehill,
Manchester
Tel: 061-834 7825/6

21 Thelby Close,
Chapel House Estate,
Skelmersdale,
Lancs

Tel: Skelmersdale 21087

London Area:
R. Lynch,
BIFU London Office

Tel: 01-248 7921

Flat 9,
15 Chatsworth Road,
London, NW2
Tel: 01-459 8478

A. Karmel,
BIFU London Office

Tel: 01-248 7921

24 Observatory,
Benson,
Oxfordshire
Tel: 0491 38879

BEAMERS, TWISTERS AND DRAWERS (HAND AND MACHINE), AMALGAMATED ASSOCIATION OF*‡

27 Every Street, Nelson, Lancashire
Tel: Nelson (0282) 64181

Formed in 1866, and reconstituted in its present form in 1889, as an amalgamation of semi-autonomous district unions. The union organises employees concerned with the weaving of cotton, linen and man-made fibres.
The Union publishes an Annual Report (for members only).
Current membership: 1,123.

OFFICIALS
President: D. Pasquill, 25 Wellington Street, St. Johns, Blackburn, Lancashire
General Secretary: F. Sumner

BLASTFURNACEMEN, OREMINERS, COKE WORKERS AND KINDRED TRADES, NATIONAL UNION OF (NUB)*

93 Borough Road West, Middlesbrough, Cleveland TS1 3AJ
Tel: Middlesbrough (0642) 242961

Originated in 1878 in Cleveland to cater for unorganised workers in the developing ore mining and iron making industry in this area and later combining federated districts operating more widely over the country. The union remains independent of the Iron and Steel Trades Confederation representing the grades of workers with which it has traditionally been concerned in all parts of the UK except Scotland.
Current membership: 14,349

OFFICIALS

President: N. Leadley
General Secretary: H.C. Smith

District Officials:
Northern District:
N. Leadley,
93 Borough Road West,
Middlesbrough, Cleveland

Welsh District:
J. Perring,
49 Talbot Road,
Port Talbot
Glamorgan

North Midlands District:
A. Chudley,
32 Mapletree Way,
Scunthorpe,
S. Humberside

South Midlands and Mines District:
B.T. Fisher,
89 New Beacon Road,
Grantham,
Lincolnshire

Executive Committee
N. Leadley,
93 Borough Road West,
Middlesbrough, Cleveland

G. Rae,
37 Lambton Road,
Grove Hill,
Middlesbrough, Cleveland,

E. Mulgrew,
47 Ennerdale Road,
Maryport,
Cumbria

J. Martin,
27 Sussex Road,
Moorside,
Consett, Co. Durham

B. T. Fisher,
9 Eaton Place,
Bingham,
Nr. Nottingham

J. Perring,
49 Talbot Road,
Port Talbot, Glamorgan

R. D. Kinneir,
25 Eskdale Avenue,
Corby,
Northants

J. Wademan,
52 Buckingham Avenue,
Scunthorpe,
S. Humberside

H. C. Smith,
93 Borough Road West,
Middlesborough, Cleveland

A. Chudley,
32 Mapletree Way,
Scunthorpe,
S. Humberside

L. James
(Finance Officer),
93 Borough Road West,
Middlesborough, Cleveland

W. J. Booth,
99 Thompson Avenue,
Lliswerry,
Newport,
Gwent

BLIND AND DISABLED, NATIONAL LEAGUE OF*†
Tottenham Trades Hall, 7 Bruce Grove, London N17 6RA
Tel: 01–808 6030

Founded in 1899 as the National League of the Blind, taking its present title in 1968. Membership is to be found in a variety of trades, e.g. bedding, upholstery, wire work, machine knitwear, cardboard box making, light engineering, weaving, boot repair, braille printing, telephone operating, basket, brush and matting trades.
Current membership: 4,250

OFFICIAL
General Secretary: M. A. Barrett

Periodical: *The Blind Advocate* (quarterly)

BOILERMAKERS, SHIPWRIGHTS, BLACKSMITHS AND STRUCTURAL WORKERS, THE AMALGAMATED SOCIETY OF (ASB)*†
Lifton House, Eslington Road, Newcastle upon Tyne NE2 4SB
Tel: Newcastle upon Tyne (0632) 813205/6

In January 1977 the Laminated and Coil Spring Workers Union officially transferred their engagements to the ASB.

Current membership: 131,051
   Males: 130,808
   Females: 243

OFFICIAL
General Secretary: J. Chalmers, CBE

Periodical: *Monthly Report*

BOOT, SHOE AND SLIPPER OPERATIVES, THE ROSSENDALE UNION OF*‡

Taylor House, 7 Tenterfield Street, Waterfoot, Rossendale BB4 7BA
Tel: Rossendale (070 62) 5657

The union was formed in 1895 and covers footwear workers mainly in the Fylde Coast and East Lancashire. It has two full-time officials, a Secretary and an Assistant Secretary. Apart from these the Executive Committee is composed of elected Area and Factory Representatives, the latter being responsible for the various departments in the industry. The President also works in the trade and is subject to election every two years by the General Meeting of members. Negotiations on behalf of that section of the industry covered by the union are conducted with the Lancashire Footwear Manufacturers Association. A General Agreement regulates the terms and conditions of employment.
Current membership: 5,809
   Males: 2,091
   Females: 3,718

OFFICIALS
President: D. Broxton
Secretary: T. Whittaker
Assistant Secretary: M. Murray

BRITISH ACTORS' EQUITY ASSOCIATION

See ACTORS' EQUITY ASSOCIATION, BRITISH

BRITISH AIR LINE PILOTS ASSOCIATION, (BALPA)*

81 New Road, Harlington, Hayes, Middlesex UB3 5BG
Tel: 01–759 9331/5

Formed in 1937 by professional airline pilots in the UK to improve and protect their conditions of service and to establish a body which could voice the opinion of professional pilots on civil aviation technical and safety matters. Membership has grown from a handful of pilots to nearly 4,500 in 1979. BALPA is governed by an Annual

Delegates Conference held in December of each year and comprising 47 pilot delegates and three full-time official delegates. Day to day running of the Association is in the hands of the National Executive Council consisting of nine elected pilot members and three full-time officials. Pilots' Local Councils are elected annually by members employed by each company or at each base.
Current membership: 4,457

FULL-TIME OFFICIALS
General Secretary: M. Young
Deputy General Secretary: D.R. Bennison
Executive Secretary: G. Arnold
Industrial Relations Officer: C. Minton
Industrial Relations Officer: R.F. Trowbridge
Technical Secretary: T.N. Staples
Assistant Technical Secretary: S.M.B. Lane
Treasurer (part-time): G. Young

Periodical: *Log* (bimonthly)

BRITISH ASSOCIATION OF COLLIERY MANAGEMENT

See COLLIERY MANAGEMENT, BRITISH ASSOCIATION OF

BRITISH DENTAL ASSOCIATION
64 Wimpole Street, London W1M 8AL
Tel: 01–935 0875

Formed in 1880. In 1952 it took over the functions of the Incorporated Dental Society and the Public Dental Services Association. It negotiates conditions of service and remuneration of all dental practitioners in the National Health Service, in the Armed Forces, and in Dental Teaching Schools.
Current membership: 13,000, including approximately 1,500 women.

FULL-TIME OFFICERS
Secretary: R.B. Allen, BChD, FDS
Assistant Secretaries: B.C. Patterson, MA, DPhil, S.H. Richardson, Ms D.M. Scarrott, MA, N.R. Webb
Accountant: J.A.C. Pugh, FCA
Editor: Mrs. M.H. Seward, MDS, FDS
Librarian: E.M. Spencer, MBE, BA, ALA

Periodical: *British Dental Journal*

BRITISH MEDICAL ASSOCIATION (BMA)
BMA House, Tavistock Square, London WC1H 9JP
Tel: 01–387 4499

Founded in 1832 as a voluntary, professional association for the promotion of the medical and allied sciences and the maintenance of the honour and interests of the medical profession. It is a company limited by guarantee and is also listed under the Trade Union and Labour Relations Act, 1974 and with a certificate of Independence under the Employment Protection Act. Recognised by the Health Departments as the negotiating body for all NHS doctors, and represents the British medical profession in the EEC. The Association deals with all matters of medico-political and medico-social nature and provides a personal service for members with professional problems. Its 600-strong Representative Body (the Doctors' Parliament) is democratically elected as are its Council and representative Committees. There are 216 Divisions in the UK and its current membership is 63,000.

In the past two years the BMA has been increasing its services to members aimed at improving the personal service and advice to the individual member at the place of work and in particular relating to the employment and other legislation of recent years and changes in terms and conditions of service. There has been an expansion in the number of regional offices, Provincial Medical Secretaries have been appointed and a Professional Relations Unit has been set up. During the 1978/9 session work began on appointing Place of Work Accredited Representatives (POWARS) and the appointment of BMA Safety Representatives under the new Health and Safety at Work regulations. A Senior Industrial Relations Officer has been appointed with a department solely devoted to helping members with their problems. Industrial Relations Officers are being appointed in the regions and four are so far in post. More emphasis has been given to helping members with employment problems and representing them before industrial tribunals.

OFFICIALS
Officers of the Association
President: Dame J. Barnes (until July 1980)
Sir J. Walton (from July 1980)
Chairman of Representative Body: Dr E.B. Lewis
Chairman of Council: A. Grabham, FRCS
Treasurer: Dr J. Miller

Senior Full-time Officials
Secretary: Dr J. Havard
Editor, *British Medical Journal*: Dr S. Lock
Financial and Estates Controller: A. Potier
Senior Industrial Relations Officer: N. Ellis
Chief Press Officer: A. Thistlethwaite

Scottish Secretary: Dr C.D. Falconer,
Scottish House,
7 Drumsheugh Gardens,
Edinburgh EH3 7QP

Welsh Secretary: Dr W. Cattell,
Welsh House,
195 Newport Road,
Cardiff CF2 1UE

Northern Ireland Office: Miss M. Donaldson,
Northern Ireland House,
609 Ormeau Road,
Belfast BT7 3JD

Regional Offices:
Cambridge Regional Office
90 Hills Road,
Cambridge

Glasgow Regional Office
9 Lynedoch Crescent,
Glasgow G3 6EI

Leeds Regional Office
24 Park Square,
Leeds

London Regional Office
British Medical Association,
BMA House,
Tavistock Square,
London WC1H 9JP

Merseyside Regional Office
Liverpool Medical Institution,
116 Mount Pleasant,
Liverpool L3 5ST

Midland Regional Office
36 Harborne Road,
Edgbaston,
Birmingham B15 3AJ

North of England Regional Office
4 Eslington Road,
Jesmond,
Newcastle upon Tyne NE2 4RH

North West Regional Office
Boyd House,
Upper Park Road,
Victoria Park,
Manchester M14 5RH

Sheffield Regional Office
Westminster House,
1–7 George Street,
Sheffield S1 2PF

Southampton Regional Office
10 College Place,
London Road,
Southampton

South West Regional Office
96c Whiteladies Road,
Clifton,
Bristol BS8 2QX

Periodicals: *British Medical Journal* (weekly), *BMA News Review*
(monthly), Specialist Journals

BRITISH ROLL TURNERS' TRADE SOCIETY

See ROLL TURNERS' TRADE SOCIETY, BRITISH

BROADCASTING AND ALLIED STAFFS, ASSOCIATION OF (ABS)*†
King's Court, 2–16 Goodge Street, London W1P 2AE
Tel: 01–637 1261/7

Formed in May 1940 as the BBC Staff (Wartime) Association. The wartime Association amalgamated with the Association of BBC Engineers in 1945 to form the BBC Staff Association. Re-registered as the Association of Broadcasting Staff in February 1956. Present title adopted in 1974. Recognised by the BBC and the IBA for representation of all categories of staff. Recognised by the independent local radio companies. Represents those who work, as permanent staff or on a temporary or short term contract or as freelances, in television, radio and allied fields involving use of sound or vision broadcasting, facsimile transmission or allied techniques for the creation and/or distribution of programmes for information, education or entertainment. Affiliated to the TUC since 1963. Also affiliated to the Scottish TUC, the Wales TUC, the National Federation of Professional Workers, the Confederation of Entertainment Unions, the Federation of Broadcasting Unions and the Radio and Television Safeguards Committee. Affiliated internationally to FISTAV (International Federation of Unions of Audio-Visual Workers). Is currently holding amalgamation discussions with the ACTT to form the Amalgamated Film and Broadcasting Union. Publishes a monthly journal, *ABStract*. A National Executive Committee of 18 elected at the annual delegate conference appoints a Chairman and two Vice-Chairmen. The annual conference determines all major policy issues.
Current membership: 14,883
    Males: 11,318
    Females: 3,565

PAID OFFICIALS
General Secretary: D.A. Hearn
Deputy General Secretary: P.S. Leech
Eight full-time and two part-time Assistant General Secretaries.

BRUSHMAKERS AND GENERAL WORKERS, NATIONAL SOCIETY OF (NSBGW)*‡
20 The Parade, Watford WD1 2AA
Tel: Watford (0923) 21950

Founded in 1747 with claims of being the union with the longest continuous existence in the world. A Brushmakers' Benevolent Institute was established in 1828 to act for all the local societies of the day, those for which records still exist including Manchester (formed 1747), Bristol (1782), Lyme Regis (1786), Leeds (1791), and London (1806), which, from the early 1800s acted as Head Society, making the

whole into a form of national union.
Current membership: 1,600

OFFICIAL
General Secretary: A.J. Parsons

CARD DRESSERS' SOCIETY
105 Whitcliffe Road, Cleckheaton, Yorkshire

Formed in 1892 with 48 members and now representing workers in the card clothing manufacturing industry consisting of the English Card Clothing Co. Ltd, the Card Clothing Co. Ltd, Messrs T. Holdsworths and Sons Ltd and Pearson Bros. Ltd. Decline in the trade has resulted in reduced membership.
Current membership: 25 male

OFFICIALS

President: B. Dolan,
17 Heaton Avenue,
Cleckheaton,
Yorkshire

Secretary: E. Brooke,
105 Whitcliffe Road,
Cleckheaton,
Yorkshire

Treasurer: H. Cawthra,
5 Second Avenue,
Windybank Estate,
Hightown,
Liversedge,
Yorkshire

CARD SETTING MACHINE TENTERS' SOCIETY*‡
36 Greenton Avenue, Scholes, Cleckheaton, West Yorkshire BD19 6DT
Tel: Cleckheaton (0274) 670022

A union of craftsmen manufacturing card clothing for use in the textile industry. Growth in the use of metallic carding in recent years has reduced the number of such craftsmen required. The present strength of the union is to be found in a few firms in Yorkshire.
Current membership: 134

GENERAL OFFICERS
President: J.W. Jessop,
21 St. Albans Avenue,
Halifax

General Secretary: G. Priestley

Treasurer: A.D. Warden,
8 The Oval,
Hightown Road,
Liversedge

Trustees: L. Higgins, J. Garside, D. Jolliffe
Executive Council Delegates: N. Scriven, R. Beaumont

CARPET TRADES UNION, NORTHERN*‡
22 Clare Road, Halifax HX1 2HX
Tel: Halifax (0422) 60492

Formed in 1892, the union originally catered exclusively for carpet weavers but in recent years has covered all sections of ancillary workers engaged in the manufacture of carpets, mainly in the north of England and in Durham. It has a Staff Section which recruits Supervisory and Management Grades. Affiliated to the TUC, the International Textile, Garment & Leather Workers' Federation, the GFTU and the National Affiliation Board to the Carpet Industry.

One of the recent major decisions was to closely examine profit sharing schemes, and a sub-committee of the National Executive Committee has been set up for this purpose.
Current membership: 2,065
    Males: 1,563
    Females: 502

OFFICIALS
General Secretary: L.R. Smith, MIWSP
President: J. Ashton

CERAMIC AND ALLIED TRADES UNION (CATU)*‡
Hillcrest House, Garth Street, Hanley, Stoke-on-Trent ST1 2AB
Tel: Stoke-on-Trent (0782) 24201/2/3

First formed around 1827 as a craft union of operative potters, later becoming the National Society of Male and Female Pottery Operatives and in 1919 the National Society of Pottery Workers. In 1970 it became the Ceramic and Allied Trades Union. At first the union organised only pottery workers, but later the other workers in the industry were included. Since then it has extended to cover clerical workers, the most recent innovation being the inclusion of the white collar workers, and this section has been successful in recruiting many new areas of non-manual workers within the ceramic industry. Membership is to be found mainly in the North Staffordshire area with approximately 50 per cent males and 50 per cent females.
Current membership: 51,219

OFFICIALS
General Secretary: L.R. Sillitoe, OBE, JP
Assistant General Secretary: A.W. Clowes
General President: J.A. Jackson (lay member)
Executive Council: 20 lay members plus officials
Organisers:
A. Martin
J.K.W. Arnold
N. Walters
H. Hammersley
Policy: It negotiates with the National Joint Council of the Ceramic

146

Industry which is composed of 12 Union Executive members and 12 Employers' representatives; with annual settlement of wages on 25th March each year. In recent years, the union has been in favour of entry into the EEC and generally supported the idea of incomes policy. An Annual Delegation decision has been taken to fight for a 35-hour week.

THE CHARTERED SOCIETY OF PHYSIOTHERAPY
14 Bedford Row, London WC1R 4ED
Tel: 01–242 1941

The Chartered Society of Physiotherapy was founded (as the Society of Trained Masseuses) in 1895 and received its Royal Charter in 1920. It is the only recognised training and examining body for chartered physiotherapists and is the professional association for the Society's members. It has been a negotiating body for its members on the Whitley Councils for the National Health Service since their inception, and in 1977 received its certificate of independence as a Trade Union under Section 8 of the Employment Protection Act 1975.

OFFICIALS:
Secretary: R.J.S. Bryant,
Industrial Relations Officer: P.H. Gray
14 Bedford Row,
London WC1R 4ED
The society does not employ full-time officials at district level but members undertake responsibilities as District Stewards. The name of a steward for a particular district may be obtained upon inquiry to the Secretary.

CHIEF AND ASSISTANT CHIEF FIRE OFFICERS' ASSOCIATION
County Fire Brigade Headquarters, The Godlands, Tovil, Maidstone ME15 6XB, Kent
Tel: Maidstone (0622) 54311

An association formed in 1974 from the previous Chief Fire Officers' Association following Local Government reorganisation. While the prime concern of the Association is to safeguard the interests of its members, the Association is actively concerned in promoting the welfare and efficiency of the Fire Service generally and giving professional advice to Local Authority Associations on any matter concerned with the management of Local Authority Fire Brigades and on any aspect of fire safety. It does this through a series of National Technical Standing Committees (serviced by the districts) which provide a forum for discussion and also provides representatives to the various Committees of the Central Fire Brigades' Advisory Council.
Current membership: 167

OFFICIALS

There are no full-time officials but the Honorary Appointments are as follows:

President: T.N. Watkins, OBE, FIFire E, AMBIM
Fire Brigade Headquarters,
The Old Hall,
Burton Road,
Littleover,
Derby DE3 6EH

Vice-President: R.J. Knowlton, QFSM, FIFire E,
Strathclyde Fire Brigade Headquarters,
Bothwell Road,
Hamilton,
Lanarkshire ML3 0EA

Hon. General Secretary: R.D.H. Doyle, FIFire E,
Fire Brigade Headquarters,
The Godlands,
Tovil,
Maidstone Kent
ME15 6XB

Hon. Treasurer: G. Clarke, FIFire E,
Fire Brigade Headquarters,
The Castle,
Winchester. Hampshire
SO23 8UA,

Hon. Assistant Secretary: C.R. Chandler,
Fire Brigade Headquarters,
St. David's,
Wray Park Road,
Reigate,
Surrey

Hon. Technical Secretary: G.K. Lockyer, OBE, QFSM, FIFire E,
Fire Brigade Headquarters,
Anstey Frith,
Leicester Road,
Glenfield,
Leicester LE3 8HD

Hon. Competitions Secretary: R.T. Ford, FIFire E,
Fire Brigade Headquarters,
Crosby Road,
Northallerton North Yorkshire
DL6 1AB

District Secretaries

W.D.C. Cooney,
Fire Brigade Headquarters,
Park Road South,
Middlesbrough,
Cleveland TS5 6LG

A.N. Lightbody, MI Fire E,
Fire Brigade Headquarters,
Walmoor House,
Dee Banks,
Chester Cheshire
CH3 5UB

T.O. Burn, QFSM, FIFire E,
Fire Brigade Headquarters,
Pirehill,
Stone,
Staffordshire ST15 0BS

K. Harden, BEM, MI Fire E,
Fire Brigade Headquarters,
Keynsham Road,
Cheltenham
Gloucestershire GL53 7PY

E.S. Faulkner, FIFire E,
Fire Brigade Headquarters,
Old London Road,
Hertford SG13 7LD

R.F. Holland-Thomas, GI Fire E,
Fire Brigade Headquarters,
Newall Terrace,
Dumfries DG1 1IE

R.B. Blackburn, QFSM,
 FIFire E, AMBIM,
Fire Brigade Headquarters,
Northgate,
Chichester,
West Sussex
PO19 1BD

W.F. Dancey, FIFire E,
Fire Brigade Headquarters,
The Mount,
Mount Street,
Swansea
West Glamorgan SA4 3HA

CINEMATOGRAPH, TELEVISION AND ALLIED TECHNICIANS, THE ASSOCIATION OF (ACTT)*†
2 Soho Square, London W1V 6DD
Tel: 01-437 8506

A small but broadly based trade union in the entertainment and communications sector whose members are mainly employed in four areas: independent television, film production, professional film processing and commercial radio. It has negotiating rights with the recognised employers' associations and is currently a signatory to five national Trade Union Agreements which cover production and technical staff in these areas. The union was formed in 1933 as the Association of Cine Technicians and in 1940 the Government accepted ACT membership as a proof of film technicians' status. The Union negotiates agreements with the Programme Contractors' Association though not with the BBC. The present title was adopted in 1956 to cover the representation of television technicians. It is discussing amalgamation with the BBC-based Association of Broadcasting and Allied Staffs and is affiliated to the International Federation of Unions of Audio-Visual Workers (FISTAV). The General Secretary is President of this organisation and a member of the General Council of the TUC.
Current membership: 20,540

OFFICIALS
President: R. Bowey
General Secretary: A. Sapper
Treasurer: P. O'Gorman
Deputy General Secretary: R.C. Lockett
Employment Officer: B. Borrows
Finance Officer: G. Maniatakis, ASCA

149

Organisers:
B. Shemmings   J. Telford
L.A. Wiles   B. Wayland
J.S. O'Connor   K. Roberts
B. Hamilton

Periodical: *Film and TV Technician* (monthly)

CIVIL AND PUBLIC SERVANTS, SOCIETY OF (SCPS)*†
(Executive and Directing Grades)
124–130 Southwark Street, London SE1 0TU
Tel: 01–928 9671

Founded over 80 years ago the Society organises executive and directing grades in the Civil Service and in other public authorities, notably the Post Office and UK Atomic Energy Authority. The greatest concentration of membership is in the South East of England and in the Civil Service, where the union has about 85 per cent of the executive grades. Approximately one sixth are women members and about 10,000 members work outside of the Civil Service. It affiliates to the TUC, STUC, Wales TUC, NFPW, Anti Nazi League, Amnesty International and the Anti Apartheid Movement.
Current membership: 106,903
    Male: 89,086
    Female: 17,817

OFFICIALS
Chairman: L.R. Keeping
General Secretary: B.A. Gillman
Deputy General Secretary: C. Christie
Assistant General Secretaries: A.W. Shute, L. Christie, D. Mackie

Periodical: *Opinion* (monthly)

Policy: Along with other public sector organisations the Society is opposed to the public expenditure cuts initiated by the Government, and against incomes policy.

CIVIL AND PUBLIC SERVICES ASSOCIATION (CPSA)*
215 Balham High Road, London SW17
Tel: 01–672 1299

The CPSA is the recognised trade union for clerical, typing and machine grades in the Civil Service and certain other public sector bodies. Its present strength grew from 383 assistant clerks who banded together in 1903 to petition the Treasury for an increase in the annual salary of £55. They formed an organisation which grew steadily and, by amalgamations with typists' associations and departmental grade societies, became in 1920 the Civil Service Clerical Association. Many of the aims of the early pioneering days (equal pay, 5-day week, removal of marriage bar) have now been achieved but some, such as all temporary service to count for pension, and the shorter working week, still feature in CPSA policy. Annual Conference 1969 decided to change the Association's name to the Civil and Public Services Association in order to maintain and recruit further members in spheres outside the Civil Service. In 1973 the Ministry of Labour Staff Association and in 1974 the Court Officers Association merged with the CPSA.

Current membership: 224,772 (35,902 employed in Post Office)

FULL-TIME OFFICIALS
There are no full-time regional or local CPSA officials. All full-time officials are centrally based at 215 Balham High Road, London SW17.
General Secretary: K.R. Thomas
Deputy General Secretary: J.A. Graham
General Treasurer: A.J. Baker
Assistant General Secretary: J. Raywood
Assistant Secretaries:

T. Adams	F. Humphries
T.G. Ainsworth	G. Lewtas
Mrs V. Bayne	J. Macreadie
C. Bush	J.J. O'Brien
M. Clarke	Mrs J. Thomason
Miss J. Drake	P. Thomason
J. Ellis	Miss D. Warwick

National Organiser: A. Ritchie
Head of Research: P. Smith

Periodical: *Red Tape* (monthly)

CIVIL SERVICE UNION (CSU)*
5 Praed Street, London W2 1NJ
Tel: 01–402 7451–60

The Civil Service Union in its present form started its life in 1945. Previously it had been known as the Government Minor and Manipulative Grades Association, which was formed in the autumn of 1917. The first paid official was appointed in the early 1930s. The union now organises many grades of worker in the Civil Service and fringe bodies. The main grades concerned are civilian instructional officers, stores supervisors, museum warders and other museum grades, security grades, messengers and paper-keepers, cleaners, reproduction grades, certain Customs and Excise grades, telecommunications grades, industrial civil servants in Metropolitan Police and Agriculture Research Services, coastguards, foresters, royal household staff, telephonists and traffic wardens.Membership is spread throughout the United Kingdom, with a significant proportion resident in the Greater London area. Although essentially non-political, in the sense that it does not affiliate to any political party, it was the first Civil Service trade union to affiliate to the Trades Union Congress. In recent years it has taken into membership cleaners employed by contractors and has been involved in the struggle to obtain fair wages and conditions of service for this group. The union occupies two seats on the Staff Side of the Civil Service National Whitley Council, on which it plays an active role, vociferously defending the interests of the lower paid civil servants. Current membership: 46,965

FULL-TIME OFFICIALS
There are no full-time Regional Officers. All the full-time Officers of the Civil Service Union are centred at its Headquarters in Praed Street.
General Secretary: L.H. Moody
Deputy General Secretary: J.D. Sheldon
Assistant General Secretary: J.P. Randall
Assistant Secretary: F.N. Phillips
Assistant Secretary: T.J. Hoyes
Assistant Secretary: W.J. Hawkins
Assistant Secretary: A. Maloney
Assistant Secretary: J.L. Delaney
Assistant Secretary: M.T. Barke
Negotiations Officer: S.M. Fagan
Negotiations Officer: K.J. Finch

National Executive Council
President: M.J. Rose
Vice-President: D. Brown
T.R. Dinsdale
H. Markan
C. Mayatt
D.A. Saunders
E. Verdon
R. F. Ivill
D. Ward
R. Barrett
A.N. Riley
Mrs M. Morrison
Mrs C. Anderson
P.R. Parsons
G.F. Richards
R.J.P. Hughes
M.H. Leigh
J. Hart
S. Glasspool
E.J.R. Eeles
C.J. Tomlinson
B.G. Venner
Miss D. Wyatt
W.H. Carey

Periodical: *The Whip* (monthly)

CLOTH PRESSERS SOCIETY*‡
34 Southgate, Honley, Nr. Huddersfield HD7 2NT
Tel: Huddersfield (0484) 661175

Founded in 1872 as the Huddersfield Cloth Pressers Society, to which the Leeds Society of Cloth Pressers (1860) transferred its engagements in 1934. It no longer has branches, members being mostly in the Huddersfield area.
Current membership: 40

OFFICIAL
General Secretary: G. Kaye

CLUB STEWARDS, NATIONAL UNION OF
Edwards Buildings, Regent Street, Hinckley, Leicester
Tel: Hinckley (0455) 614060

Formed in 1948 from members of the Yorkshire Federation of Club Stewards as the National Federation of Club Stewards and Hotel Managers, and known between 1 January 1978 and 1 January 1980 as the National Union of Club Stewards and Hotel Managers.

It now has a membership spread throughout all parts of Britain, provides legal assistance and advice and seeks, among other objectives, a national average working week of forty hours.
Current membership: 3,000

OFFICIALS
President: E. Stephenson,
Whitefield Conservative Club,
Elm Street,
Whitefield,
Nr. Manchester
Tel: 061–766 2030
General Secretary: C.L. Savage
Assistant General Secretary: Harry Scott,
344 Carlton Villas,
Gibbert Street,
Halifax
Tel: Halifax (0422) 58087
Vice-President: G. Wain,
Cockerton Band Club,
The Garth,
Cockerton,
Darlington
Tel: Darlington (0325) 66729
Treasurer: W. Clements,
Sapcote WMC.,
19 Hinckley Road,
Sapcote,
Leicester
Tel: Sapcote (045 527) 3464

No. 1 A. Baker   No. 7 L. Jenkinson
No. 2 L. Brooks   No. 8 F. England
No. 3 K. Lee   No. 9 A. Pallett
No. 4 W. Jones and N. Kelly   No. 10 B. Pitcher
  (joint)   No. 11 F. Ship
No. 5 K. Burke   No. 12 Pending
No. 6 D. Bott   No. 13 M. Weeson

The union has branch secretaries whose names can be obtained from the General Secretary.

COLLIERY MANAGEMENT, BRITISH ASSOCIATION OF (BACM)*

BACM House, 317 Nottingham Road, Old Basford, Nottingham
NG7 7DP
Tel: Nottingham (0602) 786949/785819

BACM was formed early in 1947 as a result of the nationalisation of the coalmining industry and registered as a trade union in May of that year. Initially it set out to organise and represent all managerial, technical, professional and administrative staff employed by the National Coal Board and its associated ancillary undertakings, mainly coke ovens but also producing a number of by-products. At collieries representation, broadly speaking, covers staff above the level of foreman and senior clerical officer on the surface and above the level of the colliery overman underground. The Association is accepted by the National Union of Mineworkers and the National Association of Colliery Overmen, Deputies and Shotfirers as the management trade union in the industry and demarcation agreements have avoided conflict over recruitment and representation.

The Association is affiliated to the Trades Union Congress, is a member of the Coal Industry National Consultative Council and the Coke Oven National Consultative Council, and participates in the Tripartite (Government, NCB and Mining Unions) discussions on the Coal Industry.

Current membership: 16,872
  Males: 16,157
  Females: 715

NATIONAL OFFICIALS

National President: National Vice-Presidents:
N. Schofield, CEng, FIME,   J.M. Evans,
63 Ellers Avenue,   22 Stonebridge Road,
Bessacarr,   Rassau,
Doncaster   Ebbw Vale,
                             Gwent NP3 5SN

G. Taylor,
53 Station Road,
Bagworth,
Leicestershire

National Treasurer:
M. J. Finn,
18, Littledown Road,
Cheltenham. Glos.

General Secretary:
A. Wilson
BACM House,
317 Nottingham Road,
Old Basford,
Nottingham NG7 7DP
Tel: Nottingham
(0602) 785819/786949

Regional Organising Secretaries
J.D. Mends,
BACM,
Room 12, 2nd Floor,
Exchange Buildings,
Quayside,
Newcastle upon Tyne NE1 3BJ
Tel: Newcastle upon Tyne
(0632) 22704

Scotland
North East
Gibbons Northern Brick Co.

D.F. Marsh,
BACM,
2nd Floor,
14 Hallgate,
Doncaster DN1 3NA
Tel: Doncaster (0302) 49152

North Yorkshire
South Yorkshire
Barnsley
Doncaster
Headquarters (North)
Nypro (UK) Ltd.
Thyssen (GB) Ltd.

G. Malpass,
BACM House,
317 Nottingham Road,
Old Basford,
Nottingham NG7 7DP
Tel: Nottingham (0602) 789590

North Nottinghamshire
North Derbyshire
South Nottinghamshire
South Midlands
Staveley Chemicals

A.E.Draper,
BACM,
Transport House,
1 Cathedral Road,
Cardiff CF1 9FD
Tel: Cardiff (0222) 35681

Western
South Wales
Tredmen Engineering Ltd.

E. Pate,
Regional Organiser,
BACM House.
317 Nottingham Road,
Old Basford,
Nottingham NG7 7DP
Tel: Nottingham
(0602) 786949/785819

Headquarters (South)
Associated Heat Services Ltd
Approved Coal Merchants Scheme
Opencast Executive
Compower Ltd
National Smokeless Fuels Ltd
National Fuel Distributors Ltd
SFAS
British Mining Consultants Ltd.

155

National Executive Committee
Branch Representatives

Scottish Branch
D. Paterson,
19 Glenbervie Road,
Kirkcaldy,
Fife KY2 6HR

North East Branch
H. Painter,
8 Lanchester Road,
Maiden Law,
Lanchester,
Co. Durham

Doncaster Branch
A.G.K. Kemp,
118 Croft Road,
Balby,
Doncaster

North Yorkshire Branch
G. Walker,
28 Baker Lane,
Stanley,
Nr. Wakefield,
Yorkshire

South Yorkshire Branch
J. Eadie,
7B Lindrick Road,
Woodsetts,
Nr. Worksop,

Barnsley Branch
G.C. Barber,
The Chalet,
Darton Lane,
Darton,
Barnsley

Headquarters North Branch
T. Thomas,
1 Trinity Close,
Ashby-de-la-Zouch,
Leicestershire

Western Branch
A. Wall,
19 Ivy Lane,
Alsager,
Stoke on Trent,
Staffordshire

North Nottinghamshire Branch
J.C. Rhodes,
Greendale,
67 Mansfield Road,
Edwinstowe,
Nottinghamshire

South Nottinghamshire Branch
P.W. Linsley,
Whiteleaves,
13 Park Road,
Hucknall,
Nottinghamshire

North Derbyshire Branch
H.D. Saywood,
Langwith House,
Nether Langwith,
Mansfield,
Nottinghamshire

South Midlands Branch
D. Hall,
25 Magyar Crescent,
Whitestone,
Nuneaton,
Warwickshire

South Wales Branch
T.T. Short,
37 Chestnut Drive,
Danygraig,
Newton,
Porthcawl,
Glamorgan

Headquarters South Branch
J. McDonnell,
41 Enstone Road,
Ickenham,
Uxbridge,
Middlesex

Vocational Group Representatives

Group I
W. Shawcross,
120 Newbrook Road,
Over Hulton,
Bolton,
Lancashire

Group II
P.J. Cadman,
32 Thorne Grove,
Rothwell,
Leeds

Group III
J.R. Smith,
Newith,
18 Amberley Rise,
Mill Lane,
Skellow,
Doncaster,
Yorkshire

Group IV
J.A. Rushton,
67a High Street,
Kippax,
Leeds

Group V
R. Sheldon,
2 Braemar Road,
Bulwell,
Nottingham NG6 9HN

Group VI
R. Sheldon,
2 Braemar Road,
Bulwell,
Nottingham

Group VII
W. Burrett,
31 Laverock Avenue,
Hamilton,
Lanarkshire

Group VIII
G. Fry,
1 Fraser Place,
Glenrothes,
Fife

Group IX
D. Wardle,
147 Moorland View Road,
Walton,
Chesterfield,
Derbyshire

Periodical: *National News Letter* (irregular)

COLLIERY OVERMEN, DEPUTIES AND SHOTFIRERS, NATIONAL ASSOCIATION OF (NACODS)*
2nd Floor, Argyle House, 29–31 Euston Road, London NW1 2SP
Tel: 01-837 0908

The union was known on its formation as the General Federation of Firemen's Examiners and Deputies Association of Great Britain. Its first Conference was held in York on 18 June 1910. It adopted its present title in 1947 when the coal industry was nationalised. The Association is now a federation of Area Associations situated in coalfields of Great Britain. Members are responsible for the production of coal in a supervisory capacity and for the health and safety and welfare of all men employed underground in the coalmines of Great Britain. NACODS affiliates to the Labour Party, the TUC and the Miners' International Federation.
Current membership: 19,571 males. It has no female members.

NATIONAL OFFICIALS
President:
K. Moore, JP,
(Area Secretary Midland),
19 Forest Road East,
Nottingham NG1 4HJ

National Vice-President:
K.S. Sampey,
(Area President Yorkshire),
Deputy House,
37 Church Street,
Barnsley S70 2AR

National Secretary:
A.E. Simpson, BEM,
Argyle House,
29–31 Euston Road,
London NW1 2SP

National Treasurer:
D. Skitt,
(Area Secretary N. Western),
4 Upper Dicconson Street,
Wigan WN1 2AD

Executive Committee
The following are all Area Secretaries

Durham
J.H. Benham,
John Street,
Durham City,
Co. Durham

Scotland
J. O'Connor,
19 Cadzow Street,
Hamilton,
Lanarkshire ML3 6EE

Leicestershire
E. Hunt,
15 Hotel Street,
Coalville,
Leicestershire LE6 2EQ

South Wales
E.G. Jones,
70 Neville Street,
Cardiff CF1 8LS

Area President, Staffordshire,
J. Henshall,
21 St. Mark's Close,
Shelton,
Stoke on Trent ST1 4LJ

Northumberland
M.J. McCormack,
Quayside,
Blyth,
Northumberland NE24 3AL

The following are Area Secretaries not members of the Executive Committee:

Cannock Chase
A.E. Hayward,
30 Station Road,
Hednesford,
Staffordshire WS12 4DL

Staffordshire
W. Williams,
3 Albert Street,
Newcastle,
Staffordshire ST5 1JP

Kent
S.S. Cole,
7 Milton Road,
Dover,
Kent CT16 2BJ

Yorkshire
F.R. Belfield,
Deputy House,
37 Church Street,
Barnsley S70 2AR

Cumbria
J. Ritson,
57 Fell View Avenue,
Woodhouse,
Whitehaven CA28 9LJ

All officials are elected.

Publications:
Monthly Minutes of National Executive Committee
Report of National Annual Conference
Policy: In recent years the Association has been in favour of entry into Europe, but generally opposed to any incomes policy which eroded differentials. The Association supports the Plan for Coal and an expanding coal industry and believes that more government finance should be made available for research into alternative use and efficient production of coal to meet the nation's energy needs for the future.

They are opposed to any attempts to lower the standards, responsibilities and qualifications of Her Majesty's Inspectors of Mines.

CONFEDERATION OF HEALTH SERVICE EMPLOYEES

See HEALTH SERVICE EMPLOYEES, CONFEDERATION OF

CONSTRUCTION, ALLIED TRADES AND TECHNICIANS, UNION OF (UCATT)*
UCATT House, 177 Abbeville Road, Clapham, London SW4 9RL
Tel: 01–622 2363

The development of trades unions in the building industry has a colourful history spanning nearly two hundred years and as a result of several union mergers the Union of Construction, Allied Trades and Technicians was established in 1971. In 1970 the Amalgamated Society of Woodworkers joined with the Amalgamated Society of Painters and Decorators to become the Amalgamated Society of Woodworkers and Painters (ASWP). The Association of Building Technicians, now known as the STAMP Section (Supervisory, Technical, Administrative, Managerial and Professional), joined with the new body, followed by the Amalgamated Union of Building Trade Workers. UCATT represents members in construction, civil engineering, shipbuilding, local authorities, health services, government establishments, exhibition, furnishing and related trades. As dictated by the nature of the industry approximately 99 per cent of membership is male. The union is organised on a Regional basis, twelve in all, including the Republic of Ireland. Of prime concern to the union is the development of a stable construction industry through decasualisation and rationalisation.
Current membership: 319,776

NATIONAL OFFICIALS
General Secretary: L. Wood
Executive Council members and National Officers can be contacted through the Head Office address.

REGIONAL SECRETARIES AND OFFICES

Scotland	*Northern Counties*
D. C. Macgregor,	C. E. Lowther,
6 Fitzroy Place,	Archbold House,
Glasgow C3 7RL	Archbold Terrace,
	Jesmond,
	North Shields,
	Tyne and Wear

Yorkshire
G. B. Brumwell,
Winwaed House,
64–66 Cross Gate Road,
Leeds 15

North Western
E. V. Hughes, ASW,
137 Dickenson Road,
Rusholme,
Manchester M14 5HZ

Midlands
K. Barlow,
Gough Street,
Suffolk Street,
Birmingham B1 HN

Eastern Counties
I. Jordan,
UCATT Offices,
119 Newmarket Road,
Cambridge CB5 8HA

London
L. Eaton,
11–13 Essex Road,
Dartford,
Kent

Southern Counties
A. Woods,
54 Henstead Road,
Southampton,
Hampshire SO1 2DD

South Western
R. E. Heal,
217 St. John's Lane,
Bedminster,
Bristol BS3 5AS

South Wales
W. Bowen,
61 Cowbridge Road East,
Cardiff,
Glamorgan CF1 9AE

Northern Ireland
T. Smyth,
79–81 Maystreet,
Belfast BT1 3JL

Republic of Ireland
R. P. Rice,
56 Parnell Square,
West Dublin

EXECUTIVE COUNCIL
MEMBERS
Chairman: D. Crawford
A. Utting
J. Hardman
G. Lloyd

H. D'Arcy
A. Williams
C. Kelly

NATIONAL OFFICERS
T. Graves
H.T. Potts
S.G. Reading

W. Lewis
L. Poupard
D. Sanderson

STAMP SECTION
General Secretary: A. Black
A. Verdeille

Periodicals: Viewpoint (monthly), (STAMP section), STAMP News
(quarterly)

CONSTRUCTION, ALLIED TRADES AND TECHNICIANS, UNION OF, SUPERVISORY, TECHNICAL, ADMINISTRATIVE, MANAGERIAL AND PROFESSIONAL SECTION (STAMP)*

See CONSTRUCTION, ALLIED TRADES AND TECHNICIANS, UNION OF

CO-OPERATIVE OFFICIALS, NATIONAL ASSOCIATION OF*
Saxone House, 56 Market Street, Manchester M1 1PW
Tel: 061–834 6029 and 6020

The union was formed as the National Union of Co-operative Officials in 1917, and was re-named the National Association of Co-operative Officials in 1970, upon its amalgamation with the National Co-operative Managers' Association and the Co-operative Secretaries Association. It is believed to be one of the earliest trade unions catering for managerial personnel, and is unique in the fact that its membership is drawn entirely from within the Co-operative Movement, viz. managerial personnel within Retail, Wholesale and Productive Co-operative Societies, and the Co-operative Insurance Society.
Current membership: 5,920
    Males: 5,733
    Females: 187

OFFICIALS
President: 1979–80 D.H. Carr
General Secretary: L.W. Ewing
Assistant General Secretary: K. Yorath
Assistant Secretary: D. Williams
General Council consists of 22 elected lay members.

Periodical: *Co-operative Official* (monthly), an insert in *Co-operative Marketing and Management*

COOPERS AND ALLIED WORKERS FEDERATION OF GREAT BRITAIN*
GMWU, Scottish Region, 4 Park Gate, Glasgow G3 6BD
Tel: 041–332 8641

A society of coopers with a long history of representation in the craft and membership widely spread over the country. On the 4 July 1979 the union amalgamated with the General and Municipal Workers' Union.

DOMESTIC APPLIANCE AND GENERAL METAL WORKERS, NATIONAL UNION OF (NUDAGMW)*

Imperial Buildings, High Street, Rotherham S60 1PB
Tel: Rotherham (0709) 2820

Founded in 1890 as the National Union of Stove Grate Fender and General Light Metal Workers. Members initially worked in the stove grate industry in Rotherham and district. Still predominantly a Northern based union but with members in Birmingham, London and Wales all working in the fitting, foundry and press shops of the domestic appliance industry.
Current membership: 5,200
    Males: 4,400
    Females: 800

OFFICIAL
General Secretary: R. Preston

DYERS, BLEACHERS AND TEXTILE WORKERS, NATIONAL UNION OF (NUDBTW)*†

National House, Sunbridge Road, Bradford BD1 2QB
Tel: Bradford (0274) 25642

Formed in June 1936 on the amalgamation of three textile workers' unions, namely the National Union of Textile Workers, the Amalgamated Society of Dyers, Finishers and Kindred Trades, and the Operative Bleachers, Dyers and Finishers Association. In May 1979 the Union of Jute, Flax and Kindred Textile Operatives transferred their engagements to the NUDB & TW. The union has members working in all areas of the textile industry in Great Britain. The two principal agreements to which the union is party are those covering 80,000 wool textile workers and 20,000 dyeing and finishing workers. The main concentration of membership is in the North West and Yorkshire regions. Apart from the wool textile and dyeing and finishing agreements, the union also represents its members in the negotiations under the following agreements: Scottish Woollen Trade Agreement, Scottish Hosiery Wages Agreement, West of England Wool Textile JIC, Carpets NJC, Silk JIC, Narrow Fabrics JIC, Surgical Dressing JIC, Linen and Cotton Handkerchief Wages Council and Sack and Bag Wages Council.
Current membership: 58,803

EXECUTIVE COMMITTEE

President: L. Herd

H. McGroarty	R. Connelly
?. Brandie	W. McCarthy
?.J. Humphreys	R. Pettifor
H. Hartley	P. Sanderson
A. Nutton	W. Clark
P.B. Hirst	S. Turner
	Miss K. Smith

162

General Secretary: W.H. Maddocks
Assistant General Secretary: E. Haigh
Research Officer: P.J.R. Booth

District Secretaries
No. 1 District: G. Carter
No. 2 District: J. Brannan
No. 3 District: L. Fielding
No. 4 District: B. Leach
No. 5 District: R. Gray

District Organisers

No. 1 District
J. Malone
Mrs J. Langdon
G. Sargent
G.R. Hemmins
R.L. Rooney
B. Preston

No. 2 District
A.S. Haigh
L.E. Smith
J. Jackson
J. Rutherford

No. 3 District
J. Durkin
A. Phillips
C. Harper

No. 4 District
J. Sutcliffe
J. Hall
J. Mutch

No. 5 District
J. Macfarlane
J. Park
H. Hill

West of England
H.J. Lees

Periodical: *Newsletter* (irregular)
Policy: The union's present policy is opposed to membership of the
European Economic Community. It is in favour of free collective
bargaining, retirement at 60 for males and opposes any form of racial
discrimination.

EDUCATIONAL INSTITUTE OF SCOTLAND (EIS)*†
46 Moray Place, Edinburgh EH3 6BH
Tel: 031–225 6244

Founded in 1847 and incorporated by Royal Charters in 1851, 1925
and 1978. There are approximately 48,000 members consisting of
teachers and lecturers in schools and colleges in Scotland. The
Institute holds 16 of the 22 seats on the teachers' sides of the main
negotiating bodies for Scottish teachers, the Scottish Teachers
Salaries Committee and the Scottish Teachers Service Conditions
Committee. It has an active Education Committee, which submits
views to the appropriate bodies on all important educational issues.
Close fraternal relationships exist with the National Union of
Teachers (q.v.) and the National Association of Teachers in Further
and Higher Education (q.v.) and it is affiliated to the TUC and STUC

but not to any political party. The Institute has organised militant action in support of salaries and conditions of service claims. The Institute publishes *The Scottish Educational Journal* regularly throughout the school session. It is the only educational journal to reach all schools and colleges throughout Scotland.
Current membership: 48,548

FULL-TIME OFFICIALS
General Secretary: J.D. Pollock
Deputy General Secretary: R.H.K. Thomasson
Organising Secretary: F.L. Forrester
Negotiating Secretary: R. Beattie
Accountant: R. Hodge
Assistant Secretary: Mrs S. M-C. Kreitman
Further Education Officer: A.J. Houston
Senior Field Officer: D.R.E. Sullivan

ELECTRICAL ELECTRONIC TELECOMMUNICATION AND PLUMBING UNION (EETPU)*
Hayes Court, West Common Road, Bromley BR2 7AU
Tel: 01–462 7755

The EETPU was formed in 1968 through an amalgamation between the Electrical Trades Union, founded 1889, and the Plumbing Trades Union, founded 1865. Originally formed for skilled craftsmen, the union now caters for all grades and employees in the industries covered by the name of the union and also related technologies and industries. The union also incorporates the Electrical and Engineering Staffs Association (EESA) which covers administrative, technical, supervisory and managerial employees. The union's affairs are managed by an Executive Council which is responsible to the Biennial Delegate Conference.

Since the court case of 1961, which exposed ballot-rigging by Communists, the union has been in the centre of the Labour Party politically and members of the Communist Party are ineligible for office. Industrially, it has favoured improved efficiency and productivity coupled with higher earnings for skill, responsibility and effort. To help members and officials involved in productivity bargaining, the union has created a work study department which is now the largest in the trade union movement.

The EETPU provides technical and training services in four main areas: representation on Industry Training Boards, technical publications, further technical training for adult craftsmen, and wage claims. The union owns two educational establishments, Esher College and Cudham Hall, which offer courses on a wide range of subjects.
Current membership: 450,000 (including 55,000 women)

OFFICIALS
President: T.A. Breakell
General Secretary: F.J. Chapple

Executive Councillors
Head Office
C. Lovell
E. Hammond

Division No. 1
W. Gannon,
413 Oxford Road,
Reading,
Berkshire

Division No. 2
A.B.McLuckie,
H. Barlow,
Dene House,
Westermavis Bank Avenue,
Airdrie,
Lanarkshire

Division No. 3
A.B. Davis,
3 Park Drive,
Forest Hall,
Newcastle upon Tyne NE12 9JN

Division No. 4
F. McGuffie,
T. Breakell,
137/139 Breckfield Road North,
Liverpool L5 4QU

Division No. 5
P. Gallagher,
Bury New Road,
Prestwich,
Manchester

Division No. 6
J. Ashfield,
37 Gordon Road,
West Bridgford,
Nottingham

Division No. 7
7 St. James's Crescent,
North Hill,
Swansea,
Glamorgan

Division No. 9
W.P. Hayes,
27 Balne Lane,
Wakefield,
Yorkshire

Division No. 10
W.P. Blair,
5/7 Clarendon Road,
Luton,
Bedfordshire

Division No. 11
E. Clayton,
314 Norwich Road,
Ipswich,
Suffolk

National Officers
L. Britz,
15 Abbeville Road,
London SW4 9LA

Head Office
L. Gregory
R. Sanderson
P. Adams
E. Linton
T. Rice
P. McMahon
J.K. Brewster
A. McBronse
F. Franks
J.F. Spellar

Area Officials
Area No. 1
J. Cosby,
J.B. Hanna,
I.D. Fleming,
J. Kirkwood,
C.C. Lowry,
N. McCrory,
240 Antrim Road,
Belfast BT15 2HD

Area No. 2
J. Brown,
D. Chalmers,
H. Clark,
P. O'Hanlon,
E. McShane,
J. Service,
Dene House,
Westermavis Bank Avenue,
Airdrie,
Lanarkshire

Area No. 3
M. Brennan,
2 Berkley Street,
Dublin 7

Area No. 4
D. Bremner,
B. Angles,
17 South Tay Street,
Dundee

Area No. 5
H.S. Dunnigan,
C. Henry,
A. Souza,
J.D. Wilson,
26 Abercromby Place,
Edinburgh

Area No. 6
A. Cummins,
G. Douthwaite,
D. Hepburn,
S.A. Smith,
3 Park Drive,
Forest Hall,
Newcastle upon Tyne
NE12 9JN

Area No. 7
J. Varty,
18a Crescent Road,
Windermere,
Westmorland

Area No. 8
J.C. Williamson,
K. Jackson,
F. Jardine,
196 Deepdale Road,
Preston,
Lancashire

Area No. 9
W.A. Bate,
T.N. Barr,
D. Benson,
M. Foulkes,
E. McGann,
P.J. Riley,
S.N. Simpson,
J.J. Traynor,
137/139 Breckfield Road North,
Liverpool L5 4QU

Area No. 10
E. Hughes,
A. Binks,
C. Hutchinson,
A. Pickering,
4 Longlands Road,
Middlesbrough,
Cleveland TS4 2JL

Area No. 11
E. Birch,
T. Dalton,
N. Gordon,
G. Smith,
K. Taylor,
Bury New Road,
Prestwich,
Manchester

Area No. 12
C. Chadwick,
E.W. Johnson,
R. Morton,
G.M. Nelson,
W. Moffat,
27 Balne Lane,
Wakefield,
Yorkshire
J.J. Burton,
P. Jackson,
509 Anlaby Road,
Hull HU3 6EN

Area No. 13
L.H. Hancock,
32a Doncaster Road,
Scunthorpe,
South Humberside

Area No. 14
R.M. Williams,
B. Doyley,
14a Charles Street,
Hoole,
Chester

Area No. 15
D.R. Jones,
7 St. James's Crescent,
North Hill,
Swansea

M. Aitken,
E. Jenkins,
S.N. Howe,
199 Newport Road,
Roath,
Cardiff

Area No. 16
M.E. Crofts,
W. Fitzpatrick,
L. Sturgess,
R.H. Wright,
R. Rider,
2341 Coventry Road,
Sheldon,
Birmingham

Area No. 17
F. Chapman,
J. Coventry,
A. Sansom,
J. Scoffings,
37 Gordon Road,
West Bridgford,
Nottingham

Area No. 18
D.B. Houlden,
R. Critchley,
R.J. James,
11 Belgrave Road,
Clifton,
Bristol 8

Area No. 19
M. Kearns
S. Davies,
5/7 Clarendon Road,
Luton,
Bedfordshire

Area No. 20
J.J. Cowan,
J.A. Gamble,
1 Radnor Street,
Plymouth

Area No. 21
L. Chittock,
B. Fulham,
A.J. Langley,
314 Norwich Road,
Ipswich

Area No. 22
M. Scanlon,
C.H. Croucher,
J. Davidson,
81a Bedford Place,
Southampton

Area No. 23
R.J.L. Allum,
413 Oxford Road,
Reading

Area No. 24
P. Bevis,
D. Rogers,
9 Albion Place,
Maidstone,
Kent

Area No. 25
A. Bastin,
9 Albion Place,
Maidstone,
Kent

Area No. 26
T. O'Neill,
E. Snare,
1a Civic Square,
Tilbury,
Essex

Area No. 27
D.C. Carter,
C. McKenzie,
R.T. Reno,
J.C. Riley,
15 Abbeville Road,
London SW4 9LA
J. Dormer,
A. Gray,
H. Hughes,
S. Moss,
A. Seale,
T. Spellman,
39 Highbury Place,
London N5

Periodical: *Contact* (quarterly)

Policy: In recent years the EETPU has supported the Social Contract, and urged the restoration of wage differentials for skilled craftsmen. It is opposed to the appointment of worker directors in private industry, and in favour of retirement at age 60 for males.

ENGINEERING WORKERS, AMALGAMATED UNION OF (AUEW)*
110 Peckham Road, London SE15 5EL
Tel: 01–703 4231

Originally a craft union, it began with the creation in 1826 of the 'Journeymen Steam Engine, Machine Makers and Millwrights Friendly Society'. Amalgamations in 1851 brought together a number of small societies to form the Amalgamated Society of Engineers, ASE. In 1920 a further amalgamation took place and the ASE combined with nine other unions to form the Amalgamated Engineering Union, AEU, which during the 1920s opened its ranks in an attempt to organise all workers, craftsmen and non-craftsmen working in the engineering industry, at the same time continuing the craft tradition of highly decentralised negotiations based on District Committees. Today known as the Amalgamated Union of Engineering Workers (AUEW), comprising in addition to a section for manual engineer workers other sections for Construction, Foundry and Technical/Supervisory (see respective entries: AUEW–Construction, Foundry and TASS).

Current combined membership: nearly 1.5 million

Current membership of Engineering (largest section): 1,199,309 (including nearly 160,000 women)

NATIONAL AND DIVISIONAL OFFICIALS

There are nearly 200 full-time officials and many thousand part-time or voluntary officers.

Executive Council
President: T. Duffy
General Secretary: J. Boyd, CBE
Assistant General Secretaries:
K. Brett,
R.W. Wright
Division 1: G.H. Laird
Division 2: J.G. Russell
Division 3: H. Robson
Division 4: K. Cure
Division 5: E.M. Scrivens
Division 6:
Division 7: J. Whyman

National Organisers
A. Bretherton
J.R. Bradley
J. Byrne
J.R. Foster
G.R. Lloyd
E.T. Hepple
W. P. Pritchard

Regional Officers
Division 1
T. Dougan,
AUEW House,
145/165 West Regent Street,
Glasgow G2 4RZ

Division 2
H. Lord,
AUEW Office,
46–48 Mount Pleasant,
Liverpool L3 5SE

Division 3
W.J. Bradley,
AUEW House,
Bridge Street,
Leeds LS2 7RA

Division 4
P. Povey,
4 Holloway Circus,
Birmingham 1

Division 5
E. Scott,
AUEW House,
Furnival Gate,
Sheffield S1 3HE
Tel: Sheffield (0742) 79041/3

Division 6
J.P. Weakley,
8 St. Paul's Road,
Bristol 8

Division 7
L. Choulerton,
28 Denmark Street,
London WC2

Divisional Organisers
Division 1
J. Graham,
26–34 Antrim Road,
Belfast BT15 2AA
Tel: Belfast (0232) 743271/2

Division 2
T.N. Gray,
26 South Ward Road,
Dundee,
Angus
Tel: Dundee (0382) 22710

Division 3
E. Leslie,
45 Morrison Street,
Edinburgh EH3 8AL
Tel: 031–229 8711/2

Division 4
H. Sherriff
AUEW House,
145–165 West Regent Street,
Glasgow G2 4RZ
Tel: 041–248 7131

Division 5
W. Aitken,
7 Incle Street,
Paisley,
Renfrewshire
Tel: 041–889 4334

Division 6
G. Arnold,
AUEW House,
High Street,
Gateshead,
Tyne and Wear NE8 1ER
Tel: Gateshead (0632) 774316

Division 7
W.J. Purvis
20 Yarm Road,
Stockton-on-Tees,
Cleveland
Tel: Stockton-on-Tees (0642) 65736

Division 8
H. Banks,
9–10 Cross Street,
Preston PR1 3LT
Tel: Preston (0772) 57765/7

Division 9
St. J. Binns,
AUEW House,
Bridge Street,
Leeds LS2 7RA
Tel: Leeds (0532) 34925/6

Division 10
K. Abbott,
77 St. George's Road,
Bolton,
Lancashire BL1 2BS
Tel: Bolton (0204) 27447

Division 11
J. Tocher,
AUEW House,
43 The Crescent,
Salford M5 4PE
Tel: 061–736 5206/7

Division 12
J.F. Duffy,
AUEW House,
238 Nettleham Road,
Lincoln
Tel: Lincoln (0522) 31731

Division 13
A. Knight,
AUEW House,
Furnival Gate,
Sheffield S1 3HE
Tel: Sheffield (0742) 79041/3

Division 14
D.W. Jones
210 Osmaston Road,
Derby
Tel: Derby (0332) 46617/9

Division 15
D. Gough,
46–48 Mount Pleasant,
Liverpool L3 5SE
Tel: 051–709 9561

Division 16
W. B. Jordan,
4 Holloway Circus,
Birmingham 1
Tel: 021–643 1042/4

Division 17
G.T. Butler,
61 Corporation Street,
Coventry,
Warwickshire CV1 1GQ
Tel: Coventry (0203) 27522

Division 18
T.J. Lloyd,
AUEW House,
1–3 Fitzalan Place,
Cardiff CF2 1UN
Tel: Cardiff (0222) 31271/2

Division 19
L. Gray,
8 St. Paul's Road,
Bristol 8
Tel: Bristol (0272) 39321/3

Division 20
D. Stopp (acting).
396–398 Dunstable Road,
Luton,
Bedfordshire
Tel: Luton (0582) 56271/3

Division 21
E.T. Brown,
7 Magdalen Street,
St. Botolphs,
Colchester,
Essex
Tel: Colchester (0206) 78628/9

Division 22
V.C. Evans,
52 Stuart Road,
Plymouth,
Devon PL3 4EE
Tel: Plymouth (0752) 266472

Division 23
J. D. Lye,
140 Copnor Road,
Portsmouth,
Hampshire
Tel: Portsmouth (0705) 63917

Division 24
J. Jenkins,
39 Belmont Road,
Erith,
Kent
Tel: Erith (032 24) 32182 and 33437

Division 25
A.G. Gibbard,
28 Denmark Street,
London WC2
Tel: 01–240 0625/8

Division 26
P.D. Marsden,
20 Durand Gardens,
London SW9
Tel: 01–735 1158/9

Wagon Repairing Section
J. Abernethy,
43 The Crescent,
Salford M5 4PE
Tel: 061–736 5206/7

Assistant Divisional Organisers
Division 1: J. Luney
Division 3: W.I. McWilliam
Division 4: J. Airlie
Division 5: A. Campbell
Division 6: J. Cellini
Division 7: G.N. Winship
Division 10: L. Parkinson
Division 11: E. Whalley
Division 15: G. Brown
Division 16: B. Turner
Division 17: J. Griffin
Division 18: E. Hughes
Division 19: L.M. Reay
Division 20: D.F. Stopp
Division 21: B.W. Foreman
Division 22: R.H. Baumbach
Division 23: J.D. O'Reilley
Division 25: W.E. Taylor
Division 26: A.M. Kavanagh

DISTRICT SECRETARIES
Accrington
K. Slater,
133 Blackburn Road,
Accrington,
Lancashire BB5 0AA
Tel: Accrington (0254) 31952

Andover
E.G. Harris,
2 Church Close,
Andover,
Hampshire SP10 1DP
Tel: Andover (0264) 61789

Ashton-under-Lyne
E. Stafford,
6 Margaret Street South,
Ashton-under-Lyne,
Lancashire OL7 0SH
Tel: 061–330 3116

Banbury
See Milton Keynes and Banbury

Barnsley
E. Dyson,
56–60 Silver Street,
Doncaster,
South Yorkshire
Tel: Doncaster (0302) 67269

Barnstaple
R. Turner,
43 Forches Avenue,
Barnstaple,
Devon EX32 8EF
Tel: Barnstaple (0271) 5907

Barrow
F. Ward,
114 Duke Street,
Barrow-in-Furness,
Cumbria LA14 1LW
Tel: Barrow-in-Furness (0229)
20080

Basingstoke
E.G. Harris,
2 Church Close,
Andover,
Hampshire SP10 1DP
Tel: Andover (0264) 61789

Bath
R.S. Lake,
8 Station Hill,
Chippenham,
Wiltshire
Tel: Chippenham (0249) 2572

Bedford
W.L. Robinson,
AUEW House,
34 Alexandra Road,
Bedford MK40 1JB
Tel: Bedford (0234) 54831

Birmingham East
P. Povey (Acting),
4 Holloway Circus,
Birmingham B1 1BU
Tel: 021–643 1042-4

Birmingham South
E.W. Hunt

Birmingham West
B. Benson,
4 Holloway Circus,
Birmingham B1 1BU
Tel: 021–643 1042/4

Bishop's Stortford and Harlow
E.D. French,
AUEW House,
Harberts Road,
Harlow,
Essex
Tel: Harlow (0279) 35000

Blackburn
W. Worswick,
24 Wellington Street,
St. John's,
Blackburn,
Lancashire BB1 8AF
Tel: Blackburn (0254) 51081

Blackpool and Fylde
E.M. Fail,
38–40 Station Road,
Blackpool,
Lancashire FY4 1EU
Tel: Blackpool (0253) 43236

Bolton
W. Dagnall,
AUEW House,
77 St. George's Road,
Bolton,
Lancashire BL1 2BS
Tel: Bolton (0204) 25193

Bournemouth and Poole
A.W. Gosling,
20 Lorne Park Road,
Bournemouth,
Dorset BH1 1JN
Tel: Bournemouth (0202) 23763

Bradford
J.R. Andrews,
2 Claremont,
Bradford,
West Yorkshire BD7 1BQ
Tel: Bradford (0274) 28082

Braintree, Halstead and Sudbury
See North Essex and South Suffolk
District

Brighton
P. J. Hurley,
AUEW District Office,
5a New Road,
Brighton BN1 1UF
Tel: Brighton (0273) 29691

Bristol
L. Gray,
8 St. Paul's Road,
Clifton,
Bristol BS8 1LU
Tel: Bristol (0272) 39321/4

Burnley
A.F. Robinson,
16 Hargreaves Street,
Burnley,
Lancashire BB11 1EH
Tel: Burnley (0282) 23046

Bury
P. Bramah,
12 St. Mary's Place,
Bury,
Lancashire BL9 0DZ
Tel: 061–764 1606

Carlisle
E. Nixon,
59 Dalston Road,
Carlisle CA2 5PW
Tel: Carlisle (0228) 26033

Chard
L.S. Wright,
28a High Street,
Bridgwater,
Somerset TA6 3BJ
Tel: Bridgwater (0278) 51147

Chatham
R.J. Norris,
6 New Road Avenue,
Chatham,
Kent ME4 6BB
Tel: Medway (0634) 44103

Chelmsford and Southend
R. Davis,
AEU House,
Primrose Hill,
Chelmsford,
Essex
Tel: Chelmsford (0245) 55858

Chesterfield
W.J. Mitchell,
13 West Bars,
Chesterfield S40 1AQ
Tel: Chesterfield (0246) 75329

Cirencester
J.J. Richards,
Vallis,
Farm Hill,
Stroud,
Gloucestershire

Colchester and Harwich
See North Essex and South Suffolk
District

Corby
G.H. McCart,
13 Islay Walk,
Corby,
Northamptonshire
Tel: Corby (05366) 4944

Coventry East
H. Clarke,
61 Corporation Street,
Coventry CV1 1GQ
Tel: Coventry (0203) 27522

Coventry West
R.E. Lissaman,
61 Corporation Street,
Coventry CV1 1GQ
Tel: Coventry (0203) 27522

Crewe
H.W. Ollier,
38 St. Paul Street,
Crewe,
Cheshire
Tel: Crewe (0270) 3000

Croydon
J.B. Schooling,
8 South End,
Croydon,
Surrey CR0 1DL
Tel: 01–686 3814

Darlington
H. Hammond,
66 Duke Street,
Darlington,
Co. Durham
Tel: Darlington (0325) 65791

Daventry
J. Hunter,
14 Regent Place,
Rugby CV21 2PN
Tel: Rugby (0788) 4754

Derby
W.B. Morgan,
210 Osmaston Road,
Derby DE3 8JX
Tel: Derby (0332) 46617

Dereham
See Norfolk and North Suffolk
District

Dewsbury and Wakefield
K. Garwell,
New City Chambers,
36 Wood Street,
Wakefield,
West Yorkshire WF1 2ER
Tel: Wakefield (0924) 75546

Doncaster
E. Dyson,
56–60 Silver Street,
Doncaster,
South Yorkshire DN1 1HT
Tel: Doncaster (0302) 67269

Dover
A.A. Green,
39 Albert Road,
Hythe.
Kent CT21 6BT
Tel: Hythe (0303) 67595

Dursley
See Cirencester

Enfield
A.H. Thorogood,
260 Fore Street,
London N18
Tel: 01–807 3727

Erith
L. Smith,
39 Belmont Road,
Erith,
Kent
Tel: Erith (03224) 32182

Exeter
K. Jones,
202 Sweet Briar Lane,
Exeter,
Devon
Tel: Exeter (0392) 50602

Frome
S. Sparey,
22 Foster Road,
Frome,
Somerset BA11 1NZ
Tel: Frome (0307) 61556

Gainsborough
D. Gossop,
AUEW House,
238 Nettleham Road,
Lincoln LN2 4DL
Tel: Lincoln (0522) 31731

Gloucester
W. Neale,
8 Westgate Street,
Gloucester GL1 2NL
Tel: Gloucester (0452) 24689

Grantham
G. Davis,
Oxford Hall,
Oxford Street,
Grantham
Lincolnshire NG31 6HQ
Tel: Grantham (0476) 2780

Grimsby
A.E. Salmon,
22 Dudley Street,
Grimsby,
South Humberside DN31 2AB
Tel: Grimsby (0472) 53741

Guildford and Farnborough
G. Hardy,
65 Woodbridge Road,
Guildford,
Surrey
Tel: Guildford (0483) 67055

Halifax
P Smith,
4 Rawson Street,
Halifax,
West Yorkshire HX1 1NH
Tel: Halifax (0422) 65543 and 54598

Hartlepool
F.O. Richmond,
58 Church Street,
Hartlepool,
Cleveland TS24 7DX
Tel: Hartlepool (0429) 3755

Hastings and Rye
R.V. Selden,
7 Meads Way,
St Mary's Bay,
Romney Marsh,
Kent TN29 0HE
Tel: New Romney (06793) 3095

Hatfield and Welwyn
E.D. French,
AEU House,
Harberts Road,
Harlow,
Essex
Tel: Harlow (0279) 35000

Hereford
D.D. Griffiths,
27 Marlowe Drive,
Whitecross,
Hereford
Tel: Hereford (0432) 66536

Highbridge
L.S. Wright,
28a High Street,
Bridgwater,
Somerset TA6 3BJ
Tel: Bridgwater (0278) 51147

Hinckley
J. Hunter,
14 Regent Place,
Rugby CV21 2PN
Tel: Rugby (0788) 4754

Horwich
H.D. Burke,
170 Brownlow Road,
Horwich,
Bolton,
Lancashire BL6 7EL
Tel: Bolton (0204) 67446

Huddersfield
K. Handy,
AUEW House,
42 New North Road,
Huddersfield HD1 5LL
Tel: Huddersfield (0484) 26399

Hull
W. Joester,
78 Beverley Road,
Hull HU3 1YD
Tel: Hull (0482) 25971

Ipswich and Stowmarket
R.H. Hillis,
140 St. Helens Street,
Ipswich IP4 2LE
Tel: Ipswich (0473) 52999

Isle of Wight
A.G.R. Hardy,
69 Christchurch Road,
Ringwood,
Hampshire BH24 1DH
Tel: Ringwood (042 54) 4807

Kendal
F. Ward,
114 Duke Street,
Barrow-in-Furness,
Cumbria LA14 1LW
Tel: Barrow-in-Furness (0229) 20080

King's Lynn
See Norfolk and North Suffolk District

Kingston
D.E. Wilson,
9 Grange Road,
Kingston,
Surrey KT1 2QU
Tel: 01–546 8494 and 5213

Kirkbymoorside
J. Ramsden,
AUEW Office,
Matmer House,
Hull Road,
York YO1 3JW
Tel: York (0904) 59060

Lancaster
J. Layden,
3 Burnsail Avenue,
Heysham,
Morecambe,
Lancashire LA3 2DT
Tel: Morecambe (0524) 51505

Leeds
C. Hampshire,
AUEW House,
Bridge Street,
Leeds LS2 7RA
Tel: Leeds (0532) 34925/6

Leicester
Miss B. Paton,
71 Vaughan Way,
Leicester LE1 4SG
Tel: Leicester (0533) 27758

Letchworth and Cambridge
D. Collins,
57 Nightingale Road,
Hitchin,
Hertfordshire
Tel: Hitchin (0462) 53149

Lincoln
D. Gossop,
238 Nettleham Road,
Lincoln LN2 4DL
Tel: Lincoln (0522) 31731

Liverpool
H.J. Brodrick,
46–48 Mount Pleasant,
Liverpool L3 5SE
Tel: 051–709 9561

London North
V.W. Swift,
28 Denmark Street,
London WC2
Tel: 01–240 0625/6/7/8

London South
L.G. Doust,
20 Durand Gardens,
London SW9 0PP
Tel: 01–735 1158/9

Loughborough
R.E. Ryan,
AUEW House,
63 Forest Road,
Loughborough,
Leicestershire LE11 3NW
Tel: Loughborough (0509) 61842

Lowestoft and Yarmouth
See Norfolk and North Suffolk
District

Luton
A.G. Sjogren,
AUEW House,
396 Dunstable Road,
Luton, Bedfordshire LU4 8JT
Tel: Luton (0582) 56271

Lutterworth
J. Hunter,
14 Regent Place,
Rugby CV21 2PN
Tel: Rugby (0788) 4754

Lymington
A.G.R. Hardy,
69 Christchurch Road,
Ringwood,
Hampshire BH24 1DH
Tel: Ringwood (042 54) 4807

Manchester
W. Mather,
43 Crescent,
Salford M5 4PE
Tel: 061–736 6264/5

Manchester North
D. Daniels
43 Crescent.
Salford M5 4PE

Melksham
R.S. Lake,
8 Station Hill,
Chippenham,
Wiltshire
Tel: Chippenham (0249) 2572

Melton Mowbray
R.E. Ryan,
AUEW House,
63 Forest Road,
Loughborough,
Leicester LE11 3NW
Tel: Loughborough (0509) 61842

Mid-Somerset
L.S. Wright,
28a High Street,
Bridgwater,
Somerset TA6 3BJ
Tel: Bridgwater (0278) 51147

Milton Keynes
See Milton Keynes and Banbury

Milton Keynes and Banbury
A.J. Carpenter,
13 Cofferidge Close,
Stony Stratford,
Milton Keynes MK11 1BY
Tel: Milton Keynes (0908) 566312

Minehead
L.S. Wright,
28a High Street,
Bridgwater,
Somerset TA6 3BJ
Tel: Bridgwater (0278) 51147

Newark
G. Davis,
Oxford Hall,
Oxford Street,
Grantham,
Lincolnshire NG31 6HQ
Tel: Grantham (0476) 2780

Newton Abbot
R. Main,
36 Kingskerwell Road,
Newton Abbot,
Devon
Tel: Newton Abbot (0626) 4001

Newton-le-Willows and Warrington
J.F. Coffey,
AUEW House,
Froghall Lane,
Warrington WA2 7JR
Tel: Warrington (0925) 31672

Norfolk and North Suffolk
H.G. McKenna,
13 Unthank Road,
Norwich NR2 2AB
Tel: Norwich (0603) 25772

Northampton and Wellingborough
R.P. Ward,
1 St. Giles Square,
Northampton NN1 1DA
Tel: Northampton (0604) 35788

North Essex and South Suffolk
R.J. Rouse,
AUEW Office,
7 Magdalen Street,
St Botolphs,
Colchester,
Essex
Tel: Colchester (0206) 42354

North Stafford
G. Gordon,
499 Etruria Road,
Basford,
Stoke-on-Trent,
Staffordshire ST4 6JR
Tel: Stoke-on-Trent (0782) 616020

North West Durham
J. Cranney,
Lloyds Bank Chambers,
1b Victoria Road,
Consett,
Co. Durham
Tel: Consett (0207) 502841

Northwich
A. Waddington,
68 Hatton Lane,
Greenbank,
Northwich,
Cheshire
Tel: 0606 74030

Norwich
See Norfolk and North Suffolk
District

Nottingham
R.A. Bacon,
218 Mansfield Road,
Nottingham NG5 2BU
Tel: Nottingham (0602) 606215

Oldham
J.W. Jones,
AUEW Office,
111 Union Street,
Oldham,
Lancashire OL1 1HA
Tel: 061–624 4128

Otley
J. Ramsden,
AUEW Office,
Matmer House,
Hull Road,
York YO1 3JW
Tel: York (0904) 59060

Oxford
M.W. Young,
171 Cowley Road,
Oxford
Tel: Oxford (0865) 44017

Peterborough
R. Shaw,
AUEW House,
49 Lincoln Road,
Peterborough PE1 2RR
Tel: Peterborough (0733) 54971

Plymouth
R.G. King,
52 Stuart Road,
Plymouth,
Devon PL3 4EE
Tel: Plymouth (0752) 63114

Portsmouth
C.E.Arrowsmith,
140 Copnor Road,
Portsmouth,
Hampshire
Tel: Portsmouth (0705) 63917

Preston
R. Crook,
AUEW House,
9–10 Cross Street,
Preston PR1 3LT
Tel: Preston (0772) 57765/7

Ramsgate and Margate
J. Wright,
'Briar Cottage',
Bedlam Court Lane,
Minster,
Thanet
Tel: Thanet (0843) 821512

Reading
A.J. Calow,
121 Oxford Road,
Reading,
Berkshire RG1 2DT
Tel: Reading (0734) 51706

Redditch
A. Cotton,
4 William Street,
Redditch,
Worcestershire
Tel: Reading (0527) 66460

Ringwood
A.G.R. Hardy,
69 Christchurch Road,
Ringwood,
Hampshire BH24 1DH
Tel: Ringwood (042 54) 4807

Rochdale
J. Calverley,
150 Drake Street,
Rochdale,
Lancashire
Tel: Rochdale (0706) 46333

Rugby
J. Hunter,
14 Regent Place,
Rugby CV21 2PN
Tel: Rugby (0788) 4754

St. Austell,
D.R. Brown,
101 Killigrew Road,
Falmouth,
Cornwall
Tel: Falmouth (0326) 314717

St. George's and Shrewsbury
D.W. Woodvine,
AUEW Office,
Carlton Chambers,
Queen Street,
Wellington,
Telford,
Salop
Tel: Telford (0952) 3015

Salisbury
E.G. Harris,
2 Church Close,
Andover,
Hampshire SP10 1DP
Tel: Andover (0264) 61789

Scarborough
J. Ramsden,
AUEW Office,
Matmer House,
Hull Road,
York YO1 3JW
Tel: York (0904) 59060

Scunthorpe
A.E. Salmon,
22 Dudley Street,
Grimsby,
South Humberside DN31 2AB
Tel: Grimsby (0472) 53741

Selby
J. Ramsden,
AUEW Office,
Matmer House,
Hull Road,
York YO1 3JW
Tel: York (0904) 59060

Sheffield
G. Caborn,
AUEW House,
Furnival Gate,
Sheffield S1 3HE
Tel: Sheffield (0742) 79041/3

Skinningrove
W.J. Purvis,
AUEW House,
190 Borough Road,
Middlesborough,
Cleveland TS1 2EH
Tel: Middlesborough (0642) 247827

Slough
D.E. Dean,
8 Bath Road,
Slough SL1 3SA
Tel: Slough (0753) 21444

Southall
R. Butler,
1 Woodlands Road,
Southall,
Middlesex UB1 1EG
Tel: 01–574 5361

Southampton
A. Short,
14 Mansion Road,
Freemantle,
Southampton,
Hampshire SO1 3BP
Tel: Southampton (0703) 22463

South Cornwall
D.R. Brown,
101 Killigrew Road,
Falmouth,
Cornwall
Tel: Falmouth (0326) 314717

South Essex
J.H. Mitchell,
AUEW House,
588 Rainham Road South,
Dagenham,
Essex RM10 7RA
Tel: 01–593 4891

Southport
S. Edwardson,
21 The Causeway,
Southport,
Merseyside
Tel: Southport (0704) 25884

South West Lancashire
N. Mercer,
22 Hall Street,
St. Helens,
Merseyside WA10 1DL
Tel: St. Helens (0744) 28393

Stafford and Tamworth
W.T. Setterfield,
26 Anson Street,
Rugeley,
Staffordshire
Tel: Rugeley (088 94) 2712

Stamford
G. Davis,
Oxford Hall,
Oxford Street,
Grantham,
Lincolnshire NG31 6HQ
Tel: Grantham (0476) 2780

Stockport
B. Regan,
125 Wellington Road South,
Stockport,
Cheshire SK1 3TY
Tel: 061–480 2375

Stratford-upon-Avon
W. Overy,
'Woodruff',
Ilmington,
Shipston-on-Stour,
Warwickshire
Tel: Shipston-on-Stour (0608) 430

Stroud
J.J. Richards,
'Vallis',
Farm Hill,
Stroud,
Gloucestershire GL5 4DN
Tel: Stroud (045 36) 2817

Sunderland
H. Wilkinson,
189 Roker Avenue,
Sunderland SR6 0BS
Tel: Sunderland (0783) 59570

Swindon
L.A. Thompson,
AUEW House,
Fleming Way,
Swindon,
Wiltshire SN1 1SR
Tel: Swindon (0793) 22468

Taunton
L.S. Wright,
28a High Street,
Bridgwater,
Somerset TA6 3BJ
Tel: Bridgwater (0278) 51147

Teesside
W.J. Purvis,
AUEW House,
190 Borough Road,
Middlesbrough,
Cleveland TS1 2EH
Tel: Middlesbrough (0642) 247827

Tyne
T. Johnston,
AUEW House,
High Street,
Gateshead,
Tyne and Wear NE8 1ER
Tel: Gateshead (0632) 774316

Watford
A.W. Harrison
25 Highfield Road,
Bushey,
Watford,
Hertfordshire
Tel: Watford (0932) 26342

West Cornwall
D.R. Brown,
101 Killigrew Road,
Falmouth,
Cornwall
Tel: Falmouth (0326) 314717

West Cumberland
G.L. Goldsworthy,
43 Oxford Street,
Workington,
Cumbria CA14 2AL
Tel: Workington (0900) 3112

Weston-Super-Mare
L.S. Wright,
28a High Street,
Bridgwater,
Somerset TA6 3BJ
Tel: Bridgwater (0278) 51147

Weymouth
F.G. Smith,
9 Clarendon Avenue,
Weymouth,
Dorset DT3 5BG
Tel: Upwey (030 581) 3220

Wigan
H. Costello,
100 Chapel Lane,
Wigan,
Lancashire WN3 4HG
Tel: Wigan (0924) 42373

Wirral and West Cheshire
C. Keech,
37 Old Chester Road,
Bebington,
Wirral,
Merseyside L41 9AN
Tel: 051-645 5523/4

Wolverhampton East
A. Tonkinson,
129 Horseley Field,
Wolverhampton WV1 1EQ
Tel: Wolverhampton (0902) 53022

Wolverhampton West
S. Ruthven,
129 Horseley Field,
Wolverhampton WV1 1EQ
Tel: Wolverhampton (0902) 53022

Worcester and Kidderminster
S.P. Rowlands,
AUEW Office,
29-35 Lowesmoor,
Worcester WR1 2RS
Tel: Worcester (0905) 28992

Yeovil
C.A. Hollinghurst,
13 Arundel Road,
Yeovil,
Somerset BA21 5JZ
Tel: Yeovil (0935) 5999

York
J. Ramsden,
AUEW Office,
Matmer House,
Hull Road,
York YO1 3JW
Tel: York (0904) 59060

Ireland
Ballymena
S. McKinney,
5 Mill Street,
Ballymena,
County Antrim BT43 5AB
Tel: Ballymena (0266) 42761

Belfast
J. Blair,
AEU House,
26–34 Antrim Road,
Belfast BT15 2AA
Tel: Belfast (0232) 743271

Carlow
See Southern Ireland District

Coleraine
S. McKinney,
65 Mill Street,
Ballymena,
Co. Antrim BT43 5AB
Tel: Ballymena (0266) 42761

Cork Harbour
See Southern Ireland District

Dublin
See Southern Ireland District

Dundalk
See Southern Ireland District

Galway
See Southern Ireland District

Galway West
See Southern Ireland District

Larne
S. McKinney,
65 Mill Street,
Ballymena,
Co. Antrim BT43 5AB
Tel: Ballymena (0266) 42761

Limerick
See Southern Ireland District

Londonderry
S. McKinney,
65 Mill Street,
Ballymena,
Co. Antrim BT43 5AB
Tel: Ballymena (0266) 42761

Lurgan
G.A. Leatham,
17 Charles Park,
Portadown,
Craigavon,
Co. Armagh
Tel: Craigavon (0762) 2939

Northern Counties
S. McKinney,
65 Mill Street,
Ballymena,
Co. Antrim BT43 5AB
Tel: Ballymena (0266) 42761

Offaly
See Southern Ireland District

Southern Ireland
F. Callaghan,
'Emmett House',
20 St. Charles Street,
Dublin,
Eire
Tel: Dublin 740703

Omagh
S. McKinney,
65 Mill Street,
Ballymena,
Co. Antrim BT43 5AB
Tel: Ballymena (0266) 42761

Waterford
See Southern Ireland District

Wexford
See Southern Ireland District

Wicklow
See Southern Ireland District

Scotland
Aberdeen
J. McConnachie,
AUEW House,
24 Adelphi,
Aberdeen AB1 2BL
Tel: Aberdeen (0224) 22027

Ayrshire
J.M. Paton,
65 King Street,
Kilmarnock,
Ayrshire
Tel: Kilmarnock (0563) 22878

Border
J. Douglas,
42 Howdenburn Court,
Jedburgh,
Borders

Brechin
D.K. Todd,
9 Strachans Park,
Brechin,
Angus
Tel: Brechin (035 62) 2651

Buckie
J. McConnachie,
AUEW House,
24 Adelphi,
Aberdeen AB1 2BL
Tel: Aberdeen (0224) 22027

Caithness
See Highlands and Islands District

Dumbarton
J. McKee,
69 Glasgow Road,
Dumbarton G82 1RE
Tel: Dumbarton (0389) 62103

Dundee
H. McLevy,
AUEW House,
26 South Ward Road,
Dundee DD1 1TR
Tel: Dundee (0382) 22406

Edinburgh
J. Keddie,
145 Morrison Street,
Edinburgh EH3 8AL
Tel: 031–229 8711

Falkirk
T.W. Adam,
11 Grahams Road,
Falkirk,
Stirlingshire FK1 1LD
Tel: Falkirk (0324) 21327

Fife
B.G. Simpson,
214 High Street,
Kirkcaldy,
Fife KY1 1JT
Tel: Kirkcaldy (0592) 60524

Fraserburgh
J. McConnachie,
AUEW House,
24 Adelphi,
Aberdeen AB1 2BL
Tel: Aberdeen (0224) 22027

Glasgow
J. McKenzie,
145–165 West Regent Street,
Glasgow G2 4RZ
Tel: 041–248 7131

Greenock
J. McKee,
69 Glasgow Road,
Dumbarton G82 1RE
Tel: Dumbarton (0389) 62103

Highlands and Islands
I.L. McFarlane,
22 Lawyers Way,
Inverness
Tel: Inverness (0463) 38127

Invergordon
See Highlands and Islands

Inverness
See Highlands and Islands

Inverurie
J. McConnachie,
AUEW House,
24 Adelphi,
Aberdeen AB1 2BL
Tel: Aberdeen (0224) 22027

Kilbirnie
J.M. Paton,
65 King Street,
Kilmarnock,
Ayrshire
Tel: Kilmarnock (0563) 22878

Lewis
See Highlands and Islands

Lochaber
See Highlands and Islands

Mid Lanarkshire
A.D. Milligan,
AEU House,
81 Hamilton Road,
Motherwell,
Lanarkshire
Tel: Motherwell (0698) 62076

Moray
J. McConnachie,
AUEW House,
24 Adelphi,
Aberdeen AB1 2BL
Tel: Aberdeen (0224) 22027

Paisley
M. Mackay,
AUEW House,
7 Incle Street,
Paisley,
Renfrewshire PA1 1HW
Tel: 041-889 4371

Peterhead
J. McConnachie,
AUEW House,
24 Adelphi,
Aberdeen AB1 2BL
Tel: Aberdeen (0224) 22027

Thurso
See Highlands and Islands

Turriff
J. McConnachie,
AUEW House,
24 Adelphi,
Aberdeen AB1 2BL
Tel: Aberdeen (0224) 22027

Zetland
See Highlands and Islands

Wales
Blackwood
L.H.C. Richards,
139 High Street,
Blackwood,
Gwent NP2 1AB
Tel: Blackwood (0495) 225720

Caernarfon
R.G. Jones,
111 Gae Mur,
Caernarfon,
Gwynedd
Tel: Caernarfon (0286) 3580

Cardiff
D.J. Guy,
1-3 Fitzalan Place,
Cardiff CF2 1UN
Tel: Cardiff (0222) 31271/2

Deeside
R. Bull,
AUEW Office,
17 Ash Grove,
Deeside,
Clwyd CH5 1AF
Tel: Deeside (0244) 812947

Llandudno
A. Ward,
33 Llanelian Road,
Old Colwyn,
Clywd LL29 9UT1
Tel: Colwyn Bay (0492) 55683

Llanelli
J.P. Weakley (Acting),
AUEW House,
4 Queen Victoria Road,
Llanelli,
Dyfed SA15 2TL
Tel: Llanelli (055 42) 3969

Llanidloes
J. Holliday,
Devil Bridge Street,
Rhayader,
Powys
Tel: Rhayader (059782) 825

Llantrisant
T.H. Evans,
AUEW House,
Sardis Road,
Pontypridd,
Mid. Glamorgan CF37 1DU
Tel: Pontypridd (0443) 402867

Merthyr
A. John,
AUEW Office,
Swan Street,
Merthyr Tydfil,
Mid. Glamorgan
Tel: Merthyr Tydfil (0685) 3841

Mid Glamorgan
F.C. Evans,
19 Victoria Gardens,
Neath,
West Glamorgan
Tel: Neath (0639) 2760

Milford Haven
F.D. Jones,
'Bryn-Hyfryd',
Priory Road,
Milford Haven,
Dyfed SA73 2EA

Newport
T.R. Golightly,
AUEW House,
34-38 Stow Hill,
Newport
Gwent NPT 1JE
Tel: Newport (0633) 65650

North West Gwynedd
W.R. Rowlands,
'Fron',
Llanddona,
Beaumaris,
Gwynedd LL58 8UN
Tel: Beaumaris (0248) 810 560

Pembroke Dock
J.P. Weakley (Acting),
AUEW House,
4 Queen Victoria Road,
Llanelli,
Dyfed SA15 2TL
Tel: Llanelli (055 42) 3969

Portmadoc
K. Winstanley,
'Stabel Mael',
Talsarnau,
Penrhyndeudraeth,
Gwynedd
Tel: Penrhyndeudraeth (076 674) 625

Swansea
N. Davies,
AUEW House,
34 Orchard Street,
Swansea SA1 5AW
Tel: Swansea (0792) 54398

Periodicals: *AUEW Journal* (monthly), *The Way* (irregular)

Policy: Each section has its own autonomy within a general overall policy which includes the increasing of employment by raising purchasing power, the re-establishing of free collective bargaining, substantial increases in public ownership and enterprise, large scale redistribution of wealth, and massive re-investment in industry.

ENGINEERING WORKERS, AMALGAMATED UNION OF, CONSTRUCTIONAL SECTION*
Construction House, 190 Cedars Road, Clapham, London SW4 0PP
Tel: 01–622 4451

This section of the AUEW originated in 1924 as a section of the British Iron, Steel and Kindred Trades Association and until amalgamation with the AUEF in 1970 it was known as the Constructional Engineering Union. It organises all grades of workers in engineering construction – site erectors, riggers, crane drivers, fitters, welders, and has national agreements with the Engineering Employers' Federation as well as agreements on specific construction sites.
Current membership: 35,000

NATIONAL OFFICIALS
President: F. Miller
General Secretary: J. Baldwin, OBE
Assistant General Secretary: L.F. Spackman

Executive Council
A.J. Connolly
J. Craigie
A. Jameson
A. Sparrock
T. Gaynor

F. Miller
G. Douglas
D. Downes
J. Aberdein

REGIONAL OFFICIALS

London Division
South West London Office
D. Bond,
22 Worple Road SW19
Tel: 01-947 5344

Dartford Office
H. Barr,
27 Essex Road,
Dartford,
Kent
Tel: Dartford (0322) 21874

Dagenham Office
D. Wheaton,
588 Rainham Road South,
Dagenham,
Essex
Tel: 01-593 3390

Scottish Division
Aberdeen Office
T. Lafferty,
59 Dee Street,
Aberdeen AB1 2EE
Tel: Aberdeen (0224) 55454

Edinburgh Office
R. Sneddon,
Trade Union Centre,
12-14 Picardy Place,
Edinburgh EH1 3JT
Tel: 031-557 0285

Paisley Office
T. MacLean, A. Gray,
17 Lynedoch Street,
Charing Cross,
Glasgow

North East Division
Middlesbrough Office
W. Walker, T. Woods,
78 Borough Road,
Middlesbrough,
Cleveland TS1 2JM
Tel: Middlesbrough (0642) 42383

Sheffield Office
G. Garbett,
AUEW House,
Furnival Gate,
Sheffield S1 3HE
Tel: Sheffield (0742) 25453

Leeds Office
H. Wainwright,
Room No. 3,
Winwaed House,
64-66 Crossgates Road,
Leeds LS15 7NN
Tel: Leeds (0532) 644044

Midlands Division
Birmingham Office
C. Connell,
6th Floor,
St. Martins House,
Bull Ring,
Birmingham B5 5DT

Nottingham Office
K. Antell,
9 St. James Terrace,
Nottingham NG1 6FW
Tel: 0602 45840

North West Division
Manchester Office
W. Charles,
43 The Crescent,
Salford M5 4PE
Tel: 061-736 5311

Liverpool Office
S.E. Howard,
AUEW House,
48 Mount Pleasant,
Liverpool
Tel: 051-709 4888

South Wales and South West Division
Bristol Office
P. Jones,
8 St. Paul's Road,
Clifton,
Bristol BS8 1LU
Tel: Bristol (0272) 32634

Neath Office
T. King,
Ty Can Olog,
25 Victoria Gardens,
Neath
Tel: Neath (0639) 56700

ENGINEERING WORKERS, AMALGAMATED UNION OF, FOUNDRY SECTION*

164 Chorlton Road, Brook's Bar, Manchester M16 7NU
Tel: 061-226 1151/2

The Foundry Workers section of the AUEW is the only trade union dealing exclusively with foundry workers, particularly for those associated with the engineering industry. It is among the unions with the oldest continuous existence, tracing its origins to the Friendly Iron Moulders Society founded in 1809.
Current membership: 58,728

OFFICIALS
President: G.R.Howieson
General Secretary: R. Garland
Assistant General Secretary: J. Shaw
Assistant Secretaries: J. Brock and A. McIver

Executive Council
G.R. Howieson (Vice-Chairman)
G.P. Burns
W. Prince
D.H. Cornwall, MBE
J. D. Bradshaw

National Organisers
National Organiser: B. Salt
Dresser Organiser: Vacant

Divisional Organisers
No 1
J. Taylor,
11 Graham's Road,
Falkirk
Tel: Falkirk (0324) 24459

J.A. Kelley,
13 Granville Terrace,
Otley,
Yorkshire LS21 3EJ
Tel: Otley (09434) 51448

No. 2
J. Blair,
AEU Office,
145 West Regent Street,
Glasgow G2 4RZ
Tel: 041-221 2425

No. 5
K.W. Smith,
Star Buildings,
71 Vaughan Way,
Leicester LE1 4SG
Tel: Leicester (0533) 21395

No. 3
J.W. McDonald,
AUEW House,
2nd Floor,
High Street,
Gateshead NE8 1JB
Tel: Gateshead (0632) 770 403

No. 6 (North)
D. O'Flynn,
AUEW House,
588 Rainham Road South,
Dagenham,
Essex RM10 7RA
Tel: 01-593 4893

No. 4
L. Crossley,
2 Victoria Street,
Barnsley
Tel: Barnsley (0226) 203775

No. 6 (South)
W. Chapman,
4 Southview Close,
Shoreham by Sea,
Sussex

W. Baker and W. Law,
67 Old Meeting Street,
West Bromwich,
Staffordshire
Tel: 021–553 3876

No. 7
W. Haynes,
AEU House,
43 The Crescent,
Salford M5 4PE
Tel: 061–736 2465

No. 9
W.A. Cooper,
AEF Office,
3rd Floor,
1–3 Fitzalan Place,
Cardiff CF2 1UN
Tel: Cardiff (0222) 31271

No. 8
P.H. Smith,
67 Old Meeting Street,
West Bromwich,
Staffordshire
Tel: 021–553 3876

Periodical: *Foundry Worker* (Monthly)

ENGINEERING WORKERS, AMALGAMATED UNION OF, TECHNICAL, ADMINISTRATIVE AND SUPERVISORY SECTION (AUEW-TASS)*
Onslow Hall, Little Green, Richmond, Surrey TW9 1QN
Tel: 01–948 2271

The union was formed as the Association of Engineering and Shipbuilding Draughtsmen on Clydeside in 1913. In 1922 the Tracers' Association was brought into membership. The organisation changed its name to the Draughtsmen and Allied Technicians Association in 1961. This reflected the growing spread of membership into new and developing technical areas within the engineering industry. In 1970 the union participated in a merger with the Amalgamated Engineering and Foundry Workers Union and the Construction Engineering Union to form the Amalgamated Union of Engineering Workers.

Formerly confining its recruitment to drawing office and associated technical employees, TASS now seeks to organise all staff in engineering and manufacturing industries. The union retains a very substantial base of technical membership.
Current membership: 201,000

FULL-TIME OFFICIALS
General Secretary: K. Gill
Deputy General Secretary: E. Winterbottom
Assistant Secretary (Administration): J. Tuchfield
National Organiser: J. Jones
National Women's Organiser: J. Hunt

Above officials located at Headquarters.

Divisions 13 & 14
V. Gapper/F. Hyde,
AUEW-TASS,
71 Vaughan Way,
Leicester
Tel: Leicester (0533) 27177

Divisions 17 & 19
D. Carr/D. Yeomans,
AUEW-TASS,
65 Baldwin Street,
Bristol BS1 1ZZ
Tel: Bristol (0272) 299456

Division 18
K.W.E. Lane,
AUEW-TASS,
57 Above Bar,
Southampton SO1 0DZ
Tel: Southampton (0703) 30779

B. Sanderson,
Onslow Hall,
Little Green,
Richmond TW9 1QN
Tel: 01-948 0094

Division 20
R. Longworth,
AUEW-TASS,
Sardis Road,
Pontypridd CF37 1DU
Tel: Pontypridd (0443) 406311

Division 21
D. Blockley,
AUEW-TASS,
140 St. Helen's Street,
Ipswich IP4 2LE
Tel: Ipswich (0473) 212136

Divisions 22, 23 & 24
I. Benson/B. King/J. Thomas,
AUEW-TASS,
25 Highfield Road,
Bushey WD2 2HD
Tel: Watford (0932) 49044

Divisions 25 & 26
L. Brooke/C. Darke/D. Perkins,
AUEW-TASS,
Onslow Hall,
Little Green,
Richmond TW9 1QN
Tel: 01-948 0094

Periodical: *Tass Journal* (monthly)

Policy: The union has for the past decade been opposed to British entry into the EEC and to the operation of any form of incomes policy. It has campaigned actively against the growth of racialist ideas and is in favour of an extension of public ownership.

ENGINEERS AND MANAGERS' ASSOCIATION (EMA)*
Station House, Fox Lane North, Chertsey, Surrey KT16 9HW
Tel: Chertsey (093 28) 64131/4

Formed in 1913 under the name of Association of Electrical Station Engineers, the name was changed in 1918 to the Electrical Power Engineers' Association. The membership of the EPEA was open to technical, scientific and managerial staff in the electricity supply industry until April 1976 when a decision was made at the Annual Delegate Conference to recruit engineers and managers in other occupations and industries. Following this decision the name of the enlarged association was changed in April 1977 to the Engineers' and Managers' Association (EMA) with the title of EPEA being retained by the members employed in the electricity supply industry, who became the founder constituent group within the EMA. Since the creation of the EMA other Groups have been constituted as a result

of the transfer of engagements of other unions and staff associations. These include the Association of Supervisory and Executive Engineers (ASEE), Shipbuilding and Allied Industries Management Association (SAIMA), the Aerospace Association (this particular Group comprising two staff associations within British Aerospace). There is a Central Group which holds directly recruited members to the EMA from which in the near future a new Engineering Group will be formed. Members of the EMA are located throughout England, Wales, Scotland and Ireland.
Current membership: 51,000

FULL-TIME OFFICIALS
General Secretary EMA and EPEA: J. Lyons
Deputy General Secretary EMA and EPEA: S. Petch

National Officers
EMA:
D. Sweaney,
Wix Hill House,
West Horsley,
Leatherhead,
Surrey

EPEA: H.R. Page, D.C. Bound, Head Office
Research Officers EMA and EPEA:
P.W. Davies, Mrs C. Pillay, Head Office

EMA Negotiating Officers/Organisers:
A. Askew,
2nd Floor,
Roberts House,
80 Manchester Road,
Altrincham,
Cheshire
T. Lane,
Wix Hill House,
West Horsley,
Leatherhead,
Surrey
C. Finnerty,
30 New Street,
Musselburgh,
Midlothian

Central Group & ASEE Secretary:
D. Sweaney,
Wix Hill House,
West Horsley,
Leatherhead,
Surrey

Aerospace Association Secretary:
P. Fairley, OBE,
39 High Street,
Wheathampstead,
St. Albans,
Herts AL4 8DG

SAIMA Secretary:
S. J. Alger,
140 Lower Marsh,
London SE1 7AE

EPEA Area Secretaries;
F.I. Adamson,
Castle Dale,
Chepstow,
Gwent N96 5LR

D.T. Bellamy,
140 Lower Marsh,
London SE1 7AE

R.A. Blackburn,
4th Floor,
West Wing,
Yorkshire House,
Greek Street,
Leeds LS1 5SH

H. Brockelsby,
2nd Floor,
Roberts House,
80 Manchester Road,
Altrincham,
Cheshire

D.A. Carter,
Castle Dale,
Welsh Street,
Chepstow,
Gwent N96 5LR

G.E. Knighton,
6th Floor,
James House,
Welford Road,
Leicester LE2 7AE

D. Rowbottom,
2nd Floor,
Roberts House,
80 Manchester Road,
Altrincham,
Cheshire

R. K. Score,
12f Barclays Bank Chambers,
London Road,
Pitsea,
Essex

R.G. Stevenson,
140 Lower Marsh,
London SE1 7AE

S.R. Wallace,
30 New Street,
Musselburgh,
Midlothian

FELT HATTERS AND ALLIED WORKERS, AMALAGAMATED SOCIETY OF JOURNEYMEN*‡
14 Walker Street, Denton, Manchester
Tel: 061-336 2450

Formed in 1879 by the amalgamation of the Hatters' Mutual Association and the Felt Hat Body Makers. The union organises men only and shares a common general secretary with the Felt Hat Trimmers and Wool Formers of Great Britain.
Current membership: 563

OFFICIAL
General Secretary: H. Walker

FELT HAT TRIMMERS AND WOOL FORMERS, AMALGAMATED ASSOCIATION OF*‡
14 Walker Street, Denton, Manchester
Tel: 061-336 2450

Formed in 1888 from a number of organisations dating from 1884. A trade union for women sharing a common general secretary with the Felt Hatters and Allied Workers.
Current membership: 623

OFFICIAL
General Secretary: H. Walker

FILM ARTISTES' ASSOCIATION (FAA)*
61 Marloes Road, London W8 6LF
Tel: 01-937 4567/8

Founded in 1932, catering almost entirely for crowd artistes.
Current membership: 2,203

OFFICIAL
General Secretary: S. Brannigan

FIRE BRIGADES' UNION (FBU)*
Bradley House, 59 Fulham High Street, London SW6 3JN
Tel: 01-736 2157

The Fire Brigades' Union was formed in London in 1918. From very
small beginnings it now has in membership over 90 per cent of all
uniformed personnel (wholetime firemen of all ranks) in the 65 local
authority fire brigades of Great Britain and Northern Ireland. All the
main conditions of service, e.g. pay and hours, are negotiated
nationally between the union and representatives of the local
authorities on the National Joint Council for Local Authorities' Fire
Brigades. The union also plays an important part in the work of the
Central Fire Brigades' Advisory Council, which is responsible to the
government and deals with standards of fire cover, numbers of
firemen employed, types of appliances, fire-fighting equipment,
uniforms, fire prevention legislation, training of personnel, etc.
Current membership: 35,000

OFFICIALS
President: W. Barber, MBE
General Secretary: T. Parry, CBE
Assistant General Secretary: R. Foggie
National Officers: T.R. Martindale, D. Riddell, K. Cameron and M.R.
Fordham

Executive Council

Region 1	*Region 3*
W. Craig,	J.L. Cairns,
32 Wallace Gardens,	62 Dunelm Road,
Stirling,	Thornley,
	Co Durham DH6 3HW
Region 2	
A. Culbert,	*Region 4*
39 Delamont Park,	S. Fitzsimmons
Belfast BT6 9RJ	32 Brander Road,
	Leeds 9,
	Yorkshire

Region 5
J. Haworth,
10 Dorlan Avenue,
Gorton,
Manchester 18

Region 6
P. Rockley,
Herdebi,
School Lane,
Harby,
Leicestershire

Region 7
J.B. Goodwin,
41 Taunton Avenue,
Fordhouses,
Wolverhampton WV10 6PL

Region 8
J.D. Higgs,
17 Golden Grove,
Derwen Estate,
Rhyl,
Clwyd

Region 9
T. Fields,
20 John Hunter Way,
Sefton,
Bootle,
Merseyside

Region 10
W. Deal (Vice-President),
81 Hawkesbury Road,
Canvey Island,
Essex

Region 11
D. Chaloner (National Treasurer),
6 Pointalls Close,
Finchley,
London N3

J. Lewis,
9 Orchard Hill,
Lewisham,
London SE13

Region 12
D.M. Shephard, JP,
12 Frenchgate Road,
Hampden Park,
Eastbourne,
Sussex

Region 13
J.F. Wynn,
28 Curlew Road,
Bournemouth,
Dorset BH8 9QB

Region 14
A.R. Totterdell,
51 Sutherland Avenue,
Downend,
Bristol BS16 6QW

Periodical: *Firefighter* (monthly)

FIRE OFFICERS, NATIONAL ASSOCIATION OF
6 Westow Hill, Upper Norwood, London SE19 1RX
Tel: 01–670 5474

Organises officer and junior officer ranks in the public fire service in
England, Wales, Scotland and Northern Ireland, on the basis of
Brigade Branches and a district organisation of 20 districts. The
association represents these ranks on the National Joint Council for
Local Authorities' Fire Brigades, and on the autonomous Officers'
Committee. More than two-thirds of serving officers are in
membership. The association has concerned itself particularly with
the maintenance of differentials in current social conditions in the
service.
Current membership: 4,500

FIRST DIVISION CIVIL SERVANTS, ASSOCIATION OF (FDA)*

17 Northumberland Avenue, London WC2N 5AP
Tel: 01–839 7406

Formed in 1918 to represent senior grades within the then Administrative Class, in recent years its membership has been extended to include Museum Keepers, Statisticians, Economists, Lawyers and HM Inspectors of Schools. Within these occupational groupings, the FDA represents staff ranging from the newly recruited Administration Trainee (and equivalent grades) to Permanent Secretary level. The FDA is organised on a branch basis by Government Departments and fringe bodies. It is a constituent organisation of the Civil Service National Whitley Council – Staff Side, and affiliated to the TUC in July 1977. In 1974 a close working arrangement was established with the Association of HM Inspector of Taxes (AIT) the aim being to establish a single body to formulate and pursue common policy on national issues. This is done, at present, by the AIT having representation of the FDA Executive Committee.

Also affiliated to the FDA are the Diplomatic Service Association, Senior Officers' Association (Northern Ireland Civil Service), New Town Chief Officers Association, Procurators Fiscal Society. Current membership of the FDA is 6,159, the AIT 2,518 and the affiliated bodies about 1,280.

FOOTWEAR, LEATHER AND ALLIED TRADES, NATIONAL UNION OF (NUFLAT)*†

The Grange, Earls Barton, Northampton NN6 0JH
Tel: Northampton (0604) 810326

Formed in 1971 by amalgamation between the National Union of Boot and Shoe Operatives, the Amalgamated Society of Leather Workers, the National Union of Leather Workers and Allied Trades, and the National Union of Glovers and Leather Workers. The first of these unions organised workpeople employed in the manufacture or repair of footwear of any kind, or in the manufacture of component parts; the second and third unions covered workers engaged in the production of leather (including fellmongering), made-up leather goods (including saddlery) and allied trades (including the production and processing of synthetic materials); the fourth covered workers employed in glove manufacture.

Current membership: 65,323. In 1978 there were 54,519 in Footwear Trade Group, 10,804 in Leather Trade Group)
Males: 31,544
Females: 33,779

NATIONAL OFFICIALS
General President: H. Comerford, JP,
NUFLAT, The Grange, Earls Barton, Northampton NN6 0JH
General Secretary: S.F. Clapham,
NUFLAT, The Grange, Earls Barton, Northampton NN6 0JH
Assistant General Officer: G.G. Stewart,
NUFLAT, The Grange, Earls Barton, Northampton NN6 0JH
National Secretary, Leather Trade Group: E. Mallon,
Leeds Trades Council Club, 21 Saville Mount, Leeds 7

General Executive Council

H. Comerford, JP	R. Hughes, Preston
S.F. Clapham	E. Moore, London
G.G. Stewart	M.T.W. Murray, Banbridge,
E. Mallon	N. Ireland
O. Combe, Hawick	H. Needham, Earl Shilton,
D. Cupitt, Harworth	Leicester
J.E. Dodds, Kendal	
A. Edmond, Beverley	J.N. Nevin, Bristol
R.E. Hart, JP, Northampton	R.B. Stevenson, Street
Mrs B.V. Holt, Leicester	

National Organisers

Footwear Trade Group	Leather Trade Group
G.F. Browett,	J. Firth,
28 Chesterfield Way,	13 Centre Gardens,
Barwell,	Bolton,
Leicestershire	Lancashire

T. Cheesmond, JP,
34 Church Lane,
Anstey,
Leicester LE7 7AF

AREA AND DIVISIONAL OFFICIALS
Area Officer, Footwear Trade Group:
D. Cupitt,
66 Baulk Lane, Harworth, Doncaster, South Yorkshire DN11 8PT

Divisional Officers, Leather Trade Group:

O. Combe,	J. Knight,
Exchange Arcade,	128 Drake Street,
Towerdykeside,	Rochdale,
Hawick,	Lancashire OL16 1PN
Roxburghshire,	
Scotland TD9 9EA	

J. Walsh,
8 Ashfield Road,
Birstall,
Batley,
Yorkshire WF17 0EF

G. Belben,
Unity Hall,
Vicarage Street,
Yeovil,
Somerset

E. Moore,
256 Richmond Road,
Hackney,
London E8 3QW

J. Donegan,
105–107 Overstone Road,
Northampton NN1 3JW

Full-Time Branch Officers, Footwear Trade Group:

Barwell, Earl Shilton and Hinckley
J.L. Dick,
H. Needham,
NUFLAT Offices,
3 Shilton Road,
Barwell,
Leicester LE9 8HB

Bristol, Kingswood and South Wales
C.J. Hern,
J.N. Nevin,
NUFLAT Offices,
15–17 High Street,
Kingswood,
Bristol BS15 4AA

Cockermouth
L. Blackwood, JP,
NUFLAT Offices,
Lorton Street,
Cockermouth,
Cumbria CA13 9RH

Higham and Rushden
R.H. Parker,
D.W. Richardson
P.A. Robinson,
NUFLAT Offices,
13 Higham Road,
Rushden,
Northamptonshire NN10 9DG

Kendal, Furness and Lancaster
J.E. Dodds,
NUFLAT Offices,
6–10 Gillinggate,
Kendal,
Cumbria LA9 4JE

Kettering
L. Walpole,
NUFLAT Offices,
Club Street,
Kettering NN16 8RB

Leeds
J. Scott,
NUFLAT Offices,
9 Queen Square,
Leeds LS2 8AJ

Leicester and Sileby
W.L. Barber,
Mrs B.V. Holt,
Mrs J.K. Smitten, JP,
R.G. James,
NUFLAT Offices,
Hill Street,
Leicester LE1 3PS

Metropolitan and Thurrock
R.C. Lloyd,
NUFLAT Offices,
256 Richmond Road,
Hackney,
London E8 3QW

W. Burroughs,
NUFLAT Offices,
64 Orsett Road,
Grays,
Essex RM17 6NL

Northampton
G. Dickens,
R. Hart, JP,
F. Tero,
NUFLAT Offices,
105–107 Overstone Road,
Northampton NN1 3JW

Northern Ireland
M.T.W. Murray,
NUFLAT Offices,
1b Dromore Street,
Banbridge,
Co Down,
Northern Ireland

195

Norwich
W. Critten,
J.C. Braithwaite,
Mrs B.M. Tunmore,
NUFLAT Offices,
St. Crispin Hall,
2–6 Botolph Street,
Norwich NR3 1DU

Preston, Glossop and District
R. Hughes,
NUFLAT Offices,
86 Deepdale Road,
Preston PR1 5AR

Scottish Footwear
T. Ferguson,
NUFLAT Offices,
1 John Dickie Street,
Kilmarnock KA1 1HW

Stafford, Stone and Wolverhampton
W.F. Bowers,
L. Bratt,
NUFLAT Offices,
Sheridan Hall,
Sandon Road,
Stafford ST16 3HF

Street
I. Elliot,
R.B. Stevenson,
A.A. Tume,
NUFLAT Offices,
41 Vestry Road,
Street,
Somerset BA16 0IIX

Periodical: *NUFLAT Journal and Report*

Policy: NUFLAT continues to pursue a policy against unfair imports of low labour cost and state subsidised commodities which it sees as the main cause of the problems in the industries covered. It continues its involvement in any joint negotiations, at national, European or international level which will ensure more orderly marketing arrangements within the footwear and leather industries.

FUNERAL SERVICE OPERATIVES, NATIONAL UNION OF (NUFSO)

Formed in 1917 as the British Funeral Workers' Association. It represented all grades of staff in the industry (including supervisory), and recently began to accept into membership employees in allied trades, car hire workers and florists for example. In September 1978 this union merged with the Furniture, Timber and Allied Trades Union.
1977 membership 1,375

FURNITURE, TIMBER AND ALLIED TRADES UNION (FTAT)*‡
Fairfields, Roe Green, Kingsbury, London NW9 0PT
Tel: 01–204 0273

Formed in 1971 from the merger of the National Union of Furniture Trade Operatives and the Amalgamated Society of Woodcutting Machinists. In 1978 the National Union of Funeral Service

Operatives and the National Union of Musical Instrument Makers amalgamated with FTAT.
Current membership: 90,000

OFFICIAL
General Secretary: B. Rubner

Periodical: *FTAT Record* (monthly)

GENERAL AND MUNICIPAL WORKERS' UNION (GMWU)*

(Formerly National Union of General and Municipal Workers)
Thorne House, Ruxley Ridge, Claygate, Esher, Surrey KT10 0TL.
Tel: Esher (0372) 62081

Formed in 1924 by amalgamation of three unions, the Gas and General Workers' Union, the National Amalgamated Society of Labour and the Municipal Employees' Association. Since the time of amalgamation membership of the union has almost trebled, with approximately one–third female members. Recent amalgamations with smaller unions include the Salt and General Chemical Workers (1962), the National Union of Water Works Employees (1972), the United, Rubber, Plastic and Allied Workers of Great Britain (1974), the Scottish Professional Footballers' Association (1975), and the Coopers' and Allied Workers' Federation of Great Britain (1979). The GMWU organises all grades of worker in virtually all industries. Though its membership is predominantly non-craft manual workers, it also has a large number of skilled workers and white-collar workers in membership. Since 1972, there has been a white collar section, the Managerial, Administrative, Technical and Supervisory Association (MATSA) which is an integral part of the GMWU but with separate branches and separate for industrial purposes. MATSA membership in 1978 was 72,000. The main concentration of GMWU membership is in the following industries:

    (a) Engineering and shipbuilding;
    (b) Local Government and the NHS;
    (c) Public utilities (gas, electricity, water);
    (d) Process industries (chemicals, rubber, glass);
    (e) Food and drink manufacturing;
    (f) Building materials industries;
    (g) Hotel and catering.

The union is party to 140 National Industrial Agreements and 16 Wages Councils.

The GMWU is divided into 10 regions. Since 1975, the union Executive Council has consisted of 20 lay members (two from each region) plus the General Secretary and the 10 Regional Secretaries, i.e. the senior full-time officers in each region. The supreme policy-making body of the union is the Annual Congress. There are also

Regional Councils which meet at least twice a year, and National and Regional Industrial Conferences, which cater for the different industrial groups of membership.
Current membership: 964,836
    Males: 638,484
    Female: 326,352

EXECUTIVE COUNCIL

Birmingham
J.C. Mason
(Regional Secretary)
R. Bull
N. Hough, JP

Lancashire
J.F. Eccles, JP
(Regional Secretary)
R. Pickering
J. Yates, JP

Liverpool
W.H. Alldritt, JP
(Regional Secretary)
S. Kelly
D. O'Donoghue, JP

London
H. Robertson, JP
(Regional Secretary)
W. Milne
H.H. Raveney

Midland – East Coast
C.A. Unwin, JP
(Regional Secretary)
H. Hickling, JP
S.R. Simpson

Northern
W. Rickelton, JP
(Regional Secretary)
R. Dickinson
K. Smith

Lancashire
J. Eccles
(Member of General Council of the Trades Union Congress)
36 Station Road,
Cheadle Hulme,
Cheadle,
Cheshire SK8 7AB

Liverpool and North Wales and Irish
W. Alldritt,
99 Edge Lane,
Liverpool L7 2PE

London
H. Robertson,
154 Brent Street,
London NW4 2DP

Midland and East Coast
C. Unwin,
542 Woodborough Road,
Nottingham NG3 5FJ

Northern
W. Rickelton,
77–78 West Road,
Newcastle upon Tyne NE15 6RB

Southern
D. Gladwin, OBE, JP
205 Hook Road,
Chessington,
Surrey KT9 1EP

South Western
I.G. Dunn,
17 Newport Road,
Cardiff CF2 1TB

Yorkshire and North Derbyshire
F. Booth
Concord House,
Park Lane,
Leeds LS3 1NB

Periodicals: *GMW Journal* (monthly), *GMW Herald* (quarterly)

GMWU — HOTEL AND CATERING WORKER'S UNION
Thorne House, Ruxley Ridge, Claygate, Esher, Surrey KT10 0TL
Tel: Esher 62081

This new union was formed on 14 February 1980 to look after the special needs of hotel workers. It was created by the General and Municipal Workers' Union as a separate section within their organisation.
Approximate Membership: 30,000

OFFICIAL
National Officer: F. Cooper

GENERAL UNION OF ASSOCIATIONS OF LOOM OVERLOOKERS

See LOOM OVERLOOKERS, GENERAL UNION OF ASSOCIATIONS OF

GOLD, SILVER AND ALLIED TRADES, NATIONAL UNION OF (NUGSAT)*
Kean Chambers, 11 Mappin Street, Sheffield SD1 4DT
Tel: Sheffield (0742) 21668

Founded in 1910 by a number of local trade unions. The union was originally known as the Amalgamated Society of Gold, Silver and Kindred Trades (1912). It adopted its present title in 1914 after amalgamation with the Birmingham Silversmiths and Electroplate Operatives. In 1969 the union absorbed the Society of Goldsmiths, Jewellers and Kindred Trades.
Current membership: 2,600

OFFICIAL
General Secretary: B.H. Bridge

Periodical: *Newsheet* (irregular)

GOVERNMENT SUPERVISORS AND RADIO OFFICERS, ASSOCIATION OF (AGSRO)*
90 Borough High Street, London SE1 1LL
Tel: 01–407 4866/7

Formed in 1955 by amalgamation between the Association of Government Foremen and Technical Staff and the Civil Service Radio Officers Association. The AGF and TS organised supervisory staff and the CSROA radio operating and maintenance staff in the Civil Service. Since the amalgamation AGSRO has expanded by

further amalgamations to cover Barrack Accountants and Station Wardens, the Technical Supervisors in Dockyards and the Electronic Technical Staff in the Civil Aviation Authority. Membership is located throughout the British Isles and at various stations abroad. All the membership is non-manual. The union is affiliated to the Staff Sides of the Civil Service National Whitley Council, Departmental Whitley Councils and Local Whitley Councils, and the equivalent bodies in the UKAEA and CAA.
Current membership: 12,259

FULL-TIME OFFICIALS
General Secretary: T. Casey
Deputy General Secretaries: D. Burns, A.L. Macpherson
Finance Officer: G.S. Petche

Periodical: *Monitor* (monthly)

Policy: As a union catering primarily for civil servants and staff in closely related organisations under the control of Ministers of the Crown, the union is strictly non-political and avoids any involvement which could be seen to be a party political issue as opposed to purely industrial matters.

GRAPHICAL AND ALLIED TRADES, SOCIETY OF (SOGAT)*
SOGAT House, 274–288 London Road, Hadleigh, Benfleet, Essex SS7 DE
Tel: Southend on Sea (0702) 553131/40

The union was formed in 1786 by an amalgamation of three bookbinding lodges in London and since then has extended to cover workers in general printing, newspapers (both national and provincial), bookbinding, paper and board making and the conversion of paper or board, polythene, polypropothene or other products such as fibreboard, cartons, multiwall sacks, rigid boxes, paper bags, paper boxes, plastic bags and boxes. The union has 123 branches many of which have full-time officers and officials. A Biennial Delegate Council is the governing body of the society and determines its policy. The most recent amalgamation has been with the Scottish Graphical Association. The society has an Art, Technical, Administrative and Sales Branch.
Current membership: 203,524 of which 34 per cent are female members.

GENERAL OFFICERS

		Head Office
General Secretary:	W.H. Keys	,,
General President:	A.E. Powell, JP	,,
Organising Secretary:	H. Finlay	,,
General Officer, Papermaking, Boardmaking, Conversion:	J. O'Leary	,,
General Officer:	H.W. Miles	.,,
Divisional Officers:	D. Sergeant	,,
	J.A.O. Pointing	,,
Financial Secretary:	D.G. Bartlett	,,
Divisional Officer:	F. Smith, JP	136 West Regent Street, Glasgow G2 2R2

ORGANISERS

Head Office
M.S. Dar
R.W. Finch
C.J. Phillips

L.G. Theobald
G. Beattie

London
R. Felton
A. Fowler
M. Bollands
M. Suckling
42 Doughty Street,
London WC1N 2LF

Edinburgh
W. Brown
R.W. Scott
39 Constitution Street,
Edinburgh EH6 7BG

Lancashire
K. Mallinson
828 Manchester Road,
Castleton,
Nr. Rochdale,
Lancashire OL11 3AW

Leicester
R.H. Martin,
Community House,
133 Loughborough Road,
Leicester LE4 5LX

Cambridge
G. Harrop
15/16 Trumpington Street,
Cambridge CB2 1QD

County Durham
J. Boyce,
2 Tubwell Row,
Darlington,
Co Durham DL1 1NU

Bristol
L.C. Stephen
Equity Law Building,
36/38 Baldwin Street,
Bristol BS1 1NR

Devon
L. Whittle
36 Longbrook Street,
Exeter,
Devon

Periodical: *SOGAT Journal* (monthly)

GRAPHICAL ASSOCIATION, NATIONAL (NGA)*

Graphic House, 63–67 Bromham Road, Bedford MK40 2AG
Tel: Bedford (0234) 51521

Formed in 1964 by an amalgamation between the former Typographical Association and the London Typographical Association, the NGA has grown since as a result of the transfers of the engagements of the Association of Correctors of the Press, National Society of Electrotypers and Stereotypers, National Union of Press Telegraphists and Amalgamated Society of Lithographic Printers. It therefore organises craft workers in the printing, publishing and packaging industry.

It has over 100,000 members of whom 89,666 are working as compositors, letterpress and lithographic printers, printers' readers, telecommunications and electronics workers, and stereotypers and electrotypers, White Collar workers and Members promoted to staff posts in the industry are entitled to join an Art, Technical, Clerical and Administration section of the union.

The democratic control of the union lies in the members organised in chapels in firms recognised as 'fair' by the NGA. Each chapel is related to one of 117 branches, about 38 of which have full-time secretaries and administrations. The branches are arranged in seven regions covering the whole of the United Kingdom and Ireland. Between Biennial Delegate Meetings the control of the union is vested in a 30-man National Council, the General Secretary, General President, Assistant General Secretary and seven National Officers. In 1979 terms were negotiated for a transfer of engagements with the

National Union of Wallcoverings, Decorative and Allied Trades which was successful and takes effect from 1 October 1979.
Current membership: 110,902 including 2,495 women

NATIONAL OFFICERS
General President: L.S. Dixon
General Secretary: J.F. Wade
Assistant General Secretary: A.D. Dubbins
Financial Secretary: C. James

National Officers:
R. Tomlins
G. Colling
F. Tanner
K. Haughton
J.A. Ibbotson
A. Pearson
J. Willats

NATIONAL COUNCIL
London
A.J. Bonner   J. Beck
C. Harding

South Eastern
D. Baker   J. Pinkerton
I. Cummings   P.C. Witham

Northern
K. Brindley   T. Pilling
E. Heald   R. Benson

Midland
R.H.L. Baldock   A. Bowater

South Western
J. Ralph   M.J. Holland

Ireland
W.L. Dunbar

Wales
J. Christopher

Scotland
D.L. Emmerson

Trade Group Board Representatives
Letterpress: Lithographic:
D. Baker   R. Pritchard
H. Crawley   J. Ellerton
J. Bolton   R.A. Meldrum
J. Bunn   C. Perrin

News:
C. Brindley
A. Berry
D. Truttero

REGIONAL SECRETARIES

Irish
W.R. Trulock,
29 Lower Abbey Street,
Dublin 1,
Eire
Tel: Dublin 746320

London
W.T. Booroff,
12/14 Theobalds Road,
London WC1X 8PF
Tel: 01-831 7291

Midland and North Wales
D. Chaplin,
Graphic House,
35-37 Albert Street,
Rugby CV21 2SG
Tel: Rugby (0788) 73418

Northern
J.B. Griffiths,
94 Chapel Road,
Sale,
Cheshire M33 1DX
Tel: 061-962 6939

Scottish
D.L. Emmerson,
74 York Street,
Glasgow G2 8JX
Tel: 041-221 3668

South-Eastern
R. Ireland,
Graphic House,
129 Southdown Road,
Harpenden,
Hertfordshire AL5 1PU
Tel: Harpenden (05827) 68282

South Western and South Wales
A.C.D. Webber,
Graphic House,
1 Bradenham Place,
Penarth,
Glamorgan CF6 2AG
Tel: Penarth (0222) 701544

BRANCH OFFICIALS
England and Wales
Aberystwyth (Machynlleth)
R. Hodgson (*PT*),
Isfryn,
Poplar Row,
Aberystwyth
Tel: (Works) Aberystwyth 615000

Accrington (Church, Clayton-le-
Moors, Darwen, Gt. Harwood, Has-
lingden, Oswaldtwistle, Rawtenstall,
Rishton)
G. Snowden (*PT*),
65 Westwood Street,
Accrington,
Lancashire
Tel: Accrington (0254) 393971

Andover (Over Wallop)
T.R. Town (*PT*),
9 Blendon Drive,
Andover,
Hampshire
Tel: Andover (0264) 2704

Ashton-under-Lyne (Droylsden,
Dukinfield, Mossley, Stalybridge)
A. Schofield (*PT*),
1 Buxton Way,
Haughton Green,
Denton,
Lancashire
Tel: 061-320 7532

Barnsley (Deepcar, Penistone)
D. Horbury (*PT*),
22 Spring Street,
Barnsley,
Tel: (Works) Barnsley (0226) 43131
Tel: (Home) Barnsley (0226) 85469

Birmingham
A. Jordan (*FT*),
9 William Street North,
Birmingham B19 3QH
Tel: 021-236 2963
or 021-236 9330

Bishop Auckland (Crook, Shildon, Spennymoor, Willington)
B. Henry (*PT*),
11 Bainbridge Avenue,
Willington,
Crook,
Co. Durham DL15 0AZ
Tel: (Works) Bishop Auckland (0388) 5727

Blackburn (Clitheroe)
J.K. Welch (*PT*),
63 Glendale Drive,
Mellor,
Blackburn,
Lancashire
Tel: Mellor (025 481) 2459

Boston (Skegness)
M. Flint (*PT*),
Plot 40 Camelot Gardens,
Fishtoft, Boston,
Lincolnshire
Tel: Boston (0205) 65161

Bournemouth (Blandford, Christchurch, New Milton, Parkstone, Poole, Ringwood, Swanage, Verwood, Wareham, Wimborne)
G.J. Brown (*FT*),
32 East Howe Lane,
East Howe,
Bournemouth BH10 5JE
Tel: Northbourne (020 16) 4826

Bradford (Cleckheaton, Otley, Pudsey, Shipley, Stanningley)
E. Routh (*FT*),
Textile Hall,
Westgate,
Bradford 1
Tel: Bradford (0274) 22878

Brecon (Llandrindod Wells)
G.G. Turner (*PT*),
14 Heolydwr,
Hay-on-Wye,
Via Hereford
Tel: (Works) Brecon (0874) 2932

Bristol (Clevedon, Midsomer Norton, Paulton, Radstock, Warmley, Wotton-under-Edge, Wrington)
T. Cleverley (*FT*),
Print House,
65 Baldwin Street,
Bristol BS1 1QZ
Tel: Bristol (0272) 23067

Burnley (Barnoldswick, Brierfield, Colne, Earby, Nelson, Padiham)
T. Machin (*PT*),
3 Basnett Street,
Burnley
Tel: Burnley (0282) 24234

Bury St. Edmunds
K.F. Freeman (*PT*),
12 Mere Close,
Great Barton,
Bury St. Edmunds
Tel: Great Barton (028 487) 428

Caernarvon (Amlwch, Bangor, Beaumaris, Criccieth, Holyhead, Llanerch-y-medd, Llanfairfechan, Llangefni, Port Dinorwic, Pwllheli)
J. Owen (*PT*),
Penrhyn Bach,
Llanrug,
Caernarvon
Tel: (Works) Caernarvon (0286) 2018

Carlisle
R. Johnston (*PT*),
10 Broad Street,
Carlisle
Tel: (0228) 30436

Penrith Section
M.J. Holder (*PT*),
45 Brougham Street,
Penrith

Central Southern (Battle, Bexhill, Brighton, Burgess Hill, Crawley, Dorking, Eastbourne, East Grinstead, Hailsham, Hastings, Haywards Heath, Heatherfield, Horley, Horsham, Hove, Hurstpierpoint, Lancing, Lewes, Newhaven, Peacehaven, Pevensey, Polegate, Portslade, Redhill, Reigate, Rye, Salfords, Seaford, Shoreham, Southwick, Steyning, Uckfield, Worthing)
N.C. Pearce (*FT*),
14–16 Sussex Road,
Haywards Heath,
Sussex
Tel: Haywards Heath (0444) 51607

Chester (Ellesmere Port, Mold, Northwich, Shotton, Winsford)
T.E. Jones (*PT*),
100 Philip Street,
Hoole,
Chester
Tel: Chester (0244) 46372

Chesterfield (Bakewell, Bolsover, Brimington, Clay Cross, Pilsley, Staveley Town)
W.A. Tagg (*PT*),
70 Highfield Lane,
Chesterfield
Tel: Chesterfield (0246) 78230

Chichester (Arundel, Bognor Regis, Littlehampton, Midhurst)
R.F. Harris (*PT*),
68 Orchard Side,
Hunston,
Chichester
Tel: Chichester (0243) 786091
Tel: (Works) (0243) 789942

Chiltern and Thames Valley (Ascot, Aylesbury, Beaconsfield, Buckingham, Burnham, Chalfont St. Peter, Chesham, High Wycombe, Langley, Maidenhead, Marlow, Princes Risborough, Slough, Tring, Uxbridge, West Drayton, Windsor)
T.J. Fowler (*FT*),
Graphic House,
The Broadway,
Farnham Common,
Slough,
Berkshire
Tel: Farnham Common (028 14) 2426

Colchester (Braintree, Brightlingsea, Clacton-on-Sea, Coggeshall, Dovercourt, Halstead, Rowhedge, Silver End, Sudbury, Tiptree, Witham, Wivenhoe)
P.L. Emeny (*FT*),
12 Headgate,
Colchester CO3 3BT
Tel: Colchester (0206) 47293

Conway & Vale of Clwyd (Blaenau Festiniog, Colwyn Bay, Llandudno, Llanrwst, Penmaenmawr, Prestatyn, Rhuddlan, Rhyl, St. Asaph)
M. Jones (*PT*),
52 St. George Drive,
Deganwy
Tel: (Works) Deganwy (0492) 84321, 81067

Coventry
W. Harvey (*PT*),
196 Earlsdon Avenue,
Coventry CV5 6GP
Tel: Coventry (0203) 76045

Darlington (Barnard Castle, Newton Aycliffe, Richmond)
T.W. Todd (*PT*),
28 Melsonby Crescent,
Darlington,
Co. Durham
Tel: Darlington (0325) 52049

Denbigh
D.H. Vaughan (*PT*),
10 Eldon Villas,
Beacon's Hill,
Denbigh LL16 3UA
Tel: (Works) Denbigh (0745 71) 2020
(Home) Denbigh (074–571) 4463

Devon and Somerset (Axminster, Barnstaple, Bideford, Bradninch, Braunton, Bridgwater, Burnham-on-Sea, Chard, Cheddar, Combe Martin, Crediton, Dawlish, Exeter, Exmouth, Glastonbury, Holsworthy, Honiton, Ilfracombe, Lyme Regis, Shepton Mallet, Sidmouth, South Molton, Street, Taunton, Teignmouth, Tiverton, Wellington, Wells, Weston-super-Mare, Williton)
L.J. Arnold (*FT*),
Graphic House,
16 Paul Street,
Taunton,
Somerset TA1 3PF
Tel: Taunton (0823) 71561

Doncaster (Epworth, Thorn)
R. Maguire (*PT*),
53 Melford Drive,
Balby,
Doncaster DN4 9AT
Tel: Doncaster (0302) 852580

Dunstable (Leighton Buzzard)
S. Bedwell (*PT*),
3 Garrett Close,
Dunstable LU6 2EG
Tel: Dunstable (0582) 603669

Durham (Birtley, Chester-le-Street, Consett)
J. Morgan (*PT*),
16 Moor Crescent,
Gilesgate Moor,
Durham
Tel: (Works) Durham (0385) 2542

Dyfed (Cardigan, Carmarthen, Gorseinon, Haverfordwest, Lampeter, Llandyssul, Llanelli, Narbeth, Pembroke Dock, Pontardulais, Tenby, Whitland)
T.H. Bearne (*PT*),
3 Ffynnon Drain,
Carmarthen,
Dyfed
Tel: Carmarthen (0267) 31396

Grays (Stanford-le-Hope, Tilbury, Upminster)
W.B. Butler (*PT*),
175 Hathaway Road,
Grays,
Essex
Tel: (Works) Grays Thurrock (0375) 4865

Grimsby
A. Taylor (*PT*),
64 Beverley Close,
Holton-le-Clay,
Lincolnshire DN36 5HG
Tel: (Works) (0472) 56158
(Home) 0472 823616

Harrogate (Boroughbridge, Ripon)
E.A. Green (*PT*),
6 St. John's Grove,
Harrogate
Tel: Harrogate (0423) 60790

Hartlepool
W. Henderson (*PT*),
117 Mowbray Road,
Fens Estate,
Hartlepool
Tel: Hartlepool (0429) 870992

Hull (Anlaby, Beverley, Brough, Catwick, Cottingham, Driffield, Dunswell, Ferriby, Howden, Roos, Scunthorpe),
L. Braithwaite (*FT*),
36 George Street,
Hull
Tel: Hull (0482) 23367

Ipswich (Diss, Halesworth, Leiston)
P.E. Smith (*PT*),
20 Ruskin Road,
Ipswich IP4 1PT
Tel: Ipswich (0473) 50083

Isle of Man (Douglas, Peel, Port Erin, Ramsey)
J.J. Cannell (*PT*),
3 Hibbin Way,
Anagh Coar,
Douglas,
Isle of Man
Tel: (Works) Douglas (0624) 3074

Isle of Thanet (Birchington, Broadstairs, Margate, Ramsgate, Westgate-on-Sea)
M.J. O'Neill (*PT*),
14 Farley Road,
Margate CT9 4EP
Tel: Thanet (0843) 22336

Jersey
T. McNally (*PT*),
Le Jardin du Mourin,
Maufant Village,
St. Martin,
Jersey,
Tel: Jersey (0534) 51031

Kent (Ashford, Borough Green, Canterbury, Chatham, Cranbrook, Crowborough, Deal, Dover, Faversham, Folkestone, Frindsbury, Gillingham, Gravesend, Greenhithe, Hawkhurst, Herne Bay, Hythe, Lower Stoke, Maidstone, Northfleet, Paddock Wood, Rainham, Rochester, Sevenoaks, Sheerness, Sittingbourne, Snodland, Southborough, Strood, Swanscombe, Tonbridge, Tunbridge Wells, Westerham, Whitstable)
R.C. Allen (*FT*),
Graphic House,
15 Albion Place,
Maidstone,
Kent
Tel: Maidstone (0622) 63988

Kidderminster (Bewdley, Stourport-on-Severn)
K. Whitehead (*PT*),
14 Malvern View,
Chaddesley Corbett,
Kidderminster
Tel: (Works) Kidderminster (0562) 2491

King's Langley
J. Herbert (*PT*),
133 Rucklers Lane,
King's Langley,
Hertfordshire
Tel: (Works) King's Langley (092
77) 62271

Lancashire and Lakes (Ambleside,
Barrow-in-Furness, Blackpool,
Carnforth, Chorley, Dalton,
Euxton, Garstang, Grange-over-
Sands, Heysham, Kendal, Lancas-
ter, Leyland, Millom, Morecambe,
Ormskirk, Preston, Sedbergh,
Southport, Ulverston, Windermere)
J.W. Waring (*FT*),
Graphic House,
18 Fox Street,
Preston PR1 2AB
Tel: Preston (0772) 52851

Lea Valley (Bishop's Stortford,
Epping, Harlow, Harpenden, Hert-
ford, Hoddesdon, Radlett, St.
Albans, Ware, Welwyn Garden
City)
G. Davies (*FT*),
Perpetua House,
Albion Road,
St. Albans,
Hertfordshire
Tel: St. Albans (0727) 56311

Leeds (Bramley, Castleford, Hors-
forth, Morley, Rothwell)
E. Heald (*FT*),
Graphic House,
3 Hanover Avenue,
Leeds LS3 1BG
Tel: Leeds (0532) 452813/4

Leicestershire (Anstey, Ashby-de-la-
Zouch, Coalville, Hinckley, Leices-
ter, Loughborough, Melton
Mowbray, Shepshed)
R. Upton (*FT*),
2 Newtown Street,
Leicester
Tel: Leicester (0533) 547076

Letchworth (Baldock, Hitchin, Ste-
venage, Stotfold)
S.R. Green (*PT*),
73 Marymead Drive,
Stevenage,
Hertfordshire
Tel: Stevenage (0438) 51091

Lincoln (Alford, Horncastle, Louth,
Mablethorpe, Market Rasen, Slea-
ford, Spalding, Spilsby)
S. Dufton (*PT*),
38 Uffington Avenue,
Harstholme,
Lincoln LN6 0AD
Tel: Lincoln (0522) 63781

Liverpool (Birkenhead, Bootle,
Great Crosby, Prescot, Runcorn, St.
Helens, Seaforth, Wallasey, Water-
loo, Widnes)
R. Williams (*FT*),
1st Floor, Graphic House,
107 Duke Street,
Liverpool L1 4JR
Tel: 051–708 8604

Manchester (Altrincham, Buxton,
Eccles, Hazel Grove, Pendlebury,
Pendleton, Reddish, Salford, Stret-
ford, Urmston)
A.S. Perrin (*FT*),
Graphic House,
Moseley Road,
Manchester M19 2LH
Tel: 061–248 6011

Mexborough (South Elmsall,
Swinton, Wath-upon-Dearne)
R. Charity (*PT*),
9 Kings Road,
Mexborough,
Yorkshire
Tel: Mexborough (070 988) 3400

Mid-Anglia (Burwell, Cambridge,
Cottenham, Downham Market, Ely,
Everard, Fordham, Foxton, God-
manchester, Haverhill, Huntingdon,
King's Lynn, Long Sutton, March,
Newmarket, Papworth, Peterbo-
rough, Royston, Saffron Walden, St.
Ives, Sawston, Soham, Sutton
Bridge, Hunstanton, Wisbech)
B.R. Harris(*FT*),
Graphic House,
Ferrars Road,
Huntingdon,
Cambridgeshire
Tel: Huntingdon (0480) 56384 or
55246

Mid-Counties (Ampthill, Aspley Guise, Bedford, Bletchley, Kettering, Luton, New Bradwell, Newport Pagnell, Northampton, Olney, Rushden, Stony Stratford, Thrapston, Towcester, Wellingborough, Wolverton)
J.W. Butler (*FT*),
67 Harpur Street,
Bedford
Tel: Bedford (0234) 50389 or 211064

Middlesbrough (Carlin How, Guisborough, Loftus-in-Cleveland, Marske-by-the-Sea, Redcar, Saltburn-by-the-Sea, South Bank, Stokesley)
F.H.A. Munro,
34 Brompton Street,
Linthorpe,
Middlesbrough,
Tel: (Home) Middlesbrough (0642) 85100
(Works) Middlesbrough (0642) 45401

Mid-Shropshire (Ludlow, Market Drayton, Shrewsbury, Wellington, Whitchurch)
P.E. Wynn (*PT*),
176 Conway Drive,
Telford Estate,
Shrewsbury,
Salop
Tel: Shrewsbury (0743) 61863
(Works) Telford (0952) 44377 Extn 236

Newcastle (Alnwick, Ashington, Bedlington, Blaydon, Felling, Gateshead, Hebburn, Hexham, Jarrow, Killingworth, Morpeth, North Shields, Pelaw, South Shields, Swalwell, Whitley Bay, Wallsend)
A. Turner (*FT*),
Carliol Square,
Newcastle upon Tyne NE1 6UQ
Tel: Newcastle (0632) 27745

Newton-le-Willows (Ashton-in-Makerfield, Earlestown, Golborne, Newton-in-Makerfield)
L. Jones (*PT*),
1 Conway Drive,
Newton-le-Willows,
Merseyside
Tel: Newton-le-Willows (092 52) 6955

Newtown (Llanidloes, Welshpool)
W.K. Parkes (*PT*),
11 Oldford Rise,
Welshpool,
Powys
Tel: (Works) Welshpool (0938) 2260
(Home) Welshpool (0938) 2594

Northallerton (Bedale)
T. Oxendale (*PT*),
3 Cherry Garth Road,
Romanby,
Northallerton
Tel: (Works) Northallerton (0609) 3131, Ext. 214

Norwich (Attleborough, Aylsham, Cromer, Dereham, Fakenham, Great Yarmouth, Holt, Hunstanton, North Walsham, Thetford, Wells, Wymondham)
B. Holmes (*FT*), Watton
Graphic House,
120 Thorpe Road,
Norwich NR1 1RT
Tel: Norwich (0603) 24733

Nuneaton (Atherstone)
C.J. Robinson (*PT*),
73 St. Nicholas Park Drive,
Nuneaton
Tel: (Works) Nuneaton (0682) 382251

Oswestry (Ellesmere)
I. Parry (*PT*),
Craig Wen,
Rock Lane,
Cefn Mawr,
Wrexham,
Clwyd
Tel: Ruabon (097 881) 7438

Oxfordshire and Berkshire (Abingdon, Banbury, Basingstoke, Bicester, Brackley, Bracknell, Chipping Norton, Henley, Newbury, Oxford, Reading, Thame, Wallingford, Witney, Wokingham)
E.W. Corner (*FT*),
Graphic House,
Horseshoe Road,
Pangbourne,
Reading,
Berkshire
Tel: Pangbourne (073 57) 2201

Rugby (Daventry)
K.S. Sweetman (*PT*),
21 Bath Street,
Rugby,
Warwickshire
Tel: Rugby (0788) 4204

Salisbury (Shaftesbury)
H.D. Scott (*PT*),
1 Bungalow Flats,
Church Lane,
Amesbury,
Wiltshire
Tel: Amesbury (098 02) 3174
(Works) Salisbury (0722) 4261

Scarborough (Bridlington, Filey,
Pickering, Whitby)
E. Pickering (*PT*),
20 Newlands Park Grove,
Scarborough,
Yorkshire
Tel: Scarborough (0723) 60196

Sheffield (Dronfield, Ecclesfield,
Rotherham)
B.P. Smith (*FT*),
30 Rockingham Lane,
Sheffield S1 4FW
Tel: Sheffield (0742) 25232

Sherwood Forest (Brigg, Eastwood,
Gainsborough, Grantham,
Hucknall, Ilkeston, Long Eaton,
Mansfield, Newark, Nottingham,
Retford, Stapleford, Sutton-in-
Ashfield, Worksop)
T.G. Brady (*FT*),
Ground Floor,
36 The Ropewalk,
Nottingham
Tel: Nottingham (0602) 47724

Solent (Cowes, Eastleigh,
Emsworth, Fareham, Gosport,
Havant, Hayling Island, Isle of
Wight, Newport, Petersfield,
Portsmouth, Romsey, Ryde,
Sandown, Shanklin, Southampton,
Ventnor, Winchester)
S.G. Johns (*FT*),
Graphic House,
Castle Street,
Portchester,
Hampshire
Tel: Cosham (0705) 382931

South Essex (Basildon, Benfleet,
Billericay, Brentwood, Canvey,
Chelmsford, Eastwood, Hadleigh,
Hockley, Leigh, Maldon, Rayleigh,
Rochford, Shoebury, Southend-on-
Sea, Thundersley, Wakering,
Westcliff, Wickford)
R. Tottle (*FT*),
Graphic House,
152–154 High Street,
Rayleigh,
Essex SS6 7DA
Tel: Rayleigh (0268) 773377

South Wales (Abercynon, Aberdare,
Abergavenny, Abersychan,
Abertillery, Ammanford, Bargoed,
Barry, Bridgend, Brynmawr,
Caerphilly, Cardigan, Cardiff,
Chepstow, Cowbridge, Crickhowell,
Cwmbran, Ebbw Vale, Gorseinon,
Haverford-West, Kenfig, Lampeter,
Llandeilo, Llandyssul, Llanelli,
Maesteg, Merthyr Tydfil, Mountain
Ash, Narbeth, Neath, Newbridge,
Newport, Panteg, Pembroke Dock,
Penarth, Pontardulais, Pontllan-
fraith, Pontypool, Pontypridd, Port
Talbot, Rhondda Valleys, Risca,
Swansea, Tenby, Tredegar,
Whitland, Ystalyfera)
K.J. Smith (*FT*),
Graphic House,
1 Bradenham Place,
Penarth,
Glamorgan
Tel: Penarth (0222) 703539

South West Peninsula (Bodmin,
Bugle, Camborne, Falmouth,
Helston, Kingsbridge, Launceston,
Lelant, Liskeard, Newquay,
Padstow, Penryn, Penzance,
Plymouth, Redruth, Saltash, South
Brent, St. Austell, St. Blazey, St.
Ives, Tavistock, Torpoint, Truro,
Wadebridge)
N.D.A. Crowley (*FT*),
Graphic House,
72 Mutley Plain,
Plymouth PL4 6LF
Tel: Plymouth (0752) 266577

Stamford (Bourne, Oakham, Uppingham)
E.D. Armstrong *(PT)*,
10 Poplar Crescent,
Bourne,
Lincolnshire PE10 9SA
Tel: (Home) Bourne 3760

Stockport (Alderley Edge, Bredbury, Chapel-en-le-Frith, Cheadle, Cheadle Heath, Cheadle Hulme, Denton, Glossop, Hadfield, Hazel Grove, Heaton Mersey, Heaton Moor, Heaton Norris, Hollingworth, Hyde, Marple, Mottram, New Mills, Offerton, Reddish, Whaley Bridge, Wilmslow, Woodley)
A.T. Scott *(PT)*,
6 Layton Close,
Hawfield Gardens,
Offerton,
Stockport,
Cheshire SK1 4EE
Tel: 061–480 9337

Stockton (Billingham, Thornaby)
D. Gray *(PT)*,
46 Ashton Road,
Norton,
Stockton-on-Tees,
Cleveland
Tel: Stockton-on-Tees (0642) 552833

Stratford-upon-Avon
D. Chaplin (Pro Tem) *(FT)*,
Graphic House,
35–37 Albert Street,
Rugby,
Tel: Rugby (0788) 73418

Sunderland (Easington, Hetton-le-Hole, Houghton-le-Spring, Seaham Harbour, Southwick, Washington)
C. Collinson *(PT)*,
34 Beaumaris,
Bourn Moor,
Co. Durham
Tel: Fence Houses 3445

Three Shires (Bromyard, Cheltenham, Cinderford, Cirencester, Coleford, Droitwich, Dursley, Evesham, Gloucester, Hereford, Ledbury, Leominster, Lydney, Malvern, Moreton-in-Marsh, Newham, Northleach, Pershore, Ross-on-Wye, Stroud, Tewkesbury, Upton-on-Severn, Winchcombe, Worcester)
B.G.W. Gay *(FT)*,
Graphic House,
Greyfriars,
Gloucester GL1 1TS
Tel: Gloucester (0452) 32813

Torbay and District Graphical Society–NGA (Bovey Tracey, Brixham, Dartmouth, Newton Abbott, Paignton, Torquay, Totnes)
J. Fradley *(PT)*,
15 Old Torquay Road,
Preston,
Paignton,
Devon
Tel: Paignton (0803) 522092

Trent and Derwent (Alfreton, Belper, Biddulph, Bollington, Burslem, Burton-on-Trent, Cannock, Castle Donnington, Cobridge, Congleton, Crewe, Derby, Eccleshall, Gresley, Hanley, Heanor, Hednesford, Leek, Longton, Macclesfield, Matlock, Newcastle-under-Lyme, Rugeley, Stafford, Stoke-on-Trent, Stone, Swadlincote, Tunstall, Tutbury, Uttoxeter, Wirksworth)
J.E. Ellerton *(FT)*,
Graphic House,
124 City Road,
Stoke-on-Trent ST4 2PH
Tel: Stoke-on-Trent (0782) 44246/7

Warrington (Cadishead, Irlam, Knutsford, Risley)
L. Harding *(PT)*,
19 Elizabeth Road,
Partington,
Urmston,
Manchester M31 4PU
Tel: 061–775 9812

Warwick and Leamington
(Kenilworth, Leamington Spa,
Shipston-on-Stour, Southam)
J. Prior (*PT*),
68 Greatheed Road,
Leamington Spa CV31 2LG
Tel: Leamington Spa (0926) 30160

Watford (Berkhamsted, Hemel
Hempstead)
A.L. Robinson (*FT*),
11 Station Road,
Watford WD1 1RR
Hertfordshire
Tel: Watford (0923) 23505 or 42695

Waveney Towns (Beccles, Bungay,
Lowestoft, Southwold)
D. Gladwell (*FT*),
6B Smallgate,
Beccles,
Suffolk NR34 9AD
Tel: Beccles (0502) 713141

Wessex (Bath, Devizes, Frome,
Swindon, Trowbridge)
G.R. Robinson (*FT*),
7 Church Walk,
Trowbridge,
Wiltshire
Tel: Trowbridge (022 14) 61010

West Midlands (Bewdley, Bilston,
Blackheath, Bridgnorth, Brierley
Hill, Bromsgrove, Cradley Heath,
Darlaston, Dudley, Gornal,
Halesowen, Kidderminster,
Lichfield, Lye, Oldbury, Old Hill,
Redditch, Sedgeley, Smethwick,
Stourbridge, Stourport-on-Severn,
Tamworth, Tipton, Walsall, Wed-
nesbury, West Bromwich, Willen-
hall, Wolverhampton)
T.E. Lowe (*FT*),
Graphic House,
15–18 New Road,
Willenhall,
West Midlands WV13 2BG
Tel: Willenhall (0902) 62706

West Pennine (Atherton, Bacup,
Bamfurlong, Bolton, Bury,
Castleton, Chadderton, Failsworth,
Farnworth, Greenfield, Heywood,
Hindley, Hollinwood, Horwich,
Ince, Lees, Leigh, Littleborough,
Middleton, Newhey, Oldham,
Plattbridge, Prestwich, Radcliffe,
Ramsbottom, Rochdale, Royton,
Shaw, Skelmersdale, Tyldesley,
Uppermill, Walkden, Waterfoot,
Westhoughton, Whitefield, Wigan)
N. Taylor (*FT*),
Graphic House,
3 The Rock,
Bury BL9 0JP
Tel: 061–764 9670

West Yorkshire (Batley, Bingley,
Birstall, Bradley, Brighouse, Colne
Valley, Crosshills, Dewsbury,
Elland, Featherstone, Gargrave,
Halifax, Haworth, Heckmondwike,
Holmfirth, Horbury, Huddersfield,
Innfield, Keighley, Liversedge,
Luddenden Foot, Meltham, Ossett,
Pontefract, Ravensthorpe, Scissett,
Silsdan, Skipton, Slaithwaite,
Sowerby Bridge, Stainland,
Todmorden, Wakefield)
P. Cooke (*FT*),
Graphic House,
4–6 Silver Street,
Halifax HX1 1HS
Tel: Halifax (0422) 56432

Weymouth (Dorchester)
R. Genge (*PT*),
73 Newstead Road,
Weymouth,
Dorset DT4 0AS
Tel: (Home) Weymouth (03057)
76060
(Works) Weymouth (03057) 4804
Extn 1

Wey Valley (Addlestone, Aldershot, Ashford, Byfleet, Camberley, Chertsey, Cobham, Esher, Farnborough, Farnham, Godalming, Guildford, Haslemere, Mychett, Odiham, Staines, Sunbury-on-Thames, Tongham, Walton-on-Thames, Weybridge, Woking)
H.W. Goddard (*FT*),
Graphic House,
1 Hermitage Road,
St. Johns,
Woking,
Surrey
Tel: Woking (048 62) 69629

Whitehaven (Cleator Moor, Egremont, Salterbeck)
A.L. Stephenson (*PT*),
81 Calder Avenue,
Corkickle,
Whitehaven,
Cumberland CA28 8AT
Tel: Whitehaven (0946) 4862

Wombwell
B. Dawson (*PT*),
11 Rectory Close,
Wombwell,
Barnsley,
South Yorkshire
Tel: (Works) Barnsley (0226) 753167
(Home) Barnsley (0226) 756930

Workington (Cockermouth, Harrington, Maryport)
J.W. Relph (*PT*),
1 Nairn Street,
Flimby,
Maryport,
Cumbria
Tel: (Works) Workington (0900) 2454 Extn 8

Wrexham (Cefn Mawr, Coedpoeth, Corwen, Llangollen, Rhos, Ruthin)
R. Lube
43 Maes Pengwern,
Llangollen
Tel: Wrexham 758392
(Works) (0978) 860316

Dolgelley Section:
J.H. Evans,
Solva,
Pondyrodyn,
Dolgellau,
Merionethshire

Yeovil (Castle Cary, Shaftesbury, Sherborne, Wincanton)
R.F. Boulton (*PT*),
52 Rivers Road,
Yeovil,
Somerset
Tel: Yeovil (0935) 24765

York (Malton, Pocklington, Selby, Tadcaster)
W.E. Hoggard (*PT*),
152 Albemarle Road,
York
Tel: York (0904) 53260

Ireland
All Part Time Administration
Except N. Ireland Graphical Society

Athlone (Ballinasloe, Edenderry, Roscommon, Tullamore)
J. McGonigle,
9 Wolfe Tone Terrace,
Athlone,
Co. Westmeath,
Eire

Longford Section:
H. Farrall,
Majella,
Park Road,
Longford,
Ireland

Mullingar Section:
M. Neary,
Rathdrishogue,
Castledown-Geo,
Co. Westmeath,
Eire

Bray and Wicklow
M. Carroll,
24 Killarney Park,
Bray,
Co. Wicklow,
Eire
Tel: Bray (Works) 862997/8

Carlow
M. O'Sullivan,
33 St. Kilhans Crescent,
Carlow,
Eire

L

Clonmel (Cashel, Carrick-on-Suir)
M. Cussen,
33 Kickham Street,
Thurles,
Co. Tipperary,
Eire

Thurles Section:
C. Keogh,
13 Silver Street,
Nenagh,
Eire

Tipperary Section:
J. Lyons,
13 Lacey Villas,
Tipperary

Cork
F. Lynch,
12 Frankfield Villas,
Windmill Road,
Cork,
Eire
Tel: (Works) Cork 26661

Skibbereen Section:
Father of Chapel,
Star Office

Drogheda
D. Gargan,
3 Lourdes Square,
Drogheda,
Co. Louth,
Eire

Dublin
N.S. Broughall,
29 Lower Abbey Street,
Dublin 1,
Eire
Tel: Dublin 747241

Dundalk
B. McKeever,
46 Seatown,
Dundalk,
Eire
Tel: Irish Republic All-Figure
Number (042) 32112

Galway
M. Geary,
10 St. Joseph's Avenue,
Galway,
Eire

Kilkenny
M. Brett,
80 High Street,
Kilkenny,
Eire

Limerick
C. Power,
9 Laurel Court,
Caherdavin Lawn,
Limerick,
Eire

Birr Section:
F. McGilten,
8 Cappaneale,
Birr,
Co. Offaly

Ennis Section:
A. Butler,
16 Gallows Hill,
Ennis,
Co. Clare

Nenagh Section:
M. Moylan,
Farnamurry,
Tyone,
Nenagh,
Co. Tipperary

Charleville Section:
J. O'Donoghue,
Ballysally,
Charleville,
Co. Cork

Naas
P. O'Reilly (Pro Tem),
'Balboy House',
Connolly Crescent,
Naas,
Co. Kildare,
Eire

Celbridge Section:
L. Byrne,
Loughlinstown,
Celbridge,
Co. Kildare

Portlaoise Section:
N.S. Finnegan,
c/o *Leinster Express*,
Portlaoise

Sligo
P. Shannon,
Station Road,
Boyle,
Co. Roscommon,
Eire

Ballina Section:
H. Lynch,
The Brook,
Ardnaree,
Ballina,
Eire

Ballyshannon Section:
J. Cassidy,
c/o *Democrat Office*,
Ballyshannon,
Co. Donegal,
Eire

Boyle Section:
P. Shannon,
Station Road,
Boyle,
Co. Roscommon

Carrick-on-Shannon Section:
S. Stanford,
30 St. Patrick's Park,
Carrick-on-Shannon,
Co. Leitrim,
Eire

Castlebar Section:
T. Burke,
Moonden,
Castlebar

Westport Section:
T. Slevin,
c/o *Mayo News*,
James Street,
Westport,
Co. Mayo

Tralee and Killarney
M.J. Fitzgerald,
3 O'Connor's Terrace,
Tralee,
Co. Kerry,
Eire
Tel: (Works) Tralee 21666 or 22816

Waterford (Dungarvan)
S. Casey,
42 Richardson's Folly,
Waterford,
Eire

Wexford (New Ross)
J.G. O'Flaherty,
37 McDermott Street,
Wexford,
Eire

Enniscorthy Section:
M. Nolan,
18 John Street,
Enniscorthy,
Co. Wexford,
Eire

Scotland
Aberdeen
T.M. Kemp(*PT*),
217 Cairncry Road,
Aberdeen
Tel: Aberdeen (0224) 40827

Edinburgh
H.T. Clark (*PT*),
12 Picardy Place,
Edinburgh EH1 3JT
Tel: 031-556 4114

Glasgow
D.L. Emmerson (*FT*),
74 York Street,
Glasgow G2 8JX
Tel: 041-221 3668

Periodical: *Print* (monthly)

GREATER LONDON COUNCIL STAFF ASSOCIATION (GLCSA)*

150 Waterloo Road, London SE1 8SD
Tel: 01–633 5927

Constituted on 14 May 1909 as the London County Council Staff Association. The majority of its members work for the Greater London Council and Inner London Education Authority, although substantial numbers are also employed by the Thames Water Authority, the five Inner London Polytechnics, the London Ambulance Service and the Outer London Probation and After Care Committees. The membership includes staff in the administrative, professional, technical, executive and clerical grades and some 500 analogous grades, including schoolkeepers and laboratory technicians.

Because the bulk of its members are employed within the Greater London area, the Association is able to maintain a committee system which provides excellent communication with grass roots membership. The General Committee (the Association's governing body) is elected annually on a departmental and grade basis providing one representative for each 40 members. The General Committee normally meets monthly. Other main committees, e.g. the Executive and Service Conditions Committees, meet more frequently as required. The areas of industry covered are principally local government, education and water, although within these spheres many disciplines are encompassed, including architecture, planning, mechanical, electrical and public health engineering, housing, recreation and law. GLCSA affiliates to the National Federation of Professional Workers.

Current membership: 17,186 (approximately 60% male and 40% female)

OFFICIALS
President: Harry Luxton,
GLC Housing Department,
D.O. 22,
Homer Road,
London E9

Secretary: F.T. Hollocks
Deputy Secretary: A. Capelin
Assistant Secretaries: D. Small, P. Seares, Miss A. Robertson, Mrs J. Caley, F. Ladd

Secretariat officials are appointed.

Periodical: *London Town* (monthly)

Policy: The objects of the Association are to improve the conditions and protect the interests of the Association's members; to regulate the relations between such members and their employers; to promote the efficiency of the Council's staff; to secure thrift and benevolent facilities; and to do all such other lawful things as are conducive to the attainment of the aforementioned objects.

HEAD TEACHERS, NATIONAL ASSOCIATION OF
Holly House, 6 Paddockhall Road, Haywards Heath, West Sussex RH16 1RG
Tel: Haywards Heath (0444) 53291/2

Founded in 1897 when representatives of a number of Head Teacher Associations already in existence in some of the larger cities met and discussed the value of forming a Federation. Today the union embraces 377 Local Associations and County Federations of Head Teachers. A particular feature of the NAHT is that each of its Local Associations consists of Head Teachers of schools of all types in the area served by the Local Association, e.g. nursery, infant, junior, secondary (of all types) and special.

The majority of members are Head Teachers of schools in the maintained sector, although Heads of independent schools are eligible for membership and are members of many Local Associations.

Full membership of the NAHT is open to –

1. Head Teachers of schools and Principals of other educational establishments.
2. Peripatetic Head Teachers holding definite appointments as such.
3. Former Head Teachers rendered redundant by reorganisation.
4. Temporary or Acting Head Teachers who are appointed for a period of at least twelve months. In such cases membership will last for the period of the employment.
5. Former Head teachers who have become Heads of other educational establishments (e.g. Community Centres, Teachers' Centres) who may, at the discretion of the NAHT's National Council, be permitted to retain full membership.

The National Council is the Executive Committee of the NAHT and comprises 30 elected members representing the 30 districts which cover the country.

The Association is represented on the Burnham Committee, which regulates teachers' salaries, and on the Schools Council, which deals with matters relating to schools' curricula and examinations. It is also represented on every major national body concerned with education matters.

Current membership: 20,400

FULL-TIME OFFICIALS
General Secretary/Association's Solicitor: D.M. Hart
Deputy General Secretary: D.W. Foster, DFM, DipEd, DipPsychEd
Senior Assistant Secretary: C.P. Hayes
Assistant Secretary: Mrs P.M. Sharpe, BA(Hons),DipEd
Assistant Secretary: P.R. Hellyer, DMA

Officers (1979/80)
President: F.G. Grimshaw, BA
Vice-President: M.H. Brighouse
Ex-President: M.J. Cammish, BSc
Hon. Treasurer: A. Pendlebury-Green, TD

COUNCIL (1979–80)
(Date of election in brackets)

District 1A Northumerland, Tyne and Wear MDs
K.J. Dyos, BSc(Hons), MSc, ARCS, MRI, JP (1975)

Hylton Red House School,
Rutherglen Road,
Sunderland SR5 5LN
Tel: Sunderland (0783) 481054

2 Roker Park Terrace,
Sunderland SR6 9LY
Tel: Sunderland (0783) 57012

District 1B Durham, Cleveland
D. Blenkinsopp (1972),

Coundon JM School,
Victoria Lane,
Coundon,
Bishop Auckland
Tel: Bishop Auckland (0388) 5396

24 Lambton Drive,
Bishop Auckland,
Co. Durham DL14 6LG
Tel: Bishop Auckland (0388) 603298

District 2A Cheshire, Stockport MD
P.W. Batts (1979)

Ryles Park Co High School,
Ryles Park Road,
Macclesfield,
Cheshire SK11 8AJ
Tel: 0625 29621

28 Ryles Park Road,
Macclesfield,
Cheshire SK11 8RH

District 2B Merseyside MDs and West Lancs District, Isle of Man, Northern Ireland
H.P. Eckersley, BA, DipEd (1974)

Christ the King RC Comp S
Stamford Road,
Birkdale, Southport
Merseyside PR8 4EK
Tel: Southport 65121 or 87024

32 Osborne Road,
Ainsdale,
Southport,
Merseyside
Tel: Southport 78855

District 2C MDs of Bolton, Bury, Manchester, Salford, Trafford, Wigan, plus Blackburn District (Lancashire)
H.L. Hough (1975)

Hilton Lane CP School,
Madam's Wood Road,
Little Hulton,
Worsley
Manchester M28 6JY
Tel: 061–790 4357

123 Church Road,
Urmston,
Manchester M31 1ET
Tel: 061–748 6959

218

District 2D MDs of Oldham, Rochdale, Tameside, plus Burnley, Hyndburn,
Pendle, Ribble Valley and Rossendale Districts of Lancashire
F.G. Grimshaw, BA (1972) (President)

The Heys CP School,   38 Lindale Avenue,
Herries Street,   Royton,
Ashton-under-Lyne   Oldham,
Lancashire OL6 9PL   Lancashire OL2 6UU
Tel: 061–330 1847   Tel: 061–633 4678

District 2E Cumbria plus Blackpool, Chorley, Fylde, Lancaster, Preston, South
Ribble and Wyre Districts of Lancashire
M.A. Turner, MA (1978)

Dowdales School,   'Craighurst',
Dalton-in-Furness,   Low Stott Park,
Cumbria LA15 8AH   Newby Bridge,
Tel: 0229 62535   Nr. Ulverston, Cumbria
                         Tel: Newby Bridge
                         (044–83) 406

District 3A MDs of Bradford, Calderdale, Kirklees and Leeds, plus Harrogate
and Skipton Districts of North Yorkshire
J.H. Rex, BA (1978)

Halton Middle School,   52 Moor Grange View,
Templegate Walk,   West Park,
Leeds LS15 0EU   Leeds LS16 5BJ
Tel: 0532 606203   Tel: 0532 759589

District 3B MDs of Barnsley, Doncaster, Rotherham, Sheffield and Wakefield
J. Holmes (1978)

Hallam Middle School   393 Manchester Road,
Hallam Grange Crescent,   Sheffield S10 6DS
Sheffield S10 4BD   Tel: Sheffield (0742) 685044
Tel: Sheffield (0742) 305287

District 3C East Riding and Hull Districts of Humberside plus Northallerton,
Scarborough and York Districts of North Yorkshire
P.L. Scudamore, BSc (1979)

South Holderness School,   7 Alison Garth,
Preston, Hull   Hedon,
North Humberside   Kingston upon Hull
HU12 8UZ   HU12 8LW
Tel: 0482 899315   Tel: 0482 896171

District 4A Mid, South and West Glamorgans, Dyfed and Gwent
I. Williams (1969)

Pennard Primary School,   3 Tir-mynydd,
Pennard Gower,   Three Crosses,
Swansea,   Swansea,
Glamorgan   Glamorgan
Tel: Bishopston (044 128) 3343 Tel: Swansea (0792) 87–2290

District 4B Clwyd, Gwynedd and Powys
D.L. Phillips, BA (1975)

Frongoch Junior School,   Bryn Collen,
Denbigh,   68 Vale Street,
Clwyd LL16 3UU   Denbigh,
Tel: Denbigh (074571) 2410   Clwyd LL16 3BW
                         Tel: Denbigh (074571) 2375

District 5A Hereford and Worcester, Birmingham and Dudley MDs
Mrs. V.J. Leeke (1978)

Four Dwellings
Junior School,
Quinton Road West,
Quinton,
Birmingham B32 1PJ
Tel: 021-422 3351

120 Northfield Road,
Kings Norton,
Birmingham B30 1DX
Tel: 021-458 3738

District 5B Leicestershire, Northamptonshire, Warwickshire and Coventry and Solihull MDs
J.H. Halsall (1977)

The Parkland Cty Jun School,
St Thomas' Road,
South Wigston,
Leicester LE8 2TA
Tel: Leicester (0533) 782142

62 Main Street,
Queniborough,
Leicester LE7 8DA
Tel: Leicester (0533) 605506

District 5C Salop, Staffordshire and MDs of Sandwell, Walsall and Wolverhampton
D.M. Wilkinson, BA (1972)

Wolgarston High School,
Cannock Road,
Penkridge,
Stafford ST19 5RX
Tel: Penkridge (078 571) 2466

20 Princefield Avenue,
Penkridge,
Stafford ST19 5HG
Tel: Penkridge (078 571) 2068

District 6A Humberside (Scunthorpe and Grimsby Districts), Lincolnshire
J.A. Teall (1979)

Crosby Junior School,
Fordingham Road,
Scunthorpe,
South Humberside DN15 7NL
Tel: 0724 844216

13 Jacklins Approach,
Scunthorpe,
South Humberside DN16 3PF
Tel: 0724 65265

District 6B Derbyshire, Nottinghamshire
K.W. Blockley, (1977)

Sawley County Jun School,
Wilmot Street,
Sawley, Long Eaton,
Nottingham NG10 3DQ
Tel: 060 76 3626

Derwent Ridge,
Bullhurst Lane,
Weston Underwood,
Derby DE6 4PA
Tel: 033 528 561

District 7A Cambridgeshire, Norfolk, Suffolk
M.H. Brighouse (1972) (Vice-President)

Great Heath CP School,
St John's Close,
Mildenhall,
Suffolk IP28 7NX
Tel: 0638 713430

'Hornbeams'
Santon Downham,
Brandon,
Suffolk IP27 0TG
Tel: 0842 810610

District 7B Bedfordshire, Hertfordshire and London Boroughs of Barnet,
Enfield, Haringey and Waltham Forest
F.C. Mills, DipLit(London) (1965) (P)

Marshalswick Sec School,	20 Gilpin Green,
The Ridgeway,	Harpenden,
St. Albans,	Hertfordshire
Hertfordshire	
Tel: 0727 51780	

District 7C Essex and London Boroughs of Newham and Redbridge
J.P. Swallow, BA (1975)

Ongar Comp School,	37 Malford Grove,
Fyfield Road,	Woodford,
Ongar,	London E18 2DX
Essex CM5 0AW	Tel: 01–530 5445
Tel: Ongar (02776) 3232	

District 8 Inner London (2 Members)
Mrs M. Bright-Thomas (1966) (N of Thames)

Orchard Infants School	33 Lower Kenwood Avenue,
Holcroft Road,	Enfield,
London E9 7BB	Middlesex EN2 7LT
Tel: 01–985 7785	Tel: 01–366 0689

Mrs M. Broadley, FTC, LGSM (1975) (S of Thames)

Dick Sheppard School,	6 Maple Close,
Tulse Hill,	Clarence Avenue
London SW2 2QA	London SW4 8LL
Tel: 01–674 9421	Tel: 01–674 2200

District 9A Buckinghamshire, Oxfordshire and London Boroughs of Brent,
Ealing, Harrow, Hillingdon, Hounslow and Richmond
D.C. Best, MA (1976)

Vyners School,	33 Birchmead Avenue,
Warren Road,	Pinner,
Ickenham,	Middlesex HA5 2BQ
Middlesex HB10 8AB	Tel: 01–866 6584
Tel: Uxbridge (0895) 53554	

District 9B Berkshire, Surrey and London Boroughs of Croydon, Kingston,
Merton and Sutton
T.C.J. Cunningham, FTCL, ACP
(1979)

Devonshire School.	148 Northey Avenue.
Devonshire Avenue,	Cheam,
Sutton,	Surrey SM2 7HF
Surrey	Tel: 01–643 1187
Tel: 01–643 1174	

District 10A Kent and London Boroughs of Barking, Bexley, Bromley and
Havering
G.G. Peiser, BA (1977)

The Wilderness School,	140 Lancing Road,
Seal Hollow Road,	Orpington
Sevenoaks,	Kent BR6 0QZ
Kent TN13 3SN	Tel: 0689 24165
Tel: Sevenoaks (0732) 54617	

L

District 10B East and West Sussex
A.S. Robinson (1973)
West Hove Middle School,   41 Meadway Crescent,
Portland Road,   Hove,
Hove, Sussex   Sussex BN3 7NJ
Tel: Brighton (0273) 733415   Tel; Brighton (0273) 776368

District 10C Guernsey CI, Hampshire, Isle of Wight, Jersey CI
E. Jeffares (1971)
Greenfields Junior School,   Tara,
Green Lane,   31 Vicarage Road,
Hartney Wintney,   Alton,
Basingstoke,   Hampshire GU34 1NZ
Hampshire RG27 8DQ   Tel: Alton (0420) 85069
Tel: 025126 3822

District 11A Avon, Gloucestershire, Somerset
Mrs S.A. Laver (1975)
Enmore VCP School,   Rivers End
Enmore,   Allandale Road,
Bridgwater,   Burnham-on-Sea,
Somerset TA5 2DX   Somerset TA8 2HG
Tel: Spaxton (027 867) 370   Tel: Burnham (0278) 787313

District 11B Dorset, Wiltshire
A.D. Bott, BA (1975)
Walcot Sec School,   Little Court,
Sadler Walk, Swindon,   23 Manor Close,
Wiltshire SN3 3AQ   Shrivenham, Swindon
Tel: Swindon (0793) 36178   Wilts SN6 8AE
                                    Tel: Swindon (0793) 782357

District 11C Cornwall, Devon
I. Temple-Smith (1964) (P)
Whitleigh Junior School,   55 Dunraven Drive,
Lancaster Gardens,   Derriford,
Plymouth,   Plymouth,
Devon PL5 4AA   Devon PL6 6AT
Tel: (0752) 706382   Tel: (0752) 779822
(P) denotes Past President

Ex-President
M.J. Cammish, BSc
Drove Secondary School,   235 Marlborough Road,
Drove Road,   Swindon,
Swindon, Wiltshire   Wiltshire SN3 1NN
Tel: (0793) 22071   Tel: (0793) 35407

Hon Treasurer
A. Pendlebury-Green, TD
St. Mary's CE Primary Sch,   Cliffe Haven,
Dover Road,   The Bayle,
Folkestone,   Folkestone,
Kent CT20 1LA   Kent CT20 1SQ
Tel: 0303 51390   Tel: 0303 55396

Finance & General Purposes F.C. Mills. ALAM. DipLit(London)
Salaries & Pensions D. Blenkinsopp
Professional Advice K.J. Dyos. BSc (Hons). MSc. ARCS. MRI. JP
Education (Academic) A.D. Bott. BA
Educational Administration J.H. Halsall
Membership & Organisation I. Williams
Conference A.S. Robinson

Periodicals: *The Head Teachers' Review, Newsletter* and some 'occasional' papers

HEALDERS AND TWISTERS TRADE AND FRIENDLY SOCIETY, HUDDERSFIELD*‡

Room 8, Friendly and Trades Societies Club, Northumberland Street, Huddersfield HD1 1RL
(Saturday morning 10am to 12 noon)

A small craft union formed in 1896. The union is based on Huddersfield and organises in the weaving side of the wool textile industry. It has been a member of the National Association of Unions in the Textile Trade since its inception in 1917.
Current membership: 195 all male.

OFFICIALS
The union has no full-time officials.
President: J. Womersley
Secretary: G. Booth,
20 Uppergate, Hepworth, Huddersfield HD7 1TG
Tel: Holmfirth (048 489) 4509

HEALTH SERVICE EMPLOYEES, CONFEDERATION OF (COHSE)*

Glen House, High Street, Banstead, Surrey SM7 2LH
Tel: Burgh Heath (07373) 53322

Formed in 1946 from the merger of the Mental Hospital and Institutional Workers' Union (1930) and the National Union of County Officers (1930). The union is represented on National Joint and Whitley Councils for Local Authorities and the National Health Service.
Current membership: 230,000

OFFICIAL
General Secretary: E.A.G. Spanswick

Periodical: *Health Services* (monthly)

223

HEALTH VISITORS' ASSOCIATION (HVA)*
36 Eccleston Square, London SW1V 1PF
Tel: 01–834 9523

Formed in 1896 as Women Sanitary Inspectors' Association and known since 1962 by its present name, the majority of the 11,500 members holding the Health Visitor Certificate. Other community nursing staff eligible for membership are School Nurses, Clinic Nurses, District Nurses, Family Planning Nurses and Student Health Visitors. All members must have a basic nursing qualification and the Association has always served in the dual capacity of professional association and trade union. There are 93 branches in England, Wales and Northern Ireland. Affiliated to the TUC since 1924 and represented on the Nurses and Midwives Whitley Council. The Association is non-political. It makes representations to Government departments and other interested bodies and has recently given evidence to the Royal Commission on the National Health Service. Current membership: 11,500

OFFICIALS
President: Dowager Countess of Radnor, OBE
Chairman: Mrs J. Hudson
Vice-Chairman: Mrs J. Smith, Miss S. Mowat
Hon. Secretary: Miss V. Packer
Hon. Treasurer: Miss C. Herbert
General Secretary: Mrs J. Wyndham-Kaye

Periodical: *Health Visitor* (monthly)

HOSIERY AND KNITWEAR WORKERS, NATIONAL UNION OF (NUHKW)*‡
55 New Walk, Leicester LE1 7EB
Tel: (0533) 56791

The National Union of Hosiery and Knitwear Workers was formed in 1945 as a result of amalgamation of several small district unions situated in the Midlands area. The approximate total membership at that time was 22,430. Since those early days, the union has developed into a national organisation and at present has members in over 700 factories throughout England, Scotland and Wales. In recent years, a number of craft unions engaged in the hosiery and knitwear industry have joined the organisation. The National Union of Hosiery and Knitwear Workers is the trade union which is party to the National Joint Industrial Council of the Hosiery Trade.

The NUHKW is also a party to the Scottish Knitwear Trade Wages Agreement which fixes working conditions for the majority of knitwear workers in Scotland. In the Midlands the NUHKW represents workers engaged in lace manufacture and those workers engaged in the dyeing and finishing of knitted fabric and products.

The NUHKW organises all workers in the knitwear industry, knitters, sewing machinists, mechanics, supervisors, clerical workers, dyers and finishers and designers, as well as auxiliary workers such as those people working in warehouses, canteens, etc. The Union has a special section, the Clerical, Administrative, Technical, and Supervisory Association for the Hosiery Industry, to cater for staff employees in the industry.

The NUHKW is affiliated to the Trades Union Congress, Scottish TUC, Wales TUC, The General Federation of Trade Unions, and the International Textile, Garment and Leather Workers' Federation.
Current membership: 72,858
    Male: 20,483
    Female: 52,375

OFFICIALS
General President: H.L. Gibson, OBE
General Secretary: D.A.C. Lambert

DISTRICT OFFICES
Hinckley
9 Clarendon Road,   Hinckley area of
Hinckley,   Leicestershire,
Leicestershire   Staffordshire, Mid Wales

Ilkeston
2 Mundy Street,   North West
Heanor,   Nottinghamshire,
Derbyshire   Derbyshire

Leicester
14 West Walk,   City of Leicester, East and
Leicester   South East Leicestershire

Leicester (Finishers)
14 West Walk,   Operatives in dyeing and
Leicester   finishing section in
                          Leicester and Loughborough

Loughborough
35 Factory Street,   Loughborough and environs,
Loughborough,   part of Derbyshire
Leicestershire

Mansfield and Sutton
85 Outram Street,   North East
Sutton-in-Ashfield,   Nottinghamshire
Nottinghamshire

North Eastern
Circle House,   Yorkshire, Durham,
Lady Lane,   Northumberland
Leeds

North Western	
63 Window Lane,	Cheshire, Lancashire,
Garston,	Westmorland, Cumberland,
Liverpool	North Wales
Nottingham	
Union House,	Centre of Nottingham and
Church Street,	Lincolnshire
Old Basford,	
Nottinghamshire	
Nottingham (Finishers)	
Union House,	Trimming and finishing
Church Street,	operatives in the
Old Basford,	Nottinghamshire and
Nottinghamshire	Derbyshire area, and
	Lacemakers' Branch
Scotland	
44 Kelvingrove Street,	Scotland
Glasgow	
Southern	
5 Parade Court,	South of England including
Bourne End,	South Wales from borders of
Buckinghamshire	Leicestershire,
	Lincolnshire and
	South Warwickshire
Staff Section	
14 West Walk,	Responsible for organising
Leicester,	workers such as supervisors,
Leicestershire	mechanics, warehousemen,
	clerical staff, designers, etc,
	in fact all workers ancillary
	to the knitting and making-up
	process.

Periodical: *Hosiery and Knitwear Worker* (quarterly)

Policy: Besides wages and conditions in the industry the union of late has been much concerned with future employment prospects in the industry. The Union has been respresented at many Government and European Economic Commission meetings to discuss problems associated with low-cost imports, the Multi-Fibre Arrangement, problems associated with new countries joining the EEC, and any EEC plan for textiles.

HOSIERY AND TEXTILE DYERS AND AUXILIARY ASSOCIATION‡
67 Station Road, Hinckley, Leicestershire

Formed in 1912 by a few workers who dyed cotton hose. Now

represents dyers, finishers and auxiliary workers in hosiery, knitwear and fabric dyeing and finishing in the Leicestershire and Nottinghamshire area.
Approximate membership: 450
    Males: 250
    Females: 200

OFFICIALS
All officials are part-time.
President: W. Compton,
7 Sunnyhill, Burbage, Leicestershire
Secretary: L.F. Ellis, JP

HOSPITAL CONSULTANTS AND SPECIALISTS ASSOCIATION*

The Old Court House, London Road, Ascot, Berkshire
Tel: Ascot (0990) 25052

The Regional Hospital Consultants and Specialists Association was founded at the start of the National Health Service. In 1969 the organisation was reformed and in 1972 Senior Hospital Doctors from Teaching Hospitals became eligible to join. The Association was then renamed the HCSA. Current membership is approximately 40 per cent of Senior Hospital Doctors eligible to join the association.

All National and Regional Officers are members and are elected every two years.

The Hospital Consultants and Specialists affiliated to the TUC on 1 October 1979.
Current membership: 5,000

OFFICIAL
Chief Executive: R. Brownlow Martin

Policy: The main aims of the HCSA are to promote a better hospital service; to guarantee adequate representation of the views of consultants and specialists in major Health Service policy decisions; to improve the terms and conditions of service of senior hospital doctors.

HUDDERSFIELD HEALDERS AND TWISTERS TRADE AND FRIENDLY SOCIETY

See HEALDERS AND TWISTERS TRADE AND FRIENDLY SOCIETY, HUDDERSFIELD

INLAND REVENUE STAFF FEDERATION (IRSF)*
7 St George's Square, London SW1V 2HY
Tel: 01–834 8254

A trade union with membership open to any officer employed in the
Inland Revenue Department but in practice with little recruitment
among fully trained tax inspectors, professional grades in the
Valuation Office or members of the General Services Grades.
Originally formed in 1936 as a Federation of two independent tax
officials' unions. A third union entered the Federation in the
following year. In 1938 all three unions merged into a single
organisation, while retaining the title Inland Revenue Staff
Federation. The Rt Hon. James Callaghan MP was a full-time
Assistant Secretary of the union from 1936 to 1947. At the end of 1978
membership was estimated to be over 93 per cent of potential
recruitment possibility.
Current membership: 67,614
    Males: 26,029
    Females: 41,585

OFFICIALS
President: S.C. Walters (elected lay member for two years, 1978–80)

Full-time Officers
General Secretary: A.M.G. Christopher
Deputy General Secretary: F.D. Swift
Assistant Secretaries:
C. Brooke, E. Elsey, Miss E. Symons
General Treasurer: Miss V.M. Frost
Editors: K.J. Bovington, J. Willman

Periodicals: *Taxes* (monthly), *Federation News*

INSTITUTION OF PROFESSIONAL CIVIL SERVANTS

See PROFESSIONAL CIVIL SERVANTS, INSTITUTION OF

INSURANCE WORKERS, NATIONAL UNION OF (NUIW)*
22 Worple Road, Wimbledon, London SW19 4DD
Tel: 01–947 6333

Formed in 1964 by amalgamation between the National
Amalgamated Union of Life Insurance Workers and the National
Federation of Insurance Workers. Both unions recruited their
membership from the Home Service Insurance Industry Field Staffs;
NAULAW however consisted of Agents only whereas the NFIW
membership included Agents, Officials, Inspectors and Field Office
Clerical Staffs. The NUIW continues to recruit its membership from

Field Staff employees of the Home Service Insurance Industry only. Membership for each Company or Society operates as an autonomous Section, with its own full-time General Secretary, National Committee and Officership drawn from the Companies' Field Staff on a national basis. Membership is spread throughout the United Kingdom. Most of the sections are non-political; only the Prudential Section is affiliated to the Labour Party.
Current membership: 20,131

OFFICIALS
The General Secretary of each section is a full-time Officer, each holding an honorary office within the NUIW as follows:
Prudential Section
(President NUIW) General Secretary: E. Lorenz,
91–93 Gray's Inn Road, London WC1X 8TX
(Minute Secretary NUIW) Deputy General Secretary: R. Main
Periodical: *The Gazette* (monthly)

Liverpool Victoria Section
(Hon. Gen. Secretary NUIW) General Secretary: J.P. Brown,
22 Worple Road, Wimbledon, London SW19 4DD
Periodical: *Victoria Gazette* (monthly)

Royal Liver/Composite Section
(Treasurer NUIW) General Secretary: J.E. Flunder,
73a Nuxley Road, Belvedere, Kent
Periodical: *The Journal* (quarterly)

Royal London Section
(Vice-President NUIW) General Secretary: F.H. Jarvis,
185 Woodhouse Road, London N12 9BA

Periodical: *The Gazette* (monthly)

IRON AND STEEL TRADES CONFEDERATION (ISTC)*
Swinton House, 324 Gray's Inn Road, London WC1X 8DD
Tel: 01–837 6691

The ISTC was formed in 1917 by amalgamation of the British Steel Smelters, Mill Iron and Tinplate Workers, The Associated Iron and Steel Workers of Great Britain and the National Steelworkers Association, Engineering and Labour League. It was joined later by the Amalgamated Association of Steel and Iron Workers of Great Britain and by the Tin and Sheet Millmen's Association in 1921. For a time the National Union of Clerks was within the Confederation. In the late 1960s ISTC rapidly expanded its staff membership, and now organises all grades within the industry, including middle management. The General Secretary of ISTC traditionally chairs the TUC Steel Industry Consultative Committee which negotiates all matters other than wages on behalf of the nationally recognised unions with the British Steel Corporation.

In 1976, the first ISTC annual conference was held. Recorded membership in early 1979 was about 114,000 but is likely to be affected by the closure programme being pursued by the BSC. It is grouped in seven divisions which reflect the traditional geographical pattern of steelmaking in Britain and a London area primarily grouping non-ferrous membership in the south.

Current membership: 114,000

OFFICIALS
General Secretary: W. Sirs
Assistant General Secretary: R.L. Evans
National Officer (Staff): H.A. Feather
National Officer: K. Clarke

DIVISIONAL OFFICERS

Division No. 1
A. Bell,
8 Royal Crescent,
Glasgow G3 7SL

Division No. 2
P. Woods,
Drinkwater House,
210–212 Marton Road,
Middlesbrough,
Cleveland TS4 2ET

Division No. 3
J.E. Pickles,
Edgcumbe House,
The Crescent,
Doncaster Road,
Rotherham,
South Yorkshire S65 1NL

Division No. 4
J.A. Gavin,
Mere Green Chambers,
338 Lichfield Road,
Four Oaks,
Sutton Coldfield,
West Midlands B74 4BH

Division No. 5
J. Foley,
34–38 Stow Hill,
Newport,
Gwent NPT 1JE

Division No. 6
S.E. Biddiscombe,
83 Mansel Street,
Swansea SA1 5TY

Division No. 7
G. Cooper,
Holly House,
Mobberley Road,
Knutsford,
Cheshire WA8 84T

London Area
L.H. Bambury,
Swinton House,
324 Gray's Inn Road,
London WC1X 8DD

Periodical: *Man and Metal* (Ten times yearly)

Policy: ISTC affiliates to the Labour Party through which it pursues its political ends. ISTC's main ambitions at present are to secure the retention of an adequate UK steel making capacity, and to achieve a higher earnings, single status industry.

ISTC meets most large private steel firms collectively through the Independent Steel Employers Association. Many smaller re-rollers participate with ISTC in the Midland Wages Board, a joint Conciliation body.

JOURNALISTS, NATIONAL UNION OF (NUJ)*
Acorn House, 314–320 Gray's Inn Road, London WC1X 8DP
Tel: 01–278 7916

The NUJ was formed in 1907. Previously there had been trade-union type organisations of working journalists in the larger cities and towns and it was these bodies which came together to form the national union. Today, the NUJ is the largest single trade union for journalists in the world, with members in Great Britain and the Republic of Ireland. It also has members working in various parts of the world, notably in Europe, where the union has branches in Brussels and Paris.

The NUJ has grown through its own organisational effort and its history does not include major amalgamations. With its beginnings in newspaper journalism – today still the largest single group, accounting for more than a half of total membership – the union has expanded into the fields of magazine journalism, press and public relations, radio and television and, most recently into the editorial areas of book publishing. The NUJ affiliates to the National Federation of Professional Workers, the National Council for Civil Liberties and Amnesty International.
Current membership: 30,978
    Male: 23,257
    Female: 7,721

FULL-TIME OFFICIALS
General Secretary: K. Ashton
Deputy General Secretary: C. Harkness
Assistant Secretary: R. Norris
National Organisers
M. Smith (Technology). Ms L. Rogers
N. Howell
J. Foster (Radio and Television)
Ms P. Van Der Bergh (Freelance and Press and Public Relations), J. Nash until October 1979 only (Retires)
G. Parker: Education and Research Officer
R. Knowles: Editor, *The Journalist* (the newspaper of the NUJ)

Regional Organisers
Scotland
D. Syme,
65 Buchan Street.
West Coltness.
Wishaw ML2 7HU.
Lanarkshire.
Scotland
Republic of Ireland and Northern Ireland
J. Eadie,
Irish Office,
NUJ Liberty Hall, Dublin 1

Northern Regional Organiser
M. Bower.
NUJ Regional Office.
26 Brittania House.
Love Street.
Sheffield 3.
Yorkshire
G. Morton: Magazine and Book members (Industrial Organiser)
Branch Secretary: G. McLean,
London Central Branch,
43 Fleet Street, London EC4

Periodical: *The Journalist* (monthly)

JUTE, FLAX AND KINDRED TEXTILE OPERATIVES, UNION OF (UJFKTO)‡

Formed in 1906, the union's membership is confined to Angus in Scotland and has been subjected to fluctuation based on the state of the jute and flax industry from which membership was drawn. In May 1979 the union transferred their engagements to the National Union of Dyers, Bleachers and Textile Workers.
1977 membership: 1,740
Males: 1,000
Females: 740

LACE AND TEXTILE WORKERS UNION, SCOTTISH†‡
62 Main Street, Newmilns, Ayrshire KA16 9DE
Tel: Darvel (0560) 21228

Established in 1890, originally responsible for all lace and textile workers in Scotland but at present only for factories in Darvel and Newmilns and in Kilmarnock (Irvine Valley). Affiliated for many years with the Lacemakers Union in Nottingham, but when they amalgamated with the Hosiery Union, became independent and negotiated separately.
Approximate membership: 1,123
    Males:456
    Females: 667

OFFICIALS
President: G. Mair,
5 Queen's Crescent, Newmilns, Ayrshire
General Secretary: R. Connell
Office Secretary: Ms M. Currie
Vice-President: J. McChristie,
32 John Morton Crescent, Darvel, Ayrshire

Executive Members

H. Gallacher, 16 Castleview Avenue, Galston, Ayrshire	R. Thompson, 9 Muir Drive, Darvel, Ayrshire
J. Auld, 45 High Street, Newmilns, Ayrshire	J. Paton, Drumclog Crescent, Darvel, Ayrshire
J. Young, 6 Mill Crescent, Newmilns Ayrshire	

LANCASHIRE AMALGAMATED TAPE SIZERS' ASSOCIATION ‡
238 Manchester Road, Nelson, Lancashire BB9 7DE
Tel: Nelson (0282) 64613

The Lancashire Amalgamated Tape Sizers' Association was formed in 1882 by the amalgamation of the ten district societies of textile craftsmen known as tape sizers who, although few in number (1704 in September 1920), processed every yard of the cotton warp yarn used by the Lancashire cotton industry. Because of the contraction of the textile industry two branches of the association merged with neighbouring towns, leaving eight. The membership is composed of all skilled textile sizing technicians in the cotton and man-made fibre industry, at present all male. The union affiliates to the GFTU and the Northern Counties Textile Trades Federation.
Current membership: 360

OFFICIALS
President: A. Hargreaves,
8 Moorside Avenue, Blackburn, Lancashire
General Secretary: H. Howorth,
238 Manchester Road, Nelson, Lancashire BB9 7DE
Treasurer: A. Miller,
37 London Terrace, Darwen, Lancashire

Executive Council

G. Singleton,	D. Airey,
64 Westwood Street,	67 Two Trees Lane,
Accrington	Denton,
	Manchester
J. Hill,	
172 Paulhan Street,	H. Beerman,
Bolton	54 Fairview Road,
	Bacup,
W. Goodwill,	Rossendale
27 Emily Street,	
Burnley	F. Bamford,
	10 Glendale Grove,
	Preston

With the exception of A. Miller (Darwen District was merged with Blackburn in 1968) the above officers and officials act as District Secretaries for the districts in which they reside.

LANCASHIRE BOX, PACKING CASE AND GENERAL WOODWORKERS SOCIETY ‡
50 Burton Road, Withington, Manchester M20 9EB
Tel: 061–434 6650

A craft union dating from 1825 with members from tradesman packing case makers and machinery packers with a proportion of apprentices and ancillary workers. The union caters for the

manufacture of all types of timber packing cases and the export packing of heavy engineering products, machine tools and electronic equipment, etc. The membership covers Greater Manchester and outer districts.
Approximate membership: 550

OFFICIAL
General Secretary: A. Smith
The General Secretary is the only full-time official, all other officials being lay members.

Policy: Opposed to any form of incomes policy, being in favour of responsible free collective bargaining.

LECTURERS IN COLLEGES OF EDUCATION IN SCOTLAND, THE ASSOCIATION OF (ALCES)†
Craigie College of Education, Ayr KA8 0SR
Tel: Ayr (0292) 60321

One of the major unions in Scotland organising lecturers in its respective sector. It is affiliated to the STUC and forms part of the Federation of Associations of College Lecturers in Scotland. ALCES has ten branches.
Current membership: 1,100

OFFICIALS 1977–79
Chairman: Dr R.D. Lobban.
Moray House College of Education,
Edinburgh

National Secretary: Roger M.
Hollins.
Craigie College of Education,
Ayr KA8 0SR

LICENSED HOUSE MANAGERS, NATIONAL ASSOCIATION OF (NALHM)*‡
9 Coombe Lane, London SW20 8NE
Tel: 01–947 3080/5941

NALHM officially came into being on the 1st October, 1969. It resulted from the National Managers' Committee of the National Federation of Licensed Victuallers Association deciding to form an autonomous Association of Managers.

Membership is open to managers and their wives of licensed houses, off-licenses and steak bars and is organised in 145 branches throughout England, Scotland and Wales. Administered within 11 regional areas by 12 full-time organisers.

In September, 1975, NALHM was accepted into affiliation to the Trades Union Congress and the General Federation of Trade Unions and is represented on the Hotel & Catering Industry Committee of the TUC and on the Hotel & Catering Industry Training Board.

The Association has negotiating rights with almost all major brewery companies and has signed a number of Post Entry Closed

Shop Agreements. Since the advent of NALHM there has been a dramatic improvement in the status of managers and their wives and substantial increases in salaries and related benefits.
Current membership: 16,211
    Males: 11,057
    Females: 5,154

OFFICIALS
National President: J. Cossar
National Secretary: H. Shindler

HEAD OFFICE STAFF
Personal Assistant to the National Secretary: Mrs H. O'Byrne
Snr. Administrative Officer: J.II. Walker
Secretary to Snr. Administrative Officer: Mrs S. Hornibrook
Membership Secretary: Mrs S.A. Fenner
Head of Accounts: Mrs M.R. Harding
Senior Vice-President: A.C. Clements
Junior Vice-President: D. Houghton
National Treasurer: A.E. Wilson

NATIONAL COMMITTEE MEMBERS:
R.L. Crump, K. Butt, N. Hoppitt, W.N.J. Davies, G. Weaver, J. Taylor, H. Bennett, M. Jones, B. Clutton, G. Harris, P. Edgar, J. Hall, C. Maxwell

ORGANISING STAFF
L. Adams,
Snr. Regional Organiser,
14 Birmingham Road,
Walsall WS1 2NA

A. Carter,
Midlands Regional Organiser,
14 Birmingham Road,
Walsall WS1 2NA

To be Appointed,
Scottish Regional Organiser,
22 Milton Street,
Edinburgh EH8 8HF

J.A. Cooper,
South West Regional Organiser,
205 Wells Road,
Knowle,
Bristol BS4 2DF

To be Appointed,
South Wales Regional Organiser,

R.F. Heaps,
North East Regional Organiser,
83 North Road,
Wallsend,
Tyne & Wear NE28 8RL

D. Smith,
North West Regional Organiser,
258–260 Earle Street,
Earlestown,
Newton-le-Willows. Merseyside

D. Allen.
West Pennines Regional Organiser,
258–260 Earle Street,
Earlestown,
Newton-le-Willows. Merseyside

J. Smith,
Yorkshire Regional Organiser,
93 Netherhall Road,
Doncaster, Yorks.

W.T. Parfitt,
South East Regional Organiser,
13 Approach Road,
Raynes Park, S.W.20

A.W. Wilson,
Greater London Regional Organiser,
13 Approach Road,
Raynes Park, S.W.20

To be Appointed,
Eastern Regional Organiser,

Periodical: *NALHM News* (quarterly)

Policy: The Union is deeply involved in matters intimate to the licensed trade and maintains close liaison with MPs on all sides of the House in the promotion of legislation to this end.

In particular, they seek legislation to ban those convicted of assaults on licensees and their staffs from any licensed premises for a period of time to be determined by the sentencing Magistrates.

The Union is bitterly opposed to any legislation to alter the existing licensing hours in Britain. Such a step, they believe, would have serious social consequences and worsen the conditions of managers by requiring them to work even longer hours than at present.

LITHOGRAPHIC ARTISTS, DESIGNERS, ENGRAVERS AND PROCESS WORKERS, SOCIETY OF (SLADE)*
55 Clapham Common South Side, London SW4 9DF
Tel: 01-720 7551

Established in 1885 by practising lithographic artists, designers and writers, and copperplate and wood engravers, the union caters for those engaged in the production and reproduction of pictures, illustrations, designs and images in printing, including lithographic artists, designers, geographical draughtsmen, operators and retouchers, etchers, electronic engraving machine and electronic scanning machine operators, in lithography, letterpress, photogravure and all other printing processes. The wallpaper and textile section, formed in 1972, following the transfer of engagements by the United Society of Engravers, caters for those engaged in the manufacture of cylinders for the printing of wallpapers, textiles and plastics. The SLADE Art Union is an independent section within the union created in 1974 for members engaged in the preparation and production of art and photographic copy for reproduction in print, particularly in studios and agencies. Membership of SLADE and PW (including SLADE Art Union) is spread throughout the United Kingdom and Republic of Ireland.
Current membership: 25,561 (including SLADE Art Union: 8,000)

OFFICIALS
General Secretary: J.A. Jackson
Assistant General Secretary: A.E. Parish
National Assistant Secretary: D.A. Anderson
National Organiser: E.J. Martin
National Financial Secretary: H.G. Richford

FULL-TIME BRANCH OFFICIALS
Birmingham
R.J. Gillott,
134 Bromsgrove Street,
Birmingham B5 6RN

East Midlands
B.W.R. Wood,
218 Mansfield Road,
Nottingham NG5 2BU

Glasgow
N. Dennison,
160 Hope Street,
Glasgow C2

Leeds
E. Gill,
13–14 Park Place,
Leeds 1

Liverpool
D.L. Walker,
66 Rodney Street,
Liverpool L1 9AF

London
F.R. Carvell,
54 Doughty Street,
London WC1N 2NA

Manchester
A. Akers,
SLADE House,
297–299 Chapel Street,
Salford M3 5JT

North East
L. Pye,
6 Clifton,
York

South East
P.B. Page,
39 Bell Street,
Reigate,
Surrey

South and West
W.G. Mitchell,
Liverpool Victoria Building,
172 Wells Road,
Bristol BS4 2AR

Watford
H.R. Pluckwell,
107 High Street,
Berkhamsted,
Hertfordshire

Periodical: *SLADE Journal* (monthly)

LOCAL AUTHORITY CHIEF EXECUTIVES, ASSOCIATION OF
Municipal Offices, Town Hall Square, Grimsby, South Humberside
DN31 1HU
Tel: Grimsby (0472) 59161

An Association formed in 1973 with membership open to the Chief
Executives of Local Authorities in England, Scotland and Wales, the
vast majority of which have become members.
Current membership: 500

OFFICIAL
The Association has no full-time officials.
Hon. Secretary: F.W. Ward, OBE, LLM

**LOCK AND METAL WORKERS, NATIONAL UNION
OF (NULMW)*‡**
Bellamy House, Wilkes Street, Willenhall WV13 2BS
Tel: Willenhall (0902) 66651/2

Formed on 9 March 1889, with its Head Office in the centre of Willenhall, the traditional home of the lock industry. Over the years, a number of small societies amalgamated to form the National Union of Lock and Metal Workers. The union has two sections: (a) hourly paid operatives and (b) clerical, technical and supervisory staff. National negotiations are undertaken at Joint Industrial Council level with the National Union as the sole representative of employed persons and the employers being represented by the British Lock Manufacturers' Association.
Current membership: 7,000

FULL TIME OFFICERS
General Secretary: J. Martin
Assistant Secretary: D.R. Thomas
Staff Officer: J.F. Torrington
National Officer: L.H. Wells

LAY MEMBERS
President: T.G. Sadler
Vice-President: L. Richards
Executive Council:

R. Armstrong	S. Smith
G. Groves	R. Ward
G. Guest	R. Wilkes
G. Mills	D. Wiskin
L. Price	Mrs M. Brand
G. Sands	Mrs M. Brown
L. Shakespeare	Mrs L. Collins

LOCOMOTIVE ENGINEERS AND FIREMEN, ASSOCIATED SOCIETY OF (ASLEF)*
9 Arkwright Road, Hampstead, London NW3 6AB
Tel: 01–435 6300/216

Founded in 1880 as a trade union for locomotive drivers and staff in the line of promotion to that grade (Drivers' assistants, traction trainees). It is party to negotiation with the British Railways Board through the Railway Staff Joint Council and the Railway Staff National Council and also in London Transport. ASLEF has consistently sought to preserve its craft traditions, and pursues the policy that the technical and organisational changes which have taken place on the railways since World War II have not affected the craft nature and status of the work performed by footplatemen. The union organises approximately 98 per cent of eligible staff on British Railways.
Current membership: 27,738
    Males: 27,719
    Females: 19

OFFICIAL
General Secretary: R.W. Buckton

Periodical: *Locomotive Journal* (monthly)

LONDON SOCIETY OF TIE CUTTERS

See TIE CUTTERS, LONDON SOCIETY OF

LOOM OVERLOOKERS, GENERAL UNION OF ASSOCIATIONS OF*‡
1st Floor, 3 Manchester Road, Bury
Tel: 061–764 4244

A union of autonomous local associations of loom overlookers originally formed in 1885 and now comprising 14 such associations; see also British Federation of Textile Technicians.
Current membership: 2,516

GENERAL OFFICERS
President: R. Richardson,
Overlookers' Institute, Jude Street, Nelson
Vice-President: N. Harper,
130 Drake Street, Rochdale,
General Secretary: H. Brown

LOCAL SECRETARIES

Accrington
H. Sellars,
2 Hodder Street,
Accrington
Tel: Accrington (0254) 31456

Blackburn
J. Sowerby,
Overlookers' Office,
9 Wellington Street,
St. John's,
Blackburn BB1 8AF
Tel: Blackburn (0254) 51760

Bolton
J. Ratcliffe,
80 St. George's Road,
Bolton BL1 2DD
Tel: Bolton (0204) 32787

Church and Oswaldtwistle
W. Long,
255 Queen's Road West,
Church,
Accrington
Tel: Accrington (0254) 33102

Colne
E. Marco,
Overlookers' Institute,
2 Knowsley Street,
Colne
Tel: Colne (028 24) 3021

Haslingden
D. Fletcher,
5 Holly Avenue,
Haslingden,
Rossendale BB4 6QD
Tel: Rossendale (070 62) 6175

Heywood
H. Page, JP,
249 Bury and Rochdale Old Road,
Heywood
Tel: Heywood (0706) 68196

Hyde
J.A. Bradshaw,
14 George Street,
Denton,
Manchester M34 3DJ
Tel: 061–320 0501

National
H. Astley,
14 Banastre,
Astley Park,
Chorley,
Lancashire
Tel: Chorley (025 72) 73002

Nelson
G.E. Waite,
Overlookers' Institute,
Jude Street,
Nelson
Tel: Nelson (0282) 64066

Oldham
G. Hartshorne,
4 Milford Avenue,
Hollins,
Oldham OL8 3UP
Tel: 061–682 6138

Preston
A. Rothwell,
Overlookers' Office,
172 St. Paul's Road,
Preston PR1 1PX
Tel: Preston (0772) 52450

Skipton
C. Reid,
139 Colne Road,
Earby,
Yorkshire
Tel: Skipton (0756) 3471

United
N. Harper,
130 Drake Street,
Rochdale OL16 1PN
Tel: Rochdale (0706) 46448

MACHINE CALICO PRINTERS, THE TRADE SOCIETY OF
317 Corn Exchange Buildings, Manchester M4 3BT
Tel: 061–832 4979

OFFICIAL
General Secretary: J. Eckersley

MANAGEMENT AND PROFESSIONAL STAFFS, ASSOCIATION OF (AMPS)
175 Station Road, Swinton, Manchester M27 2BU
Tel: 061–793 7054

Founded in 1972 by the member bodies of the Council of Science and Technology Institutes and has since amalagamated with the British Association of Chemists dating from 1917. Membership is open to persons who hold an appointment at a professional or managerial level in a science based industry. Evidence is provided by a degree, membership of a professional institute or similar qualifications but managers and others who hold appointments at an equivalent level may also become members. Associated membership is available to those following a part-time course of study leading to a qualification making them eligible for full membership. Of the current membership 75 per cent is drawn from the chemical and allied industries located mainly in the North and North West England, Wales, and Yorkshire/Humberside but still having a strongly based section in Greater London and the South East. The union adopted its present name at their 1978 annual conference – having previously been known as the Association of Professional Scientists and Technologists.
Current membership: 10,000

OFFICERS
President: Dr M.B. Green
Executive Secretary: Dr. M.I. Gillibrand, PhD
Administrative Secretary: P.H. Unna
Membership Secretary: Mrs S. Morris
National Officials: J.H. Golds (Harley Street), L.P. Bunt, E.A. Daws, R. McEvoy

AMPS is affiliated to FIMPA (Federation of Industrial Management and Professional Associations) and to the MP&SLG (Management and Professional Staff Liaison Group).

MANAGERS' AND OVERLOOKERS' SOCIETY

Managers' and Overlookers' Society was founded as a textile trade union in 1912 as the Yorkshire Managers' and Overlookers' Society and changed to its present title in 1921. In October 1977 the union became an autonomous section of the Association of Scientific, Technical and Managerial Staffs.
1977 membership: 1,185

MERCHANT NAVY AND AIRLINE OFFICERS' ASSOCIATION (MNAOA)*
Oceanair House, 750–760 High Road, Leytonstone, London E11 3BB
Tel: 01–989 6677

Formed under its present title in 1956, by amalgamation between the Navigators' and Engineer Officers' Union (formed 1936) and the Marine Engineers' Association (formed 1887). Represents merchant navy officers and staff in other services ancillary to shipping, as well as flight engineers in civil aviation. Negotiates centrally through the National Maritime Board and the National Joint Council for Civil Aviation. Liaises with other shipping unions through the British Seafarers' Joint Council. Involved in training, safety and other technical matters, on a national and international level. Affiliated to the TUC and to the International Transport Workers' Federation (ITF).
Current membership: 43,750

Council: Elected Members (1977–81)
Navigating Officers
Capt J. Ibester
Capt P.A. Messinger
J.C. Roberts (Chairman)
D.J. Walker
Capt B.F. Hoare
D. Seaman
M. Birchmore
Capt A.R. Tinsley
G.W. Wilson

241

Engineering Officers
J.F. Birch
M.S. O'Brien
H. Topping
M.J.A. Powell

A. Thomas
D.R. Hamilton
R.J.C. Gammie
D. Bayliss
R.G. Webb

Civil Aviation Officers
R.C. Bricknell (Vice-Chairman)
B.C.H. Ferdinando

Purser/Catering Officers
P.J. Newman
R.R.L. Judd

Electrical Engineer Officers
J.C. Corney

Other Categories
W.J. Connolly

Head Office
General Secretary: E. Nevin
Assistant General Secretary: P.J. Newman
Director of Professional and Welfare Services: D. Seaman
Research Officer: C. Bulford
National Secretaries: G.W. Wilson, T. Harding, S.J. Rendell, B.D. Orrell
Legal: M. Rogers
Income Tax: R. Verralls
Accounts: K. Clacy
Registrar and Librarian: A. MacCarthy
Data Processing: V. Carthy

REGIONAL OFFICIALS
London Region:
Bank Chambers,
130 Whitechapel High Street,
London E1 7PU
01–247 6769.

Regional Secretary: M.E. Bourne
District Officials: W.J. Ross,
J. Peterson, G. Gurman &
S.G. Morrison
Full-time official, Dover:
E. Howe,
16 Dryden Road,
Dover,
Kent.
Tel: 03047–2348

N.W. Region:
134 The Albany,
Old Hall Street,
Liverpool,
Merseyside L3 9EY
Tel: 051–236 1943

Regional Secretary: R.S. Elliot
Senior District Official: I.F. Hughes
District Official: R. Hart

Full-time Official, Belfast:
L. Attwood,
Imperial Buildings,
72 High Street, Belfast BT1 2AD
Tel: 0232–21344

Bristol Channel Region:
108 Bute Street,
Cardiff CF1 6AT
Tel: Cardiff (0222) 26920

Regional Secretary: R.I. Mason
District Officials: H.J. Windsor &
W. Harrison

Part-time Official, Milford Haven:
J.W.J. Roberts,
"Otaio",
Puncheston,
Haverfordwest,
Dyfed.
Tel: Puncheston 367

South Coast Region:
34/35 Oxford Street,
Southampton,
Hants. SO1 1DS
Tel: 0703–26606

Regional Secretary: J. Powell
District Official: C. Friskney

Scottish Region:
5th Floor, Baltic Chambers,
50 Wellington Street,
Glasgow G2 6HJ
Tel: 041-221 2868

Regional Secretary: R. Barclay
District Official: J.A. Scrimgeour

Part-time Official, Aberdeen:
A. Clark
67 Fraser Drive,
Westhills,
Skene, Nr. Aberdeen.
Tel: 0224-741051

North East Region
29 King Street,
South Shields,
Tyne and Wear NE33 1DA
Tel: South Shields (0632) 555775

Regional Secretary: G.R. Boyle
District Official: B. Parker

East Coast Region:
Bridge Chambers,
Century Buildings,
Monument Bridge,
Kingston-upon-Hull,
North Humberside HU1 2JX
Tel: Hull (0482) 25390

Regional Secretary: M. Johnston
District Official: H.V. Shaw

Full-time Official, Grimsby:
D.W. Hawley,
170 Cleethorpe Road,
Grimsby,
Humberside
Tel: 0472-42635

Periodical: *The Telegraph* (monthly)

METAL MECHANICS, NATIONAL SOCIETY OF (NSMM)*‡
70 Lionel Street, Birmingham B3 1JG
Tel: 021-236 0726

The NSMM, originally a union for Birmingham brass workers, now
has membership in the metal and engineering trades generally,
especially in the Midlands and Greater London but also in the West
and North.
Current membership: 50,494

NATIONAL OFFICIALS
General Secretary: J.H. Wood
Assistant General Secretary: J.A. Green
President (lay member): F. Troth
Vice-President: E.A. Clayton

National Executive Council

L.W. Stride	E. Goddard
V. Smith	Mrs T.M. Bates
J. Dennis	Miss F.E. Howells
W. Phillips	R. Chivers
J.C. Philips	H.O. Walker
E. Powles	D. O'Reilly
A. Mann	M. Taylor
W. Capon	

Full-time Regional Officials
Midlands
R.J. Wood,
C. McCarthy,
J.E. Morgan,
70 Lionel Street,
Birmingham B3 1JG
Tel: 021–236 0726

L. Brown,
224 Long Ley,
Heath Town,
Wolverhampton

W. Fernie,
Regent House,
26 Queen's Road,
Coventry CV1 3DQ
Tel: Coventry (0203) 23126

H. Nicholls,
70 Lionel Street,
Birmingham B3 1JG
Tel: 021–236 0726

J. Langford,
70 Lionel Street,
Birmingham B3 1JG
Tel: 021–236 0726

H. Brown,
15 Charnwood Street,
Derby DE1 2GT
Tel: Derby (0332) 44135

South
W. Hunt,
A.E. Heitzmann,
1 Renmuir Street,
Tooting,
London SW17 9SR
Tel: 01–672 3033

West
G. Halliday,
7 King Square,
Bristol BS2 8JD
Tel: Bristol (0272) 47903

North
W. Daly,
G. Husband,
25 St. John Street,
Deansgate,
Manchester M3 4DT
Tel: 061–834 0887

R. Gormley,
1st Floor, Cardigan Chambers,
27 Lord Street,
Liverpool 2
Tel: 051–236 1095

G.L. Capon,
1st Floor, Cardigan Chambers,
27 Lord Street,
Liverpool 2
Tel: 051–236 1095

52 Nether Hall Road,
Doncaster,
Yorkshire
Tel: Doncaster (0302) 26782

S.H. Hallam,
59a Derby Road,
Nottingham NG1 5BA
Tel: Nottingham (0602) 43404

S. Hill,
1 Stanley Place,
Chester CH1 2LU
Tel: Chester (0244) 26986

Periodical: *Metal Mechanics NEWS* (Bi-Monthly Newspaper)

METALWORKERS' UNION, ASSOCIATED (AMU)*‡
92 Deansgate, Manchester M3 2QG
Tel: 061–834 6891

Founded in 1868 as the Iron, Steel and Metal Dressers Society.
Current membership: 6,037

OFFICIAL
General Secretary: E. Tullock

MILITARY AND ORCHESTRAL MUSICAL INSTRUMENT MAKERS TRADE SOCIETY*

47 Mornington Terrace, Regents Park, London NW1

Founded in 1894, and known until 1926 as the Military Musical Instrument Makers' Trade Society.
Current membership: 185

OFFICIAL
General Secretary: J.N. Barker

MINEWORKERS, NATIONAL UNION OF (NUM)*

222 Euston Road, London NW1 2BX
Tel: 01-387 7631/8

The National Union was formed in 1945 (with effect from 1 January). Having advocated nationalisation of the mines for a great number of years previously, it was logical to want a National Union. Previously, some 40 separate mining unions had been in a loose federation known as the 'Miners' Federation of Great Britain'. Agreement on a National Union was finally achieved at a Nottingham Conference in 1944, and a ballot of all mineworkers showed the acceptance of the proposals by 430,630 to 39,666.

The scheme on which the National and Area Rules are based provided for:

1   The industrial activities of the separate district associations to become the responsibility of the National Union.
2   The district associations to retain full control of those funds which were provided to meet the benefits (other than normal industrial benefits) as applying to the particular districts.
3   The district associations to become Areas of the Union. As far as the day to day administration of the union was concerned, this was to be carried on through the Areas, acting under the jurisdiction of the National Executive Committee, which would administer the business of the union in accordance with the directions given from time to time by Annual or Special Conference.
4   Area Officials and Committees were to be responsible to the National Executive Committee for supervising and co-ordinating the action of the branches in accordance with the agreed policy of the union.

The union is composed of workers employed in, or connected with, the mining industry of Great Britain and ancillary undertakings.
Current membership: 254,887

FULL-TIME NATIONAL OFFICIALS

President: J. Gormley, OBE
Vice-President: M. McGahey*
Secretary: L. Daly

Also members of the
National Executive
Committee

The office of Vice-President is not a full-time post and the official present holding is also a full-time official in Scottish Area.

NATIONAL EXECUTIVE COMMITTEE

Cokemen
H. Close
5 Victoria Road,
Barnsley,
Yorkshire S70 2BA

Cumberland
W.S. Proud
Miners' Offices,
6 Nook Street,
Workington,
Cumberland CA14 4EG

Derbyshire
P.E. Heathfield
Miners' Offices,
Saltergate,
Chesterfield,
Derbyshire S40 1LG

Durham
T. Callan
Miners' Offices,
Red Hill,
Durham DJ1 4BB

Kent
J. Collins
8 South View,
Hersden,
Canterbury,
Kent

North Western
S.G. Vincent
Miners' Offices,
Bridgeman Place,
Bolton,
Lancashire BL2 1DL

Leicester
J. Jones
Miners' Offices,
Bakewell Street,
Coalville,
Leicestershire LE6 3BA

Midlands
J. McKie
47 Station Road,
Hednesford,
Staffordshire

Northumberland
S. Scott
150 North Seaton Road,
Ashington,
Northumberland

North Wales
E. McKay
Miners' Offices,
Bradley Road,
Wrexham,
North Wales

Nottingham
L.A. Clarke
Miners' Offices,
Berry Hill Lane,
Mansfield,
Nottinghamshire NG18 4JU

J. Whelan
Miners' Offices,
Berry Hill Lane,
Mansfield,
Nottinghamshire NG18 4JU

Scotland
W. McLean
5 Hillside Crescent,
Edinburgh EH7 5DZ

South Derbyshire
K. Toon
Miners' Offices,
Alexandra Road,
Swadlincote,
Burton-on-Trent DE11 9AZ

246

South Wales
G. Rees
AEU Building,
Sardis Road,
Pontypridd,
Glamorgan CF37 1DU

E. Williams
AEU Building,
Sardis Road,
Pontypridd,
Glamorgan CF37 1DU

Yorkshire
O. Briscoe
730 Doncaster Road,
Barnsley,
Yorkshire

P. Tait
55 Lamb Lane,
Monk Bretton,
Barnsley,
Yorkshire S71 2DX

A.Scargill,
Miners' Offices,
2 Huddersfield Road,
Barnsley,
Yorkshire

Group No. 1
T.E. Bartle
26 The Avenue,
Durham DH1 4ED

Group No. 2
F. Gormill
209 St. Vincent Street,
Glasgow G2 5QQ

COSA
L.D. Story
14a Bond Street,
Wakefield,
Yorkshire

Power Group
J.R. Ottey
4 Broad Street,
Hanley,
Stoke-on-Trent ST1 4HL

Power Group No. 2
L. Atkinson
Concord House,
Park Lane,
Leeds LS3 1NB

AREA SECRETARIES
Cokemen
H. Close
5 Victoria Road,
Barnsley,
Yorkshire S70 2BA
Tel: Barnsley (0226) 84006/8

Cumberland
W.S. Proud
Miners' Offices,
6 Nook Street,
Workington,
Cumberland CA14 4EG
Tel: Workington (0900) 3238

Derbyshire
P.E. Heathfield
Miners' Offices,
Saltergate,
Chesterfield S40 1LG
Tel: Chesterfield (0246) 34135/6

Durham
W. Malt
Miners' Offices,
Red Hill,
Durham DH1 4BB
Tel: Durham (0385) 3515/7

Kent
J. Dunn
10 Maison Dieu Road,
Dover,
Kent CT16 1RW
Tel: Dover (0304) 206661/206271

Leicester
J. Jones
Miners' Offices,
Bakewell Street,
Coalville,
Leicestershire LE6 3BA
Tel: Coalville (0530) 32085, 31568

Midlands
J.T. Lally
12 Lichfield Road,
Stafford ST17 4LB
Tel: Stafford (0785) 3358/9

Northumberland
S. Scott
Burt Hall,
Northumberland Road,
Newcastle-upon-Tyne NE1 8LD
Tel: Newcastle-upon-Tyne (0632) 27351/2

North Wales
E. McKay
Miners' Offices,
Bradley Road,
Wrexham,
North Wales
Tel: Wrexham (0978) 2106

North Western
S.G. Vincent
Miners' Offices,
Bridgeman Place,
Bolton,
Lancashire BL2 1DL
Tel: Bolton (0204) 21680

Nottingham
L. Martin
Miners' Offices,
Berry Hill Lane,
Mansfield,
Nottinghamshire NG18 4JU
Tel: Mansfield (0623) 26094/5

Scotland
W. McLean
5 Hillside Crescent,
Edinburgh EH7 5DZ
Tel: 031–556 2323/7

South Derbyshire
K. Toon
Miners' Offices,
Alexandra Road,
Swadlincote,
Burton-on-Trent DE11 9AZ
Tel: Swadlincote (0283) 221200

South Wales
G. Rees
AEU Building,
Sardis Road,
Pontypridd,
Glamorgan CF37 1DU
Tel: Pontypridd (0443) 404092/5

Yorkshire
O. Briscoe
Miners' Offices,
Barnsley,
Yorkshire S70 2LS
Tel: Barnsley (0226) 84006/9

Group No. 1
Group Secretary:
T.E. Bartle
Durham Colliery
Mechanics Association
T.E. Bartle
26 The Avenue,
Durham DH1 4ED
Tel: Durham (0385) 61375/6

Northumberland Mechanics
R. Wallace
56 William Street,
Blyth,
Northumberland NE24 2HR
Tel: Blyth (06706) 2279

Durham County Enginemen
R.H. Short
17 Hallgarth Street,
Durham DH1 3AT
Tel: Durham (0385) 64828

Group No. 2
Group Secretary:
F. Gormill
Scottish Enginemen
F. Gormill
209 St. Vincent Street,
Glasgow G2 5QQ
Tel: 041–221 0700 or 0709

COSA
L.D. Story
14a Bond Street,
Wakefield,
Yorkshire
Tel: Wakefield (0924) 63228

Power Group
J.R. Ottey
222 Euston Road,
London NW1 2BX
Tel: 01–387 7631/8

4 Broad Street,
Hanley,
Stoke-on-Trent ST1 4HL
Tel: Stoke-on-Trent (0782) 262759

Power Group No. 2
L. Atkinson
Concord House,
Park Lane,
Leeds LS3 1NB
Tel: Leeds (0532) 450608

Periodical: *The Miner* (monthly)

MUSICAL INSTRUMENT MAKERS, NATIONAL UNION OF (NUMIM)

Established in 1879 and incorporating the Organ Builders' Trade Society. In 1978 NUMIM amalgamated with the Furniture, Timber and Allied Trades Union.

MUSICIANS' UNION (MU)*
60/62 Clapham Road, London SW9 0SS
Tel: 01-582 5566

The present union was formed in 1921 by an amalgamation of two organisations, both formed in 1893. It organises the whole of the music profession including symphony orchestras, broadcasting orchestras, theatre orchestras, bands in night clubs, bands and groups in ballrooms, rock and other groups. It is thought to be the second largest musicians' union in the world, second only to the American Federation of Musicians. The union has collective agreements with all major employers of musicians including the BBC, the Independent Television companies, British Phonographic Industry, the Association of British Orchestras, the Theatrical Management Association, the British Resorts Association, Mecca Limited. The union plays a prominent role in the International Federation of Musicians and General Secretary, John Morton, is President of that body. The union and British Actors' Equity form a Performers' Alliance with which the Writers' Guild of Great Britain is associated. It is also involved in all the entertainment industry bodies such as the Confederation of Entertainment Unions, the Federation of Broadcasting Unions, Federation of Theatre Unions and Federation of Film Unions.
Current membership: 42,000

OFFICIALS
General Secretary: J. Morton
Assistant Secretaries:
S. Hibbert, J. Stoddart

Session Organiser: D. Smith

Music Promotions and Public Relations: B. Blain

Group Organiser: M. Evans

NATIONAL EXECUTIVE COMMITTEE

Scotland
J. Turnbull
B. Devine

North
D. Watchman
G. Turner

North West
T. Mather
R. Hurst

North East
E. Taylor
A. Field

East
T. Thompson
S. Barrett

Midlands
J. Patrick
T. Richards

South East
J. King
P. Garnham

South West
C. Hawke
B. Thomas
S. Evans

London
S. Faulkner
L. Monte
L. Worsley
D. Scard

DISTRICT ORGANISERS AND PERMANENT OFFICIALS

London
Musicians' Union,
60/62 Clapham Road,
London SW9
Tel: 01–582 5566

East District and North East
T. Yates
33 Blandfold Drive,
Walgrave,
Coventry
Tel: (0203) 619556

Birmingham Branch Secretary
P. Boothroyd
Musicians' Union,
14–16 Bristol Street,
Birmingham B5 7AA
Tel: 021–622 3870

**North West District and
Manchester Branch Secretary**
Musicians' Union
4 Roby Street,
Manchester 1
Tel: 061–236 1764

Midland
J. Forman
Musicians' Union,
56 Villiers Street,
Nuneaton,
Warwickshire
Tel: Nuneaton (0682) 383659

South East
Refer to National Office

North and North East
T. Griffin
16 Osbourne Walk,
Harrogate,
Yorkshire
Tel: Harrogate (0423) 62486

**Scottish District and Glasgow
Branch Secretary**
J. Jenkins
Musicians' Union,
135 Wellington Street,
Glasgow G2
Tel: 041–248 3723

London Branch Secretary
B. Parris
Musicians' Union,
60/62 Clapham Road,
London SW9
Tel: 01–582 5566

South West
K. Cordingley
'Rosedene',
New Road, Trull,
Taunton,
Somerset

Special Project Organiser
J. Fagan
17 Lynnburn Avenue,
Bellshill,
Lanarkshire ML4 1DR
Tel: Bellshill (0698) 843592

Scottish District Branches
Aberdeen
I. Millar
7 Pittengullies Circle,
Peterculter
Aberdeen
Tel: (0224) 733817

Airdrie
G. Reid
19 Crowwood Crescent,
Calderbank,
Lanarkshire
Tel: Airdrie (0236) 63677

Alloa
D. Anderson
12 Abbey Road Place,
Stirling,

Clydebank
T. Whelan
60 Sunnyside Drive,
Blairdardie,
Glasgow

Cowal
J. Peel
50 Ardenslate Road,
Dunoon,
Argyll
Tel: Dunoon (0369) 2786

Cumnock
A. Anderson
16 Meagher Court,
Cumnock
Tel: 0290 21161

Dumfries
c/o Jack Jenkins
135 Wellington Street,
Glasgow G2

Fife
J. Hearn
41 Haigh Crescent,
Dunfermline,
Fife
Tel: 0383 35684

East Kilbride
T. Sheldon
4 Sydney Drive,
East Kilbride,
Glasgow G75 8OH
Tel: 035–522 6464

Edinburgh
J. Rutherford
15 Windsor Street,
Edinburgh EH7 54A
Tel: 031–556 4485

Falkirk
I. Ramsay
94 Tryst Road,
Stenhousemuir,
Falkirk
Tel:(032) 453682

Glasgow
J. Jenkins
Musicians' Union,
135 Wellington Street,
Glasgow G2
Tel: 041–248 3723

Greenock
T. McAnerney
5 Hole Farm Road,
Greenock,
Renfrewshire
Tel: Greenock (0475) 26647

Inverness
G.A. Cushnie
40A Tomnahurich Street,
Inverness

Irvine
W. Fletcher
8 Hopetown Bank,
Bourtree Hill,
Irvine,
Ayrshire
Tel: (0294) 213050

Motherwell
B. Devine
105 Thorndean Avenue,
Bellshill,
Lanarkshire
Tel: Bellshill (0698) 842858

Paisley
D. Finnie
26 Brown Street,
Paisley,
Renfrewshire

Perth
J. Hall
42 Crieff Road,
Perth

Strathkelvin
c/o John Fagan
17 Lynnburn Avenue,
Bellshill,
Lanarkshire

Tayside
R. Bruce
247 Charleston Drive,
Dundee

West Lothian
J. Monaghan
62 The Green,
Bathgate,
West Lothian
Tel: (0506) 53980

North District
Cumberland, Northumberland,
Durham and North Riding of
Yorkshire, excluding Scarborough
Branches

Berwick
D. Crawford
19 The Oval,
Tweedmouth,
Berwick-on-Tweed,
Northumberland

Darlington
A.G. Butler
Bath Cottage,
Dinsdale Park,
Middleton St. George,
Co. Durham
Tel: Darlington (0325) 732723

Durham
A. Walton
43 Villa Real Road,
Consett,
Co. Durham DH8 6BC
Tel: (0207) 503992

Houghton-le-Spring
J. Wilson
71 Cathedral View,
Newbottle,
Houghton-le-Spring,
Co. Durham DH4 4HN
Tel: Houghton-le-Spring
(0783) 843349

Middlesbrough
Mrs K. Moore
14 Lothian Road,
Middlesbrough,
Cleveland
Tel: Middlesbrough (0642) 44050

Newcastle-upon-Tyne
G. Turner
Musicians' Union,
28 Ridley Place,
Newcastle-upon-Tyne NE1 4PQ
Tel: Newcastle-upon-Tyne
(0632) 25900

Redcar
N.L. Nawton
19 Chiltern Avenue,
Redcar,
Yorkshire
Tel: Redcar (064 93) 77057

South Shields
R. Simpson,
4 Chester Gardens,
South Shields

Stockton-on-Tees
T. Shaw
5 Park Drive,
Darlington Lake,
Stockton-on-Tees,
Cleveland
Tel: Stockton-on-Tees (0642) 67696

Sunderland
D. Watchman
137 Nursery Road,
Elstob,
Sunderland,
Co. Durham
Tel: Sunderland (0783) 285448

Workington
D. Best
Greenview,
Shore Street,
Maryport,
Cumberland

North West District
Westmorland, Lancashire, Cheshire,
North Wales and Isle of Man
Branches
Barrow
G. Sear
11 Cliffe Lane,
Barrow-in-Furness,
Lancashire
Tel: Barrow (0229) 24898

Blackburn
H. Greenwood
5 Sunny Bower Close,
Sunny Bower,
Blackburn,
Lancashire
Tel: Blackburn (0254) 54535

Blackpool
S.H. Anderson
40 Haddon Road,
Norbreck,
Blackpool,
Lancashire
Tel: Blackpool (0253) 52080

Bolton
P. Hickman
889 Wigan Road,
Bolton,
Lancashire
Tel: Bolton (0204) 61542

Bury
E. Willan
17 Alexander Drive,
Unsworth,
Bury,
Lancashire BL9 8PF
Tel: 061-796 8113

Chester
C.R. Butler
75c Dee Banks,
Chester
Tel: Chester (0244) 24070

Isle of Man
E. Kelly
4 Ballaterson Road,
Peel,
Isle of Man
Tel: Peel (062 484) 2548

Kendal & South Lakes
J. Bailey
3 Windermere Bank,
Lake Road,
Bowness-on-Windermere
Cumbria LA23 2JJ
Tel: 092-62 3155

Liverpool
R. Hurst
11 Camden Street,
Liverpool 3
Tel: 051-207 1326

Manchester
4 Roby Street,
Manchester 1
Tel: 061-236 1764

Morecambe
c/o NWDO

North Wales Coast
R. Morgan Borthwick,
14 Patrick Avenue,
Rhyl,
Clwyd
Tel: Rhyl (0745) 53264

Preston
W. Stuttard
26 Oxley Road,
Preston,
Lancashire PR1 5QH

Southport
R. Taylor,
Flat 32,
Sandown Court,
Albert Road,
Southport PR9 0HE
Tel: Southport (0704) 41401

Stockport
G. Jones
20 Greystroke Street,
Stockport,
Cheshire
Tel: 061-480 7080

Wigan
H. Oakes
66 Masefield House,
Worseley Mesnes North,
Wigan,
Lancashire
Tel: Wigan (0942) 43052

North East District
Yorkshire, other than the North
Riding, but including Scarborough,
Lincolnshire and Rutland
Branches
Barnsley
D. Fellowes
3 North Close,
Kirkfield Way,
Royston,
Barnsley,
Yorkshire
Tel: Royston 3297

Boston
c/o T. Yates

Bradford
W. Rathmell
174 Upper Castle Street,
West Bowling,
Bradford
Yorkshire
Tel: Bradford (0274) 31374

Bridlington
L. Wilkinson
214 Quay Road,
Bridlington,
Yorkshire
Tel: Bridlington (0262) 6959

Dewsbury
L. Brunton
32 Windermere Road,
Dewsbury,
Yorkshire
Tel: Dewsbury (0924) 463176

Doncaster
A. Hodgson
148 Sandringham Road,
Intake,
Doncaster
Tel: Doncaster (0302) 21764

Grimsby
J.E. Taylor
15 Westhill Road,
Grimsby,
Lincolnshire
Tel: Grimsby (0472) 3392

Harrogate
J. Dearlove
Flat 2,
57 East Parade,
Harrogate,
Yorkshire
Tel: Harrogate (0423) 64863

Huddersfield
T. Darryl-Gee
13 Howard Road,
Lindley,
Huddersfield,
Yorkshire
Tel: Huddersfield (0484) 27082

Hull
T.W. Glenton
32 Moffat Close,
Lambwath Road,
Hull HU8 0AU
Tel: Hull (0482) 74427

Leeds
G. Cope
23 Barr Lane,
Garforth,
Leeds LS25 2ED
Tel: Garforth (097 38) 860755

Lincoln
R. Renshaw
27 King's Way,
Nettleham,
Lincoln
Tel: 0522 52458

Scarborough
T. Turner
26 Holbeck Mill,
Scarborough,
Yorkshire
Tel: Scarborough (0723) 65577

Sheffield
R. Brightman
43 The Oval,
North Anston,
Sheffield S31 7BX
Tel: Dinnington (090 978) 3074

York
A. Field
17 Shirley Avenue,
Boroughbridge Road,
York
Tel: York (0904) 798202

East District
Norfolk, Suffolk, Cambridgeshire,
Huntingdonshire, Bedfordshire,
Hertfordshire and Essex
Branches
Cambridge
S. Barrett
64 Victoria Park,
Cambridge
Tel: Cambridge (0223) 50924

Clacton and Colchester
S. Calcutt
52 Anchor Road,
Clacton,
Essex
Tel: Clacton (0255) 24462

Great Yarmouth
G. Askew
25 California Avenue,
Scratby,
Great Yarmouth,
Norfolk
Tel: Gt. Yarmouth (0493) 731150

Harlow
J. Raymond
128 Spring Hills,
Harlow,
Essex
Tel: Harlow (0279) 21587

Ipswich
J. Halliday
15 Woodthorpe Close,
Hadleigh,
Suffolk IP7 5IH
Tel: 047 338 2662

Lowestoft
I. Cleveland
56 Park Road,
Lowestoft,
Suffolk
Tel: 0502 64139

Luton
J. Stead,
56 Montrose Avenue,
Luton,
Bedfordshire
Tel: 0582 29115

Mid-Herts
T. Vincent
22 Windridge Close,
St. Albans,
Hertfordshire
Tel: St. Albans (0727) 56 62727

Norwich
D. Buck
69 Middletons Road,
Norwich,
Norfolk
Tel: Norwich (0603) 49983

Peterborough
Mrs C. Locker
406C Fulbridge Road,
Peterborough,
Northamptonshire
Tel: 0733 71100

Southend
F. Blow
50 Nutcombe Crescent,
Rochford,
Essex
Tel: Southend (0702) 544717

Midland District
Derbyshire, Nottinghamshire,
Leicestershire, Warwickshire,
Northamptonshire, Herefordshire,
Worcestershire, Staffordshire and
Shropshire
Branches
Birmingham
P. Boothroyd
Musicians' Union,
14–16 Bristol Street,
Birmingham B5 7AA
Tel: 021–622 3870

Burton
W.A. Bailey
12 Kingsley Road,
Burton-on-Trent,
Staffordshire

Chesterfield
E.W.R. Pygall
298 Old Road,
Brampton,
Chesterfield,
Derbyshire 540 3QN
Tel: Chesterfield (0246) 77740

Coventry
K. Francis
11 Chesford Crescent,
Hall Green,
Coventry CV8 7LP
Tel: 0203 619556

Leamington Spa
L. Spreckley
43 Villiers Street,
Leamington Spa,
Warwickshire
Tel: Leamington Spa (0926) 28625

Leicester
G. Simpson
19 Thurmaston Lane,
Humberstone,
Leicester LE5 0TE
Tel: Leicester (0533) 767520

Mansfield
A. Birks
7 Bathgate Drive,
Sutton Road,
Mansfield,
Nottinghamshire
Tel: Mansfield (0623) 35528

Northampton
V. Williams
164 Balfour Road,
Northampton

Nottingham
D. Spink
51 Mountfield Drive,
Bestwood Park,
Nottinghamshire
Tel: Nottingham (0602) 264626

Nuneaton
M. McCathy
24 Windermere Avenue,
Nuneaton,
Warwickshire

Rugby
C.H. Aland
62 St. Annes Road,
Rugby
Tel: Rugby (0788) 812513

Stoke-on-Trent
G. Simpson
20 The Avenue,
Harpfield,
Stoke-on-Trent,
Staffordshire
Tel: Stoke-on-Trent (0782) 614374

Wolverhampton
T.N. Richards
22 Balfour Crescent,
Wolverhampton,
Staffordshire
Tel: Wolverhampton (0902) 751901

Worcester
L. Harber
418 Wylds Lane,
Worcester
Tel: 0905 351682

South East District
Kent, Middlesex, Sussex, Surrey,
Hampshire, Berkshire, Oxfordshire
and Buckinghamshire
Branches
Aldershot
L.J. Coleman
Pangbourne,
328 Vale Road,
Ash Vale,
Aldershot
Tel: Aldershot (0252) 24930

Banbury
J.C. Prickett
4 Howard Road,
Banbury,
Oxfordshire
Tel: 0295 4945

Basingstoke
J. Borrill
13 Henshaw Crescent,
Newbury RG14 6ES
Tel: Newbury (0635) 47104

Bognor Regis
D. Barnes
Clamps,
93 North Bersted Street,
Bognor Regis,
Sussex
Tel: Bognor Regis (024 33) 23377

Bournemouth
B. Collins
14 Campbell Road,
Boscombe,
Bournemouth,
Dorset BH1 4EP
Tel: Bournemouth (0202) 38121

Brighton
P. Barrs
93 High Street,
Shoreham-by-Sea,
Sussex
Tel: 079 17 5730

Eastbourne
P. Hellier
Cambridge House,
6 Cambridge Road,
Eastbourne,
Sussex
Tel: Eastbourne (0323) 21100

Folkestone
P. Stacey
10 Elmstead Place,
Folkestone,
Kent
Tel: Folkestone (0303) 53760

Hastings
A.D. Knight
36 Fairlight Avenue,
Hastings TN35 5HP
Sussex
Tel: 0424 436486

Medway
D. Young
71 Brewer Street,
Maidstone,
Kent
Tel: Maidstone (0622) 55085

Oxford
R. Woodley
1 Melton Drive,
Didcot,
Berkshire OX11 7JP
Tel: Didcot (0235) 813410

Portsmouth & Isle of Wight
R. Bannistra
28 Alhambra Road,
Southsea,
Hampshire
Tel: Portsmouth (0705) 33146

Reading
F.J. Boucher
49 Harveys Nurseries,
Peppard Road,
Caversham,
Reading
Tel: Reading (0734) 474427

Southampton
Mrs J. Lock
55 Oakleigh Crescent,
Rushington,
Totton,
Hampshire
Tel: 0227 60985

Thanet
D. Mannouch
23 Lanfranc Gardens,
Harbledon,
Canterbury
Kent
Tel: 0227 60985

South-West District
Cornwall, Devonshire, Wiltshire,
Dorsetshire, Somerset, Monmouth-
shire, Gloucestershire, South
Wales and Channel Isles
Branches
Bath
R. Harrup
60 Lower Oldfield Park,
Bath,
Somerset
Tel: Bath (0225) 24962

Bristol
K. Lewis
86 Mortimer Road,
Filton,
Bristol BS12 7LQ
Tel: Bristol (0272) 692160

Cardiff
A.I. Jones
39 Elgar Crescent,
St. Mellons Rise,
Llanrumney,
Cardiff
Tel: Cardiff (0222) 791334

Cornwall
Mrs M. Thomas
8 Coronation Terrace,
Truro,
Cornwall
Tel: Truro (0872) 77173

Devon North
W. Brown
24 Green Bank,
Torrington,
North Devon
Tel: Torrington (080 52) 2644

Exeter
S. Gillick
3 Danesway,
Pinhoe,
Exeter,
Devon
Tel: Exeter (0392) 66466

Gloucestershire
C. Robinson
54 Naunton Crescent,
Cheltenham,
Gloucestershire

Jersey
P. Moignard
1 Pine Court,
Grouville,
Jersey,
Channel Islands
Tel: Jersey East (0534) 51058

Llanelli
M. Lord
7 Blodwen Terrace,
Penclawdd,
Swansea SA4 3XY
Tel: 044 123 267

Newport
F. Fahy
2 Heath Park Avenue,
Cardiff
Tel: Cardiff (0222) 752839

Plymouth
W. Thomas
12 Caroline Place,
Stonehouse,
Plymouth,
Devon
Tel: Plymouth (0752) 64007

Port Talbot
D. Partington
'Opus One',
John Street,
Cefncribwr,
Bridge End,
Mid-Glamorgan
Tel: Kenfig Mill 741914

Rhondda
T. Bennett
34 Bank Street,
Penycraig,
Rhondda,
Glamorgan

Salisbury
K. Daubney
38 Waters Road,
Salisbury,
Wiltshire
Tel: Salisbury (0722) 28110

Swansea
L. Humphreys
St. Brendan,
11 Robert Street,
Manselton,
Swansea,
Glamorgan
Tel: Swansea (0792) 53642

Swindon
R. Grant
27 Northern Road,
Swindon,
Wiltshire
Tel: Swindon (0793) 36162

Taunton
F. Knighton
Marsh View,
Fore Street,
Seaton,
Devon EX12 2AN
Tel: Seaton (0297) 21907

Torbay
J. Jenkins
Mount Royal,
Clennon Heights,
Paignton,
Devon
Tel: 0803 551977

Wessex
M. Rose
118 Belgrave,
Southill Garden Drive,
Weymouth,
Dorset
Tel: 030 57 74678

West Wales
F. De'ath
High Havens,
Wisemans Bridge,
Saundersfoot,
Dyfed
Tel: Saundersfoot (0834) 813479

London District
Metropolitan Police Area of
London
and the City of London
Branches
Central London
Bernard Parris
60/61 Clapham Road,
London SW9 0JJ

East London	South London
P. Bottrell	S. Faulkner
36 Oak Road,	49 Beverley Road,
Rochford,	Whytleafe,
Essex	Surrey CR3 0DU
Tel: 0702 547488	Tel: 01–660 5918

North London	West London
A. Banner	H. Goodman
54 Beresford Road,	621 London Road,
London E4,	Isleworth,
Tel: 01–529 0264	Middlesex
	Tel: 01–560 5571

South East London	
G. Hyde	Kingston
13 Downsbank Avenue,	C. Mantell
Barnehurst,	75 Cobham Road,
Kent DA7 6RS	Kingston,
Tel: 38 35360	Surrey
	Tel: 01–546 7050

Periodical: *The Musician* (quarterly)

NATIONAL AND LOCAL GOVERNMENT OFFICERS ASSOCIATION (NALGO)*
1 Mabledon Place, London WC1H 9AJ
Tel: 01–388 2366

Founded in 1905 as the National Association of Local Government Officers, with a membership of about 5,000. In 1920 it was certificated as a trade union under the Trade Union Act 1913. By 1946 it had become the eighth largest union in Britain with nearly 150,000 members. In that year National Schemes of Conditions of Service were agreed for English and Scottish local government officers and the NALGO constitution was amended to enable it to recruit officers in other public services. The membership now includes clerical, administrative, professional and technical staffs in the national health, gas, electricity, new towns, water, transport and university services. In 1952 the name of the association was amended to its present form to reflect this wider membership. Total membership had grown to over 300,000 by 1964 when NALGO affiliated to the TUC and today (1979) NALGO represents over 720,000 local government and service employees and is by far the largest white collar union in the country. Apart from its participation in the national negotiating machinery for all the above mentioned groups, the Association provides a range of legal, educational, research, welfare and recreational services for its members. Between annual conferences the controlling body is the National Executive Council, elected on an annual basis and served by a staff of some 600 full-time officers, some 200 of which are deployed in its 12 district offices.
Current membership: 729,405 (as at 31 October 1978)

PRINCIPAL OFFICERS

General Secretary: G.A. Drain
Deputy General Secretary: W.R. Rankin
Assistant General Secretary (Service Conditions): J. Daly
Assistant General Secretary (Administration): B. Holland
Local Government Service Conditions Officer: A. Jinkinson
Organising Officer for Electricity Staffs: J. Lockwood
Organising Officer for Gas Staffs: D. Stirzaker
Organising Officer for Health Staffs: Ms A. Maddocks
Organising Officer for Water/Transport: E.J. Roberts
Organising Officer for Universities/New Towns: A. Thompson
Research and Statistical Officer: J.S. Thane
Financial Officer: C.L. Read
Legal Officer: Ms P. Grant
Publicity Officer: E. Smythe
Education Officer: Ms R. Kibel
International Relations Officer: H. Bynger

District Organisation Officers

Eastern
C. Cronin
30–33 Townfield Street,
Chelmsford,
Essex CM1 1UW
Tel: Chelmsford (0245) 84691

East Midland
L.B. Briggs, DFC
Pearl Assurance House,
Friar Lane,
Nottingham NG1 6BY
Tel: Nottingham (0602) 45756

Metropolitan
A. Jack
34 Gloucester Gardens,
Bishop's Bridge Road,
London W2 6BP
Tel: 01-402 5227

North Eastern
J.D. Williamson
Milburn House (A),
Dean Street,
Newcastle upon Tyne, NE1 1LE
Tel: Newcastle upon Tyne (0632) 24900

North Western and North Wales
E. Baxendale, AICA
18 Lloyd Street,
Manchester M2 5WA
Tel: 061-834 6443

Scottish
C.C. Drury
Hellenic House,
87–97 Bath Street,
Glasgow G2 2ER
Tel: 041-332 0006

Southern
L.G. Jones
Kennet House,
80–82 Kings Road,
Reading,
Berkshire RG1 3BX
Tel: Reading (0734) 57229

South Wales
S. Bradley
Third Floor,
1 Cathedral Road,
Cardiff CF1 9SB
Tel: Cardiff 398333

South Western
B. Bailey, OBE, JP
16 The Crescent,
Taunton,
Somerset TA1 4DU
Tel: Taunton (0823) 88031

West Midland
S. Platt
Lichfield House,
Smallbrook,
Queensway,
Birmingham B5 4JD
Tel: 021-643 6943

Yorkshire and Humberside
J. Fitches
Bridge House,
Westgate,
Leeds LS1 4NW
Tel: Leeds (0532) 39782/3

South Eastern
D. Kennedy, JP
Queensberry House,
104–109 Queen's Road,
Brighton BN1 3XF
Tel: Brighton (0273) 29445

Periodical: *Public Service* (monthly). Editor: C.E. Timaens

NATIONAL ASSOCIATION OF COLLIERY OVERMEN, DEPUTIES AND SHOTFIRERS

See COLLIERY OVERMEN, DEPUTIES AND SHOTFIRERS, NATIONAL ASSOCIATION OF

NATIONAL ASSOCIATION OF CO-OPERATIVE OFFICIALS

See CO-OPERATIVE OFFICIALS, NATIONAL ASSOCIATION OF

NATIONAL ASSOCIATION OF FIRE OFFICERS

See FIRE OFFICERS, NATIONAL ASSOCIATION OF

NATIONAL ASSOCIATION OF HEAD TEACHERS

See HEAD TEACHERS, NATIONAL ASSOCIATION OF

NATIONAL ASSOCIATION OF LICENSED HOUSE MANAGERS

See LICENSED HOUSE MANAGERS, NATIONAL ASSOCIATION OF

NATIONAL ASSOCIATION OF PROBATION OFFICERS

See PROBATION OFFICERS, NATIONAL ASSOCIATION OF

NATIONAL ASSOCIATION OF SCHOOLMASTERS AND UNION OF WOMEN TEACHERS

See SCHOOLMASTERS AND UNION OF WOMEN TEACHERS, NATIONAL ASSOCIATION OF

NATIONAL ASSOCIATION OF TEACHERS IN FURTHER AND HIGHER EDUCATION

See TEACHERS IN FURTHER AND HIGHER EDUCATION, NATIONAL ASSOCIATION OF

NATIONAL ASSOCIATION OF THEATRICAL, TELEVISION AND KINE EMPLOYEES

See THEATRICAL, TELEVISION AND KINE EMPLOYEES, NATIONAL ASSOCIATION OF

NATIONAL ASSOCIATION OF YOUTH HOSTEL WARDENS

See YOUTH HOSTEL WARDENS, NATIONAL ASSOCIATION OF

NATIONAL GRAPHICAL ASSOCIATION

See GRAPHICAL ASSOCIATION, NATIONAL

NATIONAL LEAGUE OF THE BLIND AND DISABLED

See BLIND AND DISABLED, NATIONAL LEAGUE OF THE

NATIONAL SOCIETY OF BRUSHMAKERS AND GENERAL WORKERS

See BRUSHMAKERS AND GENERAL WORKERS, NATIONAL SOCIETY OF

NATIONAL SOCIETY OF METAL MECHANICS

See METAL MECHANICS, NATIONAL SOCIETY OF

NATIONAL SOCIETY OF OPERATIVE PRINTERS, GRAPHICAL AND MEDIA PERSONNEL

See PRINTERS, GRAPHICAL AND MEDIA PERSONNEL, NATIONAL SOCIETY OF OPERATIVE

NATIONAL TILE, FAIENCE AND MOSAIC FIXERS SOCIETY

See TILE, FAIENCE AND MOSAIC FIXERS SOCIETY, NATIONAL

NATIONAL UNION OF AGRICULTURAL AND ALLIED WORKERS

See AGRICULTURAL AND ALLIED WORKERS, NATIONAL UNION OF

NATIONAL UNION OF BANK EMPLOYEES

See BANKING INSURANCE, AND FINANCE UNION

NATIONAL UNION OF BLASTFURNACEMEN, ORE MINERS, COKE WORKERS AND KINDRED TRADES

See BLASTFURNACEMEN, ORE MINERS, COKEWORKERS AND KINDRED TRADES, NATIONAL UNION OF

NATIONAL UNION OF CLUB STEWARDS

See CLUB STEWARDS, NATIONAL UNION OF

NATIONAL UNION OF DOMESTIC APPLIANCE AND GENERAL METAL WORKERS

See DOMESTIC APPLIANCE AND GENERAL METAL WORKERS, NATIONAL UNION OF

NATIONAL UNION OF DYERS, BLEACHERS AND TEXTILE WORKERS

See DYERS, BLEACHERS AND TEXTILE WORKERS, NATIONAL UNION OF

NATIONAL UNION OF FOOTWEAR, LEATHER AND ALLIED TRADES

See FOOTWEAR, LEATHER AND ALLIED TRADES, NATIONAL UNION OF

NATIONAL UNION OF FUNERAL SERVICE OPERATIVES

See FUNERAL SERVICE OPERATIVES, NATIONAL UNION OF

NATIONAL UNION OF GENERAL AND MUNICIPAL WORKERS

See GENERAL AND MUNICIPAL WORKERS, NATIONAL UNION OF

NATIONAL UNION OF GOLD, SILVER AND ALLIED TRADES

See GOLD, SILVER AND ALLIED TRADES, NATIONAL UNION OF

NATIONAL UNION OF HOSIERY AND KNITWEAR WORKERS

See HOSIERY AND KNITWEAR WORKERS, NATIONAL UNION OF

NATIONAL UNION OF INSURANCE WORKERS

See INSURANCE WORKERS, NATIONAL UNION OF

NATIONAL UNION OF JOURNALISTS

See JOURNALISTS, NATIONAL UNION OF

NATIONAL UNION OF LOCK AND METAL WORKERS

See LOCK AND METAL WORKERS, NATIONAL UNION OF

NATIONAL UNION OF MINEWORKERS

See MINEWORKERS, NATIONAL UNION OF

NATIONAL UNION OF MUSICAL INSTRUMENT MAKERS

See MUSICAL INSTRUMENT MAKERS, NATIONAL UNION OF

NATIONAL UNION OF PUBLIC EMPLOYEES

See PUBLIC EMPLOYEES, NATIONAL UNION OF

NATIONAL UNION OF RAILWAYMEN

See RAILWAYMEN, NATIONAL UNION OF

NATIONAL UNION OF SCALEMAKERS

See SCALEMAKERS, NATIONAL UNION OF

NATIONAL UNION OF SEAMEN

See SEAMEN, NATIONAL UNION OF

NATIONAL UNION OF SHEET METAL WORKERS, COPPERSMITHS, HEATING AND DOMESTIC ENGINEERS

See SHEET METAL WORKERS, COPPERSMITHS, HEATING AND DOMESTIC ENGINEERS, NATIONAL UNION OF

NATIONAL UNION OF TAILORS AND GARMENT WORKERS

See TAILORS AND GARMENT WORKERS, NATIONAL UNION OF

NATIONAL UNION OF TEACHERS

See TEACHERS, NATIONAL UNION OF

NATIONAL UNION OF WALLCOVERINGS, DECORATIVE AND ALLIED TRADES

See WALLCOVERINGS, DECORATIVE AND ALLIED TRADES, NATIONAL UNION OF

NATIONAL WOOL SORTERS SOCIETY

See WOOL SORTERS SOCIETY, NATIONAL

NELSON AND DISTRICT ASSOCIATION OF PREPARATORY WORKERS‡

(Warpdressers, Dry Tapers, Chainbeamers, Leasers, Warpers, Highspeed Beamers)
2 Hall Street, Colne, Lancashire BB8 0DJ
Tel: Colne (028 24) 3858 (morning)
2a New Brown Street, Nelson, Lancashire BB9 7NY
Tel: Colne (0282) 64055 (afternoon)

Founded as the Warpdressers Assocation about 1892. About 1927 amalgamated with the Chainbeamers and Dry Tapers Association when it had some thousand members. Membership is now reduced to about 100 members who are working and 100 retired members. Discussions on amalgamation are being held with the Nelson and Colne Branches of Twisters and Drawers Society.
Approximate membership: 200 including retired members

OFFICIALS
President: J. Horsfall,
6 Lowther Street, Colne, Lancashire
Secretary: H. Phillips
Committee:

F. Phillip	H. Howarth
52 Spring Lane,	68 Sheridan Road,
Colne,	Laneshawbridge,
Lancashire	Lancashire
G. Shaw	S. Pretty
80 Reedyford Road,	105 Birtwistle Avenue,
Nelson,	Colne,
Lancashire	Lancashire

NORTH-EAST COAST TUGBOATMEN'S ASSOCIATION

See TUGBOATMEN'S ASSOCIATION, NORTH-EAST COAST

NORTHERN CARPET TRADES UNION

See CARPET TRADES UNION, NORTHERN

OFFICIAL ARCHITECTS, ASSOCIATION OF
66 Portland Place, London W1N 4AD
Tel: 01-580 5533

Formed in 1958 with the support and approval of the Royal Institute of British Architects. Certified as an independent trade union under the Trade Union and Labour Relations Act and the Employment Protection Act. Membership is open throughout the UK to registered architects and those who have passed parts 1 and 2 of the RIBA Final Examination who are employed in public offices including central and local government, health service and new town authorities and the nationalised industries. Membership in general is organised on the basis of the 13 RIBA regions with the addition of minority groups for members in the health service, new towns, nationalised industries, etc.

The association seeks to enhance the status, career prospects and remuneration of architects in the public sector and to promote efficiency and good management in public architectural offices. It is a founder member of the Federation of Professional Officers' Associations, care of APSPE Office, 37 Wimbledon Hill Road, London SW19 7PF. It is also one of NALGO's associated professional societies.
Current membership: in excess of 500

OFFICERS
President and Chairman: G.J. Foxley, DipArch, RIBA
Director of Development, Civic Centre, Harrow HA1 2ZX
Hon. Secretary: A. McCombe, BA, RIBA, DipTP, MRTPI
33A Upper Oldfield Park, Bath BA2 3JX
Hon. Registrar: R. Binyon, BArch, RIBA
53 Vicar's Cross Road, Chester CH3 5NN
Assistant Registrar: Mrs M.J. Clarke
31 Frogmore Street, Tring, Hertfordshire HP23 5AZ
Hon. Treasurer: J.P. McCulloch, DipArch, RIBA, ARIAS
Cairndhu, Lintwhite Crescent, Bridge of Weir, Renfrewshire PA11 3LJ

Policy: The association has no political affiliations.

PATTERN WEAVERS' SOCIETY*
New Field End, Hill Top, Cumberworth, Huddersfield HD8 8YE
Tel: Holmfirth (048 489) 2547

Founded 1930.
Current membership: 150 (all male)

General Secretary: D.G. Hawley
President: E. Ainley
Treasurer: S. McCraken

PATTERNMAKERS AND ALLIED CRAFTSMEN, ASSOCIATION OF (APAC)*

15 Cleve Road, West Hampstead, London NW6 1YA
Tel: 01–624 7085

Formed 1872 as a union catering for skilled patternmakers and continues to be concerned only with craftsmen with patternmaking skills. Membership is found mainly in the Midlands.
Current membership: 9,706
   Males: 9,704
   Females: 2

OFFICIALS
General Secretary: G. Eastwood
Assistant General Secretary: D. Stoddart

Executive Committee
General President:
D. Waters
6 Tranter Avenue,
Alvechurch,
Worcestershire B48 7PH
Tel: 021–445 3687

Area No. 1
T.R. Auchincloss
57 Cerrybank Road,
Glasgow G43 2NG
Tel: 041–637 1340

Area No. 2
J. Coulson (Pro-Tem)
10 Debussy Court,
Jarrow,
Tyne & Wear NE32 3BN

Area No. 3
W. Oakes
44 Smethurst Lane,
Pemberton,
Wigan
Tel: Wigan (0942) 213341

Area No. 4
K.G. Morris
9 Cathel Drive,
Birmingham B42 1HH
Tel: 021–357 8051

Area No. 5
K. Bowes
64 Walcot Avenue,
Luton,
Bedfordshire,
Tel: (0582) 36933

AREA OFFICIALS
Area No. 1
Organiser: A. Dorrens
13 Sandyford Place,
Glasgow G3 7NB
Tel: 041–221 4736

Area Secretary:
J. Inglis
Flat 112,
60 Kingsway Court,
Glasgow G14 9FA

Area No. 2
Organiser:
D. Firth
247 Keldregate,
Deighton,
Huddersfield,
Yorkshire
Tel: 0484 37904

NE Coast District Secretary:
A. Russell
248 Bamburgh Avenue,
South Shields
Tel: South Shields (0632) 62514

West Yorkshire and Humberside
District Secretary:
J.H. Johnson
88 Cottesmore Road,
Hessle,
North Humberside HU13 9JG
Tel: 0482 643311

Area No. 3
Organiser:
P. Bagnall
Room 3,
Savoy Chambers,
1 Wellington Street,
Stockport,
Cheshire
Tel: 061-480 7557

Lancashire and Cheshire District
Secretary:
W. Clarkson
20 Rosemary Avenue,
Blackpool FY4 2PQ
Tel: 0253 47043

Sheffield District Secretary:
F. Beeden
8 Moorlands Avenue,
Chapeltown S30 4WA

Area No. 4
Organiser:
H.J. Ashmore
14–16 Bristol Street,
Birmingham B5 7AA
Tel: 021-622 3306

Midland District Secretary:
H. Layland
152 Lincoln Road North,
Olton,
Birmingham B27 6RR
Tel: 021-706 5293

Area No. 5
Organiser:
D. Yearley
Griffon House,
1 Cinema Parade,
Green Lane,
Dagenham,
Essex RM8 1AA
Tel: 01-592 2758

London District Secretary:
K. Bowes
64 Walcot Avenue,
Luton,
Bedfordshire
Tel: Luton (0582) 36933

West of England District Secretary:
N. Rowe
1 Castle Rise,
Laira,
Plymouth,

Periodical: *Patternmaker* (monthly)

Policy: In recent years it was against entry into Europe and generally opposed to the idea of incomes policy.

POLYTECHNIC TEACHERS, ASSOCIATION OF (APT)
Throgmorton House, 27 Elphinstone Road, Southsea, Hampshire
PO5 3HP
Tel: Portsmouth (0705) 818625

Formed in May 1973 following the designation of the last of the 30 Polytechnics in England and Wales and the Polytechnic of Northern Ireland. There are autonomous local associations in all Polytechnics. Membership consists of lecturers and other academics in the designated Polytechnics, of whom about 8% are women. The

Association is affiliated to the Managerial, Professional and Staff Liaison Group (MP and SLG).
Current membership: 3,500

OFFICIALS
Full-time Official (Chief Executive): Mrs S.A. Perrin
National Secretary: Dr A.J. Pointon

EXECUTIVE COMMITTEE
Chairman:
R. Powell
Department of Electrical and
Electronic Engineering,
Trent Polytechnic,

Deputy Chairman:
Dr J.A. Simmons
Department of Physics,
Polytechnic of Central London,
115 New Cavendish Street,
London W1M 8JS
Tel: 01–486 5811

Vice Chairmen:
E.P. Zucker
Department of Physics,
Polytechnic of North London,
Holloway,
London N7 8DB
Tel: 01–607 2789

J.R. Hart
Department of Humanities,
Hatfield Polytechnic,
PO Box 109,
Hatfield,
Hertfordshire AL10 9AB
Tel: Hatfield (07072) 6811

Dr R.M. Wood
Department of Applied Physics,
Sheffield Polytechnic,
Pond Street,
Sheffield S1 1WB
Tel: Sheffield (0742) 20911

Treasurer:
A. Cameron
Department of Mechanical
Engineering,
Lanchester Polytechnic,
Priory Street,
Coventry CV1 5FB
Tel: Coventry (0203) 24166

National Secretary:
Dr A.J. Pointon
Department of Physics,
Portsmouth Polytechnic,
King Henry I Street,
Portsmouth PO1 2DZ
Tel: Portsmouth (0705) 27681

Conference Secretary:
Dr D. Burrin
Department of Biological Studies,
Lanchester Polytechnic,
Priory Street,
Coventry CV1 5FB

Chairman Legal Panel:
Sir E.F. Wilson
Advocates Library,
Elmdere-cul-de-sac,
London SE18

Minutes Secretary:
Mrs H. Eggins
Department of Humanities,
Ulster Polytechnic,
Jordanstown,
Newtownabbey
Co. Antrim BT37 0QB

Bulletin Editors:
J.R. Hart
Department of Humanities,
Hatfield Polytechnic,
PO Box 109,
Hatfield,.
Hertfordshire AL10 9AB

E.P. Zucker,
Department of Physics,
Polytechnic of North London,
Holloway,
London N7 8DB

Members:
D. Bullar
Department of Electrical
Engineering,
Brighton Polytechnic,
Moulsecoomb,
Brighton BN2 4GJ
Tel: Brighton (0273) 64141

D. Fox
Higher Education Centre,
Goldsmith House,
Trent Polytechnic,
Burton Street,
Nottingham NG1 4BU
Tel: Nottingham (0602) 48248

P.K. Koch
Department of Mechanical
Engineering,
Lanchester Polytechnic,
Priory Street,
Coventry CV1 5FB
Tel: Coventry (0203) 24166

Dr. A.R. Miller
Division of Law,
Polytechnic of South Bank,
Borough Road,
London SE1 0AA
Tel: 01-407 8989

W. Gray
Middlesex Polytechnic,
Level 4,
Bounds Green Road,
London N13 4RT

W. Anderson
School of Librarianship,
Leeds Polytechnic
28 Park Place,
Leeds LS1

J. Dawson
School of Law,
Leeds Polytechnic,
Vernon Road,
Leeds 1

Dr N.A.A. McFarlane
Department of Life Sciences,
Trent Polytechnic,
Nottingham NG1 4BU

J. Powell
Department of Biological Sciences,
Wolverhampton Polytechnic,
Wulfruna Street,
Wolverhampton WV1 1LY

A.R. White
Faculty of Engineering,
Liverpool Polytechnic,
Byrom Street
Liverpool L3 3AF

D. Johnston
Department of Chemical Science,
Huddersfield Polytechnic,
Queensgate,
Huddersfield ND1 3DN

Dr D. Walter
Department of Electrical
Engineering,
Hatfield Polytechnic,
PO Box 109,
Hatfield,
Hertfordshire AL10 9AB

LOCAL SECRETARIES
Birmingham
L.J. Wright
Department of Government
and Economics
Tel: 021–359 6721

Brighton
S.L. Harris
Mechanical Engineering
Tel: Brighton (0273) 693655

Bristol
Dr G.C. Carney
Science
Tel: Bristol (0272) 41241

Central London
(Marylebone Road)
D.A. Preddie
Civil Engineering
Tel: 01–486 5811

City of London
(Moorgate)
Dr M. Gumbrell
Physics
Tel: 01–283 1030

Hatfield
D. Chapple
Mechanical and Aeronautic
Engineering
Tel: Hatfield (070 72) 68100

Huddersfield
D. Johnston
Chemical Science,
Tel: Huddersfield (0484) 30501

Kingston
P. Wagstaff
MAP Engineering
Tel: 01–544 0151

Lanchester
(Coventry)
R.C. Adams
Mathematics
Tel: Coventry (0203) 24166

Leeds
W. Anderson
School of Librarianship
Tel: Leeds (0532) 41101

Leicester
Dr I. Davies
Pharmacy
Tel: Leicester (0533) 50181

Liverpool
P.D. Moloney
Languages
Tel: 051–207 3581

Manchester
N. Aspinall
Medlock Fine Art Centre
Tel: 061–228 2351

Middlesex
(Enfield)
G. Slattery
Engineering
Tel: 01–368 1299

Newcastle
D.J. Vaizey
Mathematics, Statistics and
Computing
Tel: Newcastle-upon-Tyne (0632)
26002

North East London
(West Ham)
R.G. Smith
Biological Sciences
Tel: 01–555 0811

North London
(Holloway Road)
K. Veale
Extension Studies
Tel: 01–607 2789

North Staffordshire
(Stoke)
B.J. Williams
Chemistry
Tel: Stoke-on-Trent (0782) 45531

Oxford
F. Stubbs
Construction
Tel: Oxford (0865) 64777

Plymouth
A.H. Moreton
Engineering Science
Tel: Plymouth (0752) 21312 Ext. 272

Portsmouth
Mrs E.M. Aldridge
Languages
Tel: Portsmouth (0705) 27681

Preston
P.R. Bissell
Physics
Tel: Preston (0772) 51831

Sheffield
Dr R.M. Wood
Applied Physics
Tel: Sheffield (0742) 20911

South Bank
(Wandsworth Road)
R. Stewart
Land Surveying
Tel: 01–928 8989

Sunderland
S.J. Overerd
Business Management
Tel: Sunderland (0783) 76191

Teesside
Dr P. Bunn
Electrical, Instrumentation and
Control Engineering
Tel: Stockton-on-Tees (0642) 44176

Thames
(Woolwich)
Dr R.A.M. Scott
Materials Science
Tel: 01–854 2030

Trent
(Nottingham)
Dr N.A.A. MacFarlane
Life Sciences
Tel: Nottingham (0602) 48248

Ulster
(Jordanstown)
Mrs H. Eggins
Humanities
Tel: Whiteabbey (0231) 65131

Wales
(Llantrisant)
Dr H. Elliott
Chemistry
Tel: Llantrisant (0443) 405133

Wolverhampton
J. Hunter
Humanities
Tel: Wolverhampton (0902) 28521

Periodicals: *Bulletin* (monthly during term time) and a variety of information publications, e.g. Health and Safety, Taxation and EDAPT, the publication of the Education Panel.

Policy: The Association is in favour of national control of the Polytechnics compatible with their national and international role and parity of provision for Polytechnics and Universities; and believes in the distinctive role of the Polytechnics for both community and vocational education.

POST OFFICE ENGINEERING UNION (POEU)*†
Greystoke House, 150 Brunswick Road, Ealing, London W5 1AW
Tel: 01–998 2981

The POEU represents members employed in the telecommunication business of the Post Office; it also represents a smaller group of staff employed on broad engineering and associated work in the postal business, and staff employed on support functions for the telecommunications side of the industry. The membership does not include Supervisory Officers. There are members throughout the whole of the UK which has 290 branches all staffed by voluntary officers and workers.
Current membership: 121,406

OFFICIALS
National Executive Council
President: J. Scott-Garner
Vice-President: F.W. Feltham,

Members			
P.A. Evers	J.D Dodds	A.R. Field	E.W. Purkis
W.A. Cox	W.J. Walker	D. Raftery	M.F. Hubbard
A.I. Young	M.G. Ronaldson	K. Thomas	L.A. Willett
P.J. Lee	G.S. Duncan	W.J. Fry	J.T. Lane
R.G. Rock	L.R. Gillard	B.E. Harper	
	T.E. Jones	W.E.P Wilcox	

General Secretary: B. Stanley
Deputy General Secretary: E.A. Webb, MA
General Treasurer: D. Norman, MA

Assistant Secretaries
Committee A: D. Bourn
Committee B: F. Berezai
Committee C: J. Rose
Establishment Committee: E.C. George, J. Regan
Education Department: L.E. Gyseman
Legal Aid Department: E. Kenworthy
Social Security Department: F.H. Edwards
Publicity Department: N. Howard
Political Organiser: J. Golding, MP
Political Officer: N. Howard
National Organisers: J. Starmer, V. Turner
London Regional Organiser: J. Dunn
Research Officer: P.H. Shaw, BA
Assistant Research Officers: Miss V. Kidd, R. Darlington
Sponsored Members of Parliament:
J. Golding, MP, (Newcastle under Lyme)
R. Stott, MP, (West Houghton)
J. McWilliams (Blaydon)

Periodical: *POEU Journal* (monthly)

POST OFFICE EXECUTIVES, SOCIETY OF (SPOE)*†
116 Richmond Road, Kingston upon Thames, Surrey KT2 5HL
Tel: 01-549 3323

Formed in 1972 by the amalgamation of the Association of Post
Office Executives and the Society of Post Office Engineers. The first
covered mostly technical and quasi-technical junior grade
supervising staff and the second middle grade supervising engineers.
The senior engineers joined in 1974 and the sales managers in 1975.
The society now represents most of Post Office Telecommunications
managers up to Senior Director, engineering managers in the Postal
Business and senior managers in the Data Processing Service.
Membership is spread throughout Great Britain and Northern
Ireland, being about 90 per cent of staff on grades for which the union
is recognised. The union affiliates to Amnesty International and the
Conservation Society.

Current membership: 22,359

FULL-TIME OFFICIALS
General Secretary: J.K. Glynn
Assistant General Secretary: Miss C.K. Palfrey
Assistant Secretary: R.M. Bunnage
Assistant Secretary: T. Wilkinson

Full-time officials are appointed by the Executive Council. The President and
Executive council are elected by Annual Conference.

President: J.O. Helleur
Council:
J.A. Brookes
R. Coombes
G.S. Evans
R.G. Humphreys
H.J. Jordan
J.C. Lashmar
H. Marchant
A. Short
J. Thorpe
M.J. Townsend
F.D. Whitehead
J. Williams

Periodical: *The Review* (monthly)

POST OFFICE MANAGEMENT STAFFS ASSOCIATION (POMSA)*
52 Broadway, Bracknell, Berkshire RG12 1AJ
Tel: Bracknell (0344) 24061

Affiliated to the TUC in July 1957.
Current membership: 18,500

OFFICIAL
General Secretary: L.F. Pratt

Periodical: *New Management* (monthly)

POST OFFICE WORKERS, UNION OF (UPW)*†
UPW House, Crescent Lane, Clapham Common, London SW4 9RN
Tel: 01–622 9977

Formed in 1920 by amalgamation between three major unions, Fawcett Association (organising sorters), Postal and Telegraph Clerks Association and Postmen's Federation, and a number of smaller unions.

Membership is spread throughout the whole of the United Kingdom and Northern Ireland. The UPW is a highly centralised organisation with only 12 full-time officials, all of whom are elected and stay in office until retirement. It represents rank and file grades in the Post Office (e.g. Postmen, Telephonists, Postal Officers, Telegraphists, Cleaners). About 20% of the union's members are women.
Current membership: 197,259

FULL-TIME OFFICIALS
General Secretary: T. Jackson
Deputy General Secretary: N. Stagg
Assistant Secretaries:
Miss J.M. McKinlay,
K. McAllister,
A.D. Reid
M.H. Styles
W.M. Tracey
A.D. Tuffin
W.H. Wolfenden
Organising Secretary: R.I. Rowley
General Treasurer: F.W. Moss
Editor: H. Burnett

EXECUTIVE COUNCIL (1979–80)
The Executive Council is elected annually at the union's conference.
Chairman: J.R. Fraser

F.J. Binks	J. Mahoney
A.J. Clarke	M. Morritt
Miss V. Clements	R. Nelson
P.W. Curtis	A. Slater
J. R. Fraser	Ms M. Spurr
R. Devine	J. Taylor
P. Grace	Mrs. B. Treble
J. Hawkins	
D. G. Hodgson	
J.T. Jacques	
H.J. Jones	

Periodical: *The Post* (monthly)

Policy: The UPW has generally supported the incomes policy but only when sponsored by the TUC.

POWER LOOM CARPET WEAVERS' AND TEXTILE WORKERS' ASSOCIATION*‡
Callows Lane, Kidderminster, Worcestershire DY10 2JG
Tel: Kidderminster (0562) 3192

Founded in 1866 as the Kidderminster and Stourport United Brussels Power Loom Carpet Weavers' Friendly Society, and two years later known as the Power Loom Carpet Weavers' Mutual Defence and Provident Association. In 1917 the union opened its membership to those textile workers, many of them women, who were not carpet weavers, at the same time changing its name to the one that still exists today with a strong membership within the carpet trade.
Current membership: 6,287
    Males: 4,113
    Females: 2,174

OFFICIALS
All officials of the union are elected.

FULL-TIME OFFICIALS:
General Secretary: D.T. Carter
Assistant and Financial Secretary: B.C. Moule
Negotiating Officer: H.T. Moore

Lay Officials:
President: H.J. Simmonds
Vice-President: D. O'Malley

Executive Committee:
Miss Millward
Mrs R. Rouse
K. Andrews
W. Andrews
A. Carter
D. Howley
G. Newton
R. White

POWER LOOM OVERLOOKERS, SCOTTISH UNION OF*‡
3 Napier Terrace, Dundee, Tayside
Tel: Dundee (0382) 612196

See British Federation of Textile Technicians
Current membership: 250

OFFICIAL
General Secretary: J. Reilly

POWER LOOM OVERLOOKERS, YORKSHIRE ASSOCIATION OF*‡
Textile Hall, Westgate, Bradford BD1 2RG
Tel: Bradford (0274) 27966

See British Federation of Textile Technicians
Current membership: 1,252

OFFICIAL
General Secretary: K. Hattersley

PRESSED GLASSMAKERS' SOCIETY‡
11 Oakfield Road, Lobley Hill, Gateshead NE11 0AA
Tel: Dunston (0632) 605099

Founded in 1872 as a craft union of members making for the most part hand-made glassware. Membership is declining as a result of

automated processes. It is affiliated to the General Federation of Trade Unions.
Current membership: 50–60

PART-TIME OFFICIALS
General Secretary: A.W. De-Vere
President: R. Punshon,
37 King Street, Gateshead, Tyne and Wear

DISTRICT SECRETARIES
Gateshead: E. Steanson,
38 Ventnor Crescent, Gateshead, Tyne and Wear
Sunderland: A. Turner,
97 Percy Terrace, South Hendon, Sunderland

PRINTERS, GRAPHICAL AND MEDIA PERSONNEL, NATIONAL SOCIETY OF OPERATIVE (NATSOPA)*

Caxton House, 13–16 Borough Road, London SE1 0AL
Tel: 01–928 1481

A union covering the national and provincial press, general printing, magazines, news agencies, advertising agencies, ink and roller making and sign and display work. Established September 1889 as the Printers' Labourers' Union, solely London based, initially with 500 members. Changing its name to the Operative Printers' Assistants Society in 1898, its activities were extended to the provinces in 1904 and the name changed to the National Society of Operative Printers and Assistants, NATSOPA, in 1912. The Stereotypers and Electrotypers Assistants' Society was dissolved, to save the expense of amalgamation proceedings, and joined as a body in 1914. The London Press Clerks Association joined in July 1920. In 1966 the union amalgamated with the National Union of Printing, Bookbinding and Paper Workers to form the Society of Graphical and Allied Trades which was subsequently dissolved in 1972, and the union name changed to the present one. October 1972 saw the Sign and Display Trade Union transfer their engagements to NATSOPA.
Current membership: 54,471

NATIONAL OFFICERS
General Secretary: O. O'Brien
National Assistant Secretaries:
J.A. Selby, E. O'Brien, J.A. Moakes
National Officer: A.B. Smith
Assistant Organisers: N. Preece, J.B. White
Sign and Display Officer and Organiser: R.W.E. Saunders
London Machine Branch
Secretary:
J. Mitchell
Assistant Secretary:
C. Cherrill
Natsopa House,
Milcote Street,
London SE1 0AL

London Branch of Clerical,
Administrative and
Executive Personnel
Secretary: C.A. Robbins
Assistant Secretary:
Mrs A. Field
Natsopa House,
Milcote Street,
London SE1 0AL

London Branch of Revisers,
Ink and Roller Makers
and Auxiliaries
Secretary:
D.E. Hutchinson
Natsopa House,
Milcote Street,
London SE1 0AL
Assistant Secretary:
K. Lucas

South Eastern
Secretary:
G.A. Allen
67 Albert Road,
South Woodford,
London E18 1LF

Eastern
Secretary:
D. Hogan
Sarel House,
193 Rickmansworth Road,
Watford,
Hertfordshire

Western
Secretary:
W.J.G. Hall
Equity Law Building,
36/38 Baldwin Street,
Bristol BS1 1NR

North Western
Secretary:
C.V. Brown
Assistant Secretary:
J. Blakey
10 Swan Street,
Manchester M4 5JN

North Eastern
Secretary:
A. Butcher
2nd Floor,
Parade Chambers,
East Parade,
Sheffield S1 2ET

Northern
Secretary:
G. Lambie
2 Clifton Street,
Glasgow G3 7LA

Newcastle Branch
Secretary: J. Nugent
5 Walker Terrace,
Gateshead,
Tyne and Wear NE8 1JR

Periodical: *Journal and Graphic Review* (monthly)

PRISON OFFICERS' ASSOCIATION (POA)*
Cronin House, 245 Church Street, Edmonton, London N9 9HW
Tel: 01–803 0255 (3 lines)

Formed in 1939, this is the recognised union for organising and representing prison officers and staffs of the special hospitals. It is a member union of the Civil Service National Whitley Council Staff Side and a TUC affiliate.
Current membership: 22,189
 Males: 20,762
 Females: 1,427

FULL-TIME OFFICIALS
General Secretary: K.A. Daniel
Deputy Secretary: P. Rushworth
Assistant Secretary: D. Evans

Periodical: *Prison Officers' Magazine* (monthly)

PROBATION OFFICERS, NATIONAL ASSOCIATION OF (NAPO)

First Floor, Ambassador House, Brigstock Road, Thornton Heath, Surrey CR4 7JG
Tel: 01–689 1116/7

NAPO was formed in 1912 and, in the main, owes its existence to developments arising from the appointment of the first Police Court Missionary in 1876 and the Probation of Offenders Act of 1908. It is the national professional association of the Probation Service and is thus concerned with advancing probation work in all its aspects. NAPO is also the negotiating body in respect of probation officers' salaries and conditions of service and was registered as an independent trade union in 1976. It is currently pursuing affiliation to the TUC. In 1977 it widened eligibility for full membership to include certain other workers, who are directly involved with the Probation Service. In addition to work involving the welfare of its members, it is actively concerned with social policy matters affecting the general community.
Current membership: 4,600

OFFICIALS
President: Lord Hunt, CBE, DSO
General Secretary: Mrs J. Kirkpatrick
Assistant General Secretaries: P.J. Bowyer, D.A. Lafferty

THE PROFESSIONAL ASSOCIATION OF TEACHERS

See TEACHERS, THE PROFESSIONAL ASSOCIATION OF

PROFESSIONAL CIVIL SERVANTS, INSTITUTION OF (IPCS)*

3 Northumberland Street, London WC2N 5BS
Tel: 01–930 9755

A trade union founded in 1919 and now representing about 100,000 professional, technical, scientific or specialist officers employed as civil servants or as employees of organisations which are financed wholly or in part by the central UK government. It does not embrace staff employed in regional or local government service, or in the National Health Service or in the nationalised industries (e.g. the Electricity Council). On the other hand, it does organise staff in the Atomic Energy Authority, the Research Councils, the Civil Aviation Authority and the National Museums.

The membership covers a very wide range of professions and

specialisms including the following: Architects, Engineers, Surveyors, Scientists, Accountants, Photographers, Cartographers, Medical Officers, Information Officers, Psychologists, Librarians, Actuaries, Conservation Officers, Fire Service Officers, Restorers, Catering Officers and very many smaller departmental grades and classes like Air Traffic Control Officers, Veterinary Officers, Patent Officers, Intelligence Officers, Lecturers, Health and Safety Inspectors, Housing and Planning Inspectors, Prison Chaplains, Social Work Officers.

The sovereign body of the IPCS is the Annual Delegate Conference attended by about 475 delegates from the 131 branches of the Institution. The ADC elects a National Executive Committee of 25 members including three National Officers. The National Executive Committee manages and transacts all matters and business in the affairs of the Institution between meetings of the Conference in conformity with the policies determined by the Conference. The Institution also has eighteen professional groups which, with the exception of one which has some executive powers, act in an advisory capacity to the National Executive Committee on matters affecting their profession across the Institution as a whole. Branches are organised on the basis of employing department or organisation.

The institution is affiliated to the Trades Union Congress, National Federation of Professional Workers, Public Services International and to a variety of other professional, trade union, social and educational bodies.

Although the Institution is primarily concerned with the pay and conditions of its members it also attaches considerable importance to the contribution it makes to policy on science and technology and on other issues which closely affect the job and professional interests of its members. It is a member of the Parliamentary and Scientific Committee which includes trade unions, MPs and other interested bodies concerned with policy on science and technology.

IPCS is the second largest trade union in the Civil Service.
Current membership: 100,000

OFFICIALS
Officers elected annually
Chairman: J.S. Sim
Vice-Chairman: V.C. Moores
Deputy Vice-Chairman: E.T. Mannins

Permanent full-time officials
General Secretary: W. McCall
Deputy General Secretaries: C. Cooper, E. Hewlett
Assistant General Secretaries: Miss M. Platt, BA, W. Wright
Assistant Secretaries:

Miss A.C. Hilton, BSc	W. Brett
B. Stevens	D. Davies, BA
C.F. Waters	R. McDowell
(Research Officer)	Miss E. Jenkins, BA
G. Janeway	Miss E. Stallibrass, BA

Mrs V. Ellis, PhD   Miss L. Cohen, BA
C. Crook, CEng, MIMechE   Miss W. Harrison, BA
                                           Miss J. Thurston, BA

Editor and Public Relations Officer: P.L. Downton
Press Officer: J. O'Dea, MBE

Periodical: *State Service* (monthly) and *IPCS Bulletin* (fortnightly)
for lay and full-time officers.

PROFESSIONAL, EXECUTIVE, CLERICAL AND COMPUTER STAFF, ASSOCIATION OF (APEX)*
22 Worple Road, London SW19 4DF
Tel: 01–947 3131

Founded in 1890 as the National Union of Clerks, the union was
primarily intended for clerks only. The union signed its first
engineering procedure agreement with the Engineering Employers
Federation in 1920. In the same year the name was changed to the
National Union of Clerks and Administrative Workers. The union's
first paid General Secretary was Herbert Henry Elvin in 1909. Upon
amalgamation with the union of the Association of Women Clerks
and Secretaries in 1940 the name was changed again to the Clerical
and Administrative Workers' Union, and the present title was
adopted in 1972. APEX now caters for computer, supervisory and
managerial staff, including security personnel, industrial nurses and
machine operators in addition to clerical grades, and has members in
civil air transport, the co-operative movement, steel, coal, the car
industry, insurance, confectionery and chocolate manufacture and
the tobacco industry, as well as engineering. In 1978 the AA Staff
Association amalgamated with APEX.
Current membership: 151,343

NATIONAL OFFICIALS
General Secretary: R. Grantham
Deputy General Secretary: T. Thomas
Assistant General Secretary: R. Edwards
Executive Secretaries:
R. Stephen
D. Lapish
K. Standring

NATIONAL EXECUTIVE COUNCIL
President: D. Howell, MP
Vice-Presidents: Miss J. Travis, K.B. Smith
Executive Council: D. Winnich, M.P., R.A. Peck

Area Council Representatives:
London and Home Counties	A.E. Hayes
Midlands	W. Linthwaite
Northern	H. Green
North East	H. Skyte

Northern Ireland   W. Davies
North West   J.F. Roberts
Scotland   C.R. Stuart
Wales   D. Sims
West England   M. Cromwell

General Treasurer: M. Barrett
Trustees:
D. Currie
Ms H. Walker
Editor: J. Jump
Finance Officer: A. Kenward
Conference arrangements: T. Ferguson

DISTRICT OFFICIALS

London and Home Counties
Area Secretary:
S.F. Vickers
Senior Organisers:
L. Gristey
A. Cheeseman
Area Organisers:
I. Trott
R. Ascough
D. Wood
K. Whyman
D. Rice
R. Carpenter
M. Tonner

North East
Area Secretary:
B. Hayward, JP
Senior Organiser:
N. Jolly
Area Organisers:
H.A. Clarke
B. Charlesworth
H. Hunt
B. Yegliss

Midlands
Area Secretary:
F.W. Leath
Organisers:
N. Evans
H.D. Bott
A.D. Gilliver
D.A. Braisted
V.H. McElhinney
L. Watson
M.W. Langford
G.A. Roberts
G. Veart
O.J. Granfield

North West
Area Secretary:
P. Scott
Senior Organiser:
M. Robinson
Organisers:
P. Goodwin
W. Gilkinson
J. Preece
D. McLaughlin

Northern
Area Secretary:
T. Hallett
Senior Organiser:
J. Creaby
Organiser:
D. Morgan

West England
Area Secretary:
F. Cole
Senior Organiser:
G. Camamile
Organiser:
J. Colville
G. Camamile

Welsh
Area Secretary:
O.C. Saunders
Area Organiser:
K. Chamberlain

Automobile Association Section
National Secretary:
J.R. Whiffin

Area Secretary:
T. Robertson
Senior Organiser:
H. Smith
Organisers:
E. Nolan
T. Reid
A. Cowan

Northern Ireland
Area Secretary:
P. McCartan
Organiser:
C. Kell

General Accident Section
General Secretary:
M. Ward

Periodical: *APEX* (monthly)

PROFESSIONAL FOOTBALLERS ASSOCIATION (PFA)
124 Corn Exchange Buildings, Hanging Ditch, Manchester M4 3BN
Tel: 061–834 7554

Formed in 1907 and confined to professional footballers within England and Wales. It is affiliated to the Radio and Television Safeguards Committee and the Federation of International Footballers Associations.
Current membership: 2,500

OFFICIALS
Chairman: G. Taylor
Secretary: C. Lloyd, OBE
Millpond, Alvanley via Warrington WA6 9HB
Tel: Helsby (092 82) 2330

The Association is governed by a Management Committee of eight members including the Chairman.

PROFESSIONAL SCIENTISTS AND TECHNOLOGISTS, ASSOCIATION OF (APST)

See MANAGEMENT AND PROFESSIONAL STAFF, ASSOCIATION OF

PUBLIC EMPLOYEES, NATIONAL UNION OF (NUPE)*
Civic House, Aberdeen Terrace, London SE3
Tel: 01–852 2842/7

Originated in 1888 under the title London County Council Employees Protection Society, and took on its present title in 1928. Membership (1979) is 712,392, having increased by more than 150 per cent in last ten years. The membership is divided in approximately the following proportions: local government 55 per cent, National Health Service 36 per cent, university non-teaching staff 5 per cent, water services 4 per cent. Women members number 450,000, the highest figure for any union in Britain. In 1975 the structure of the union was reorganised and a system of district committees, area committees, divisional councils and divisional conferences introduced; these are based on 20,000 stewards and 3,200 branch officers with the aim of extending the democratic base of the union and securing greater participation in the decision making process. Current membership: 712,392

OFFICIALS
General Secretary: A.W. Fisher
Assistant General Secretaries: W.H. Bull, B. Dix, R. Keating
National Officers: R.K. Bickerstaffe, R.L. Jones
Assistant National Officers: H.E. Wild, R. Poole

Divisional Officers

N.R. Wright,
6 Sherwood Rise,
Nottingham NG7 6JS

D. Gregory,
158–159 St. Helens Road,
Swansea

B. Shuttleworth,
Monaco House,
Bristol Street,
Birmingham B5 7AS

H. Barker,
13–15 Stockwell Road,
London SW9 9AT

R. Curran,
18 Albany Street,
Edinburgh EH1 32B

F. Huff,
853 Fishponds Road,
Fishponds,
Bristol

L. Sawyer,
Southend,
Fernwood Road,
Jesmond,
Newcastle-upon-Tyne NE2 1TH

W. Gregory,
Blackgates House,
Bradford Road,
Tingley,
Yorkshire

B. Couldridge,
Garland Hill House,
Sandy Lane,
St. Paul's Cray,
Kent

C. Barnett,
222 Stamford Street,
Ashton-under-Lyne,

In addition there are 20 Assistant Divisional Officers and 119 Area Officers operating within the Divisions for which the Divisional Officers are responsible.

Periodical: *Public Employees* (monthly)

PUBLIC SERVICE FINANCE OFFICERS, ASSOCIATION OF
Terminus House, The High, Harlow, Essex CM20 1TZ
Tel: Harlow (0279) 34443/4

The association was formed in 1920 for professionally qualified accountants in the Local Government service. It gradually widened its interests and now covers staff in the Health Service and the Water Industry having changed its name from the Association of Local Government Financial Officers to its present one in 1975. It is certified as an independent trade union under the current industrial relations legislation. Membership includes an increasing number of women and the union is represented on the national negotiating machinery covering Local Government and the Water Service. It is a member of the Federation of Professional Officers' Associations. Current membership: 3,000

OFFICIALS
Executive Committee
President: J.F. Hicks, IPFA
Hon. Secretary: D.B. Chynoweth, BA, IPFA, MBIM
General Secretary: Mrs E. Farrow (full-time)
Six additional committee members

Executive Council: 31 members

RADIO AND ELECTRONIC OFFICERS' UNION (REOU)*
4–6 Branfill Road, Upminster, Essex RM14 2XX
Tel: Upminster (04022) 22321/2

Established in 1912 by a small group of Wireless Operators serving in the Merchant Navy, the union grew rapidly and by 1918 a permanent Secretariat and office had been set up in London. In 1921 the Cable and Telegraph Operators Assocation amalgamated with the Association of Wireless Telegraphists and the combined union was re-named The Association of Wireless and Cable Telegraphists. To accord with the change in duties of its members the title was changed to the Radio Officers' Union in 1937 and to the Radio and Electronic Officers' Union in 1967. Current membership comprises Radio and Radio Electronic Officers in the Merchant Navy and fishing fleets, Radio Officers and Technicians on oil rigs, and Technicians and Radio/Electronic Engineers employed in ancillary shore industries.
    The MN Radio Officer membership includes 33 female Radio Officers.
Current membership: 3,926

OFFICIALS
Full-Time Officers
General Secretary/Treasurer: K.A. Murphy
Assistant General Secretary: J. Bromley
National Organiser: P. Curwell

Executive Committee
These are not full-time officials and are elected for three year periods.
Chairman: H. Allan
Vice-Chairman: A.E. Fell

M.L. Bird	H.G.J.A. Loane
A.E. Burbidge	J.J.B. Toomey
R.G. Campbell	M.G. Ridehalgh
D.A. Drummond	T.P. Twomey
M. Prior	D.J.B. Haines
S. Harding	W.E. Meeks

R.A. White
Assistant to General
Secretary (East Coast),
Radio and Electronic
Officers' Union,
Bridge Chambers,
Alfred Gelder Street,
Hull HU1 2JQ

Assistant to General
Secretary(West Coast):
vacant

Periodical: *Signal* (bimonthly)

RAILWAYMEN, NATIONAL UNION OF (NUR)*
Unity House, Euston Road, London NW1 2BL
Tel: 01-387 4771
(The NUR expects to move in March 1980 to Bentley House, Eastern
Road, London NW1, the telephone number will remain the same.)

An industrial union catering for all grades formed in 1913 by the
amalgamation of the Amalgamated Society of Railway Servants with
two other railway unions. Members are employed mainly by British
Railways Board and subsidiary companies, e.g. British Rail
Engineering Ltd and British Transport Hotels Ltd. Substantial
membership is employed by LTE, NCL and Freightliners Ltd.
Membership also includes staff employed in subsidiary companies of
the National Bus Company, principally in the West Country.
    For many years the NUR has advocated the introduction of an
integrated and co-ordinated transport system with an increasing role
for public transport.
Current membership: 180,000

FULL-TIME OFFICIALS
President: A. Rees
General Secretary: S. Weighell
Senior Assistant General Secretary: R. Tuck
Assistant General Secretaries: F. Cannon, C. Turnock
Headquarters Officer: A. Dodds, B. Arundel
Divisional Officers (17) based in different areas of the country.
The union is administered by an Executive Committee of 24 members
operating from Head Office.

Periodical: *Transport Review* (weekly)

RETAIL BOOK, STATIONERY AND ALLIED TRADES EMPLOYEES' ASSOCIATION, THE
7 Grape Street, Shaftesbury Avenue, London WC2H 8DW
Tel: 01-836 4897

ROLL TURNERS' TRADE SOCIETY, BRITISH (BRTTS)*
24 Moreton Parade, May Bank, Newcastle, Staffordshire ST5 0JD
Tel: 0782 617685

Founded in 1898, and recognised in the steel industry mainly in Lancashire, Midlands and South Wales.
Current membership: 723

OFFICIAL
General Secretary: D. Storer

ROSSENDALE UNION OF BOOT, SHOE AND SLIPPER OPERATIVES

See BOOT, SHOE AND SLIPPER OPERATIVES, ROSSENDALE UNION OF

ROYAL COLLEGE OF MIDWIVES LIMITED, THE
15 Mansfield Street, London W1M 0BE
Tel: 01–580 6523/4/5

The College was founded in 1881 as the Midwives Institute and received a certificate as an Independent Trade Union in 1976. In membership today are approximately 70 per cent of practising midwives. The College is administered by a Council elected by a postal ballot. It is the negotiating body for all midwives, having representatives on the Nurses and Midwives Whitley Council. The aim of the College is to advance the art and science of midwifery and to maintain high professional standards. Under the Midwives Acts the College has representatives on the statutory bodies for midwives of the United Kingdom and also represents midwives on appropriate Government and other national committees. It maintains a centre of information on midwifery. The library is open to the public for reference purposes. Exchange of information and ideas on the profession of midwifery throughout the world is encouraged and efforts are made to improve international understanding.
Current membership: 18,000

OFFICIALS
President: Mrs W.A. Andrews, CBE, RFN, SCM, HV(Cert)
General Secretary (Acting): Miss R.A. Ashton, SRN, SCM, MTD

Industrial Relations Department
Director: Mrs A.M. Hardie, SRN, OHNC
Labour Relations Officers: Mrs M.A. Stansfield, SRN, SCM, MTD,
K.W.H. Limington, FHA, FSS,
Miss H.C. Butler, RGN, SCM, ONC, RCI (Edinburgh)

RCM Scottish Board
Secretary: Miss J. Savage, SRN, SCM, MTD
37 Frederick Street, Edinburgh EH2 1EP

SAWMAKERS' PROTECTION SOCIETY, SHEFFIELD*
27 Main Avenue, Totley, Sheffield S17 4FH
Tel: Sheffield (0742) 361044

The date of formation of the Sawmakers Society is unknown.
Documents belonging to the Society are in the safekeeping of the
Sheffield City Central Library Archives Dept and date back to 1797.
Amongst them there is a document which implies that there was in
existence in 1740 'a Society of Sawmakers'. The Society is totally
independent apart from affiliation to the Trades Union Congress in
1944 and is based in Sheffield. In addition to their trade union duties,
all the officers are employed full-time at sawmaking establishments
throughout the city.
Current membership: 241
    Males: 232
    Females: 9

OFFICIALS
President: H. Jones
33 Dryden Road, Sheffield 5
Secretary: A. Marples
27 Main Avenue, Totley, Sheffield S17 4FH
Assistant Secretary: C.H. Frost
61 Richmond Park Rise, Sheffield 13

Policy: The Society fully supported entry into Europe and the
previous Government's Pay Policies (phases 1 and 2) but is in favour
of a gradual return to free collective bargaining.

SCALEMAKERS, NATIONAL UNION OF (NUS)*
71 Cornwall Street, Birmingham B3 2EE
Tel: 021–236 8998

Founded in 1909, adopting the present title in 1930.
Current membership: 1,800

OFFICIAL
General Secretary: A. F. Smith

SCHOOLMASTERS AND UNION OF WOMEN TEACHERS, NATIONAL ASSOCIATION OF (NAS/UWT)*

P.O. Box 65, Swan Court, Hemel Hempstead, Hertfordshire HP1 1DT
Tel: Hemel Hempstead (0442) 42971/4

The NAS/UWT was formed on 1 January 1976 by the amalgamation of the National Association of Schoolmasters and the Union of Women Teachers.

The NAS was formed in 1919 by men returning from the Great War and who were disillusioned by the prospect of depressed salaries for schoolmasters. The UWT was founded in 1965 as a corollary of the NAS, and after 10 years of co-operation the decision to amalgamate was taken.

The NAS/UWT has in membership qualified teachers in all types of schools and colleges, excluding universities, in England, Wales, Scotland and Northern Ireland. It is now the second largest teachers' trade union.

The Association is affiliated to the TUC, but in all other aspects is non-political and non-sectarian. Within recent years contact has been established with other teacher unions in Europe through membership of the European Teachers' Trade Union Committee and on the international scene with affiliation to the International Federation of Free Teacher Unions.

Current membership: 120,000

OFFICIALS
General Secretary: T.A. Casey, CBE, KHS
Assistant General Secretaries: B.F. Wakefield, F.A. Smithies
Assistant Secretary: W.J. Heron, K. Ronald, K.J. Ellis, N. de Gruchy

Administrative Centre:
Hillscourt Education Centre, Rose Hill, Rednal, Birmingham B45 8RS
Tel: 021–453 7221

REGIONAL AND AREA OFFICIALS

Scottish Secretary
R. McClement,
SSA Office,
41 York Place,
Edinburgh EE1 3HP
Tel: 031 556 8825

Welsh Regional Official
H.H Thomas,
'Sealands',
Llanfairfechan,
Gwynedd LL33 0DY
Tel: 0248 680675

NI Regional Official
T. McKee, BA,
NAS/UWT Regional Office,
16 Donegal Square South,
Belfast BT1 5JK
Tel: 0232 26065

NW Regional Official
E.R. Holden, ACP, MSIT
37 Overton Crescent,
Sale, Cheshire M33 4EG
Tel: 061 969 1517

Northern Regional Official
C.J. McInnes,
Regional Office,
NAS/UWT Education Centre,
Spout Lane,
Washington Village,
Tyne and Wear NE38 7HP
Tel: 0632 465381

Yorkshire Regional Official
M. Calvert, DPE
'Tynecroft',
Tweedy Street,
Wilsden,
Bradford,
West Yorkshire BD15 0AE
Tel: 09766 60677

AREA OFFICIALS
W.L. Bolitho,
NAS/UWT N. West Area Office,
'Camelot',
6 Elmsley Road,
Liverpool L18 8AZ
Tel: 051 724 1724/1930

M.A. Langdell, BSc, ARCM
2 Warner road,
Hornsey,
London N8 7ED
Tel: 01–340 7869

G.J. Lewis,
156 Stanway Road,
Shirley,
Solihull,
West Midlands B90 3JH
Tel: 021–744 6125

G.F. Limburn,
7 Church Croft,
Edlesborough,
Nr Dunstable
Bedfordshire LU6 2HU
Tel: 0525 220759

A.A.J. Riley,
41 Combe Street Lane,
Yeovil,
Somerset BA21 3PD
Tel: 0935 22314

A.J. Smyth,
27 Aigburth Hall Avenue,
Liverpool L19 9EA
Tel: 051–427 3186

E.F. Tomkins,
Brook House,
Lower Middle Hill,
Pensilva,
Liskeard,
Cornwall PL14 5QF
Tel: 0579 62692

F. Woodcock,
55 Cliff Gardens,
Scunthorpe,
South Humberside DM15 7PH
Tel: 0724 3682

EXECUTIVE LIST 1979–80
OFFICERS
President:
Miss C. Skeavington, MEd, FRSA,
28 Ralegh Avenue,
St. Helier,
Jersey, CI
Tel: *H* 0534 30888,
     S 0534 35541

Senior Vice-President:
C.F. Abraham,
Croyle House,
Kentisbeare,
Cullompton,
Devon
Tel: *H* Kentisbeare 355
     S Exeter (0392) 67773

Junior Vice-President
A.M.S. Poole,
'Springbank',
124 World's End Lane,
Chelsfield,
Orpington,
Kent BR6 6AS
Tel: *H* Farnboro' (Kent) (0689)
         55984
     S 01–648 1450

Hon. Treasurer
R.B. Cocking,
Spindrift,
Old House Lane,
Dayhouse Bank,
Romsley,
Halesowen,
Worcestershire
Tel: *H* 0562 710570
     S 021–453 3234

Ex-President
C.S. Jones,
580 Daws Heath Road,
Hadleigh,
Benfleet,
Essex SS7 2NL
Tel: *H* 0702 555506
    S 02774 55191

MEMBERS OF EXECUTIVE
District
16
G.G. Barnes,
7 St. Margarets' Close,
Upton,
Norwich,
Norfolk NR13 6BD
Tel: *H* 0493 750770
    S 0493 2177

2
A. Bellarby, JP,
40 Ennerdale Avenue,
Workington CA14 3JT
Tel: *H* 0900 3244
    S 0946 830427

*
Mrs A. Boone,
8 Cromdale Avenue,
Bolton BL1 4PS
Tel: *H* 0204 40970
    S 0204 23280 Greenland Road,
Farnworth, Bolton
    S 0204 71850 Harrowby Street,
Farnworth, Bolton

7
J. Boone,
8 Cromdale Avenue,
Bolton BL1 4PS
Tel: *H* 0204 40970
    S 0204 23280 Greenland Road,
Farnworth, Bolton
    S 0204 71850 Harrowby Street,
Farnworth, Bolton

4
B.A. Clegg, BSc,
14 Northwood Park,
Woodlesford,
Leeds LS26 8PF
Tel: *H* 0532 821668
    S 0924 823135

26
W.P. Coakley, MA,
26 Upper Park Road,
Camberley,
Surrey
Tel: *H* 0276 27589
    S 0932 46162

3
F.A. Coleman,
25 Clairville Road,
Middlesbrough,
Cleveland
Tel: *H* 0642 211525
    S 0642 219299

4
L. Cooper, BSc,
17 Hillingdon Way,
Leeds LS17 7QX
Tel: *H* 0532 678571
    S 0977 682442

18
R.A. Darke,
72 Addison Close,
Exeter
Tel: *H* 0392 50839
    S 0392 76110

13
D.L. Davies,
15 Avondale,
Droitwich,
Worcestershire
Tel: *H* 09057 4231
    S 0905 42306

10
I.J. Donaldson,
11 Cedar Avenue,
Shawbury,
Shrewsbury SY4 4JA
Tel: *H* 0939 250295
    S 0952 44895

5
L.W. Dore, BSc,
65 Rydal Road,
Hambleton,
Blackpool FY6 9BL
Tel: *H* 0253 700632
    S 03917 2843/2668

20
I.M. Frampton,
'Sutherland',
Broad Oak,
Sturminster Newton,
Dorset
Tel: *H* 0258 72905
    S 0258 72796

1
H. Gardner,
'Heatherlea',
Dipton,
Stanley,
Co. Durham DE9 9FL
Tel: *H* 0207 570231
    S 0207 70396

25
D.M. Griffiths, BA,
16 Campbell Close,
Chelmsford,
Essex CM2 9BE
Tel: *H* 0245 81813
    S 040 23 71334

17
D. Gwyn Jones, FRGS, LTCL,
Broomhills Farmhouse,
Little Burstead,
Billericay,
Essex CM12 9TR
Tel: *H* 02774 57549
    S 02774 56563

15
P. Harrison, BA(Hons), ACP,
3 Salwey Crescent,
Broxbourne,
Hertfordshire EN10 7NJ
Tel: *H* 09924 66769
    S 0992 54242 Ext 5115 up to
1.30
5114 after 1.30

27
J.P. Hennessey,
7 Gordon Road,
Sevenoaks,
Kent TN13 1HE
Tel: *H* 0732 51424
    S 0732 56592/55133

23
P. Herbert, MA(Oxon),
107 Cubitt House,
Poynders Road,
London SW4
Tel: *H* 01–673 8673
    S 01–788 3421

11
J.M. Inman, BA, NDA, DipREd,
The Grove Farm,
Waterfall,
Waterhouses,
Stoke-on-Trent,
Staffordshire
Tel: *H* 0538 6364
    S 0538 385737

29
R. Jenkins,
'Glynelroy',
1 Myrtle Road,
Cimla,
Neath,
West Glamorgan SA11 3UF
Tel: *H* 0538 6364
    S 063974 238

14
Mrs A. Jones, BSc,
5 Highfield Court,
Highfield Way,
Hazlemere,
High Wycombe,
Buckinghamshire HP15 7UX
Tel: *H* 0494–81 4670
    S 0494 23924

6
G. Kavanagh,
70 Woolacombe Road,
Liverpool L16 9JQ
Tel: *H* 051 722 3294
    S 051 263 6388

23
G.W. Lee, JP,
64 Lambeth Road,
London SE1 7PP
Tel: *H* 01–928 9714
    S 01–703 3455

7
M. Littlewood,
14 Sherbourne Road,
Middleton,
Manchester M24 3EH
Tel: *H* 061–643 6002
    S 061–643 5116

22
P.E. Lord,
11 Bosworth Road,
New Southgate,
London N11 2SY
Tel: *H* 01–889 1547
    S 01–889 6761

1
P. Matthews,
26 St. Michael's Crescent,
Heighington,
Darlington,
Co. Durham DL5 6RJ
Tel: *H* 0325 312483
    S 0388 720255

32
J. Milgrew, BSc, MIBiol,
47 Berelands Road,
Prestwick,
Ayrshire,
Scotland
Tel: *H* 0292 70917
    S 041 423 8932

*
Mrs B.M.W. Morgan,
92 Winston Road,
Withycombe Raleigh,
Exmouth,
Devon EX8 4LR
Tel: *H* 03952 77099
    S 03952 4761 Ext. 280 or 228

6
R.W. Morley, BSc,
2 Greenville Drive,
Maghull,
Liverpool L31 7DE
Tel: *H* 051 526 6236
    S 051 521 1734

31
E. O'Kane, MA, DipEd,
18 Bristol Avenue,
Belfast BT15 4AJ
Tel: *H* 0232 778274
    S 0232 770011

30
E.E. Powell, BA, FRGS
37 Lon-y-Dail,
Rhiwbina,
Cardiff CF4 6EA
Tel: *H* 0222 67339
    S 0222 30278

9
W. Ridealgh, MEd, DipEd,
242 Ings Road,
Hull HU8 0LZ
Tel: *H* 0482 783544
    S 0482 854687

8
H. Russon,
56 Barholm Road,
Sheffield S10 5RS
Tel: *H* 0742 301885
    S 0742 392531

21
R.P. Shore,
19 Maddoxford Way,
Botley,
Southampton SO3 2DW
Tel: *H* 04892 4156
    S 0703 23289

13
J.E. Skiffington,
48 Meadowfield Road,
Rubery,
Rednal,
Worcestershire B45 9BZ
Tel: *H* 021–453 8305
    S 021–476 8211 Ext. 345

24
G.K. Terrell, BA, DipEd,
1 Marion Court,
Griffiths Road,
Wimbledon,
London SW19
Tel: *H* 01–542 6218
    S 01–542 1212

12
G.S. Whelbourn,
60 Valley Prospect,
Newark,
Nottinghamshire NG24 4QW
Tel: *H* 0636 704680
    S 0602 264609

28
J. Wilce, BA, DipEd
10 Salisbury Road,
Wrexham,
Clwyd LL13 7AS
Tel: *H* 0978 262003
    S 0978 51211

19
G.W. Wills,
'Philmar',
Merriott Road,
Hinton St. George,
Somerset TA17 8SL
Tel: *H* 0460 72095
       S 0460 72677

Womens Advisory Committee
(Co-opted Members)
Mrs A Boone
Mrs B. M. W. Morgan

Periodical: *Schoolmaster and Career Teacher* (monthly)

Policy: The Association is committed to policies for the improvement of the education service and while recognising that the national budget is limited believes that adequate expenditure on education is vital to the future welfare and well-being of the nation. In particular the Association is committed to the view that the greatest improvement in the service can come about by the improvement of standards among teachers. The achievement of an all graduate profession is within sight and the union is continually urging the necessity of improving the quality and quantity of in-service training opportunities available to serving teachers. It has at Rednal near Birmingham its own Residentail Education Centre which is used to train its local officers and provide professional courses for its own members.

SCIENTIFIC, TECHNICAL AND MANAGERIAL STAFFS, ASSOCIATION OF, (ASTMS)*
10–26a Jamestown Road, Camden Town, London NW1 7DT
Tel: 01–267 4422

Formed in 1968 by a merger between the Association of Supervisory Staffs, Executives and Technicians (ASSET) and the Association of Scientific Workers (AScW). Both unions were basically engineering-orientated and held master procedure agreements with the Engineering Employers' Federation, ASSET's base being in the supervisory grades whilst the AScW's base was technical. Both unions recruited members outside the engineering industry – ASSET notably in transport (especially Civil Air Transport) and AScW in the Universities.

Since the formation of ASTMS there have been mergers with over 30 other unions. ASTMS is now the largest trade union in the insurance industry, and has membership in other financial institutions; the Medical Practitioners Union and the United Commercial Travellers Association have both merged with ASTMS, as have many para-medical groups – pharmacists, opticians, speech therapists, etc. At the same time there has been a steady increase in membership in other sectors, including voluntary agencies, semi-public and public bodies, the petro-chemical industry, North Sea oil, electronics and data processing. ASTMS now covers more industries and more separate grades of staff than any other union in the United Kingdom. Engineering still accounts for nearly one half of the membership.

The basic form of organisation within ASTMS is the *Group*. This, typically, will consist of members within one company, or one department of a company, with an elected chairman and secretary and Group Committee. The tasks of the Group include collecting members' subscriptions, communications, negotiations and recruiting.

The *Branch* is the basic unit in the union's policy-making system. All members of a Group are entitled to attend meetings of their Branch. There are two types of Branch in addition to those still existing within the merged sections of the union. A general Branch is geographically based, and usually will have members from a number of different companies and industries. A closed Branch is based on a particular undertaking or industry. Every Branch has administrative and financial responsibilities, as well as important democratic rights and duties concerned with elections, delegations and affiliations. Branches are responsible for electing the ASTMS President, Vice-President, National, Regional and Divisional Executive Committee members, the Appeal Court and the three National Trustees, in whom the union's investments and property are vested.

There are sixteen *Divisional Councils*. They consist of delegates from each Branch within the Division and they elect officers and a Divisional Executive Committee. One task of the Divisional Council is to act as an advice centre for Branches.

The union's premier policy-making body is the Annual Delegate Conference, which consists of delegates from each Branch. Between Conferences, the union's affairs are managed by a National Executive Council, elected by the Branches.

In addition to the elective structure there are the services provided by the union's full-time officers. There is a network of Divisional Officers and National Officers responsible for particular sections of industry. Above this level are three Assistant General Secretaries, whose responsibilities cover groups of industries, and the General Secretary with overall responsibility. Other officers are in charge of Head Office services, including Research, Finance, Medical, Legal and the Editor of the Journal.

Current membership: 450,000

OFFICIALS
General Secretary: C. Jenkins
Assistant General Secretaries:
M. Turner, S. Davison, R. McCusker

National Executive Council (May 1979)
President: E.D. Hoyle, MP
Vice-President: L.H. Wells
National Members:
F.R.J. Allenby, A. Edmondson

Regional Executive:
H. Seddons, A. Kellet, P. Elliman, P.A. Bell

DIVISIONAL MEMBERS
T. Pearson
R. Ford
S. Jefferson
I. Read
K. O'Hanay
J. Gilham
O. Loughan
A. Sier
F. Lott
J. Aherne
D. Clarke
C. Fulton
R. Crew
B. Webster
N. Morson
M.T. Walker
Dr D.R.I.M. Poirier

DISTRICT OFFICIALS
(NO, DO, TO denote National, Divisional and Trainee Officer, respectively)
Head Office
NO   R. Bird
NO   R. Lyons
NO   R. Miller
NO   T. Webb
NO   J. McKie
(Finance Officer)
NO   P. Kennedy
A. Brown
(Editor)
B. Sherman
(Director of Research)

Aberdeen
DO   C. Reid

Belfast
DO   H. Cavan
TO   R. Jeary

Birmingham
NO   D. Mathison
DO   D. Groves
DO   J. Higgins
DO   C. Crabb
DO   B. Holmes
DO   K. Orme
DO   T. Dolan

Bristol
DO   D.G. Mainwaring
DO   J. Heenan

DO   A. Taylor

Coventry
DO   B. Cairns
DO   J. Fisher

Dublin
NO   J. Hall
DO   B. Aylward
TO   B. Horah

Durham
DO   A. Wilson
DO   P. Ray
DO   B. Fox

Eastleigh
DO   T. Bull

Glasgow
NO   J. Langan
DO   W. Anderson
DO   W. McLatchie
DO   I. Fulton
DO   G. Craig
NO   P. Talbot

Harrow
DO   P. Amoss
DO   J. Mercer
DO   C. Carter

Haverhill
DO   R. Spiller

Hounslow
DO   M. Godfrey
DO   E. Mackenzie
DO   J. Sheppard
DO   T. Mahoney
DO   P. Taylor
DO   D. Jacks
DO   P. Wallis

Kendal
DO   A. Stubbs
DO   E. Hazelwood

Knutsford
DO   R. Tomlinson
DO   M. Moss

Leeds
DO   R. Walker
DO   D. Jeffery

DO   A. Clark

Liverpool
DO   P. Leverton
DO   B. Howard
DO   D. Bird
DO   A. Whipp
DO   G. Murray
DO   J.F. Hall
DO   A. Miller

London Sutton House
DO   R. Ward
DO   C. Ball
DO   D. Haber
NO   T. Comerford
DO   D. Barr
DO   D. Ingram
DO   J. Chowcat
DO   K. Rose

London Wardrobe Court
DO   M. Kennedy
DO   F. Dowling
DO   W. Walsh
DO   J. Terry

Manchester
NO   R. Beson
DO   F. Sharp
DO   H. Glass
DO   S. Wyatt
DO   J. Wall
DO   S. Marshall

Bradford
DO   L. Smith

Nottingham
DO   M. Hill
DO   M. Teague
DO   J. Paine

Oxford
DO   T. Murray
DO   C. Fletcher

Sheffield
DO   D. Sequerra
DO   G. Johnson

South Wales
DO   K. Gomm
DO   N. Hufton

Uttoxeter Office
DO   R. Lear
DO   J. Hoard
DO   C. Luker

Whitehall College
Lecturers:
G. Fordham, H. Forrest
Health and Safety Officer:
S. McKechnie

Periodicals: *ASTMS Journal* (bimonthly), *Medical World, Finance News, Selling Today*

Policy: In recent years ASTMS has been opposed to incomes policies, and to Britain's entry into the EEC; it has been in favour of the NEB and planning agreements and for the creation of a more attractive working life. The union has its own residential college with both resident and visiting lecturers.

SCOTTISH CARPET WORKERS' UNION†
83 Carlton Place, Glasgow G5 9TU
Tel: 041–429 5199

Current membership is not available

OFFICIAL
General Secretary: J. Deighan

SCOTTISH FURTHER EDUCATION ASSOCIATION (SFEA)†
111 Union Street, Glasgow GS1 3SS
Tel: 041–221 0118

The association was founded in 1966 by a number of trade union activists who felt that the unions of which they were members did not effectively represent the lecturers in Scottish Further Education Colleges. Members are all lecturers in Further Education, and comprise about half of the organised lecturers in this sector of Scottish education. The Association is affiliated to the STUC and is registered under the Employment Protection Act, 1975.

The distinctive philosophy underlying the recent growth and development of the SFEA is the desire for unity of all lecturers in the Tertiary Sector of education in Scotland, comparable to the philosophy of NATFHE in the rest of the United Kingdom.

Following the Houghton Report, 1974, a common grading and salary structure was established for the Colleges of Education, Further Education Centres and Central Institutions in Scotland. In January 1978 the SFEA joined with the Association of Lecturers in Colleges of Education in Scotland (ALCES) and the Association of Lecturers in Scottish Central Institutions (ALSCI) to form the Federation of Associations of College Lecturers in Scotland (FACLS).

The Federation has responsibility for all areas of policy on which there are common negotiations, a field which will be greatly extended by the formation of common negotiating machinery for the Tertiary Sector in Scotland.

In recent years the SFEA has achieved full recognition on negotiating and consultative bodies at all levels. It is represented on the Scottish Teachers' Salaries Committee, the Scottish Teachers' Service Conditions Committee and the Teachers' Superannuation Working Party.

Current membership: 1,800

OFFICIALS
General Secretary: D. Bleiman, MA
Administrative Assistant: Mrs M. Mitchell

Officers
President: D. Baillie, Cardonald College
Vice-President: J. Frame, Glasgow College of Technology

SCOTTISH LACE AND TEXTILE WORKERS UNION

See LACE AND TEXTILE WORKERS UNION, SCOTTISH

SCOTTISH SECONDARY TEACHERS' ASSOCIATION†
15 Dundas Street, Edinburgh EH3 6QG
Tel: 031–556 5919 and 0605

Formed in 1944 by the members of the Scottish Secondary Teachers' Defence Association to oppose the policy of a common maximum salary for all teachers adopted by the then sole Scottish teachers' union, the Educational Institute of Scotland. Objects are to advance education in Scotland, particularly secondary education, and to safeguard and promote the interests of Scottish secondary teachers. The association remains in favour of reasonable salary differentials based on academic qualifications and sector of education in which teacher employed. It has successfully opposed several attempts to have common maximum salary policy introduced and it advocates establishment of an independent review body to determine teachers' salaries, believing that existing 'negotiating machinery' does no more than share out global sum previously determined by government of day. Consistently maintains a non-political stance. Affiliated to the Scottish Trades Union Congress.
Current membership: 8,500.

OFFICIALS
General Secretary: J. Docherty
Depute General Secretary: D. Miller

SCOTTISH UNION OF BAKERS AND ALLIED WORKERS

See BAKERS AND ALLIED WORKERS, SCOTTISH UNION OF

SCOTTISH UNION OF POWER LOOM OVERLOOKERS

See POWERLOOM OVERLOOKERS, SCOTTISH UNION OF

SCREW, NUT, BOLT AND RIVET TRADE UNION*‡
368 Dudley Road, Birmingham B18 4HH
Tel: 021–429 2431

Founded in 1914 and currently having all its membership in Guest, Keen and Nettlefolds in Birmingham where it recruits all grades of workers.
Current membership: 2,500

OFFICIAL
General Secretary: H. Cater

SEAMEN, NATIONAL UNION OF (NUS)*
Maritime House, Old Town, Clapham, London SW4 0JP
Tel: 01-622 5581 and 5587

Formed in 1887, and the sole organisation representing ratings employed in the British Shipping industry. Changes in ship technology and the decline of the UK shipping industry have reduced union membership. The first official strike since 1911 took place in 1966 from which time the union has taken a more militant stance particularly with respect to disciplinary matters and the employment of Asian seamen on British ships. The union is affiliated to the Labour Party and the International Transport Workers Union. Current membership: 44,000

OFFICIALS
General Secretary: J. Slater
Assistant General Secretary and Treasurer: S. McCluskie
National Secretaries:
E. Brown
R. Spruhan

Assistant National Secretaries:
R. Wilkins, R. Fleming, J. Kenny

Executive Council
Chairman: W. Brankley
General Secretary: J. Slater
Assistant General Secretary–Treasurer: S. McCluskie
National Secretaries: E. Brown, R. Spruhan

J. Allen	R. Hickman
P. McGregor	A. Musa-Nogan
A. Skinner	J. Lawler
R. Hazelaar	J. Polson
J. Kennedy	T. Ablett
M. Hawkins	T. Clare
R. Mardell	T. Richards
J. McGill	N. Finlayson

BRANCH SECRETARIES
Branch secretaries are elected by the executive council

Aberdeen
H. Bygate,
3 Commerce Street,
Aberdeen AB2 18U

Avonmouth
D. Tedder,
Gloucester Road,
Avonmouth,
Bristol BS11 9AQ

Belfast
W. Henderson,
11 Victoria Street,
Belfast,
Northern Ireland BT1 3GA

Cardiff
B. Keating,
Britannic Quay,
Cardiff CF1 5UP

Douglas
4 Fort Street,
Douglas,
Isle of Man

Dover
Maritime House,
Snargate Street,
Dover,
Kent

Dublin
B. Crossan,
112 Marlborough Street,
Eden Quay,
Dublin 1

Falmouth
J. Couch,
Armyn House,
Bar Road,
Falmouth,
Cornwall

Glasgow
L.L. Green,
9–15 James Watt Street,
Glasgow G2 8NF

London
L. W. Larkin,
325 Newham Way,
London E16 4ED

Grimsby
I.C. Hanson,
8 Cleethorpe Road,
Grimsby,
Lincolnshire

Harwich
R. Williams,
7 Kingsway,
Dovercourt,
Essex

Holyhead
E. Morrisey,
3 Stanley Terrace,
Holyhead
Anglesey LL65 O8Y

Hull
A. Holden,
8 Posterngate,
Hull,
Yorkshire HU1 2JN

Leith
H. Dillon,
8 Shore,
Leith,
Edinburgh EH6 6QN

Liverpool
J. McPherson,
Maritime House,
47–49 Paradise Street,
Liverpool L13 EH

Malta
Ph. Hili (Union Representative),
The Annexe,
Seafarer's Memorial Club,
Lascari's Wharf,
Valetta,
Malta, GC

Manchester
P. Neary,
94 Smith Street,
Salford,
Lancashire M5 3DE

Middlesbrough
J. Woods,
7 North Street,
Middlesbrough,
Cleveland

Milford Haven
Serviced from
Swansea branch

Plymouth
J. O'Keefe,
64 Vauxhall Street,
Plymouth,
Devon

Southampton
M. Bailey,
Havelock Chambers,
Queen's Terrace,
Southampton SO1 1BP

South Shields
J. McMullan,
4 Coronation Street,
South Shields,
Co. Durham

Sunderland
Serviced from
South Shields,
15 Borough Road,
Sunderland,
Co. Durham SR1 1EQ

Swansea
O.P. Willis,
Room 17,
Pembroke Buildings,
Cambrian Place,
Swansea,
Glamorgan

Periodical: *The Seaman* (monthly)

SECONDARY HEADS ASSOCIATION
29 Gordon Square, London WC1H 0PS
Tel: 01-388 1765

Formed on 1 January 1978 by amalgamation between the
Association of Headmistresses founded 1874 and the Headmasters'
Association inaugurated in 1890. The membership consists of
headmasters and headmistresses of schools, both maintained and
independent, whose pupils are predominantly of secondary school
age. Membership is open to secondary school heads in England,
Wales, Scotland and Northern Ireland. Within current membership
there are 2,900 full members, 100 are affiliates and 1,250 are associate
members.

Current Membership: 4,250 approximately

OFFICIALS
President 1979/80: J.R.K. Sayer, MA
General Secretary: D.A. Frith
Deputy Secretaries: Miss S.M. Chapman, BA, R.F. Glover, MA

Periodical: *S.H.A. Review* (twice yearly)

SHEET METAL WORKERS, COPPERSMITHS, HEATING AND DOMESTIC ENGINEERS, NATIONAL UNION OF (NUSMWC, H and DE)*
75-77 West Heath Road, London NW3 7TL
Tel: 01-455 0053

A union representing sheet metal workers, coppersmiths and, since
1967, heating and domestic engineers. Formed from a number of
sheet metal working unions, dating from the beginning of the 19th
century and since 1875 incorporating local societies, the last being the
Birmingham and Midland Society with which it amalgamated in June
1973. Membership fluctuates around 75,000–80,000, about two-
thirds of whom are skilled craftsmen and the remainder semi-skilled
including a very small group of women.
Current membership: 75,000

FULL-TIME OFFICIALS
National President: W. Benson
General Secretary: L.G. Guy
National Officers: T. Nelson, R.A. Marsh, S. Nugent

National Executive Committee

F. Cooper	W. Lawrenson
F.J. Harris	R. Lofting
J. Holborn	J. Lowe
H. Patterson	S. Seymour
A. Rae	E. Vaughton
R. Steele	A.G. Wigfield
A. Sweet	

Periodical: *The Journal* (quarterly)

Policy: The union was opposed both to incomes policies and to entry into Europe.

SHEFFIELD SAWMAKERS PROTECTION SOCIETY

See SAWMAKERS PROTECTION SOCIETY, SHEFFIELD

SHEFFIELD WOOL, SHEAR WORKERS TRADE UNION

See WOOL, SHEAR WORKERS TRADE UNION, SHEFFIELD

SHOP, DISTRIBUTIVE AND ALLIED WORKERS, UNION OF (USDAW)*
Oakley, 188 Wilmslow Road, Manchester M14 6LJ
Tel: 061–224 2804

Formed in January 1947 on the amalgamation of the National Union of Distributive and Allied Workers (NUDAW) and the National Amalgamated Union of Shop Assistants, Warehousemen and Clerks (NAUSA). USDAW has a membership approaching half-a-million in Great Britain and Northern Ireland, over 60 per cent of which are women. The majority of members are employed in retail and wholesale distribution but considerable numbers are employed in service trades, such as catering, laundries, hairdressing, milk industry, meat trades, mail order, food manufacturing and chemical processing. The union's members are located in eight territorial divisions covering Great Britain and Northern Ireland and are serviced by approximately 120 full-time organisers under the control of divisional officers based in Cardiff, Liverpool, London, Manchester, Birmingham, Leeds and Glasgow. In addition there are 27 area offices in various parts of the country. In January 1978 the

304

Scottish Union of Bakers and Allied Workers (q.v.) merged with USDAW as its Scottish Bakers' Section. The union also has a specialist Insurance Section and a white-collar section known as SATA (Supervisory, Administrative and Technical Association).

USDAW's supreme policy-making body is the Annual Delegate Meeting, consisting of delegates from all the Union's thousand branches, which meets for four days at the end of April each year. The Executive Council is the ruling Authority between ADMs and consists of the President, elected nationally, and two members elected by each of the eight divisions (for two-year periods) plus the General Secretary – elected nationally till retirement age. There are eight Divisional Councils each of which has ten elected members. The Divisional Officer, his Deputy and the team of Area Organisers are all appointed by the executive Council, as are all National Officials apart from the General Secretary.

Current membership: 462,178

PRINCIPAL OFFICIALS
President: S. Tierney, MP
General Secretary: W.H.P. Whatley
Deputy General Secretary: J. Flood

EXECUTIVE COUNCIL:

D.E. Andrews	T.A. McLean
R. Caton	Mrs C.E. Page
J.J. Coleby	R.J. Scherer
J.L. Foweather	R.J. Stonehouse
P.E. Howitt	Mrs E. Wardle
P. Hunter	A.C. Waterfield
J. McEwan	Mrs L. Woolston
F. Kaye	E.T. White

CENTRAL OFFICIALS AND DEPARTMENT HEADS
Administration Officer: H.L. Booth
Central Treasurer and Executive Officer: A.W. Hilton
Audit Officer: S.H. Hardcastle
Education Officer: P.L. Rosenfeld, MBE
Legal Officer: A.C. Heywood, LL.B
O&M Officer: V. Lowe
Public Relations Officer: P.H. Jones
Research Officer: Diana Jeuda, BA
Finance Department: J.H. Wilson

NATIONAL OFFICERS
L.H. Watson: (Retail Co-op, Milk & Laundry Trades)
W.J. Connor: (Retail Multiple Food Trades)
T.F. Sullivan: (Retail Multiple Non-Food Trades)
G. Kiely: (Baking, Soap/Fats Industry and Transport)
D.G. Davies: (CWS, Warehousing and Catering)
M. Gordon: (Meat, Hairdressing and Credit Trades)
S. Williams: (Chemical Industry)
W. Cowan: (Insurance Section)

Divisional and Area Offices
South Wales and Western Division
Bristol
65 Woodland Road,
Bristol BS8 1UW
Tel: Bristol (0272) 20431

Cardiff
W.J. Jones, MBE, JP,
Second Floor,
Caerwys House,
1 Windsor Lane,
Cardiff CF1 3RN
Tel: Cardiff (0222) 25626

Plymouth
Second Floor,
Prudential Building,
115 Armada Way,
Plymouth PL1 1HJ
Tel: Plymouth (0752) 65951

Swansea
5 Mansel Street,
Swansea SA1 5SF
Tel: Swansea (0792) 55121 and 54638

North Western Division
Belfast
First Floor,
Leicester House,
61–63 Royal Avenue,
Belfast BT1 1NN
Tel: Belfast (0232) 41851

Liverpool
J.W. Gardner, JP
145 Edge Lane,
Liverpool L7 2PG
Tel: 051-263 7521

Port Sunlight
1 Boundary Road,
Bebington,
Cheshire L62 5ER
Tel: 051-645 4719

Preston
81 Garstang Road,
Preston PR1 1LD
Tel: Preston (0772) 54952

Eastern Division
Cambridge
72 Regent Street,
Cambridge CB2 1DP
Tel: Cambridge (0223) 65203

Ipswich
8 Neale Street,
Ipswich IP1 3JB
Tel: Ipswich (0473) 51530

London Area
T.P. Callinan
Dilke House,
Malet Street,
London WC1E 7JA
Tel: 01–580 8641

Luton
20 Leagrave Road,
Luton,
Bedfordshire LU4 8HY
Tel: Luton (0582) 423218

Norwich
11 Chapel Field North,
Norwich,
Norfolk NR2 1NY
Tel: Norwich (0603) 24380

Manchester Division
Hanley
Norwich Union House,
40 Trinity Street,
Hanley,
Stoke-on-Trent ST1 5LJ
Tel: Stoke-on-Trent (0782) 29801

Insurance Section
Oakley,
188 Wilmslow Road,
Fallowfield,
Manchester M14 6LJ
Tel: 061-224 2804

Manchester
J.C. Callahan
Maythorpe,
13 Warwick Road,
Old Trafford,
Manchester M16 0QX
Tel: 061-872 3527

Midlands Division
Birmingham
J. Toogood
First Floor,
Gloucester House,
Smallbrook Queensway,
Birmingham B5 4HT
Tel: 021-643 4377

Leicester
98 New Walk,
Leicester LE1 7EA
Tel: Leicester (0533) 56861

Nottingham
20 Regent Street,
Nottingham NG1 5DF
Tel: Nottingham (0602) 47301 and
45371

North Eastern Division
Carlisle
Second Floor,
National Westminster Bank
Chambers,
Blackfriars Street,
Carlisle CA3 8AA
Tel: Carlisle (0228) 22453

Hull
36 George Street,
Hull HU1 3AS
Tel: Hull (0482) 29031

Leeds
N.B. Capindale
Concord House,
Park Lane,
Leeds LS3 1EJ
Tel: Leeds (0532) 41881

Middlesbrough
132 Borough Road,
Middlesbrough,
Cleveland TS1 2ES
Tel: Middlesbrough (0642) 242326

Newcastle
47 Leazes Terrace,
Newcastle upon Tyne NE1 4LZ
Tel: Newcastle upon Tyne (0632)
20531 and 23731

Sheffield
10 High Court,
Sheffield S1 1PJ
Tel: Sheffield (0742) 24997

Scottish Division
Aberdeen
Provincial House,
9 Holburn Street,
Aberdeen AB1 6BS
Tel: Aberdeen (0224) 23289

Periodical: *DAWN* **(monthly)**

Dundee
43 South Tay Street,
Dundee DD1 1NP
Tel: Dundee (0382) 26380

Edinburgh
30 Walker Street,
Edinburgh EH3 7HU
Tel: 031–225 4901

Glasgow
A. Forman, CBE
Muirfield,
342 Albert Drive,
Glasgow G41 5PG
Tel: 041–427 1121

Scottish Bakers' Section
Baxterlee,
127 Fergus Drive,
Glasgow
Tel: 041–946 4213

Southern Division
London Area
R.A. Hammond
Dilke House,
Malet Street,
London WC1E 7JA
Tel: 01–580 8641

Kent
1 East Street,
Faversham ME13 8AD
Tel: Faversham (079 582) 2637

Portsmouth
51 Charter House,
Lord Montgomery Way,
Portsmouth PO1 2SH
Tel: Portsmouth (0705) 21850

South East London
20 Greens End,
Woolwich SE18 6LA
Tel: 01–854 0171

South West London
Ruskin House,
23 Coombe Road,
Croydon,
Surrey CR0 1BD
Tel: 01–688 4800 and 6145

Basingstoke
9 Wote Street,
Basingstoke,
Hants.
Tel: Basingstoke (0265) 51545

SHUTTLEMAKERS, SOCIETY OF*‡
21 Buchan Towers, Manchester Road, Bradford, West Yorkshire
Tel: Bradford (0274) 33620

Formed in 1891 by a small group of shuttlemakers in Lancashire and Yorkshire. After World War II membership increased to 600, this being 90 per cent of the shuttlemakers in Great Britain. The Society has been affiliated to the Trades Union Congress, General Federation of Trades Unions and the Labour Party for over fifty years. With the introduction of the shuttleless loom and the loss of Indian markets. membership has gradually decreased over the last 11 years.

OFFICIALS
The Society has no full-time officers.

President: R. Turner,
36 Lamlash Road, Shadsworth, Blackburn, Lancashire
General Secretary: E.V. Littlewood,
21 Buchan Towers, Manchester Road, Bradford, West Yorkshire
Treasurer: B. Sharpe, 59 Rillington Mead, Greengates, Bradford

Executive Committee
R. Turner,
36 Lamlash Road,
Shadsworth,
Blackburn,
Lancashire

H. Bentley,
55 Hollins Road,
Todmorden,
Lancashire

A. Partington,
113 Bury New Road,
Heywood,
Lancashire

K. Sanderson,
17 Rook Street,
Nelson,
Lancashire

Branch Secretaries
Blackburn
F. Erry,
239 Mosely Street,
Blackburn,
Lancashire

Bradford
M. Lee,
143 Reevy Road,
Bradford 6,
West Yorkshire

Todmorden
H. Bentley,
55 Hollins Road,
Todmorden,
Lancashire

Heywood
T.W. Heath,
15 South Avenue,
Heywood,
Lancashire

Nelson
D. Horsefield,
3 Belmont Terrace,
Barrowford,
Nelson,
Lancashire

SOCIETY OF CIVIL AND PUBLIC SERVANTS

See CIVIL AND PUBLIC SERVANTS, SOCIETY OF

SOCIETY OF GRAPHICAL AND ALLIED TRADES

See GRAPHICAL AND ALLIED TRADES, SOCIETY OF

SOCIETY OF LITHOGRAPHIC ARTISTS, DESIGNERS, ENGRAVERS AND PROCESS WORKERS

See LITHOGRAPHIC ARTISTS, DESIGNERS, ENGRAVERS AND PROCESS WORKERS, SOCIETY OF

SOCIETY OF POST OFFICE EXECUTIVES

See POST OFFICE EXECUTIVES, SOCIETY OF

SOCIETY OF SHUTTLEMAKERS

See SHUTTLEMAKERS, SOCIETY OF

SPRING TRAPMAKERS' SOCIETY*
Bellamy House, Wilkes Street, Willenhall, West Midlands WV13 2BS
Tel: Willenhall (0902) 66651

Formed in 1890 as the Wednesbury Spring Trapmakers' Society, changing to its present name in 1916. It has been associated with the National Union of Lock and Metal Workers since 1924.
Current membership: 90

OFFICIAL
General Secretary: J. Martin

STEEL INDUSTRY MANAGEMENT ASSOCIATION (SIMA)
Leet Court, 14 King Street, Watford WD1 8BR
Tel: Watford (0932) 25909 and 27341

Formed in 1968 after the nationalisation of the steel industry to represent senior and middle management staff. It holds national recognition and procedure agreements with the British Steel Corporation and with a number of undertakings in the private sector of the industry. Membership is largely concentrated in the steel making areas of the United Kingdom. Cornerstones of its policies are a belief in the 'managerial obligation' of the manager in the enterprise in which he is engaged, the position of manufacturing managers as a 'third force' in industry and a determination to secure improved levels of rewards for them. Nevertheless, it is a genuine independent trade union and, with reluctance, has taken industrial action in the public sector to promote adequate salary levels for its members. Current membership: 12,000

OFFICIALS
General Secretary: R.A.C. Muir
Deputy General Secretary: F. Collins
Assistant General Secretary: (post vacant)
Regional Secretary Midlands: L. Middleton,
National Deposit House, 1 Waterdale, Doncaster DN1 3HX
Regional Secretary Wales: G.G. Evans,
41 John Street, Porthcawl, Mid Glamorgan
Regional Secretary North East: G.G. Sherry,
15 West Dyke Road, Redcar, Cleveland,
Regional Secretary Scotland: M. Tierney,
77 Hamilton Road, Motherwell, Lanarkshire

TAILORS AND GARMENT WORKERS, NATIONAL UNION OF (NUT and GW)*‡
Radlett House, West Hill, Aspley Guise, Milton Keynes MK17 8DT
Tel: Milton Keynes (0908) 583099

An industrial union catering for all workers, manual and non-manual, employed in all sectors of the clothing industry and in that part of the textile industry which is closely associated with clothing. It represents a merger of a number of unions in the clothing sector, with the major mergers taking place during the 1930's. The latest union to join was the Manchester-based Waterproof Garment Workers' Trade Union, founded in 1907. Trade union activity in the clothing sector has a long history reaching back into the fifteenth century. In 1824, the activities of Francis Plaice, a London master tailor, played a major part in the repeal of the Combination Acts. The largest concentration of union members is in the men's and boys' tailored outerwear sector. The Union's membership is divided into eight divisions, London and South (7,700), East and Midlands (11,917), Western (including Wales) (11,785), Leeds and Yorkshire (20,362), North East (15,714), North West (18,878), Scotland (18,055) and Ireland (11,723).

The Clerical and Supervisory Section was established in 1972 and currently has 4,700 members. Under the rules of the Union Executive Board members are elected for a two-year term of office, and a General Conference takes place biennially. The major subjects for discussion at the last General Conference held in April 1979 were

310

wages, hours of work, holidays and working conditions.
Current membership: 116,134 of which 90 per cent are women.

NATIONAL OFFICERS
General Secretary: Alec Smith
Deputy General Secretary: Anne Spencer
National Officer: Colin Tindley

DIVISIONAL OFFICERS

Leeds and Yorkshire
H. Yates,
Circle House,
29 Lady Lane,
Leeds 2
Tel: Leeds (0532) 31818

Western
A.J. Hawkins,
14 North Road,
Cardiff CF1 3DY,
South Wales
Tel: Cardiff (0222) 28164

North West
T. Evans,
409 Wilmslow Road,
Withington,
Manchester M20 9NB
Tel: 061–224 6212/3

North East
S. Yeoman.
4 Cloth Market,
Newcastle upon Tyne NE1 1EX
Tel: Newcastle upon Tyne (0632)
29688

East and Midlands
Trade Union Offices,
Club Street,
Kettering,
Northamptonshire
Tel: Kettering (0536) 2534

London and Southern
C. Wilson
16 Charles Square,
London N1
Tel: 01–253 1137/8/9

Scotland
F. Dickinson,
Albany Chambers,
534 Sauchiehall Street,
Charing Cross,
Glasgow G2 3LX
Tel: 041–331 2747/8

Ireland
W. Wallace,
44 Elmwood Avenue,
Belfast BT9 6BB
Northern Ireland
Tel: Belfast (0232) 662942

FULL-TIME OFFICERS
Leeds and Yorkshire Division
Leeds No. 1
C. Mason,
Circle House,
29 Lady Lane,
Leeds 2
Tel: Leeds (0532) 31818

Leeds No. 2
H. Fudge,
Circle House,
29 Lady Lane,
Leeds 2
Tel: Leeds (0532) 31818

Leeds No. 3
T. Price,
Circle House,
29 Lady Lane,
Leeds 2
Tel: (0532) 31818

Yorkshire
H. North,
Circle House,
29 Lady Lane,
Leeds 2
Tel: Leeds (0532) 31818

P. Wingrove,
Circle House,
29 Lady Lane,
Leeds 2
Tel: Leeds (0532) 31818

Hebden Bridge
Trades Club,
Hebden Bridge,
Yorkshire
Tel: Hebden Bridge (042 284) 2124

Western Division
Exeter
G. Baldwin,
45/47 Fore Street,
Heavitree,
Exeter,
Devon
Tel: Exeter (0392) 34687

South Wales
Mrs L. Teague,
14 North Road,
Cardiff CF1 3DY
South Wales
Tel: Cardiff (0222) 28164

South West
J.S. Ferns,
92 Gloucester Rd,
Bristol BS7 8BN
Tel: Bristol (0272) 47866

North West Division
Manchester
D. Cattell,
409 Wilmslow Road,
Withington,
Manchester M20 9NB
Tel: 061–224 6212/3

Liverpool
V. Fairbrother,
Room 46,
Imperial Chambers,
62 Dale Street,
Liverpool 2
Tel: 051–227 5665

Wigan
Miss M.A. Ryder,
28 Upper Dicconson Street,
Wigan,
Lancashire
Tel: Wigan (0942) 42062

East Lancashire
Mrs J. Platt,
9 Manchester Road,
Walkden,
Manchester
Tel: 061–790 2577

Crewe
C. Whitehurst,
213a Nantwich Road,
Crewe,
Cheshire
Tel: Crewe (0270) 213810

North East Division
Middlesbrough
A. Burton,
114 Borough Road,
Middlesbrough,
Cleveland
Tel: Middlesbrough (0642) 246953

Newcastle
R. Bales,
Mrs P.D. Wraith.
4 Cloth Market,
Newcastle upon Tyne NE1 1EX
Tel: Newcastle upon Tyne (0632)
29688

Sunderland
G. Bowen,
18 Norfolk Street,
Sunderland
Tel: Sunderland (0783) 57961

East and Midlands Division
Cannock
D. Thomas,
6 Hallcourt Crescent,
Cannock,
Staffordshire
Tel: Cannock (054 35) 5215

Ipswich
F.H. Phelps,
31 Lower Brook Street,
Ipswich IP4 1AQ
Suffolk
Tel: Ipswich (0473) 55259

Kettering
A. Garley,
Trade Union Offices,
Club Street,
Kettering,
Northamptonshire
Tel: Kettering (0536) 2534

Nottingham
K.W. Simpson,
35 Waverley St,
Nottingham, NG7 4DX
Tel: Nottingham (0602) 703614

London and Southern Division
Ms M. Foy and A. Hillier,
18 Charles Square,
London N1
Tel: 01–253 1137/8/9

Reading
Room 1b,
Trade Union Club,
56–59 Minster Street,
Reading,
Berkshire
Tel: Reading (0734) 51460

South East
M.W. Juniper,
45 Axe Street,
Barking,
Essex
Tel: 01–594 5487

London Tailors and Tailoresses
S. Keston,
3rd Floor,
20 Great Chapel Street,
London W1

Scotland
C. Brown, D. Farrell,
J. Easdale. F. Mundie. J. Howard.
Albany Chambers,
534 Sauchiehall Street,
Charing Cross,
Glasgow G2 3LX
Tel: 041–332 0353

Ireland
Belfast
Miss F. Maguire,
J. Nixon,
44 Elmwood Avenue,
Belfast BT9 6BB
Tel: Belfast (0232) 662942

North West Ireland
F.McCrossan,
Northern Counties Buildings,
Custom House Street,
Londonderry
Tel: Londonderry (0504) 3515

Senior Officer Dublin
S. Walsh,
7 Eustace Street,
Dublin 2
Tel: Dublin 771681

Periodical: *Garment Worker* (monthly)

TEACHERS IN FURTHER AND HIGHER EDUCATION, NATIONAL ASSOCIATION OF (NATFHE)*
Hamilton House, Mapledon Place, London WC1H 9BH
Tel: 01–387 6806

NATFHE was formed on 1 January 1976 through the amalgamation of the Association of Teachers in Technical Institutions and the Association of Teachers in Colleges and Departments of Education. NATFHE is the only union for all post-school public sector further education teachers and represents about 85 per cent of these employees with membership in England, Wales and Northern Ireland. In September 1977 another 2,700 approximately were added under a new joint membership scheme with the Educational Institute of Scotland Further Education Lecturers' National Section. NATFHE's main concern in recent years has been the effect of the public expenditure cuts upon educational provision and upon the conditions of service and jobs of staff employed in educational institutions.
Current membership: 65,269

East Midlands, Cambridgeshire,	Yorkshire and Humberside
Norfolk, Suffolk	P. Harrigan,
W. Hilbourne,	Sanderson House,
16 The Jamb,	Station Road,
Corby,	Horsforth,
Northamptonshire	Leeds
Tel: Corby (053 66) 3245	

North Western
I. Mackay,
2 Grove Street,
Liverpool L15 8HU

Periodical: *NATFHE Journal* (monthly)

Policy: The association nationally and locally campaigns to resist the attacks on public services. A major focus of attention currently and over the next few years will be the reorganisation of teacher education which is taking place in the worst possible circumstances, i.e. during a period of rundown in the size of the teacher education system and of unprecedented cutbacks in expenditure. The association has negotiated two major agreements on conditions of service and trade union facilities in recent years and negotiations to secure local implementation of these agreements are proceeding apace. On salaries NATFHE is concerned to restore, in real terms, teachers' pay to the levels established by the settlement which followed the report of the Houghton Committee of Inquiry.

TEACHERS, NATIONAL UNION OF (NUT)*

Hamilton House, Mabledon Place, London WC1H 9BD
Tel: 01-387 2442

The National Union of Teachers (NUT) is the principal teachers' organisation in England and Wales. It has members working in every type of teaching establishment including primary, secondary, middle and special schools, community homes, sixth form colleges and colleges of education. Moreover, it covers the whole spectrum of teaching posts from students to head teachers. Founded in 1870, the year of the Forster Education Act, the union combines the functions of a professional association and a trade union. The NUT represents the interests of its members in all matters relating to salary, conditions of service and working conditions, but also works to secure the improvement of educational services and opportunity. In this respect it is very much a campaigning body. The union plays the leading role in representing teachers on all major national and local representative bodies, for example, on the Teachers' Panel of the Burnham Committee which negotiates salaries, and in the Schools Council for the curriculum and examinations.

The union's services to members include legal advice and

assistance, insurance facilities, travel services and its own building society specifically catering for teachers. There is also an extensive library service provided for members whilst all schools receive a free copy of the influential weekly newspaper *The Teacher*. As well as its London headquarters, the union has twelve regional offices providing on-the-spot professional help for members and a residential training college in Lincolnshire which is used for a whole range of courses, meetings and conferences.

NUT membership is organised through Local Associations, each with its own officers and committees. Counties and Metropolitan Divisions of the union are based on the same boundaries as local education authorities and seek to provide facilities for negotiation and consultation. Each division appoints officers and committees from Local Association representatives. The NUT Executive consists of 46 members elected every two years and includes four representatives of the National Association of Teachers in Further and Higher Education, and one of the Association of Teachers of Domestic Services, with which the union has a partnership agreement.

Current membership: 298,500

THE NUT EXECUTIVE
President: J. O. Murphy
17 St. Leonard's Way, Woore, Crewe CW3 9SS
Tel: Pipe Gate (063–081) 581

Vice-President: P.J. Kennedy
Gt. Wakering County Primary School, High Street, Gt. Wakering, Essex SS3 0EJ
Tel: Southend on Sea (0702) 219435

Ex-President: D. G. Bonner
Llwyncrwn Primary School, Beddan, Nr. Pontypridd
Tel: 044–362 3557

Treasurer: J. Gray, BA
Goyt Bank Secondary Comprehensive School, The Fairway, Offerton, Stockport SK2 6BY
Tel: 061–483 9336

124 Mile End Lane, Stockport SK2 6BY
Tel: 061–483 3502

Districts
1: Cumbria, Durham and
Northumberland

D.W. Armstrong, BA,	Turf Moor,
Deerness Valley Comprehensive	Butterknowle,
School,	Bishop Auckland,
Ushaw Moor,	Co. Durham DL13 5ST
Durham	Tel: Cockfield (038887) 485
Tel: Durham (0385) 730336	

2: Tyne and Wear MC
D. Winters,
Hilton Primary School,
Blakelaw,
Newcastle upon Tyne NE5 3RN
Tel: Newcastle (0632) 869297

2 The West Rig,
Newcastle upon Tyne NE3 4LR
Tel: Newcastle (0632) 853070

3: Cleveland and North Yorkshire
A.B. Budd,
Roseberry County Junior School,
Great Ayton,
Middlesbrough,
Cleveland,
Tel: Great Ayton (064 945) 2883

19 Welburn Grove,
Ormesby,
Middlesbrough,
Cleveland
Tel: Middlesbrough (0642) 34352

4: West Yorkshire MC
Miss B. Lynn,
Beach Hill Primary School,
Halifax
Tel: Halifax (0422) 65474

9 Westbury Place,
West End,
Halifax
Tel: Halifax (0422) 65496

C. Morris,
Kippax North Junior School,
Brexdale Avenue,
Kippax,
Leeds LS25 7EJ
Tel: Leeds (0532) 864274

12 Breck's Lane,
Kippax,
Leeds LS25 7EG
Tel: Leeds (0532) 864704

5: South Yorkshire MC
H. Dowson,
Earl Marshal School,
Earl Marshal Road,
Sheffield
Tel: Sheffield (0742) 389391

40 Chorley Drive,
Sheffield S10 3RR
Tel: Sheffield (0742) 305099

6: Humberside and Lincolnshire
J.W. Wiggen, BA
Bransholme High School,
Kingston-upon-Hull
Tel: Hull (0482) 826207

27 South Street,
Cottingham,
North Humberside
Tel: Hull (0482) 848306

7: Lancashire and Isle of Man
D.I. Morgan, MA,
WR Tuson College,
St. Vincent's Road,
Fulwood,
Preston PR2 4UR
Tel: Preston (0772) 716511

Serendip,
19 Oxford Road,
Fulwood,
Preston PR2 3JL
Tel: Preston (0772) 718383

8: Greater Manchester MC
Miss J.C. Davenport,
Woodhouse Park Infant School,
Cornishway,
Wythenshawe,
Manchester M22 6NW
Tel: 061–437 1899

51 Milwain Road,
Levenshulme,
Manchester M19 2PT
Tel: 061–224 5775

T.M. Jones,
Werneth Junior School,
Coppice Street,
Oldham,
Lancashire OL8 4BL
Tel: 061–624 3749

18 George Street,
Chadderton,
Oldham,
Lancashire OL9 9HY
Tel: 061–624 5501

9: Cheshire and Merseyside MC
E.M. Brash,
Garston RC Junior Mixed and
Infants' School,
Liverpool L19 1RT
Tel: 051–427 7515

317

14 Gwydrin Road,
Calderstones,
Liverpool L18 3HA
Tel: 051-722 8171

H.B. Jones,
Warrington Road County Primary
School,
Castle Street,
Widnes,
Cheshire
Tel: 051-424 2918

50 Hillside Drive,
Liverpool 25
Tel: 051-428 5934

10: Derbyshire and Nottinghamshire
W.A. Rippon,
Redwood Junior School,
Redwood Road,
Sinfin,
Derby
Tel: Derby (0332) 26587

44A High Street,
Repton,
Derbyshire
Tel: Burton on Trent (0283) 903226

*11: Leicestershire and
Northamptonshire*
J.D. Perry,
English Martyrs' R.C. School,
Anstey Lane,
Leicester
Tel: Leicester (0533) 57740

21 St. Albans Road,
Leicester
Tel: 0533 546752

12: Shropshire and Staffordshire
F. Howker.
Cheadles County Primary School,
Stoke on Trent
Tel: 053 84 3227

Wendover,
8 Moorland Road,
Leek,
Staffs.
Tel: 053 83 82802

13: West Midlands MC
J.F. Bowdler,
Nordley School,
Bellamy Lane,
Wednesfield,
Wolverhampton
Tel: Wolverhampton (0902) 736331
ext. 33

1 Somers Road,
Pleck,
Walsall WS2 9AX
Tel: Walsall (0922) 29064

W.G. Green,
Primrose Hill Comprehensive
School,
Shannon road,
King's Norton,
Birmingham 38
Tel: 021-459 4451/2/3

20 Beech Hurst,
King's Norton,
Birmingham 38
Tel: 021-458 4710

*14: Gloucestershire, Hereford,
Worcestershire and Warwickshire*
B.W. Meakin,
Rigby Hall School,
Rigby Lane,
Bromsgrove,
Worcs. B60 2EN
Tel: Bromsgrove (0527) 75475

61 Manor Court Road,
Bromsgrove,
Worcs. B60 3NP
Tel: Bromsgrove (0527) 32561

*15: Cambridgeshire, Norfolk and
Suffolk*
Dr W. Roy, CBE
Hewett School,
Cecil Road,
Norwich NOR 78D
Tel: Norwich (0603) 28181

Magnolia House,
Chester Place,
Norwich NR2 3DG
Tel: Norwich (0603) 52355

16: Bedfordshire and Hertfordshire
A. Noonan,
Holy Rood RC Junior Mixed School,
Greenbank Road,
Watford,
Hertfordshire
Tel: Watford (0923) 27099

105 Mildred Avenue,
Watford
Hertfordshire
Tel: Watford (0923) 24173

17: Essex and British Families' Education Service Association
P.C. Cotgrove,
Blenheim Junior School,
Leighview Drive,
Leigh on Sea,
Essex
Tel: 0702 74684

10 Woodfield Gardens,
Leigh on Sea,
Essex
Tel: 0702 78598

18: Berkshire, Buckinghamshire and Oxfordshire
C. Metcalf,
Willink School,
Hollybush Lane,
Burghfield Common,
Reading RG7 3JP
Tel: Burghfield Common (073 529) 2030

23 Broomfield Road,
Tilehurst,
Reading RG3 6AJ
Tel: Reading (0734) 27689

19: Hampshire and Isle of Wight
J. Chambers,
Regents Park Secondary School,
King Edward's Avenue,
Shirley,
Southampton
Tel: Southampton (0703) 771519 and 771443

Four Winds,
Allington Lane,
Fair Oak,
Eastleigh,
Hampshire SO5 7DD
Tel: Fair Oak (042–133) 2479

20: Surrey and West Sussex
R.D. Ellis,
St Peter's CE Middle School,
Little Green Lane,
Farnham,
Surrey
Tel: 0252 714 115

West Garth,
104 Church Lane East,
Aldershot,
Hants GU11 3HW
Tel: 0252 20729

21: East Sussex and Kent
G.S. Foster,
The Towers School,
Faversham Road,
Kennington,
Ashford,
Kent
Tel: Ashford (0233) 34171

26 Chequers Park,
Wye,
Ashford,
Kent TN25 5BB
Tel: Wye (0233) 812547

22: Avon and Wiltshire
A.F. Wilshire, BSc,
Merrywood Boys' School,
Daventry Road,
Knowle,
Bristol BS4 1QB
Tel: Bristol (0272) 668561

205 Soundwell Road,
Staple Hill,
Bristol BS16 4RP
Tel: 0272 673 686

23: Dorset, Somerset and Channel Islands
B.A. White,
All Saints CE Secondary School,
Wyke Regis,
Weymouth,
Dorset
Tel: Weymouth (030 57) 3391

Roslyn,
Cross Road,
Weymouth,
Dorset DT4 9QX
Tel: Weymouth (030 57) 84285

24: Cornwall and Devon
H.L. Brokensha, BA, BSc (Econ.)
The Grammar School,
Plympton,
Plymouth,
Devon
Tel: Plymouth (0752) 337193

19 Lucas Lane,
Plympton,
Plymouth PL7 4EU
Tel: 0752 336625

25: Wales
P. Griffin,
Windsor Clive Junior School,
Grand Avenue,
Ely,
Cardiff
Tel: Cardiff (0222) 591240

31 Court Road,
Whitchurch,
Cardiff CF4 1HN
Tel: Cardiff (0222) 68779

Miss M. M. Jones,
Ysgol Bryn Golau,
Sunny View,
First Avenue,
Wheatsheaf Lane,
Gwersylt,
Wrexham
Tel: Bryn Teg (097 871) 574

6 Court Road,
Wrexham
Tel: Wrexham (0978) 52781

R.G. Jones,
Melin County Junior School,
Neath,
West Glamorgan,
Tel: Neath (0639) 55967

3 New Well Lane,
Newton,
Mumbles,
Swansea
Tel: Swansea (0792) 60217

26: Inner London
R. Richardson,
William Penn Comprehensive
School,
Red Post Hill,
London SE24 9JH
Tel: 01-737 2336

37 Daneswood Avenue,
Bellingham,
London SE6
Tel: 01-698 4140

R.C. North,
Dick Sheppard School,
Tulse Hill,
London SW2 2QA
Tel: 01-674 9421

5 Rommany Road,
London SE27 9PY
Tel: 01-670 8100

27: Outer London
L.J. Claisse,
Picardy School (Beeches Site)
Halt Robin Road,
Belvedere,
Kent
Tel: Erith (38) 47738

Hillview,
Botsom Lane,
West Kingsdown,
Kent
Tel: West Kingsdown (047 485) 2914

M. Horne
Willesden High School,
Doyle Gardens,
London NW10
Tel: 01-965 5976

Chatterings,
Orchard Grove,
Chalfont St Peter,
Bucks
Tel: Gerrards Cross (028 13) 83739

D.M. Streeter,
Fairchildes High School,
New Addington,
Croydon CR0 9AA
Tel: Lodge Hill (0689) 2545

39 Harewood Gardens,
Sanderstead,
Surrey CR2 9BU
Tel: 01-657 5865

Mrs. J. Moseley,
Uphall Remedial Centre,
Uphall Road,
Ilford,
Essex
Tel: 01-478 0410

42 Grosvenor Court,
Vicarage Road,
Leyton,
London E10
Tel: 01–556 2289

ATDS
Miss M Mason.
Ravenscroft School,
Barnet Lane,
London N20
Tel: 01–445 9205

Flat 2,
48 Somerset Road,
New Barnet,
Barnet,
Hertfordshire
Tel: 01–440 8903

NATFHE
F. Cammaerts,
Rolle College,
Exmouth,
Tel: Exmouth (039 52) 5344

3 Fairfield Road,
Exmouth,
Devon
Tel: Exmouth (039 52) 4196

W.J Richardson,
Sydney Webb School of Education,
(Polytechnic of Central London),
9–12 Barrett Street,
London W1M 6DE
Tel: 01–487 5911

56 Vernon Drive,
Stanmore,
Middlesex HA7 2BY

Dr P. Knight,
Plymouth Polytechnic,
Plymouth,
Devon
Tel: Plymouth (0752) 21312

The Mount,
30 Manor Lane,
Laira,
Plymouth,
Devon
Tel: 0752 28664

J.W. Tyrrell,
Kingston College of Further
Education,
Kingston Hall Road,
Kingston-on-Thames,
Surrey KT1 2AQ
Tel: 01–546 2151

265 Jersey Road,
Osterley,
Isleworth,
Middlesex TW7 4RF
Tel: 01–560 8758

OFFICIALS
General Secretary: F.F. Jarvis, MA
Deputy General Secretary: D.N. McAvoy
Senior Solicitor: H. Pierce, BA
Solicitor: G. Clayton, MA

Senior Officers:
A. Evans, BSc(Econ)
Education

C.E. Gorham
Accountant

Miss Toni Griffiths, BA(Hons)
Publicity

M.J. Power
Membership

Miss A. Sutherland
Administration

Vacancy
Salaries and Superannuation

Officials
R.P. Boland
Action

Miss J.H. Farrall
Women's Official

G.B. Fawcett
Salaries and
Superannuation

A. Jarman, BSc
Education

J. Rowe
Education

J. Sprach
Membership

Regional Officers
J. Alderson, BA, DipEd,
NUT Regional Office,
3 Sunderland Road,
Durham DH1 2LH
Tel: Durham (0385) 67238
Home Tel: Peterlee (0783) 862008

V.G. Botterill, BA
NUT Regional Office,
Summerland Street,
Exeter,
Devon EX1 2AT
Tel: Exeter (0392) 58028

28 Collins Road,
Pennsylvania,
Exeter,
Devon EX4 5DY

B.A. Carter,
West Midlands Regional Office,
16 Salter Street,
Stafford ST16 2NQ
Tel: Stafford (0785) 44129
Home Tel: Stafford (0785) 58714

B.J.F. Curtis,
108 High Street,
Newmarket,
Suffolk
Tel: Newmarket (0638) 4538
Home Tel: (0683) 2711

R. Fox, BA
NUT Regional Office,
Kendrick House,
Wharf Street,
Newbury,
Berkshire
Tel: Newbury (0635) 43158 and
43571
Home Tel: Newbury (0635) 44941

D.A. Grant,
NUT Regional Office,
Stoke Rochford Hall,
Stoke Rochford,
Grantham,
Lincolnshire
Tel: Grantham (0476) 83 401/2
Home Tel: Grantham (0476) 68182

D.J. Gregory, JP
NUT Regional Office,
2 Roberts Road,
Doncaster,
South Yorkshire
Tel: Doncaster (0302) 62448
Home Tel: Retford (0777) 2879

H.E. Perrin,
Hamilton House,
Mabledon Place,
London WC1H 9BD
Tel: 01–388 2763

T.W. Stone,
14–16 Sussex Road,
Haywards Heath,
West Sussex RH16 4EA
Tel: Haywards Heath (0444) 52073
Home Tel: Lewes (079 16) 6399

J.A. Heaslip,
NUT Regional Office,
30 Chorley New Road,
Bolton BL1 4AP
Tel: 0204 35299 and 21434
Home Tel: 0704 33050

J. Swift,
Hamilton House,
Mabledon Place,
London WC1H 9BD
Tel: 01–388 5368
Home Tel: Upminster (040 22) 25869

H. Vaughan,
Welsh Office,
NUT,
3rd Floor,
34 Queen Street,
Cardiff CF1 4BW
Tel: Cardiff (0222) 29989 and 396899
Home Tel: Raglan (0291) 690648

Accounts Manager:
G.A. Jones,
Hamilton House,
Mabledon Place,
London WC1H 9BD
Tel: 01–387 2442

Action Officer:
R.P. Boland,
Hamilton House,
Mabledon Place,
London WC1H 9BD
Tel: 01-387 2442

Head of Research Unit:
Dr H. Quigley,
Hamilton House,
Mabledon Place,
London WC1H 9BD
Tel: 01-387 2442

Negotiations Officer:
D. MacFarlane, MA
Hamilton House,
Mabledon Place,
London WC1H 9BD
Tel: 01-387 2442

District Officers:
S. Bradley,
Hamilton House,
Mabledon Place,
London WC1H 9BD
Tel: 01-388 4734
Home Tel: 01-478 8386

R. Card,
NUT Regional Office,
Kendrick House,
Wharf Street,
Newbury,
Berkshire
Tel: Newbury (0635) 43158 and
43571
Home Tel: 025 082 3080

B.J. Marshall,
NUT Regional Office,
2 Roberts Road,
Doncaster,
South Yorkshire
Tel: Doncaster (0302) 62448

T.J. Harrison,
14–16 Sussex Road,
Haywards Heath,
West Sussex RH16 4EA
Tel: Haywards Heath (0444) 52073

T.R. Palframan,
NUT Regional Office,
30 Chorley New Road,
Bolton,
Lancashire
Tel: Bolton (0204) 35299 and 21434
Home Tel: Bolton (0204) 40517

A. Pearce,
NUT Regional Office,
16 Salter Street,
Stafford ST16 2NQ
Tel: Stafford (0785) 44129
Home Tel: Stoke-on-Trent (0782)
264866

D. Roberts,
3rd Floor,
34 Queen Street,
Cardiff CF1 4BW
Tel: Cardiff (0222) 29989 and 396899
Home Tel: Cardiff (0222) 43214

R. Ruffle,
NUT Regional Office,
Summerland Street,
Exeter,
Devon EX1 2AT
Tel: Exeter (0392) 58028
Home Tel: Exeter (0392) 76792

I. Whittaker,
NUT Regional Office,
3 Sunderland Road,
Durham DH1 2LH
Tel: Durham (0385) 67238
Home Tel: Durham (0385) 64097

A.H. Williams,
NUT Regional Office,
108 High Street,
Newmarket,
Suffolk
Tel: (0638) 4538
Home Tel: (0638) 742 191

A.J. Woodward, BA, DipEd,
NUT Regional Office,
Stoke Rochford Hall,
Stoke Rochford,
Grantham,
Lincolnshire
Tel: Grantham (0476) 83 401/2
Home Tel: Grantham (0476) 68572

Regional Field Officer:
A.M. Woolley, MA
NUT Regional Office,
30 Chorley New Road,
Bolton BL1 4AP
Tel: 0204 35299 and 21434
Home Tel: 07062 28911

Periodical: *The Teacher* (weekly)

Policy: The union is currently occupied, and has been for some years, with the effects of cuts in educational expenditure and the related problems of oversize classes and teacher unemployment. The Union has always fought for the *expansion* of educational opportunity including such issues as the mandatory provision of nursery education, a broader curriculum and the reform of the examination system. In addition, it strongly supports the comprehensive principle in secondary and higher education and played a leading part in the successful campaign to end selection of pupils at eleven-plus.

Recent NUT publications
1. The Case against the Cuts (August 1979)
2. Comprehensive Education—Does Mrs Thatcher know what she is doing? (August 1979)
3. Campaign for Nursery Education (July 1979)
4. Kept Behind—The Teachers' Case for Fair Pay (January 1979)
5. Middle Schools: deemed—or doomed? (March 1979)
6. Falling Rolls—introduction (April 1979)

Issues discussed at the 1979 Annual Conference included salaries, falling school rolls, racialism, nursery education, comprehensive schools, as well as the closure of rural schools, early retirement; sex discrimination in (*a*) conditions of service and (*b*) the curriculum; the appointment and promotion of teachers.

TEACHERS, THE PROFESSIONAL ASSOCIATION OF
5 Wilson Street, Derby DE1 1PG
Tel: Derby (0332) 372337/8/9
This association was formed in 1970 as a non-militant professional trade union for teachers in all types of educational institutions and is registered with the Certification Office as an independent trade union under the relevant statutes. From small beginnings it has grown to a membership of over 17,000 in more than 150 branches throughout England, Scotland and Wales. It is affiliated to the federation of politically independent trade unions. (M.P.&S.L.G.)
Current membership: over 17,000

President: R.V. Bryant, 11 Pentland Grove, Darlington, County Durham
Chairman: W. Lunt, 84 Greenloons Drive, Formby, Merseyside
Hon. Secretary: B.D. Round, 11 Nup End Lane, Wingrave, Aylesbury, Bucks
Hon. Treasurer: D. Walker, Stable Cottage, Morley Hall, Wymondham, Norfolk

The above elected honorary officers are supported by full-time staff at Head Office under the direction of:
Chief Executive: James M. Snowdon, BA, DipEd, ATh, FCIS
Field Officer: Geoffrey Gospel
Chief Administrative Assistant: Mary W. Archer (Mrs)

Council
Area A
N.G. Henderson,
29 Campion Drive,
Guisborough,
Cleveland

B. Jefferson,
19 The Green,
Piercebridge,
Darlington,
Co. Durham

Area B
P. Frost,
284 Windsor Road,
Oldham,
Lancs. OL3 4HL

Miss C. Leonard,
5 Grafton Street,
Claughton, Birkenhead,
Merseyside

Area C
H. Butler,
1 The Crescent,
Totley,
Sheffield,
S. Yorks.

Mrs J. McCulloch,
25 Hatfield House,
St. James Street,
Doncaster

Area D (0)
M. Best,
15 Lowans Hill View,
Redditch,
Worcs.

Miss M. Johnson,
46 Dewsbury Avenue,
Coventry CV3 4LF,
W. Midlands

Area D (1)
R. Ramsey,
Handsworth Wood Girls School,
Church Lane,
Handsworth Wood,
Birmingham

Harvey H. Jones,
40 Somerset Road,
Erdington,
Birmingham 23

Area E
J. Brind,
6 Marshall Close,
Llandaff,
Cardiff

J. Andrews,
1 Chaseley Gardens,
off Elder Lane,
Burntwood,
Nr. Walsall

Area F
G.C. Eldridge,
Westover,
Greater Lane,
Edington,
Westbury,
Wilts.

J. Green,
6 Kennall Park,
Ponsanooth,
Truro,
Cornwall

J.G. Spiers,
11 Mount Pleasant Avenue,
Wells,
Somerset

Area G
R. Jane,
334 Woodlands Road,
Woodlands,
Nr. Southampton,
Hants.

P.A. Howlett,
Redbank,
22B Priory Crescent,
Southsea,
Hants.

Area H
Mrs J. Edwards,
1A Sandgate Road,
Folkestone,
Kent

Miss C. Croudson,
40 Rackham Road,
Worthing,
Sussex

Area J
P. Murphy,
78 Drakefield Road,
London SW17

Mrs A. Kerr,
49 Redcliffe Square,
London SW10

P.J. Howe,
67 Wentworth Road,
Barnet,
Herts.

Area K
Mrs D. Womack,
11 South Road,
Saffron Walden,
Essex CB11 3DG

Area L
Mrs D. Smith,
19 Cainhoe Road,
Clophill,
Beds.

Area M
Mrs J. Hoogerwerf,
The Crest,
22 Lime Avenue,
Derby

J. Bell,
14 Bideford Road,
Evington,
Leicester LE5 6XE

Area N
M. Woolston,
2A Cissplatt Lane,
Keelby,
Grimsby,
S. Humberside

Mrs J. Tomlin,
Marsh Cottage,
Easington,
Hull,
N. Humberside

Area O
N.C.P. Griffin,
15 Orchard Avenue,
Southgate,
London N14

Area P
W. Thomson,
Catherinefield School House,
Edinburgh Road,
Dumfries DG1 3NT

J. Robertson,
O'Neil Corse School House,
Craigievar,
Alford,
Aberdeen,
Scotland

W. Thomson,
Scottish Officer

D. Mackinnon,
Welsh Officer—Shalom,
82 Station Road,
Llandaff North,
Cardiff

Area Q
K.D. Shaw,
10 Southcroft Avenue,
West Wickham,
Kent

K. Barritt,
99 Stag Leys,
Ashtead,
Surrey

SECRETARIES OF LOCAL ASSOCIATIONS
Electoral Area A
County Councils of Cumbria, Lancashire, Northumberland, North Yorkshire, Durham, Cleveland, and districts in Metropolitan Counties of Tyne & Wear, (Newcastle-Upon-Tyne, North Tyneside, South Tyneside, Gateshead and Sunderland).

Cumbria
Joint Branch Press Sec.,
R. Acland, S. Mullaney,
57 Currock Road,
Carlisle,
Cumbria (Plate)

York & District
M. G. Fife,
77 Millfield Lane,
Nether Poppleton,
Yorks
Tel: York (0904) 795905

Darlington & District
I. Moore,
105 Geneva Road,
Darlington,
Co. Durham,
Tel: (School) Newton Aycliffe 314572

Cleveland
N.G. Henderson,
29 Campion Drive,
Guisborough, Cleveland TS14 8DY

Durham
Mrs. M. Morgan,
77 Swinside Drive
Belmont,
Durham

Northumbria
Mrs A. Graham,
6 Mayfield,
Whickham,
Newcastle-Upon-Tyne NE16 4PJ
Mrs. J. Fox,
4 Croftdale Road,
Blaydon on Tyne,
Tyne & Wear
Blaydon (0632) 5153 (Sch)
Blaydon (0632) 5131 (Hm)

Nidderdale
R.E.M. Imeson,
Pear Tree Cottage,
High Street,
Pateley Bridge,
Harrogate,
North Yorkshire HG3 5JU
Tel: Pateley Bridge 388

Electoral Area B
County Council and Districts in Metropolitan Counties of: Cheshire, Merseyside, (Wirral, Liverpool, Sefton, Knowsley and St. Helens) and Greater Manchester, (Wigan, Bolton, Bury, Rochdale, Salford, Trafford, Manchester, Stockport, Tameside and Oldham).

Liverpool
G. Ross,
31 Gotham Rd,
Spital,
Bebington,
Wirral,
Cheshire

F.R. Blackburn,
41 Birch Rd.,
Meols,
Wirral
Cheshire

Chester Branch
Mrs J.E. Bucknall,
10 Tintern Avenue,
Upton by Chester,
Cheshire

Stockport
Mrs D. Smith,
11 Sevenoaks Avenue,
Heaton Moor,
Stockport

Manchester County
Mrs A. Bancroft,
7 Bardsley Vale Avenue,
Bardsley,
Oldham,
Lancashire
Tel: 061–665 3460

Rochdale & District
A.E. Marsden-Jones,
High Birch,
Market Street,
Whitworth,
Rochdale,
Lancs. OL12 8RU

Sefton
Mrs W.A. Lunt,
84 Greenloons Drive,
Formby,
Nr. Liverpool,
Merseyside

Southport
Mrs J. Lamb,
5 Chesterfield Road,
Ainsdale
Southport,
Merseyside
Tel: 0704 76241

Bolton
Rev. W.G. Spedding,
26 Milverton Close,
Lostock,
Bolton,
Lancs.

Tameside
R.C. Phillips,
33 Cote Green Road,
Marple Bridge,
Stockport
Tel: 061–427 2504

Bury
R.J. Joynson,
58 Hathaway Road,
Bury,
Lancs. BL9 8GG

Trafford
E.G. Durden,
7 Cranbourne Road,
Heaton Moor,
Stockport,
Cheshire SK4 4LD

S. Ribble
W. Joynson,
8 Greenway,
Eccleston,
Chorley,
Lancs. PR7 5SH

East Lancashire
Mrs Audrey Smith,
1 Lowerfield,
Langho,
Blackburn BB6 8HE
Tel: Blackburn 49699

Wigan & District
A. McGillard,
29 Park Road,
Golborne,
Warrington,
Lancs.
Tel: Ashton-in-Makerfield 78002

Electoral Area C.
Districts in the Metropolitan counties of West Yorkshire, S. Yorks, (Leeds, Bradford, Calderdale, Kirklees and Wakefield), and (Barnsley, Doncaster, Sheffield and Rotherham)

Bradford
Mrs M. Boulton,
61 Rose Avenue,
Horsforth,
Nr. Leeds,
Yorks.
Tel: Horsforth 87492

Kirklees
Mrs S. Beaumont,
Avon Lea,
Greenway,
Henley,
Huddersfield
Tel: 661 856

Sheffield & District
Mrs S. Longden,
40 June Road,
Woodhouse,
Sheffield

Doncaster
Mrs P.K. Jepson,
The Summit,
90 Rotherham Road,
Tickhill,
Doncaster

Leeds & Wakefield
(S. Yorks)
Mrs M. Gallon,
Manor House,
Whitwood,
Castleford
Tel: 552438

Mrs J.C. Gough,
25 Tatefield Grove,
Kippax.
Leeds
Tel: 860064

Electoral Area D
County Council of Staffordshire, Warwickshire, Hereford, Worcester and Salop and Districts in the Metropolitan County of the West Midlands (Wolverhampton, Walsall, Dudley, Sandwell, Birmingham, Solihull and Coventry.)

Birmingham
M. Burston,
151 Rocky Lane,
Perry Barr,
Birmingham B42 1QZ
Tel: Home 021–356 4080
School 021–351 1345

Coventry/Warwicks
Mrs J. Hayes,
73 The Mount,
Cheylesmore,
Coventry
Tel: Coventry 504401

Hereford/Worcester
Mrs Ann Bowker,
Priory House,
Priory Road,
Malvern
Tel: 4079

Solihull
Mrs M. Scanes,
36 Broad Oaks Road,
Solihull,
West Midlands
Tel: 621–705 3723

Burton-on-Trent
H.R. Curtis,
54 Eaton Road,
Burton-On-Trent,
Staffs DE14 2SW

Rugby (Joint)
Mrs P. Morris,
The Rectory,
Churchover,
Rugby

Mrs G. Dale,
170 Lower Street,
Hillmorton,
Rugby

L

Dudley
Mrs P. Cowell,
14 Hawne Close,
Halesowen,
West Midlands
Tel: Cradley Heath 65317
School 021–550 1566

Nuneaton
Mrs S.R. Teagle,
49 Birmingham Road,
Coleshill,
Birmingham B46 1DJ

N. Staffs.
Mrs A. Page,
37 Lancaster Road,
Newcastle-Under-Lyme,
Staffs.
Tel: Newcastle 618965

Walsall
Mrs P. Bayley,
21 Sandymount Road,
Walsall,
West Midlands

West Bromwich College
N. A. Davies,
'Meon',
8 Copper Beech Drive,
Kingswinford,
West Midlands

Sandwell
Mrs J. Bannister,
112 Cherry Tree Avenue,
Walsall,
West Midlands
Tel: 27711

Electoral Area E
County Councils of Avon, Gloucestershire, Salop and Wales

Avon
Miss B. Jervis,
109 Somerville Road,
St. Andrews,
Bristol BS6 5BX

Glos. & District
Miss G. Jones,
26 Oxstalls Way,
Longlevens,
Glos. GL2 9JG

Stroud & District
Mrs J. French,
Hazelhanger,
Far End,
Sheepscombe,
Stroud,
Glos. GL3 7RL
Tel: Painswick 812 040

Cheltenham
Mrs M. Ader,
64 Andover Road,
Cheltenham,
Glos
Tel: Cheltenham 54026

Wales Fed.
Miss M. Gardner,
12 Adare Terrace,
Treorchy,
Glam.
Tel: Treorchy 772003

R.J. Brind,
6 Marshall Close,
Llandaff,
Cardiff CF5 2JJ

Salop
Mrs H. Baty,
The Rectory,
Hope Bowdler,
Church Stretton,
Salop SY6 7DD

N. Clwyd
Mrs R. McQuillen,
Penrhos,
Glyn Circle,
Kimmel Bay,
Rhyl,
Clywd
Tel: Rhyl 55978

Gwent
T.I. (Lyn) Evans,
Bryn Hafod,
Ponthir Road,
Caerleon.
Gwent
Tel: 422242

Wrexham
May 1979
G. Hodges,
Rivendell,
Mountain View,
Hope,
Wrexham

Gwynedd (Joint)
G. Williams,
Tair Lon,
Edern,
Pwllheli
Tel: Nefyn 341,

Miss S. Probin,
19 Gwynan Park,
Penmaenmawr
Tel: 2511

West Glam
Mrs B. Quick,
65 Pennard Drive,
Swansea,
Glam.

Electoral Area F.
County Councils of Cornwall, Devon, Dorset, Somerset, Wiltshire

Wells (Somerset)
Mr J. Spiers,
11 Mount Pleasant Avenue,
Wells,
Somerset

Wiltshire
G.C. Eldridge,
Westover,
Greater Lane,
Edington,
Westbury,
Wilts.
(Local Contact)

Exeter
St. Lukes
J.R. Field,
Rowancroft House,
Heavitree,
Exeter

Sedgmoor
Miss R. Saunders,
Little Bickley,
Milverton,
Taunton TA4 1PZ,
Somerset

Cornwall
Mrs A. Martin,
"Bunnys Hall",
71 Melvill Road,
Falmouth,
Cornwall FA1
Tel: 312353

Dorset
Mrs J.A. Jay,
30 Downland Place,
Adastral Road,
Canford Heath,
Poole,
Dorset

W. Devon
C. W. Garven,
20 California Gdns.,
Little America,
Efford,
Plymouth,
Devon

S. Devon (Joint)
Mrs. A. Callard,
2A Haslam Road,
Torquay
Contact Thro- Torquay 26978

Miss M. Dobson,
49 Thatcher Avenue,
Torquay
Tel: Torquay 23041

Electoral Area G
County Councils of Berkshire, Hampshire, Isle of Wight

Solent
B. Jones,
30 Hillside Avenue,
Widley,
Portsmouth,
Hampshire PO7 5BB
Tel: Cosham (07018) 82061

South Hampshire
M.St.J. Fancourt,
Springacre,
Walhampton Hill,
Lymington,
Hampshire

Reading
Mrs S.P. Shaw,
6 Pottery Road,
Tilehurst,
Reading

Thames Valley
Mrs Ann Robertson,
21 Mallard Close,
Twyford,
Berkshire
Tel: 345802

Electoral Area H
County Councils of Kent, Surrey, East Sussex, West Sussex

Ashford (Kent) & District
Mrs M.M. Russell,
6 Greenside,
High Halden,
Ashford,
Kent

Canterbury & District
J. Viner,
13 Sweechgate,
Broad Oak,
Canterbury
Tel: (Sch) Faversham 2496

Dartford & Swanley
Mrs W.M. Parsons,
76 Watling Street,
Dartford,
Kent DA2 6AE
Tel: 24879

Eastbourne
S.G. Wentworth,
27 Terminus Road,
Bexhill on Sea,
E. Sussex TN39 3LS

Farnham
Sec. Miss E.R.C. Astbury,
14 Cranmore Lane,
Aldershot,
Hants. GU11 3AS

Gravesham
Miss J. Wall,
3 Orchard Avenue,
Gravesend

Kent (Fed.)
J. Whisson,
159 Canterbury Road,
Kennington,
Ashford,
Kent TN24 9RB

Lewes
Miss J.M. Mitchell,
2 Sherrington Road,
Woodingdean, Brighton BN2 6QJ,
E. Sussex

Maidstone
D. Rattenbury,
5 Rayner Road,
Maidstone,
Kent

Medway Towns
Mrs J.C. White,
48 Pattens Lane,
Rochester,
Kent
Tel: Medway 45363

Shepway & Dover
Mrs S. Dunstall,
51 Canterbury Road,
Folkestone,
Kent
Tel: Folkestone 54719

South Surrey
A.G. Groom,
6 Grove Court,
Falkland Grove,
Dorking,
Surrey RH4 3DL

Sussex Fed.
Miss J.M. Kennedy,
33 Gannett House,
6 Hartington Place,
Eastbourne,
E. Sussex

W. Sussex (North)
Mrs B. Cobbett,
37 Horsham Road,
Pease Pottage,
Crawley

W. Sussex (South)
O. Smith-Boyes,
51 West Court Road,
Worthing BN14 7DJ,
W. Sussex

W. Sussex (West)
Miss J. Bishop,
Bishop Otter College,
College Lane,
Chichester,
W. Sussex PO19 4PE

Tunbridge Wells & District
Mrs S.M. Bishop,
13 Birling Drive,
Tunbridge Wells,
Kent
Tel: Tunbridge Wells 30008

West Surrey
Miss S. Bacon,
117A Collingwood Crescent,
Boxgrave Park,
Guildford,
Surrey GU1 2PF

Electoral Area J (I)
I.L.E.A.

London Area
Federation Secretary:
D. Riddick,
4 Montpelier Road,
Purley,
Surrey

Camden Div. 2
Miss B. Morgan,
1 Paul Court,
Windsor Road,
Finchley,
London N3 3SP

Hackney
I.L.E.A. Div 4
M. Sanders,
19 Cass House,
Harrowgate Road,
Hackney,
London E9 7BP

Greenwich I.L.E.A.
Miss I.M. Gelderd,
5 Willersley Avenue,
Sidcup,
Kent

Southwark Branch
I.L.E.A. 8 & Lewisham I.L.E.A. 7
A.J. Parfott,
161 Green Lane,
New Eltham,
London SE9 3SZ
Tel: (Home) 01-850 1777
(School) 01-237 5243

South West London I.L.E.A. 9 & 10
Mrs D.I. Turner,
144 Abbeville Road,
Clapham,
London SW4 9LP

Woolwich Coll. (Div. 5)
J.H. Harrison,
Engineering Dept.,
Woolwich College,
Villas Road,
London SE18

I.L.E.A. I Hammersmith,
Kensington & Chelsea
Mrs J.K. Davis,
20 Ducie House,
Chartfield Avenue,
Putney,
London SW15

London Boroughs of Barking, Bexley, Brent, Bromley, Croydon, Ealing,
Enfield, Haringey, Harrow, Havering, Hillingdon, Hounslow, Kingston-
Upon-Thames, Merton, Newham, Redbridge, Richmond, Sutton and
Waltham Forest

London Borough of Bexley
W.L. Everest,
8 Torbrook Close,
Bexley,
Kent DA5 1ES

London Borough of Bromley
Mrs P.M. Miles,
4 Kelsey Way,
Beckenham

London Borough of Brent
R.W. Parnell,
51 Dunster Drive,
Kingsbury,
London NW9 8EH
Tel: 01-205 5953

London Borough of Croydon
Miss D. Holdaway,
413 Wickham Road,
Shirley,
Nr. Croydon,
Surrey
Tel: 01-777 1812

London Borough of Hounslow
Mrs C. Bowden,
111 Ringway,
Southall,
Middlesex

London Borough of Ealing
Mrs M.J. Sangster,
120 Brunswick Road,
Ealing,
London W5 1AW

Kingston College of F.E.
K. Barritt,
99 Stags Leys,
Ashtead,
Surrey
Tel: 01-546 2151 Ext. 272
(Col) Ashtead 73009 (H)

London Borough of Hillingdon
Miss V. Preston,
163 High Street,
Northwood,
Middlesex

London Borough of Enfield
L.H. Bull,
44 Bush Hill Road,
Winchmore Hill,
London N21 2DT
Tel: 804-1769

North London
Miss M.M. Wurr,
2 Park View Road,
Finchley,
London N3 2JB

London Borough of Merton
Miss C. Wigmore,
40 Villiers Avenue,
Surbiton,
Surrey

Newham
R.G. Fleming,
279 Upton Lane,
Forest Gate,
London E7 9PR
Tel: (Home) 01-472 5929
(School) 01-511 1231

Harrow College
Mrs V.L. Fox,
3 Manor Park Drive,
North Harrow,
Middlesex.

London Borough of
Waltham Forest
Miss B. Jones,
9 Bloxhall Road,
Leyton,
London E10 7LW

Havering
Miss J.O. Baskett,
Brookside Junior School,
Dagnam Park Drive,
Harold Hill,
Romford,
Essex
Tel: Ingrebourne 43074

Redbridge (Essex)
Mrs O. Cushing,
Goodmayes Pri. School,
Airthrie Road,
Ilford,
Essex
Tel: 01-590 5810

Harrow
Mrs C.M. Pellicer,
5 Beresford Road,
Harrow,
Middlesex

Sutton
Mrs K. Chapman,
Woodlands,
Radcliffe Gardens,
Carshalton Beeches,
Surrey

Electoral Area K
County Councils of Cambridgeshire, Essex, Norfolk and Suffolk

Brentwood & District
Mrs M.H. Hackwell,
57 Potash Road,
Billericay

Clacton-on-Sea District
Mrs J. Vine,
15 Eastcliffe Avenue,
Clacton-on-Sea,
Essex
Tel: Clacton-on-Sea 27430

Essex N.E.
M. Coyne,
21 Brookhall Road,
Fingringhoe,
Colchester
Tel: Rowhedge 371

Norwich Branch
Mrs M.D. Herbert,
8 The Boulevard,
Sheringham,
Norfolk

Southend-on-Sea
Mrs F. Johnson,
19 Stuart Road,
Southend-on-Sea

Essex-Thurrock
Mrs E.J. Williams,
48 Hobart Road,
Tilbury,
Essex
Tel: Tilbury 70641

West Essex
G.E. Manning,
Perry's Chase,
Greensted Road,
Ongar,
Essex
Tel: Home Ongar 3159
School 01-508 5806

East Suffolk
C.P. Briscoe,
Home Farm,
Parham,
Woodbridge,
Suffolk IP13 9NW

Essex Fed.
Mrs S. Gallop,
11 Coles Green,
Loughton,
Essex

Cambs (Joint)
Mrs B. Ratcliffe,
5 Park Road,
Burwell
Tel: Newmarket 741052

Mrs J.E. Mansell,
20 Parsonage Lane,
Burwell
Tel: Newmarket 741139

Suffolk West
Miss J. Lupton,
47A Queens Road,
Bury St. Edmunds,
Suffolk IP30 9SD

L

Peterborough
Mrs Dot Byron-Evans,
9 Ibbott Close,
Stanground,
Peterborough
Tel: 42582

Electoral Area L
County Councils of Bedfordshire, Buckingham, Hertfordshire,
Northamptonshire, Oxfordshire

Bedfordshire
Mrs J. Ogilvie,
93 Dunstable Street,
Ampthill,
Bedfordshire

Buckinghamshire
D. Ray-Smith,
10 Stokes End,
Haddenham,
Bucks.
Tel: Haddenham 291695

East Herts
Miss P. Robinson,
2 Redan Road,
Ware,
Hertfordshire

West Herts
Mrs G. Nottage,
6 Highfield Crescent,
Northwood,
Middlesex
Tel: Northwood 24963

Oxford
Miss C. Ecclestone,
7 Sandringham Road,
Didcot,
Oxon OX11 8TP

N. Oxon
D.J.A. Todd,
95 Courtington Lane,
Bloxham,
Nr. Banbury,
Oxon OX15 4HS

W. Oxon
B. Lupton,
5 Perrot Close,
North Leigh,
Oxon

Northants
(Revived) Temp. Sec:
Miss E.M. Goldthorpe,
5 Pytchley Rise,
Wellingborough,
Northants
Home: Wellingborough 71481
School: Burton Latimer 2801

Milton Keynes
Miss Elaine Medlock,
81D Springfield Boulevarde,
Springfields,
Milton Keynes MK6 3HR
Tel: Milton Keynes 679037

Electoral Area M
County Councils of Derbyshire, Leicestershire, Nottinghamshire.

Derby & District
T.H. Bennet,
44 The Common,
Crich,
Matlock,
Derbyshire
Tel: Ambergate 2319

Leicester
Mrs G. Jefferson,
18 Coombe Place,
Oadby,
Leics. LE2 5TH

Mansfield
Mrs B. Parrock,
15 Granmer Grove,
Mansfield,
Notts NH19 7JR
Tel: Mansfield 29612

Nottingham & District
Miss J. Everitt,
33 Holly Road,
Watnall,
Nottinghamshire
Tel: Nottingham 382147

Longeaton & District
Mrs B.S. Grundy,
65 Risley,
Breaston,
Derby

Charnwood (Leicester)
A. Speight,
17 Beaumont Road,
Barrow On Stour,
Leicestershire.

Rutland & District
S. Seabrook,
7 Willoughby Drive,
Empingham,
Rutland

Electoral Area N
County Councils of Humberside & Lincolnshire

Lincs.
D.J. Pearson,
7 High Street,
Carlby,
Stamford,
Lincolnshire.

Grimsby & District
D. Nicholson,
11 Danesfield Avenue,
Waltham,
Grimsby

N. Humberside
Mrs S. Sarel,
54 Louis Street,
Spring Bank,
Hull,
N. Humberside HU3 1LZ

Scunthorpe
E.E. Gibbs,
38 Richdale Avenue,
Kirton Lindsey,
Gainsborough,
Lincolnshire.
Tel: Kirton Lindsey 639

Louth & District
Mrs P. Powell,
19 Ramsgate,
Louth,
Lincolnshire. LN11 0NB

Boston & District
Miss G.J. Revitt,
27 Welland Terrace,
London Road,
Spalding,
Lincolnshire. PE11 2TA
Tel: (0775) 66100

Scottish Branch Secretaries
Borders, Central, Dumfries, Fife, Grampian, Highland, Lothian, Orkneys,
Shetland, Strathclyde, Tayside, Western Isles, Moray

Angus & Dundee
J.M. Forrester,
4 Fairfield,
Arbroath,
Angus

Dumfries & Galloway
W.J. Thomson,
Catherinefield School House,
Edinburgh Road,
Dumfries
Tel: Dumfries 64156

Bearsden & Milngavie
Mrs J. Jordon,
46 Bailie Road,
Bearsden,
Glasgow G61 3AH
Tel: 041-942 0364

Edinburgh & Lothian
Miss M.I.G. Lawton,
11 Craigleith Hill Loan,
Edinburgh EH4 2JG
Tel: 031-332 5258

Glasgow East Branch
Miss L. Cammock,
8 Muiredge Court,
Uddingston, Glasgow

Fife
Miss Winifred Scott,
2 Links Place,
Leven,
Fife

Glasgow North Branch
J.T. Campbell,
9 Loskin Drive,
Glasgow G22 7QW
Tel: 041-772 1374

Aberdeen & District
R. Howard,
12 Glendee Terrace,
Cults,
Aberdeen,
Scotland AB1 9HX

Wigtownshire
Mrs J. Collier,
27 Main Street,
Glenluce,
Stranraer,
Wigtown
Tel: 058 13 308

Glasgow West Branch
Mrs J.K. Combe,
33 Airlie Street,
Glasgow G12 9TS

Lanarkshire
J.J. Ferguson,
7 Skye,
St. Leonards,
East Kilbride

Highland Branch
Mrs A.M.H. Fraser,
12 Southside Place,
Inverness,
Scotland
Tel: 04563-30484

Callender Park
College Branch
D. McLeish,
Callender Park Coll. of Education,
Falkirk,
Stirlingshire

Central Region
Mrs V. Pickering,
18 Back Yetts,
Thornhill,
By Stirling FK8 3PU

Strathclyde Federation
J. Struthers,
26 Hillhead Street,
Glasgow G12 8PX

Moray
Mrs C.T. Edwards,
Amor Villa,
77 Commerce Street,
Lossiemouth,
Moray
Tel: 2627

Orkney
J. Eccles,
Dorsgarth,
Stenness,
Orkney

Perth
Miss M. Bowen,
19 Pitcullen Terrace,
Perth,
Scotland

Periodicals: *Professional Teacher* (bi-monthly), *Noticeboard Newsletter* in the intervening months; *Off PAT* newsletter (once a term). Occasional papers have included recently *Premature Retirement*, *Maternity Benefits* and the *Student Teachers Handbook*.

TELEPHONE CONTRACT OFFICERS' ASSOCIATION, THE
15 Cranford Road, Tonbridge, Kent TN10 4HL
Tel: Tonbridge (0732) 351368

Founded in 1921 to represent Sales Representatives employed within Post Office Telecommunications. The union is organised nationally into 10 regions with a branch located at each of the 64 General Manager's Areas. The union is affiliated to the National Federation of Professional Workers.
Current membership: 1,010

OFFICIALS
Executive Council all working members, non-paid, elected at Annual Conference.
President: W.A. Meerza,
6 Longmead Road, Tooting Broadway, London SW17 8PN
General Secretary: D.L. Edwards
General Treasurer: W. Petrie
80 Ainslie Road, Cumbernauld, Glasgow G67 2ED
Minute Secretary: B. Fippard,
4 Buttermere Close, Lincoln LN6 0YD
Assistant General Secretary: R.C. Avis,
29 Hawfield Court, Woodland Grove, Isleworth, Middlesex TW7 6NU
Research Officer: D.A. Brownjohn,
Danford House, Danford Lane, Hartpury, Gloucester GL19 3BQ

Regional Officers	*North West*
London and South East	H. McPhail
H. Huggett	
	Wales
South West	W.A. Meerza
R. Avis	
	Scotland
Midland	W. Petrie
D.A. Brownjohn	
	Northern Ireland
North East	M.G. McConville
B. Fippard	

Periodical: *Pivot* (quarterly)

TESTON INDEPENDENT SOCIETY OF CRICKET BALL MAKERS
2 Invicta Villas, Malling Road, Teston, Maidstone, Kent ME18 5AP
Tel: Maidstone (0622) 812994 (home) 812230 (works)

Formed 29 December 1919 with original membership of 24, all male cricket ball makers. (The first female was introduced into the craft section (Hand stitching) of cricket ball making on 3 April 1979.) Since that time the union has extended to cover plastic made sports goods production operatives and sports equipment distribution employees. Of the members 20 are fully employed and 4 part-time in cricket ball

making, seven in plastic made sports goods and five in sports equipment distribution. The union was affiliated to the General Federation of Trade Unions from 1946 to 1973 when they were expelled for not complying with mandate, and chose to remain registered under the Industrial Relations Act 1971.
Current membership: 36
    Males: 34
    Females: 2

OFFICIAL
No full-time officials
General Secretary: D. Newick

TEXTILE CRAFTSMEN, YORKSHIRE SOCIETY OF‡
Textile Hall, Westgate, Bradford BD1 2RG
Tel: Bradford (0274) 27965

Established in 1952 as a merger between the former Yorkshire Warptwisters Society and the Bradford and District Warpdressers Association. The Textile Day Men's Union and Cloth Pattern Makers Association transferred their engagements to the society in 1968 and the Leeds and District Warpdressers, Twisters and Kindred Trades Association in 1975. The union comprises basically three different apprentice-trained 4/5 years craftsmen together with warpers and weftmen, etc. All are involved in the preparatory stage to weaving. Each branch has a committee of six members with a lay part-time secretary, from which three are appointed to the Executive Committee, making an executive of fifteen which meet not less than four times each year plus the annual and half-yearly meetings.
Current membership: 971

FULL-TIME OFFICIAL
General Secretary: F. Towers, JP

TEXTILE WORKERS AND KINDRED TRADES, AMALGAMATED SOCIETY OF (ASTWKT)*‡
Foxlowe, Market Place, Leek, Staffordshire ST13 6AD
Tel: Leek (0538) 382068

Founded in 1871 and incorporates the Trimming Weavers' Society, the Silk Pickers' Society, the Braid Workers' and Kindred Trades Society, the Silk and Cotton Dyers' Society, the Macclesfield Power Loom Silk Weavers' Association, Women Workers' Union, the Spun Silk Dressers' Union and the Spinners', Throwsters' and Reelers' Union. With the exception of the Macclesfield Power Loom Silk Weavers' Association the other seven unions amalgamated in 1919. The Macclesfield union (National Silk Workers) was merged into the

amalgamation in 1965. Members are found in all sections of the textile and clothing industry, mainly in North Staffordshire and South Cheshire. Affiliated to the TUC and the Labour Party.
Current membership: 5,959
    Males: 2,370
    Females: 3,589

OFFICIALS
General Secretary: H. Lisle, OBE, JP, Foxlowe, Market Place, Leek, Staffs ST13 6AD
Organiser and Clerical Assistant: F. Pakeman, (Address as above)
Secretary to H. Lisle: E. Woodcock, (Address as above)
Cheshire Area Secretary: C.Graves,
The Cocoon, 38 Park Green, Macclesfield, Cheshire
President: K. Wright, JP (lay member)
3 Cae Glas, Penyrheol, Caerphilly, Mid Glamorgan

Periodical: *Textile Voice* (at irregular intervals)

Policy: The union supported entry into Europe and the incomes policy with the 1977 12-month rule.

TEXTILE WORKERS' UNION, AMALGAMATED*‡
Textile Union Centre, 5 Caton Street, Rochdale, Lancashire OL16 1QJ
Tel: Rochdale (0706) 59551 and 58367

The Amalgamated Textile Workers' Union was formed as a result of a merger between several unions operating in the cotton and allied textiles' spinning and weaving industries in North West England. The unions involved were,The Amalgamated Weavers' Association, The National Union of Textile and Allied Workers, The Amalgamated Warehouse Operatives, The Operative Cotton Spinners' and Twiners' Association, and The Textile Officials' Association. The merger took effect on 1 January, 1974.
    The structure of the union is a federal one rather than a centralised organisation. It consists of fifteen district associations, each of which have a considerable degree of local autonomy. Membership is drawn from the spinning and weaving industries (all occupations) in Lancashire, Cheshire, Greater Manchester, Cumbria and North Yorkshire. The breakdown of membership is 56% male, and 44% female.
    The ATWU is affiliated to the TUC, The General Federation of Trade Unions, The International Textile and Garment Leather Workers' Federation, and the Labour Party. It holds an annual conference in Blackpool, at which union, domestic and international subjects are debated, and policy decisions reached.
Current membership: 39,864

General Secretary: J. Brown
President: J.J. Quinn
Assistant General Secretary: P.G. Walker

DISTRICT SECRETARIES

R. Bennett, JP
Amalgamated Textile Workers
Union,
(Southern Area),
193 Old Street,
Ashton-under-Lyne,
Lancashire
Tel: 061–330 1960

J. Browning, JP
Oldham Provincial Union of Textile
and Allied Workers,
Textile House,
108 Union Street,
Oldham,
Lancashire
Tel: 061–624 4135

J.J. Quinn, JP
Bolton and District Union of Textile
and Allied Workers,
AEU House,
77 St. Georges Road,
Bolton,
Lancashire
Tel: Bolton (0204) 25803

A. Belfield, JP
(Rochdale District)
NUTAW,
Newbold Buildings,
33 Oldham Road,
Rochdale,
Lancashire OL16 5QJ
Tel: Rochdale (0706) 43165

J. Farrington, JP
Northern Textile and Allied
Workers' Union,
11 Avenue Parade,
Accrington,
Lancashire BB5 6PN
Tel: Accrington (0254) 32384

D. Maurice,
(Staff Section),
NUTAW,
1st Floor,
Room 21,
Priory Buildings,
77 Union Street,
Oldham,
Lancashire
Tel: 061–624 8918

Mrs O. Sharples,
29 Wellington Street,
(St. John's),
Blackburn,
Lancashire BB1 8AF
Tel: Blackburn (0254) 55912

A. Shaw,
Weavers' Office,
95–97 Leeds Road,
Nelson,
Lancashire BB9 9UA
Tel: Nelson (0282) 64097

G.F. Jones,
Textile Centre,
6 Sedgwick Street,
Preston,
Lancashire PR1 1TP
Tel: Preston (0772) 53415

Mrs M. Lampitt,
Weavers' Office,
163 Wellington Street,
Accrington,
Lancashire
Tel: Accrington (0254) 32273

Mrs D. Lucas,
Weavers' Institute,
Bartlam Place,
Oldham,
Lancashire OL1 3SU
Tel: 061–624 4439

R.W. Hill and P.N. Willey,
(Joint Secretaries),
Colne and Craven District,
Weavers' Office,
11 Cross Skelton Street,
Colne,
Lancashire BB8 9JB
Tel: Colne (028 24) 3022

E. Garlick,
Weavers' Office,
77 St. George's Road,
Bolton,
Lancashire BL1 2BS
Tel: Bolton (0204) 22726

R. Trotter,
Cloth Hall,
150 Drake Street,
Rochdale,
Lancashire
Tel: Rochdale (0706) 43198 and
39403

R.G. Morrow
Weavers' Office,
2 Dicconson Terrace,
Wigan,
Lancashire WN1 2AF
Tel: Wigan (0942) 42133

N. Wareing,
Amalgamated Textile Operatives
Association,
(Warehousemen),
80 St. George's Road,
Bolton,
Lancashire
Tel: Bolton (0204) 25398

TEXTILE WORKERS UNION, AMALGAMATED STAFF SECTION*‡
1st Floor, Room 21, Priory Buildings, 77 Union Street, Oldham OL1 1HL
Tel: 061–624 8918

The section of the ATWU dealing with staff employees, originally derived from the Textile Officials' Association, an amalgamation in 1949 of various pockets of managers and overlookers in the Lancashire textile industry. As well as being affiliated to the TUC it belongs to the GFTU.
Current membership: 1,294 including 342 women.

NATIONAL OFFICERS
General Secretary: D. Maurice
President: W. Matthews,
89 Broadway Street, Oldham, Lancashire
Vice-President: R. Watson,
44 Hough Lane, Bromley Cross, Bolton BL7 9DB

Executive Council Members

R. Norton,
22 Hamer Close,
Ashton-under-Lyne,
Lancashire

P.J. Walsh,
48 First Avenue,
Church,
Accrington,
Lancashire

K. Jones,
2 Ford Street,
Dunkinfield,
Cheshire

D. Jones,
51 Windsor Road,
Knuzden,
Blackburn BB1 2DQ

D.G. Buckley,
4 Atherleigh Grove,
Leigh,
Lancashire

D. Needham,
51 Holmes Street,
Rochdale OL12 6AQ

P. Jones,
60 James Street,
Dearnley,
Littleborough

G. Whitham,
14 Alice Street,
Homer,
Rochdale

R. Watson,
44 Hough Lane,
Bromley Cross,
Bolton,
Lancashire

H.W. Warren,
18 Westminster Road,
Worsley,
Manchester M28 5AP

K. Smalley,
23 Leyland Avenue,
Hindley,
Wigan

H. Wheatcroft,
5 Birch Avenue,
Limeside,
Oldham

BRANCH SECRETARIES
Ashton
K. Jones,
2 Ford Street,
Dukinfield,
Cheshire

Blackburn
D. Jones,
51 Windsor Road,
Knuzden,
Blackburn BB1 2DQ

Bolton
R. Watson,
44 Hough Lane,
Bromley Cross,
Bolton BL7 9BD

Leigh
F. Yates,
29 Samuel Street,
Hindsford,
Atherton,
Manchester

Oldham
H. Wheatcroft,
5 Birch Avenue,
Limeside,
Oldham

Rochdale
P. Klieve,
37 Queen Victoria Street,
Rochdale,
Lancashire

THEATRICAL, TELEVISION AND KINE EMPLOYEES, NATIONAL ASSOCIATION OF (NATTKE)*

155 Kennington Park Road, London SE11 4JU
Tel: 01–735 9068/9 and 9060

Formed in 1890 and organised theatre workers mainly in the first years of its existence; subsequently extended to Cinemas, Film Studios, the BBC, Bingo and other parts of the entertainment industry. Today the association is mainly involved in organising the unskilled, craft and technical workers in these various branches of entertainment.

Current membership: 18,150 split almost evenly between men and women.

FULL-TIME OFFICERS
Regional Officers
London and South East
A. Carnall
S. Ogden
A. Collins
J. Downman
R. Johnson
B. Quinton
T. Lever
125 Kennington Park Road,
London SE11

Glasgow
H. McFarlane
103 Bath Street,
Glasgow

Manchester
A. Montrose,
85 Mosley Street,
Manchester

Nottingham
W. Bovey,
53 Mansfield Road,
Nottingham

Southampton
Mrs L. Wallace,
25 Portsmouth Road,
Southampton

GENERAL OFFICERS (Honorary positions)
General President: J. Tattum
General Vice-President: K. Barry
General Treasurer: J. Lascelles
General Secretary: J.L. Wilson

Periodical: *NATTKE Newsletter* (quarterly)

Policy: The union has no basic political attitudes but prefers to keep a flexible outlook since it is considered that politics play a very great part in the industry, which is protected by quota regulations from foreign competition.

TIE CUTTERS, LONDON SOCIETY OF
67 Wessex Drive, Erith, Kent DA8 3AE
Tel: Erith (032 24) 39810

Founded in 1911 by London Tie Cutters and still consisting of Silk, Lining, Swan and Machine cutters engaged in the men's tie and women's neckwear trades. Organising both men and women, the latter only since 1977, its members are all tie cutters either working at the trade or retired. Membership has recently increased and now represents 90 per cent of all tie cutters working in the South East. 1977 membership: 84

OFFICIALS
Secretary: J. McCormack

TILE, FAIENCE AND MOSAIC FIXERS SOCIETY, THE NATIONAL
186 Goswell Road, London EC1V 7DT
Tel: 01-251 2251

Formed 12 October 1892 as the Amalgamated Society of Tile and Mosaic workers and Fixers. Re-established in 1910 as the London and District Tile, Faience and Mosaics Fixers Society. Renamed the National Tile Faience and Mosaic Fixers Society 1928-9 to include Manchester and Leeds tile fixers. The Society is the only building trades craft union not now amalgamated. It received a certificate as an Independent Trade Union in August 1976.
Current membership: 325

OFFICIAL
Secretary: G.W. Foote

TOBACCO MECHANICS ASSOCIATION*‡
9 Wootton Crescent, St. Anne's Park, Bristol BS4 4AN
Tel: Bristol (0272) 773848

Formed in 1897 to cater for cigarette machine operators after the introduction of the Baron cigarette machine. It was known until 1975 as the Cigarette Machine Operators' Society.
Current membership: 351

OFFICIAL
General Secretary: W.D. Brunt

TOBACCO WORKERS' UNION (TWU)*
9 Station Parade, High Street, Wanstead, London E11 1QF
Tel: 01-989 1107

The union was originally founded in 1834 and became one of Britain's first industrial unions in 1918 when it opened its membership to all tobacco workers, male and female, skilled and unskilled. Currently the TWU has over 20,000 members, two-thirds of them female, in 42 branches and 5 districts. It seeks to organise all employees of a manual, clerical and supervisory kind and those in distribution (but not in the retail trade).
Current membership: 20,840

NATIONAL OFFICIALS
President: A.R. Martin
Full-time Officials
General Secretary: C.D. Grieve
Deputy General Secretary: Mrs T. Marsland
Financial Secretary: Miss J.E. Garwood
Information and Administration Officer: P. Duffy

No. 1 London, Ipswich, Basildon:
Miss L. Grotier,
Room 13,
Leysian Buildings,
112 City Road,
London EC1V 2NB

No. 2 Bristol, Southampton,
Swindon, South Wales:
G.R. Robertson,
272 St. Johns Lane,
Bedminster,
Bristol BS3 5AU

No. 3 Manchester, Liverpool:
K.G. Jones,
77 Lisburn Lane,
Tuebrook,
Liverpool L13 9AF

No. 4 Nottingham:
M. Mulhern,
126 Hartley Road,
Nottingham NG7 3AJ

No. 5 Glasgow, Stirling,
Newcastle, Darlington:
R.T. Brown,
108 West Rgent Street,
Glasgow G2 4RW

Periodical: *Tobacco Worker* (bimonthly)

Policy: The union was opposed to entry into the EEC and is against incomes policies. It has a long history of involvement in international trade union solidarity, dating back at least to 1871 when it was a founder-member of the Tobacco Workers International. It maintains strong contact with tobacco workers throughout the world, and is actively involved in attempts in working for a closer relationship between the ICFTU and WFTU.

TRADE SOCIETY OF MACHINE CALICO PRINTERS, THE

See MACHINE CALICO PRINTERS, THE TRADE SOCIETY OF

TRANSPORT AND GENERAL WORKERS UNION (TGWU)*
Transport House, Smith Square, London SW1P 3JB
Tel: 01-828 7788   Telex: 919009

The TGWU was formed on 1 January 1922 by amalgamation between fourteen trade unions representing 350,000 members from various industries including factory workers, dockers, stevedores, lightermen, transport workers and clerks. Since that time it has grown steadily through a combination of recruitment and amalgamation. By 1942 membership had reached a million, by 1969 a million and a half, and in 1977 the two million mark was passed. In all, more than 75 separate unions have been incorporated into the TGWU.

An essential feature of the union has always been its insistence on democratic control. From the beginning, its structures has been based on two principles: first, responsibility for union policy rests with the lay members and is exercised through their elected representatives; second, the constitution of the union is dual in character, the decision-making bodies being elected partly on a geographical basis and partly on an industrial basis.

Every member of the union is attached to a branch, and also has the right to elect a workplace representative. The growth of large-scale industry has led to more branches based on the place of work, and with the trend towards localised industrial agreements, this form of branch structure is becoming increasingly popular. The branch is the basis administrative unit in the union and is essential as a channel of communication. But increasingly the work of its officers is supplemented by that of the workshop representatives.

In the workplace the shop steward is the key figure in carrying out the union's policies. He or she speaks and acts for union members on all matters affecting their wellbeing. The greatest scope for local initiative on the part of shop stewards is in negotiations over payment systems and productivity bargaining.

In each of its eleven regions the union provides machinery for co-ordinating the work of branches, both industrially and administratively. In most regions district committees are widely established; some bring together branches within a district on a community basis, and others co-ordinate branches in particular industries. Regional trade group committees also operate in some regions.

The principal committee in the region is the regional committee, consisting of representatives of the district or trade group committees. The regional committee has a direct relationship with the union's General Executive Council. Its functions include supervising the union's activities throughout the region; co-ordinating the work of the regional trade groups and sections; educational work; and consideration of disputes in the region.

National trade group or section committees are the principal trade bodies of the union. They deal with the specific industrial interests of the group membership, including the formulation of policy relating to wages and conditions. The following industries are covered by trade groups or sections:

Administrative, Clerical, Technical and Supervisory; Vehicle Building and Automotive; Building, Construction and Civil Engineering; Building Craft Section; Chemical, Rubber and Oil Refining; Commercial Road Transport; Docks, Waterways, Fishing, etc.; Food, Drink, Tobacco (including Agriculture and Flour Milling); General Workers (including Textiles and Man-made Fibres); Passenger Services; Power and Engineering; Public Services and Civil Air Transport.

The General Executive Council is the governing body of the union. It is responsible for the general administration and management of the union, subject to the policy laid down by the Biennial Delegate Conference to which it reports. The Council reflects the dual structure of the union: the territorial representatives are elected by ballot of membership in the region concerned, and there is one representative from each national trade group committee.

The supreme policy-making authority within the union is the Biennial Delegate Conference. Nominations for delegates are made from the branches, and election is by ballot vote of regional trade groups on a membership basis.

The chief full-time officer of the union is the General Secretary, who is elected by ballot vote of all members. Between Biennial Delegate Conferences he is responsible to the GEC for all aspects of union policy and administration. He is also the spokesman of the GEC both within the labour movement and in the world outside. The Deputy General Secretary shares many of these tasks, and there are also a National Organiser, National Secretaries, National Officers and Heads of Department with special responsibilities.

Among the specialist services provided by the union to its members are legal advice, help with safety and health matters, convalescent home facilities, economic and statistical research, and education (including home study courses and a wide range of training programmes).

Current membership: 2,083,959

OFFICIAL
President: S. Pemberton,
Transport House,
Smith Square,
Westminster,
London SW1P 3JB
General Secretary: A. M. Evans
Deputy General Secretary: C.H. Urwin

REGIONAL AND DISTRICT OFFICES

No. 1
Regional Office
Woodberry,
218 Green Lanes,
London N4 2HB
Tel: 01-800 4281

District Offices
London
281 Victoria Dock Road, E16
Tel: 01-476 2647

173 Clapham Road,
Stockwell SW9
Tel: 01-274 3251

203-209 North Gower Street, NW1
Tel: 01-387 7242/5

80 West India Dock Road,
Stepney E14
Tel: 01-987 3911

43 West Ham Lane,
Stratford E15
Tel: 01-534 4187/8

164 Lower Road,
Rotherhithe SE16
Tel: 01-237 3143

137 Tooley Street, SE1
Tel: 01-407 1664

Broad House,
205 Fore Street,
Edmonton N18
Tel: 01-807 5516/7

82 Hammersmith Grove, W6
Tel: 01-748 2606

3 Woolwich New Road, SE18
Tel: 01-854 1406

74 Camberwell Church Street,
Camberwell SE5
Tel: 01–703 4228

B170–171 Fruit and Vegetable
Market,
New Covent Garden Market,
Vauxhall,
London SW8 5HH
Tel: 01–720 8344

781a London Road,
Thornton Heath,
Croydon CR4 6AW
Tel: 01–684 3757

25 Snow Hill,
Smithfield Market, EC1
Tel: 01–236 8582

66 Lewisham Way, SE14
Tel: 01–692 2214

84 High Street,
Harlesden NW10
Tel: 01–965 1671

7–9 South Road,
Southall
Tel: 01–574 1391

Rooms 83/84.
12/13 Henrietta Street. WC2
Tel: 01–240 1056

Brighton
20 Church Road,
Hove
Tel: Brighton (0273) 71737

Bury St. Edmunds
63 Churchgate Street IP33 1RJ
Tel: Bury St. Edmunds (0284) 5224

Cambridge
12 Burleigh Street,
Cambridge
Tel: (0223) 53048

Chatham
5A New Road Avenue,
Tel: Chatham (0634) 400411

Chelmsford
19b High Street
Tel: Chelmsford (0245) 53709

Colchester
Hammond House,
10 Queen Street, CO1 2PJ
Tel: Colchester (0206) 73446

Eastbourne
200 Terminus Road, BN21 3BB
Tel: Eastbourne (0323) 24224

Haverhill
Bevan House,
Camps Road
Tel: Haverhill (0440) 5773

Ipswich
Transport House,
60 Grimwade Street
Tel: Ipswich (0473) 50321/2

Lowestoft
10 Suffolk Road,
Tel: Lowestoft (0502) 3861

Luton
33 Cardiff Road
Tel: Luton (0582) 26122

Milton Keynes
670 North Row,
Secklow Gate West, MK9 3EG
Tel: Milton Keynes (0908) 678261/2

Norwich
59 Bethel Street, NOR 57E
Tel: Norwich (0603) 24052

Rainham
76 Rainham Road,
Rainham RM13 7RL
Tel: Rainham (040 27) 51722

St Albans
1 Catherine Street,
Tel: St Albans 56 66076

Tilbury
80 Calcutta Road
Tel: Tilbury (037 52) 2371

Watford
66 Leavesden Road, WD2 5EH
Tel: Watford (0932) 21267/8

Region 2
Regional Office
67–75 London Road,
Southampton SO9 5HH
Tel: Southampton (0703) 37373

District Offices:
Aldershot
67 Grosvenor Road
Tel: Aldershot (0252) 21686

Bournemouth
238 Holdenhurst Road
Tel: Bournemouth (0202) 294333

Guernsey
Norman House,
South Esplanade,
St. Peter Port
Tel: Guernsey (0481) 22133

Jersey
66 New Street,
St. Helier
Tel: Jersey (0534) 725841

Portsmouth
Victoria House,
57 Kingston Road, PO2 7DS
Tel: Portsmouth (0705) 24514

Reading
36 Kings Road
Tel: Reading (0734) 590311

Salisbury
23 Brown Street
Tel: Salisbury (0722) 5048

Region 3
Regional Office
Transport House,
Victoria Street,
Bristol BS1 6AY
Tel: Bristol (0272) 293001

District Offices
Avonmouth
Transport Hall,
Gloucester Road, BS11 9AQ
Tel: Avonmouth (027 52)
823216/823032

Bridgwater
44 St Mary Street,
Tel: Bridgwater (0278) 57051/2

Exeter
Branscombe House,
17 York Road
Tel: Exeter (0392) 73665/70854

Falmouth
50 Arwenack Street
Tel: Falmouth (0326) 312201

Gloucester
18 Worcester Street, GL1 3AE
Tel: Gloucester (0452) 22041/23546

Plymouth
65 Breton Side
Tel: Plymouth (0752) 65667/65459

St. Austell
1 High Cross Street, PL25 4AB
Tel: St. Austell (0726) 3694/5110

Swindon
39 Victoria Road
Tel: Swindon (0793) 22979 and
28993

Yeovil
Unity Hall,
Vicarage Street, BA20 1JY
Tel: Yeovil (0935) 5820

Region 4
Regional Office
1 Cathedral Road,
Cardiff CF1 9SD
Tel: Cardiff (0222) 394521

District Offices
Aberdare
29 Whitcombe Street,
CF44 7AV
Tel: Aberdare (0685) 876327

Barry Dock
Dockers' Hall,
Coronation Street, CF6 6JW
Tel: Barry (0446) 735160

Bridgend
Welsh Development Agency,
Project Office,
Waverton Industrial Estate,
Tel: Bridgend (0656) 2202

Caernarfon
17 Segontium Terrace, LL55 2PW
Tel: Caernarfon (0286) 2102

Cardiff
1 Cathedral Road, CF1 9SD
Tel: Cardiff (0222) 394521

Ebbw Vale
11 Armoury Terrace, NP3 6BE
Tel: Ebbw Vale (0495) 303086

351

Flint
64 Chester Street, CH6 5DH
Tel: Flint (035 26) 3611/2

Haverfordwest
18 Mariners Square, SA61 2EN
Tel: Haverfordwest (0437) 2304

Llanelli
107 Station Road
Tel: Llanelli (055 42) 3972

Newport
Transport House,
Cardiff Road, NPT 2EN
Tel: Newport (0633) 63086 and 65337

Newtown
2 Commercial Street,
SY16 2ES
Tel: Newtown (0686) 26300

Port Talbot
48 Talbot Road, SA13 1HM
Tel: Port Talbot (063) 882807

Shotton
Transport House,
Chester Road,
Shotton,
Deeside,
Clwyd CH5 1QG
Tel: (0244 81) 3565/6

Swansea
13 St. James Gardens, SA1 6DX
Tel: Swansea (0792) 57410, 57501 and 56377

Wrexham
65 Regent Street, LL11 1PF
Tel: Wrexham (0978) 261842 and 52141

Region 5
Regional Office
9–17 Victoria Street,
West Bromwich B70 8HX
Tel: 021–553 6051

District Offices
Birmingham
211 Broad Street,
Birmingham B15 1DE
Tel: 021–643 6221

Burton-on-Trent
2 Horninglow Street
Tel: Burton-on-Trent (0283) 61176

Coventry
Transport House,
Short Street, CV1 2LS
Tel: Coventry (0203) 27361

63 Holyhead Road, CV1 3AA
Tel: Coventry (0203) 29628

Derby
32 Charnwood Street, DE1 2HA
Tel: Derby (0332) 45851

Dudley
81 King Street, DY2 8PR
Tel: 0384 231268

Leicester
7 Bowling Green Street, LE1 6AW
Tel: Leicester (0533) 26571

Northampton
254 Wellingborough Road,
NN1 1NW
Tel: Northampton (0604) 22097

Nottingham
259 Mansfield Road, NG1 3HA
Tel: Nottingham (0602) 46784

Oxford
Transport House,
46 Cowley Road, OX4 1JA
Tel: Oxford (0865) 43506 and 47188

Redditch
16 Royal Square, B97 4HB
Tel: Redditch (073–92) 60432

Stoke-on-Trent
140 Broad Street,
Hanley,
Staffordshire ST1 4HP
Tel: Stoke-on-Trent (0782) 29800 and 24558

Tamworth
16 Kettlebrook Road
Tel: Tamworth (0827) 65622

Wellington
48 Walker Street, TF1 1BA
Tel: Telford (0952) 42930

Wolverhampton
32–33 Berry Street
Tel: Wolverhampton (0902) 26434

Worcester
8 Severn Street
Tel: Worcester (0905) 24894

Region 6
Regional Office
Transport House,
1 Crescent,
Salford M5 4PR
Tel: 061–736 1407/9; 3130; 4089;
7828/9

District Offices
Birkenhead
Transport House,
Berner Street L41 4JY
Tel: 051–647 8160

Blackburn
Refuge Buildings,
64 Ainsworth Street, BB1 6AZ
Tel: Blackburn (0254) 51375

Blackpool
44 Cookson Street, FY1 3ED
Tel: Blackpool (0253) 22140

Bolton
9/11 Moor Lane,
Tel: Bolton (0204) 22741 and 22842

Burnley
84 St. James Street, BB11 1NJ
Tel: Burnley (0282) 24918

Bury
12 Silver Street, BL9 0EX
Tel: 061–764 2171

Ellesmere Port
235 Whitby Road, L65 6RT
Tel: 051–355 5248

Fleetwood
92 Dock Street, FY7 6JW
Tel: Fleetwood (039 17) 3475

Isle of Man
Transport House,
Prospect Hill,
Douglas
Tel: Douglas (0624) 21156

Liverpool
Transport House,
Islington, L3 8EQ
Tel: 051–207 3388

4 Speke Road,
Garston, L19 2PA
Tel: 051–427 7214

42–44 Derby Road,
Bootle, L20 1AB
Tel: 051–922 5000

Northwich
27a High Street, CW9 5BY
Tel: Northwich (0606) 3034

Oldham
90 Union Street, OL1 1DS
Tel: 061–624 4496

Preston
Transport House,
228 West Strand, PR1 8UJ
Tel: Preston (0772) 729243/4

Rochdale
5 Oldham Road, OL16 1UA
Tel: Rochdale (0706) 44918

Salford
9 Dock Entrance,
Aubrey Street,
Trafford Road, M5 3DE
Tel: 061–872 1740

Skelmersdale
65 Westgate
Sandy Lane Centre,
WN8 8LE
Tel: 0695 32008

Warrington
16 Museum Street, WA1 1HU
Tel: Warrington (0925) 30233

Wigan
7 Bridgeman Terrace, WN1 1SX
Tel: Wigan (0942) 42252

Region 7
Regional Office
24 Park Circus,
Glasgow, G3 6AR
Tel: 041–332 7321

District Offices
Aberdeen
42–44 King Street, AB9 2TJ
Tel: Aberdeen (0224) 574271

Ayr
4 Dalblair Road, KA7 1UL
Tel: Ayr: (0292) 64427

Dumfries
29 Castle Street, DG1 1DL
Tel: Dumfries (0387) 4514

Dundee
61 Reform Street, DD1 15P
Tel: Dundee (0382) 27360

Dockers' Office,
West End Shed 13,
King George V Wharf,
Dundee Harbour
Tel: Dundee (0382) 457776

Dunfermline
4 Victoria Street, KY12 0NQ
Tel: Dunfermline (0383) 21685

Edinburgh
13 Claremont Crescent, EH7 4HX
Tel: 031–556 9676

Galashiels
70/72 Overhaugh Street,
Tel: Galashiels (0896) 3774

Glasgow
216 West Regent Street, G2 4DA
Tel: 041–248 6071

308 Albert Drive, G41 5RR
Tel: 041–429 3111

Portakabin,
King George V Docks, G51
Tel: 041–440 2438

Grangemouth
47 Bo'ness Road
Tel: Grangemouth (032 44) 2165

Greenock
4 Brougham Street, PA1 68AA
Tel: Greenock (0475) 26237

Inverness
Station Square
Tel: 0463 222768

Kirkcaldy
25 St. Clair Street, KY1 2QF
Tel: 0592 69106

Leith
Dockers' Office
27 Constitution Place, EH6 7DJ
Tel: 031–554 3722

Lerwick
Portacabin,
Albert Wharfe
Tel: Lerwick (0595) 3587

Paisley
129 Renfrew Road, PA3 4EA
Tel: 041–889 5176

Saltcoats
43 Vernon Street, KA21 5HF
Tel: Saltcoats (0294) 61521

Wick
15 Sinclair Terrace, KW1 5AB
Tel: Wick (0955) 4567

Wishaw
46 Main Street, ML2 7AJ
Tel: Wishaw (069 83) 74875

Region 8
Regional Office
Transport House,
Barrack Road,
Newcastle upon Tyne NE4 6DP
Tel: (0632) 28951

District Offices
Barrow-in-Furness
22 Hartington Street
Tel: 0229 29416

Carlisle
38 Cecil Street, CA1 1NT
Tel: Carlisle (0228) 22878

Darlington
22 North Road, DL1 1TL
Tel: Darlington (0325) 64904 and
61442

Middlesbrough
Transport House,
Fry Street
Tel: Middlesbrough (0642) 242314
and 243776

Stockton
62 Bishopston Lane, TS18 2AJ
Tel: Stockton (0642) 65228, 611462
and 61146

Workington
14 Oxford Street, CA14 2AH
Tel: Workington (0900) 2141

Region 9
Regional Office
22 Blenheim Terrace,
Leeds, LS2 9HF
Tel: Leeds (0532) 451587

District Offices
Bradford
36 North Parade, BD1 3JD
Tel: Bradford (0274) 21691

Doncaster
30 Nether Hall Road, DN1 2PW
Tel: Doncaster (0302) 49077

Halifax
37 Broad Street, HX1 1YA
Tel: Halifax (0422) 52028

Huddersfield
10 Byram Buildings,
Station Street, HD1 1LN
Tel: Huddersfield (0484) 30879

Sheffield
Transport House,
Hartshead, S1 1NX
Tel: Sheffield (0742) 77607

Region 10
Regional Office
Bevin House,
George Street,
Hull HU1 3DB
Tel: Hull (0482) 24167/8

District Offices
Boston
6/8 Bridge Street,
Tel: Boston (0205) 62016

Goole
80 Pasture Road
Tel: Goole (0405) 4485

Grimsby
390 Cleethorpe Road
Tel: Grimsby (0472) 55421

King's Lynn
16 Church Street,
Tel: 0553 65508

Lincoln
13 High Street,
Tel: Lincoln (0522) 22839

Peterborough
34 Cowgate
Tel: Peterborough (0733) 62152

Region 11
Regional Office
Transport House,
102 High Street,
Belfast BT1 2DL
Tel: Belfast (0232) 3238

District Offices
Ballymena
45 Wellington Street
Tel: Ballymena (0266) 6216

Banbridge
1a Dromore Street
Tel: Banbridge (076–262) 3680

Carrick-on-Suir
c/o Clonmel Office

Clonmel
20 Parnell Street
Tel: Clonmel 22809

Coleraine
27 New Row,
Tel: (0265) 3386

Cork
59 MacCurtain Street
Tel: Cork 961784

Drogheda
15 North Quay
Tel: Drogheda 041 8953

Dublin
112–113 Marlborough Street
Tel: Dublin 747995/6

Dundalk
30 Clanbrasil Street
Tel: Dundalk 4338

Dungarvan
35 O'Connell Street
Tel: Dungarvan 41246

Londonderry
56/58 Carlisle Road,
Tel: Londonderry (0504) 64851

Lurgan
5a Market Street
Tel: Lurgan (076 282) 2209

Newry
76 Hill Street
Tel: Newry (0693) 2993

Omagh
Belfast Bank Buildings,
High Street
Tel: Omagh (0662) 3326

Portadown
11k Magowan House,
West Street
Tel: Portadown (0762) 32124

Portlaw
c/o Clonmel Office

Waterford
Keyzer Street
Tel: Waterford 5438

Periodical: *The Record* (monthly)

Policy: In recent years the TGWU has opposed the entry of the UK into the EEC, and supported the voluntary pay policies negotiated by the TUC and the Labour Government in 1975–77. Current policy is to work for a return to free collective bargaining.

TRANSPORT SALARIED STAFFS' ASSOCIATION OF GREAT BRITAIN AND IRELAND (TSSA)*
Walkden House, 10 Melton Street, London NW1 2EJ
Tel: 01–387 2101

Formed in May 1897 at Sheffield under the name Railway Clerks Association. Registered as a trade union in 1900 and affiliated to Trades Union Congress in 1903. In 1951 it was decided that the name Railway Clerks Association was no longer appropriate to an organisation catering for all salaried staff in the publicly-owned transport industry. The new name, Transport Salaried Staffs' Association, was chosen to reflect the wide range of grades and undertakings covered. The association caters for approximately 70,000 members in 31 different organisations within the Transport and Travel industries, and is the only trade union catering solely for salaried staff employed in transport and travel. Membership extends nationwide, on the Continent, United States and Canada, the whole being divided into 296 branches, then grouped geographically in Divisional Councils to produce an Executive Committee of 27 members.
Current membership: 69, 479

NATIONAL OFFICIALS
President: W.H. Johnson, MP
Treasurer: J. Mills
General Secretary: Tom Jenkins
Assistant General Secretaries: C.A. Lyons, N. Hitchen

Periodical: *Transport Salaried Staff Journal* (monthly)

TRANSPORT UNION, THE UNITED ROAD (URTU)*
76 High Lane, Chorlton-cum-Hardy, Manchester M21 1FD
Tel: 061–881 6245/6

Formed in 1890 by a group of carters. Today its members are mainly drivers employed in general haulage and own account distribution. Current membership: 32,000

NATIONAL OFFICIALS
President: A. Fallon,
Laburnum Villa, 5 Sutton Lane, Middlewich, Cheshire
General Secretary: J. Moore
Assistant General Secretary: A. Hughes

Executive Committee
T. Way,
34 Carrill Grove East,
Levenshulme,
Manchester

A. Ford,
19 Anchor Avenue,
Chapel-en-le-Frith,
Derbyshire

F. Pockington,
44 Park Close,
Swinton,
Mexborough,
Yorkshire

A. Crozier,
95 Northumbria Walk,
West Denton,
Newcastle on Tyne

N. Trehearn,
100 Manor Road,
Brinsworth,
Rotherham

A. Williams,
10 Brindley Avenue,
Winsford,
Cheshire

J. Allen,
38 Boardshaw Crescent,
Middleton,
Lancs.

R. Thomas,
6 Bodnant Road,
Llandudno,
North Wales

D.M. Jones,
5 Quarella Crescent,
Bridgend,
Glamorgan

T. Stanworth,
3 Laurel Road,
Bassaleg,
Newport,
Gwent

D.C. Banks,
32 Bisley,
Stanshawe Estate,
Yate,
Bristol

DIVISIONAL OFFICIALS
W. French,
165 Atlantic Road,
Greenhill,
Sheffield

A. Taysome,
117 Sandringham Road,
The Lawn,
Swindon

M. Durant,
2 St. Clements Road,
Chorlton-cum-Hardy,
Manchester

REGIONAL OFFICIALS
A. Mottershead,
36 Charnwood Road,
Higher Blackley,
Manchester

F. Griffin,
5 Broom Street,
Newley,
Rochdale,
Lancs.

M. Billingham,
14 Mavina Drive,
Lostock Hall,
Preston

G. Farmery,
Trelawny,
6 Oakfields,
Middleton-Tyas,
Richmond,
Yorkshire

G. McGougan,
177 High Street,
Royston,
Barnsley,
Yorkshire

W. Beales,
1 Batley Close,
Marfleet Lane,
Hull

R. Abrahams,
61 Cemetery Road,
Dronfield,
Sheffield

J. Dunbreck,
1 Flaminian Way,
Ancaster,
Lincolnshire

K.J. Marron,
11 Fairview Avenue,
Rainham,
Essex

P.H. Rendall,
1 Verbena Way,
Summer Lane,
Worle,
Weston-super-Mare,
Avon

N.C. Rogers,
14 Greenway Avenue,
Alveley,
Nr. Bridgnorth,
Salop

R.T. May,
109 Greenham Wood,
North Lake,
Bracknell,
Berks.

Periodical: *Wheels* (bi-monthly) and *Your Cafe Accommodation Handbook* (Annual)

TUGBOATMEN'S ASSOCIATION, NORTH EAST COAST
47 Sibthorpe Street, North Shields, Tyne and Wear NE29 6NQ
Tel: South Shields 61515

A small association catering for tug boat crews operating on the river Tyne.

OFFICIAL
General Secretary: H.J. Malcolm

UNION OF CONSTRUCTION, ALLIED TRADES AND TECHNICIANS

See CONSTRUCTION, ALLIED TRADES AND TECHNICIANS, UNION OF

UNION OF JUTE, FLAX AND KINDRED TEXTILE OPERATIVES

See, JUTE, FLAX AND KINDRED TEXTILE OPERATIVES, UNION OF

UNION OF POST OFFICE WORKERS

See POST OFFICE WORKERS, UNION OF

UNION OF SHOP, DISTRIBUTIVE AND ALLIED WORKERS

See SHOP, DISTRIBUTIVE AND ALLIED WORKERS, UNION OF

UNITED ROAD TRANSPORT UNION

See TRANSPORT UNION, UNITED ROAD

UNIVERSITY TEACHERS, ASSOCIATION OF (AUT)*
United House, 1 Pembridge Road, London W11 3HJ
Tel: 01-221 4370

Founded in 1917, under the name of the 'Association of University Lecturers' it did not include University staff in Scotland who formed their own Scottish Association of University Teachers in 1922 and who, although united with the main body in 1949, still have separately elected representation on the national Executive Committee. In 1919, the membership was re-defined to cover all teaching staff, including Lecturers, Senior Lecturers, Readers and Professors, and the name was changed to 'Association of University Teachers'. Since its foundation, the AUT has extended its membership to cover academic library staff, senior administrative staff, research and other related grades of staff. These were eventually brought into the national salary grading structure in 1974, the national negotiating machinery for the teaching grades having been established in 1970. Affiliation to the TUC took place in 1976. Its objects are the advancement of University education and research;

the regulation of relations between University teachers and related staff and their employers; the promotion of common action by these staff; and the safeguarding of the interests of members. Its policies are determined by a Council of representatives which meets twice a year and which also elects a national Executive Committee; such policies are traditionally formed on a non-political basis.

The AUT's President, Vice-Presidents, Treasurer and Executive Committee are not full-time but are all elected from and by the members (through their Council representatives) on an honorary, unpaid basis. Its Headquarters Officials are appointed on a full-time, paid basis. There is one Regional Official, and its 80 Local Associations are organised by honorary unpaid local officials who are all working members of the association.

Current membership: 30,000

OFFICIALS 1979-80
President Dr. A. Taylor,
Department of Applied Maths & Theoretical Physics, University of Liverpool.

Headquarters Officials
General Secretary: L.J. Sapper, LLB
Deputy General Secretary: J.R. Akker, BA, DipEcon (Oxon)
Assistant General Secretaries:
Mrs A.M. Aziz, BA
Dr G.R. Talbot, BSc, PhD
Miss C.J. Day, MA

Periodical: *University Teachers' Bulletin* (bimonthly)

WALLCOVERINGS, DECORATIVE AND ALLIED TRADES, NATIONAL UNION OF*‡
223 Bury New Road, Whitefield, Manchester M25 6GW
Tel: 061–766 3645/6

Formed in 1919, as the Wall Paper Workers' Union, through an amalgamation of the Amalgamated Society of Machine Paper Stainers and Colour Mixers of Great Britain, and Paper Stainers Union of General Workers. With the subsequent acceptance of the members of the Block Printers Society and the later transfer of the engagements of the Print Block, Roller and Stamp Cutters Society it formed an industrial union for the British Wallcoverings Industry.

In July 1975 the Engagements of the Wallcoverings' Staff Association, which organised administrative, supervisory and managerial personnel in the industry, were transferred, with a subsequent name change from the Wall Paper Workers' Union to the National Union of Wallcoverings, Decorative and Allied Trades.

Whilst some 60 per cent of members are employed in the North West, the remainder are spread geographically across Great Britain.

The union transferred engagements to the National Graphical Association from 1 October 1979.
Current membership: 3,820

OFFICIALS
General Secretary: R.W. Tomlins
Assistant General Secretary: T.A. Trickett
National Officers: B. Philbin

Periodical: *Décor* (irregular)

WIRE DRAWERS AND KINDRED WORKERS, AMALGAMATED SOCIETY OF*

Prospect House, Alma Street, Sheffield S3 8SA
Tel: Sheffield (0742) 21674

Originally formed in 1840 to organise craft-apprentice trained wire drawers. In the early 1920s it changed from being a craft union to an industrial union, organising all employees engaged in the manufacture of wire and wire products. The membership is mainly centred in the areas of Warrington, Halifax, Ambergate, Birmingham, Manchester, Sheffield, North East, Cardiff and Scotland. Of the current membership, 550 are honorary members and in receipt of the Superannuation Benefit. National agreements for the majority of membership in regard to minimum terms and conditions of employment are conducted at the Joint Industrial Council for the Wire and Wire Rope Industries, the society having five representatives and the TGWU and GMWU with one each.
Current membership: 10,784

OFFICIALS

General Secretay:
L. Carr,
Prospect House,
Alma Street,
Sheffield S3 8SA

A.M. Ardron,
7 Bank Street,
South Anston,
Sheffield

National Organisers:
E.B. Lynch,
20 Ashdene Road,
Withington,
Manchester 20

T.B. Mellors,
56 Crewe Terrace,
Edinburgh 5,
Scotland

WOOL, SHEAR WORKERS' TRADE UNION, SHEFFIELD*

19 Rivelin Park Drive, Malin Bridge, Sheffield 6

Founded in 1890 and originally known as the Sheffield Wool Shear Grinders Makers Finishers, Benders Union. After changing its name

in 1912 and 1913 it adopted the present title in 1914.
Current membership: 32
Male: 30
Female: 2

OFFICIAL
General Secretary: J. Billard
President: F. Burrows, 30 Winn Gardens, Sheffield 6
Treasurer: E. Carr, 8 Harrison Road, Sheffield 6

WOOL SORTERS' SOCIETY, NATIONAL*‡
40 Little Horton Lane, Bradford BD5 0AL
Tel: Bradford (0274) 20392

Founded in 1921 with members in the textile industry.
Current membership: 757

OFFICIAL
Acting General Secretary: N. Newton, MBE, JP

WRITERS' GUILD OF GREAT BRITAIN (WGGB)*
430 Edgware Road, London W2 1EH
Tel: 01-723 8074/5/6

A writers' trade union recognised as representing writers' interests in all areas of film, television, radio and publishing, and originally formed as the Screenwriters' Guild in 1959 and currently also active on behalf of book authors and stage authors who became eligible to join in 1974. It is non-political.
Current membership: 1,500

GUILD OFFICIALS
General Secretary: Ian Roland Hill
Assistant General Secretary: Mrs M. Banks
Editor, Writers' News: J. Gratus
President: Lord Willis
Joint Chairmen: Rosemary Anne Sisson, Bruce Stewart
Deputy Chairman: Alfred Shaughnessy, Colin Spencer
Honorary Treasurer: Alice Crotch

Periodical: *Writer's News* (monthly)

YORKSHIRE ASSOCIATION OF POWER LOOM OVERLOOKERS

See POWER LOOM OVERLOOKERS, YORKSHIRE ASSOCIATION OF

YORKSHIRE SOCIETY OF TEXTILE CRAFTSMEN
See TEXTILE CRAFTSMEN, YORKSHIRE SOCIETY OF

YOUTH HOSTEL WARDENS, NATIONAL ASSOCIATION OF

Formed in 1948 as the National Federation of Wardens Associations and assumed present title and form in November 1965. The membership was spread over the whole of England and Wales but with the greatest concentration in the tourist areas, Lakeland, North Wales, Devon and Cornwall, etc. There were 11 branches of the NAYHW corresponding to the 11 regions of the Youth Hostel Association. In 1978 the union transferred engagements to the Transport and General Workers' Union.

1977 membership: 310
    Males: 190
    Females: 120

List of certified unions at 31 October 1979

Abbey National Staff Association
Accrington and District Power Loom Overlookers' Association
Alumasc Employees' Association, The
Amalgamated Association of Beamers Twisters and Drawers
  (Hand and Machine)
Amalgamated Association of Beamers Twisters and Drawers
  (Hand and Machine) Preston and District Branch
Amalgamated Felt Hat Trimmers', Wool Formers' and Allied
  Workers' Association
Amalgamated Society of Boilermakers, Shipwrights, Blacksmiths
  and Structural Workers, The
Amalgamated Society of Journeymen Felt Hatters and Allied
  Workers
Amalgamated Society of Textile Workers and Kindred Trades
Amalgamated Society of Wire Drawers and Kindred Workers
Amalgamated Society of Woolcomb Hackle and Gill Makers, The
Amalgamated Tape Sizers Friendly Protection Society
Amalgamated Textile Trades Union Wigan, Chorley &
  Skelmersdale District, The
Amalgamated Textile Warehousemen
Amalgamated Textile Warehousemen (Bolton and District
  Branch), The
Amalgamated Textile Workers' Union
Amalgamated Textile Workers' Union – Oldham AWA Division
Amalgamated Textile Workers' Union – Staff Section
Amalgamated Textile Workers' Union, Rochdale, Todmorden,
  Heywood, Bury
Amalgamated Textile Workers Union (Southern Area)
Amalgamated Union of Asphalt Workers
Amalgamated Union of Block Printers of Great Britain and
  Ireland, The
Amalgamated Union of Engineering Workers
Amalgamated Union of Engineering Workers (Constructional
  Section)
Amalgamated Union of Engineering Workers – Engineering
  Section
Amalgamated Union of Engineering Workers Foundry Section
Amalgamated Union of Engineering Workers – Technical,
  Administrative and Supervisory Section

A Monk and Company Staff Association
Anglia Hastings and Thanet Building Society Staff Association
Arts Council of Great Britain Staff Association
Assistant Masters and Mistresses Association, The
Associated Metalworkers' Union
Associated Society of Locomotive Engineers and Firemen
Association for Adult and Continuing Education
Association of Agricultural Education Staffs
Association of British Dental Surgery Assistants
Association of Broadcasting and Allied Staffs
Association of Cambridge University Assistants
Association of Career Teachers
Association of Cinematograph Television and Allied Technicians,
  The
Association of Clinical Biochemists Limited, The
Association of Community Home Schools, The
Association of Education Officers
Association of First Division Civil Servants, The
Association of Football League Referees and Linesmen
Association of Government Supervisors and Radio Officers
Association of Her Majesty's Inspectors of Taxes, The
Association of HSDE (Hatfield) Employees
Association of Local Authority Chief Architects
Association of Local Authority Chief Executives, The
Association of Local Government Lawyers
Association of London Transport Officers
Association of Magisterial Officers, The
Association of Management and Professional Staffs
Association of Managerial Staff of the National Bus Company
  and Subsidiary Companies, The
Association of National Health Service Officers, The
Association of Nurse Administrators, The
Association of Official Architects
Association of Operative Cotton Spinners of Haslingden and
  Surrounding Neighbourhood
Association of Optical Practitioners Limited, The
Association of Passenger Transport Executives and Managers
Association of Patternmakers and Allied Craftsmen
Association of Planning Officers
Association of Plastic Operatives and Engineers
Association of Polytechnic Teachers
Association of Principals of Colleges, The
Association of Professional, Executive, Clerical and Computer
  Staff (APEX)
Association of Public Service Finance Officers
Association of Public Service Professional Engineers
Association of Scientific, Technical and Managerial Staffs
Association of Somerset Inseminators, The

Association of Staff of Probation Hostels, The
Association of University Teachers
Association of Vice Principals of Colleges
Australian Mutual Provident Society Staff Association
Bakers, Food and Allied Workers' Union
Balfour Beatty Group Staff Association
Banking, Insurance and Finance Union, The
Bank of England Staff Organisation
Bank of New Zealand (London) Staff Association
Barclays Group Staff Association
Beamers, Twisters and Drawers Hand and Machine of Blackburn
    and Bolton Districts
Birmingham and District Association of Club Stewards and Hotel
    Managers
Blackburn and District Amalgamated Power Loom Overlookers'
    Association, The
Blackburn and District Tape-Sizers' Society
Blackburn and District Weavers, Winders and Warpers'
    Association, The
Bolton and District Powerloom Overlookers Trade Sick and
    Burial Association
Bolton and District Power Loom Weavers, Winders, Warpers,
    Loom Sweepers and Ancillary Workers Association, The
Bolton and District Union of Textile and Allied Workers
Bradford and Bingley Building Society Staff Association
Bradford and District Power-Loom Overlookers Society
Britannia Airways Staff Association
Britannic Assurance Chief Office Staff Association
Britannic Field Staff Association
British Actors Equity Association incorporating the Variety
    Artistes Federation
British Aerospace (Dynamics Group) Employee Association
British Aircraft Corporation Limited, Senior Staff Association
British Air Line Pilots Association
British Association of Colliery Management, The
British Association of Occupational Therapists Limited
British Cement Staffs Association, The
British Ceramic Research Association Staff Association
British Dental Association
British Federation of Textile Technicians
British Fire Service Federation, The
British Hospital Doctors Federation, The
British Medical Association
British Orthoptic Society
British Roll Turners' Trade Society
British Transport Officers' Guild, The
Burmah Engineering Senior Staff Union, The

Burnley and District Branch of the Amalgamated Association of
    Twisters and Drawers (Hand and Machine), The
Burnley Building Society Staff Association, The
Burnley and District Tape Sizers' Protective Society
Burnley, Nelson, Rossendale and District Textile Workers' Union
Cadbury Limited Representatives Association
Cadbury Schweppes Senior Managers' Association
Cadbury Typhoo Representatives' Association
Cantonian High School Staff Association, The
Card Dressers' Society, The
Card Setting Machine Tenters' Society
Carlsberg Brewery Staff Association, The
Central Trustee Savings Bank Staff Association
Ceramic and Allied Trades Union
Chartered Society of Physiotherapy, The
Chelsea Building Society Staff Association
Chemistry Societies' Staff Association
Chief and Assistant Chief Fire Officers' Association, The
Church and Oswaldtwistle Power-loom Overlookers Society
Civil and Public Services Association
Civil Service National Whitley Council – Staff Side
Civil Service Union
Clerical and Secretarial Staffs Association of the University of
    Liverpool
Clerical, Medical and General Staff Association
Cloth Pressers' Society
Colman Association of Staff, The
Colne and Craven Textile Workers' Association
Colne and District Power Loom Overlookers' Association
Colne and District Textile Warehouse Association
Colne District of the Amalgamated Association of Twisters and
    Drawers
Commercial Bank of Australia (London) Staff Association
Commercial Union Group Staff Association, The
Community and Youth Service Association, The
Confederation of Bank Staff Associations
. Confederation of Employee Organisations, The
Confederation of Health Service Employees
Communications Division of the Foreign and Commonwealth
    Office Staff Association, The
Construction Industry Training Board Staff Association
Corporation of London Staff Association
COSESA
Coventry Economic Building Society Staff Association
Cumberland Colliery Officials Association, The
Dean Clough Staff Association
Derbyshire Building Society Staff Association
Design Council Staff Association

Dexion (Hourly Paid Staff) Union
Diplomatic Service Association, The
Eagle Star Staff Association
Economists Bookshop Staff Association, The
Electrical and Mechanical Instrument Makers' Association
Electrical Electronic Telecommunication and Plumbing Union
EMI Electronics Ltd Junior and Middle Management Staff
 Association
Engineering Inspectors' Association, The
Engineering Officers Technical Association
Engineers' and Managers' Association
English China Clays Staff Association, The
English Chiropodists Association
Federation of Cadbury Schweppes Representatives' Associations,
 The
Federation of Nursing Personnel
Federation of Professional Officers' Associations
Film Artistes' Association
Fire Brigades Union, The
Football League Secretaries' Managers' and Coaches' Association,
 The
Football Pools Collectors Union, The
Foremen's Association of the British Aircraft Corporation Limited,
 Military Aircraft Division, The
Furniture Timber and Allied Trades Union
General Dental Practitioners Association, The
General Federation of Trade Unions, The
General Telephone Systems Ltd and Associated Companies Staff
 Association
General Union of Associations of Loom Overlookers, The
Greater London Council Staff Association, The
Grindlays Staff Association
Guild of County Land Agents and Valuers, The
Guild of Directors of Social Services, The
Guild of Local Authority Valuers and Estate Surveyors, The
Guild of Medical Secretaries
Guild of Professional Teachers of Dancing, The
Guild of Senior Officers of the Greater London Council and the
 Inner London Education Authority, The
Guild of Textile Supervisors
Guild of Water Service Senior Officers
Guinness Brewing Staff Association (UK)
Guinness (Park Royal) Supervisory Association
Halcrow Staff Association
Halifax Building Society Staff Association
Halifax and District Carpet Power-Loom Tuners' Association
Halifax and District Power Loom Managers' and Overlookers'
 Society

Headmasters' Conference, The
Health Visitors' Association
Hongkong Bank Group UK Staff Association, The
Hopkinsons' Senior Staff Association
Hosiery and Textile Dyers' and Auxiliary Association
Hospital Consultants and Specialists Association, The
Hospital Doctors Association •
Hospital Physicists' Association, The
HSD (Stevenage) Staff Association
Huddersfield and Bradford Building Society Staff Association, The
Huddersfield and Dewsbury Power Loom Overlookers Society
Huddersfield and District Healders' and Twisters' Trade and
    Friendly Society
Hull Trawler Officers' Guild
Hyde and District Loom Overlookers' Association, The
Imperial Group Staff Association
Imperial Supervisors' Association (Imperial Tobacco Limited)
Independent Union of Owner Operators
Inland Revenue Staff Federation, The
Inner London Schoolkeepers Society, The
Institute of Journalists, The
Institution of Professional Civil Servants, The
Inter Employees' Association
Iron and Steel Trades Confederation
Jeyes Representatives Association
Johnson Matthey Chemicals Royston Staff Society
Johnson Matthey Headquarters Staff Society, The
Joint Boots Pharmacists Association
Joint Industry Board for the Electrical Contracting Industry, The
Jones & Shipman Administrative Staff Association, The
KDG Industries Staff Association
Kosset Staff Association
Laker Airways Flight Crew Association
Lancashire Box, Packing Case and General Woodworkers' Friendly,
    Relief, Sick, Superannuation and Burial Society, The
Laurence Scott and Electromotors Foremen's Association
Leeds and District Power Loom Overlookers Society
Leek and Westbourne Staff Association
Legal and General Staff Association
Leicester Building Society Staff Association
Leicestershire Overmen, Deputies' and Shotfirers' Association
Leisure and General Holdings Staff Association
Liverpool Victoria Section of the National Union of Insurance
    Workers
Lloyds Bank Group Staff Association
Lloyd's Register (UK) Staff Association
Lloyds Staff Association
London Jewel Case and Jewellery Display Makers Union, The

369

London Society of Tie Cutters
Lufthansa Staff Association United Kingdom
Managerial Staff Association of the Provincial Insurance Group of
    Companies, The
Manchester Pilots' Association
Manchester, Salford and District Society of Brewers' and General
    Coopers
Merchant Navy and Air Line Officers Association
Military and Orchestral Musical Instrument Makers' Trade Society
Musicians' Union
Nalgo Staff Union
National Amalgamated Stevedores and Dockers
National and Local Government Officers' Association
National Association of Chief Housing Officers, The
National Association of Colliery Overmen, Deputies and Shotfirers,
    Cannock Chase Area
National Association of Colliery Overmen, Deputies and Shotfirers
National Association of Colliery Overmen, Deputies and Shotfirers,
    Durham Area
National Association of Colliery Overmen, Deputies and Shotfirers,
    Midland Area
National Association of Colliery Overmen, Deputies and Shotfirers
    (North Staffordshire Area)
National Association of Colliery Overmen, Deputies and Shotfirers
    (Northumberland Area)
National Association of Colliery Overmen, Deputies and Shotfirers,
    North Western Area
National Association of Colliery Overmen, Deputies and Shotfirers
    (South Wales Area)
National Association of Colliery Overmen, Deputies and Shotfirers
    (Yorkshire Area)
National Association of Co-operative Officials
National Association of Executives, Managers and Staffs, The
National Association of Fire Officers
National Association of Grooms
National Association of Head Teachers, The
National Association of Heads and Matrons of Assessment Centres,
    The
National Association of Inspectors and Educational Advisors
National Association of Licensed House Managers, The
National Association of NFU Group Secretaries, The
National Association of Power-Loom Overlookers, The
National Association of Probation Officers, The
National Association of Schoolmasters and the Union of Women
    Teachers
National Association of Teachers in Further and Higher Education
National Association of Theatrical Television and Kine Employees
National Association of Unions in the Textile Trade

National Federation of Sub-Postmasters, The
National Graphical Association
National League of the Blind and Disabled
National Owner Drivers Association, UK
National Society of Brushmakers and General Workers
National Society of Metal Mechanics, The
National Society of Operative Printers Graphical and Media
  Personnel
National Tile, Faience and Mosaic Fixers' Society
National Unilever Managers Association
National Union of Agricultural and Allied Workers
National Union of Blast Furnacemen, Ore Miners, Coke Workers
  and Kindred Trades
National Union of Club Stewards
National Union of Co-operative Insurance Agents
National Union of Co-operative Insurance Society Employees
National Union of Domestic Appliance and General Metal Workers
National Union of Dyers, Bleachers and Textile Workers
National Union of Flint Glass Workers
National Union of General and Municipal Workers
National Union of Gold Silver and Allied Trades
National Union of Hebrew Teachers of Great Britain and Ireland,
  The
National Union of Hosiery and Knitwear Workers
National Union of Insurance Workers
National Union of Insurance Workers Prudential Section
National Union of Insurance Workers, Royal Liver and Composite
  Section
National Union of Insurance Workers, Royal London Section
National Union of Journalists
National Union of Lock and Metal Workers
National Union of Mineworkers
National Union of Mineworkers (Cannock Chase and Pelsall
  District, Midland Area)
National Union of Mineworkers (Cokemen's Area)
National Union of Mineworkers (Colliery Officials' and Staffs'
  Area)
National Union of Mineworkers (Colliery Officials' and Staffs'
  Area) Region No. 2
National Union of Mineworkers (Colliery Officials' and Staffs'
  Area) Region No. 3
National Union of Mineworkers (Colliery Officials' and Staffs'
  Area) Region No. 4
National Union of Mineworkers (Cumberland Area)
National Union of Mineworkers (Derbyshire Area)
National Union of Mineworkers (Durham Enginemen Group No. 1
  Area)

National Union of Mineworkers (Durham Mechanics Group No. 1 Area)
National Union of Mineworkers (Kent Area)
National Union of Mineworkers (Leicester Area)
National Union of Mineworkers (Midland Area)
National Union of Mineworkers (North Stafford Federation Midland Area)
National Union of Mineworkers (Northumberland Area)
National Union of Mineworkers (Northumberland Mechanics Group No. 1 Area)
National Union of Mineworkers (North Wales Area)
National Union of Mineworkers (North Western Area)
National Union of Mineworkers (North Western Area) Pendlebury Branch
National Union of Mineworkers (Nottingham Area)
National Union of Mineworkers (Power Group Area)
National Union of Mineworkers (South Derbyshire Area)
National Union of Mineworkers (South Wales Area)
National Union of Mineworkers (Warwickshire District, Midlands Area)
National Union of Mineworkers (Yorkshire Area)
National Union of Public Employees
National Union of Railwaymen
National Union of Recreation and Sports Employees
National Union of Scalemakers
National Union of Seamen
National Union of Sheet Metal Workers Coppersmiths and Heating and Domestic Engineers
National Union of Social Workers
National Union of Tailors and Garment Workers
National Union of Teachers
National Union of Textile and Allied Workers (Rochdale Districts)
National Union of the Footwear, Leather and Allied Trades
National Westminster Staff Association
National Woolsorters' Society, The
Nationwide Building Society Staff Association
Nelson and District Association of Preparatory Workers, The
Nelson and District Branch of the Amalgamated Association of Beamers, Twisters and Drawers (Hand and Machine)
Nelson and District Clothlookers and Warehouse Association, The
Nelson and District Powerloom Overlookers' Society
Nelson, Colne and District Tape Sizers' Protective Society
New Towns Chief Officers Association, The
NFER Staff Association, The
North-East Coast Tug-Boatmen's Association, The
Northern Carpet Trades Union
Northern Colliery Officials and Staffs Association
Northern Counties Textile Trades' Federation

Northern Rock Staff Association (NORSA)
Northern Textile and Allied Workers' Union
North Lancashire and Cumbria Textile Workers Association
Nottingham and District Federation of Club Stewards
Nottingham Dyers and Bleachers Association
Oldham Association of Loom Overlookers, The
Oldham Provincial Union of Textile and Allied Workers
Organisation of CPL Technicians, The
Pattern Weavers' Society
Playboy Staff Association
PMB Staff Association
Portman Staff Association
Post Office Engineering Union
Post Office Management Staffs Association
Power Loom Carpet Weavers' and Textile Workers' Union, The
Pressed Glass Makers' Society of Great Britain
Preston and Districts Powerloom Overlookers' Association
Preston and District Tape Sizers' Association
Pride of Golborne Miners' Lodge, Trade Union and Checkweight
    Fund
Printing Trades Alliance, The
Prison Officers' Association
Professional Association of Teachers
Professional Flight Instructors Association, The
Professional Footballers' Association
Provincial Building Society Staff Association
Radio and Electronic Officers' Union
Rank Hotels Staff Association
Redifon Flight Simulation Monthly Staff Association
Retail Book, Stationery and Allied Trades Employees' Association
Retained Firefighters Union, The
Retired Officers Association
Robert Hirst Staff Association, The
Rolls-Royce Management Association
Rossendale Union of Boot, Shoe and Slipper Operatives
Rowntree Mackintosh Sales Staff Association
Royal College of Midwives, The
Royal College of Nursing of the United Kingdom, The
Royal Insurance Branch Managers Association
RSPB Staff Association, The
Rumbelows Branch Managers' Association
Schering Chemicals Representatives Association
Schweppes Limited Representatives Association
Screw, Nut, Bolt and Rivet Trade Union
Secondary Heads Associations, The
Sheffield Sawmakers Protection Society
Sheffield Wool Shear Workers' Trade Union
Skipton and District Power-Loom Overlookers Association, The

373

Société Générale Staff Association, The
Society of Authors, The
Society of Chiropodists, The
Society of Civil and Public Servants (Executive, Directing and
    Analogous Grades)
Society of Graphical and Allied Trades 1975
Society of Lithographic Artists Designers, Engravers and Process
    Workers
Society of Metropolitan and County Chief Librarians
Society of Post Office Executives
Society of Public Analysts and Other Official Analysts
Society of Radiographers, The
Society of Registration Officers (Births, Deaths and Marriages)
Society of Remedial Gymnasts, The
Society of Shuttlemakers
Society of Union Employees (NUPE), The
Squibb UK Staff Association
Stable Lads Association
Staff Association of S.W. Farmer Group of Companies, The
Staff Association of the Printing and Publishing Industry Training
    Board, The
Staffordshire Building Society Staff Association
Star Aluminium Managerial Staff Association
Steel Industry Management Association, The
Sun Alliance and London Staff Association
Sun Life Staff Association
Telecommunications Staff Association
Telephone Contract Officers' Association, The
Tempered Group (Spring Division) Staff Association, The
Teston Independent Society of Cricket Ball Makers
Textile Manufacturing Trades' Federation of Bolton and
    Surrounding Districts
Thames Water Staff Association
Tobacco Mechanics Association
Tobacco Workers' Union, The
Trade Society of Machine Calico Printers
Transport and General Workers' Union
Transport Salaried Staffs' Association
Trebor Sharps Limited Salesmen's Association
Undeb Cenedlaethol Athrawon Cymru (English translation:
    National Association of the Teachers of Wales)
Union of Construction, Allied Trades and Technicians
Union of County and District Secretaries, The
Union of Post Office Workers
Union of Shop Distributive and Allied Workers
United Association of Power Loom Overlookers
United Friendly Agents Association
United Friendly Divisional and District Managers' Association, The

United Friendly Head Office Management Association, The
United Friendly Insurance Co. Ltd, Assistant Managers'
  Association, The
United Kingdom Association of Professional Engineers
United Road Transport Union
Walsall Lock and Keysmiths Male and Female Trade Society
Whatman Reeve Angel Staff Association, The
Willerby Staff Association
Writers' Guild of Great Britain
Yorkshire Association of Power Loom Overlookers
Yorkshire Society of Textile Craftsmen

Scottish listed trade unions

Aberdeen Trawl Officers' Guild
Association of Directors of Administration in Scotland, The
Association of Lecturers in Colleges of Education in Scotland
Association of Lecturers in Scottish Central Institutions
District Nursing Association, The
Educational Institute of Scotland
Glasgow and West of Scotland Power Loom Tenters' Society
Honours Graduate Teachers Association
National Association of Colliery Overmen, Deputies and Shotfirers
  (Scottish Area)
National Union of Mineworkers Group 2 Scottish Colliery
  Enginemen Boilermen and Tradesmen's Association
Professional Staff Association of Scottish Woodland Owners
  Association (Commercial) Ltd
Scottish Approved Schools Staff Association
Scottish Association of Amenity Supervisory Staffs
Scottish Association of Local Government and Educational
  Psychologists
Scottish Association of Nurse Administrators, The
Scottish Carpet Workers' Union
Scottish Equitable Staff Association
Scottish Further Education Association
Scottish Health Visitors Association
Scottish Joint Industry Board for the Electrical Contracting
  Industry
Scottish Prison Officers' Association
Scottish Secondary Teachers' Association
Scottish Union of Power Loom Technicians

Part 4
Bibliography
of Official
Trade Union Histories

Form of Entry: Author(s), *Title*, Publication Date, (Trade Union and (if appropriate) Trade Union to which engagements have been transferred)

1 Mining

R. Challinor, *The Lancashire and Cheshire Miners*, 1972 (NUM).
Durham Miners' Association Jubilee Souvenir, 1919 (MFGB now NUM).
N. Edwards, *History of the South Wales Miners' Federation*, 1938 (MFGB now NUM).
A.R. Griffin, *The Miners of Nottinghamshire: A History of the Nottinghamshire Miners' Association*, 2 vols, 1955 and 1962 (NUM).
W.S. Hall, *A Historical Survey of the Durham Colliery Mechanics' Association*, 1879–1929 (MFGB now NUM).
F. Machin, *The Yorkshire Miners: A History*, 1958 (NUM).
Midland Area, 1908–1962: A Short History, 1962 (NACODS).
R. Page Arnot, *A History of the Scottish Miners from the Earliest Times*, 1955 (NUM).
R. Page Arnot, *South Wales Miners: A History of the South Wales Miners' Federation*, 1898–1914, 1967 (NUM).
R. Page Arnot, *The Miners*, 3 vols, 1949, 1953 and 1961 (NUM).
Vol. 1: *A History of the Miners' Federation of Great Britain, 1889–1910*;
Vol. 2: *A History of the Miners' Federation of Great Britain: Years of Struggle, from 1910 onwards*;
Vol. 3: *In Crisis and War: From 1930 onwards*.
E. Welbourne, *The Miners' Unions of Northumberland and Durham*, 1923 (MFGB now NUM).
J.E. Williams, *The Derbyshire Miners: A Study in Industrial and Social History*, 1962 (NUM).
J. Wilson, *History of the Durham Miners' Association, 1870–1904*, 1907 (MFGB now NUM).

2 Railways

G.W. Alcock, *Fifty Years of Railway Trade Unionism*, 1922 (NUR).

P.S. Bagwell, *The Railwaymen*, 1963 (NUR).

P.S. Bagwell, *The National Union of Railwaymen, 1913–1963: A Half-Century of Industrial Trade Unionism*, 1963 (NUR).

N. McKillop, *The Lighted Flame: A History of the Associated Society of Locomotive Engineers and Firemen*, 1950 (ASLEF).

Railway Clerks' Association and its Path of Progress, 1897–1928, 1928 (RCA now TSSA).

J.R. Raynes, *Engines and Men: The History of the Associated Society of Locomotive Engineers and Firemen*, 1921 (ASLEF).

Souvenir History: Amalgamated Society of Railway Servants, 1910 (ASRS now NUR).

3 Transport (other than Railways) and Docks

First Anniversary, 1891 (DWRGLUGBI now TGWU).

R. Hyman, *The Workers' Union*, 1971 (TGWU).

The Growth of the Trade Union Idea and Spirit among the Staffs of the Port of London, 1923 (TGWU).

The Story of the Seamen: A Short History of the National Union of Seamen, 1964 (NUS).

A. Tuckett, *The Scottish Carter: The History of the Scottish Horse and Motormen's Association, 1898–1964*, 1967 (SCMU now TGWU).

Unity, Strength, Progress: The Story of the Transport & General Workers' Union, 1967 (TGWU).

4 Iron and Steel and Minor Metal Trades

National Union of Gold, Silver and Allied Trades, 1911–1961, 1961 (NUGSAT).

J. Owen, *Ironmen: A Short Story of the History of the Union from 1878 to 1953*, 1953 (NUBOMCWKT).

A. Pugh, *Men of Steel by One of Them: A Chronicle of Eighty-Eight Years of Trade Unionism in the British Iron and Steel Industry*, 1951 (ISTC).

5 Engineering and Shipbuilding

A Short History of the National Union of Vehicle Builders to Commemorate the 125th Anniversary of the Union, 1834–1959, 1959 (NUVB now TGWU).

H. Bending, *Forty Years*, 1949 (NUSM).

Centenary Souvenir of the Friendly Society of Iron Founders of England, Ireland and Wales, 1909 (FSIF now AUEW–F/S).

D.C. Cummings, *A Historical Survey of the Boiler Makers' and Iron and Steel Ship Builders' Society from August, 1834, to August, 1904*, 1905 (USBISSB now ASBSBSW).

D.C. Cummings, *A Short History of the Association of Engineering and Shipbuilding Draughtsmen, 1913–1934*, 1934 (AESD now AUEW–TASS).

H.J. Fyrth and H. Collins, *The Foundry Workers: A Trade Union History*, 1959 (AUFW now AUEW–F/S).

J.B. Jefferys, *The Story of the Engineers, 1800–1945*, 1946 (AEU now AUEW–E/S).

Jubilee Souvenir, 1901 (ASE now AUEW–E/S).

A.T. Kidd, *History of the Tin-Plate Workers and Sheet Metal Workers and Braziers Societies*, 1949 (NUSMWB now NUSMWCHDE).

J.E. Mortimer, *A History of the Association of Engineering and Shipbuilding Draughtsmen*, 1960 (AESD now AUEW–TASS).

J.E. Mortimer, *History of the Boilermakers' Society, 1834–1906*, 1973 (ASBSBSW).

W. Mosses, *The History of the United Pattern Makers' Association, 1872–1922*, 1922 (UPA now APAC).

J. Nicholson, *A Hundred Years of Vehicle Building, 1834–1934*, 1934 (NUVB now TGWU).

One Hundred and Fifty Years Progress, 1961 (AEU now AUEW–E/S).

The Story of the Engineers: Centenary Souvenir, 1951 (AEU now AUEW–E/S).

G.W. Thomson, *A Short History of the AESD*, 1934 (AESD now AUEW–TASS).

A. Tuckett, *The Blacksmiths' History*, 1974 (ASBSBSW).

6 Electricity

G. Schaffer, *Light and Liberty: Sixty Years of the Electrical Trades Union*, 1949 (ETU now EETPU).

W. Stevens, *The Story of the ETU: The Official History of the Electrical Trades Union*, 1952 (ETU now EETPU).

7 Building Trades

T.J. Connelly, *The Woodworkers, 1860–1960*, 1960 (ASW now UCATT).

J.O. French, *Plumbers in Unity: History of the Plumbing Trades Union, 1865–1965*, 1965 (PTU now EETPU).

G. Hicks, *The Operative Stone Masons' Centenary, 1932–33*, 1933 (OSS now UCATT).

S. Higenbottam, *Our Society's History*, 1939 (ASW now UCATT).

W.S. Hilton, *Foes to Tyranny*, 1963 (AUBTW now UCATT).

J.R. Newman, *The NAOP Heritage: A Short Historical Review of the*

Growth and Development of the National Association of Operative Plasterers, 1860–1960, 1960 (NAOP now TGWU).

'Onlooker', *Hitherto*, 1930 (NAOP now TGWU).

Our History, Organisation and Aims, n.d., (ABT now UCATT).

R.W. Postgate, *The Builders' History*, 1923 (NFBTO now UCATT).

The Building Workers' Struggle: Centenary Souvenir, 1955 (AUBTW now UCATT).

8 Textiles, Clothing and Footwear

An Epic of Trade Unionism: Being an Account of Its Earliest Days to the Raunds Strike in 1905, 1934 (NUBSO now NUFLAT).

W. Bateson, *The Way We Came: An Historical Retrospect of the Adventures of the Pioneers of the Amalgamated Society of Dyers*, 1928 (ASD now NUDBTW).

F. Burchill and J. Sweeney, *A History of Trade Unionism in the North Staffordshire Textile Industry*, 1971 (ASTWKT).

N. Cuthbert, *The Lacemakers Society, 1760–1960*, 1962 (ASLMTW now NUHKW).

S. Elsbury and D. Cohen, *The Rego Revolt: How the United Clothing Workers' Trade Union was formed*, 1929 (UCWTU).*

Ever Since Fig Leaves came into Fashion: Tale of the Tailors' Union, 1947 (NUTGW).

A. Fox, *A History of the National Union of Boot and Shoe Operatives, 1874–1957*, 1958 (NUBSO now NUFLAT).

E. Hopwood, *The Lancashire Weavers' Story*, 1969 (AWA now ATWU).

L. Hunter and M. Stewart, *The Needle is Threaded*, 1963 (NUTGW).

W. Hustwick(?), *Yorkshire Managers' and Overlookers' Society: Celebration of the Amalgamation – March 22nd 1913*, 1913 (MOS).

W. Hustwick(?), *Managers' and Overlookers' Society Centenary Celebrations, 1827–1927*, 1927 (MOS).

W. Hustwick, *Celebration of the 50th Anniversary of the Amalgamation*, 1963 (MOS).

A. Murie, *The Carpet Weavers of Kidderminster*, 1966 (PLCWTWA).

T.F. Richard and E.L. Poulton, *Fifty Years: NUBSO, 1874–1924*, 1924 (NUBSO now NUFLAT).

M. Spiers, *One Hundred Years of a Small Trade Union*, 1972 (CSMTS).

B. Turner, *Heavy Woollen District: Textile Workers' Union*, 1917 (NUTW now NUDBTW).

B. Turner, *A Short History of the General Union of Textile Workers*, 1920 (NUTW now NUDBTW).

*The UCWTU was formed in 1929 by members of the Tailors' and Garment Workers' Union dissatisfied with the official leadership's management of the Rego dispute in the East End of London. It is doubtful if the union survived beyond 1934.

9 Printing

A Fifty Years' Record, 1849–99, 1899 (TA now NGA).

A Fifty Years' Record, 1853–1903, 1903 (STA now SGA).

A Record of Fifty Years, 1885–1935, 1935 (SLADE).

C.J. Bundock, *NUJ: A Jubilee History*, 1957 (NUJ).

C.J. Bundock, *The Story of the National Union of Printing, Book-binding and Paper Workers*, 1959 (NUPBPW now SOGAT).

S.C. Gillespie, *A Hundred Years of Progress*, 1953 (STA now SGA).

E. Howe, *The Typecasters, Monotype Casters and Typefounders Society*, 1955 (TMCTS now SOGAT).

E. Howe and J. Child, *Society of London Bookbinders, 1780–1951*, 1951 (SLB now SOGAT).

E. Howe and H. Waite, *London Society of Compositors*, 1948 (LSC now NGA).

G.W. Howe, *Jubilee of the National Union of Press Telegraphists, 1909–1959*, 1959 (NUPT now NGA).

F.J. Mansfield, *Gentlemen, the Press! Chronicles of a Crusade*, 1943 (NUJ).

J. Moran, *NATSOPA, Seventy-Five Years, 1889–1964*, 1964 (NATSOPA).

A.E. Musson, *The Typographical Association: Origins and History up to 1949*, 1954 (TA now NGA).

J. Reynolds, *The Letter Press Printers of Bradford: A Short History of the Bradford Graphical Society*, 1970 (NGA).

G.E. Rowles, *The 'Line' is On: A Centenary Souvenir of the London Society of Compositors, 1848–1948*, 1948 (LSC now NGA).

T.N. Shane, *Passed for Press: A Centenary History of the Association of Correctors of the Press*, 1954 (ACP now NGA).

Sixty Years of Service, 1961 (PKTF).

Souvenir of the Jubilee of the National Society of Operative Printers and Assistants, 1889–1939, 1939 (NATSOPA).

R.B. Suthers, *The Story of NATSOPA, 1889–1929*, 1929 (NATSOPA).

10 Agriculture

R. Groves, *Sharpen the Sickle! The History of the Farm Workers' Union*, 1949 (NUAW now NUAAW).

R.C. Russell, *'The Revolt of the Field' in Lincs.: The Origins and Early History of Farm Workers' Trade Unions*, 1956 (NUAW now NUAAW).

11 Food, Distributive and Allied Trades

P.C. Hoffman, *They Also Serve: The Story of the Shop Worker*, 1949 (USDAW).
The Tobacco Workers' Union: Centenary Souvenir, 1834–1934, 1934 (TWU).

12 Public Employees

C.D. Andrews and G.C. Burger, *Progress Report, 1909–1959: The First Fifty Years in the History of the London County Council Staff Association*, 1959 (LCCSA now GLCSA).
T.C. Barton, *A History of the Manchester Municipal Officers' Guild, Branch of the National and Local Government Officers' Association, 1906–1956*, 1956 (NALGO).
W.W. Craik, *Bryn Roberts and the National Union of Public Employees*, 1955 (NUPE).
W.W. Craik, *Sydney Hill and the National Union of Public Employees*, 1968 (NUPE).
G. Gibson, *The History of the Mental Hospital and Institutional Workers' Union from Infancy to its 21st year*, 1931 (MHIWU now COHSE).
J. Horner and T. Parry, *Fifty Years' History of the Fire Brigades Union*, 1968 (FBU).
J. Jepson, *Fifty Years of Progress*, 1960 (COHSE).
B. Morton, *Action 1919–1969: A Record of the Growth of the National Association of Schoolmasters*, 1969 (NAS).
F. Radford, *Fetch the Engine*, 1952 (FBU).
A. Spoor, *White Collar Union* – 60 Years of NALGO, 1967 (NALGO).
The First Half Century, 1904–1954, 1954 (ATTI).

13 Civil Service and Post Office

W.J. Brown, *The CSCA: Its History, Achievements and Plans for the Future*, 1925 (CSCA now CPSA).
John Golding, *75 Years: A Short History of the Post Office Engineering Union*, 1962 (POEU).
C.E. Hall, *Thirty Years of Agitation: Being a Short Account of the Origin, Work and Progress of the Postal and Telegraph Clerks' Association*, 1902 (PTCA now UPW).
How We Began: Postal Trade Unionism, 1870–1920, 1960 (UPW).
B. Newman, *Yours for Action*, 1953 (CSCA now CPSA).

14 Professional and Clerical

F. Ashton, *A History of the Guild of Insurance Officials*, 1969 (GIO now ASTMS).

F. Hughes, *By Hand and Brain: The Story of the Clerical and Administrative Workers' Union*, 1952 (CAWU now APEX).

A. Oliver, *Our Business: Story of the National Pearl Federation, 1920–1940*, 1940 (PF now NUIW–PF).

15 General Workers

Fifty Years of the National Union of General and Municipal Workers, 1939 (NUGMW).

Sixty Years of the National Union of General and Municipal Workers, 1949 (NUGMW).

KEY TO ABBREVIATIONS

ABT	Association of Building Technicians
ACP	Association of Correctors of the Press
AESD	Association of Engineering and Shipbuilding Draughtsmen
AEU	Amalgamated Engineering Union
APAC	Association of Patternmakers and Allied Craftsmen
APEX	Association of Professional, Executive, Clerical and Computer Staff
ASBSBSW	Amalgamated Society of Boilermakers, Shipwrights, Blacksmiths and Structural Workers
ASD	Amalgamated Society of Dyers
ASE	Amalgamated Society of Engineers
ASLEF	Associated Society of Locomotive Engineers and Firemen
ASLMTW	Amalgamated Society of Lace Makers and Textile Workers
ASRS	Amalgamated Socieiety of Railway Servants
ASTMS	Association of Scientific, Technical and Managerial Staffs
ASTWKT	Amalgamated Society of Textile Workers and Kindred Trades
ASW	Amalgamated Society of Woodworkers
ATTI	Association of Teachers in Technical Institutions
ATWU	Amalgamated Textile Workers' Union
AUBTW	Amalgamated Union of Building Trade Workers

AUEW–E/S	Amalgamated Union of Engineering Workers – Engineering Section
AUEW–F/S	Amalgamated Union of Engineering Workers – Foundry Section
AUEW–TASS	Amalgamated Union of Engineering Workers – Technical Administrative and Supervisory Section
AUFW	Amalgamated Union of Foundry Workers
AWA	Amalgamated Weavers' Association
CAWU	Clerical and Administrative Workers' Union
COHSE	Confederation of Health Service Employees
CPSA	Civil and Public Services Association
CSCA	Civil Service Clerical Association
CSMTS	Card Setting Machine Tenters' Society
DWRGLUGBI	Dock, Wharf, Riverside and General Labourers' Union of Great Britain and Ireland
EETPU	Electrical, Electronic, Telecommunication and Plumbing Union
ETU	Electrical Trades Union
FBU	Fire Brigades' Union
FSIF	Friendly Society of Iron Founders
GIO	Guild of Insurance Officials
GLCSA	Greater London Council Staff Association
ISTC	Iron and Steel Trades Confederation
LCCSA	London County Council Staff Association
LSC	London Society of Compositors
MFGB	Miners' Federation of Great Britain
MHIWU	Mental Hospital and Institutional Workers' Union
MOS	Managers' and Overlookers' Society
NACODS	National Association of Colliery Overmen, Deputies and Shotfirers
NALGO	National and Local Government Officers' Association
NAOP	National Association of Operative Plasterers
NAS	National Association of Schoolmasters
NATSOPA	National Society of Operative Printers, Graphical & Media Personnel
NFBTO	National Federation of Building Trade Operatives
NGA	National Graphical Association
NUAAW	National Union of Agricultural and Allied Workers
NUAW	National Union of Agricultural Workers
NUBOMCWKT	National Union of Blastfurnacemen, Ore Miners, Coke Workers and Kindred Trades
NUBSO	National Union of Boot and Shoe Operatives

NUDBTW	National Union of Dyers, Bleachers and Textile Workers
NUFLAT	National Union of Footwear, Leather and Allied Trades
NUGMW	National Union of General and Municipal Workers
NUGSAT	National Union of Gold, Silver and Allied Trades
NUHKW	National Union of Hosiery & Knitwear Workers
NUIW–PF	National Union of Insurance Workers – Pearl Federation
NUJ	National Union of Journalists
NUM	National Union of Mineworkers
NUPBPW	National Union of Printing, Bookbinding and Paper Workers
NUPE	National Union of Public Employees
NUPT	National Union of Press Telegraphists
NUR	National Union of Railwaymen
NUS	National Union of Seamen
NUSM	National Union of Scalemakers
NUSMWB	National Union of Sheet Metal Workers and Braziers
NUSMWCHDE	National Union of Sheet Metal Workers, Coppersmiths, Heating and Domestic Engineers
NUTGW	National Union of Tailors and Garment Workers
NUTW	National Union of Textile Workers
NUVB	National Union of Vehicle Builders
OSS	Operative Stone Masons' Society
PF	Pearl Federation
PKTF	Printing and Kindred Trades Federation
PLCWTWA	Power Loom Carpet Weavers and Textile Workers' Association
POEU	Post Office Engineering Union
PTCA	Postal and Telegraph Clerks' Association
PTU	Plumbing Trades Union
RCA	Railway Clerks' Association
SCMU	Scottish Commercial Motormen's Union
SGA	Scottish Graphical Association
SLADE	Society of Lithographic Artists, Designers, Engravers and Process Workers
SLB	Society of London Bookbinders
SOGAT	Society of Graphical and Allied Trades
STA	Scottish Typographical Association
TA	Typographical Association
TGWU	Transport & General Workers' Union
TMCTS	Typecasters', Monotype Casters' and Typefounders' Society

TSSA	Transport Salaried Staffs' Association
TWU	Tobacco Workers' Union
UCATT	Union of Construction, Allied Trades and Technicians
UCWTU	United Clothing Workers' Trade Union
UPA	United Pattern Makers' Association
UPW	Union of Post Office Workers
USBISSB	United Society of Boilermakers and Iron and Steel Ship Builders
USDAW	Union of Shop, Distributive and Allied Workers

386

Part 5
Addresses of Other Industrial Relations Institutions

Advisory Conciliation and Arbitration Service (ACAS)

Head Office
Cleland House, Page Street, London SW1P 4ND
Tel: 01–211 3000

Northern Region
Westgate House, Westgate Road, Newcastle-upon-Tyne NE1 1TJ
Tel: Cleveland (0632) 612191

Cumbria	Tyne and Wear	Cleveland
Northumberland	Durham	

Yorkshire and Humberside Region
City House, Leeds LS1 4JH
Tel: Leeds (0532) 38232

North Yorkshire	South Yorkshire
West Yorkshire	Humberside

London Region
Clifton House, 83–117 Euston Road, London NW1 2RB
Tel: 01–388 5100
Greater London

South Eastern Region
Clifton House, 83–117 Euston Road, London NW1 2RB
Tel: 01–388 5100

Cambridgeshire	Bedfordshire	Kent
Norfolk	Hertfordshire	Hampshire (except
Suffolk	Essex	Ringwood)
Oxfordshire	Berkshire	Isle of Wight
Buckinghamshire	Surrey	East Sussex
		West Sussex

South Western Region
16 Park Place, Clifton, Bristol BS8 1JP
Tel: Bristol (0272) 211921

Gloucestershire	Cornwall	Dorset
Avon	Devon	Ringwood
Wiltshire	Somerset	

Midlands Region
Alpha Tower, Suffolk Street, Queensway, Birmingham B1 1TZ
Tel: 021-643 9911

Derbyshire (except	Leicester	Herefordshire and
High Peak District)	Northamptonshire	Worcestershire
Nottinghamshire	Shropshire	West Midlands
Lincolnshire	Staffordshire	Warwickshire

North West Region
Boulton House, 17-21 Chorlton Street, Manchester M61 3HY
Tel: 061-228 3222

| Lancashire | Greater | High Peak District |
| Merseyside | Manchester | of Derbyshire |

Scotland
Franborough House, 123-157 Bothwell Street, Glasgow G2 7JR
Tel: 041-204 2677

Wales
Phase 1, Ty Glas Road, Llanishen, Cardiff CF4 5PH
Tel: Cardiff (0222) 762636

Industrial Tribunals

England and Wales
The Secretary,
Central Office of the Industrial Tribunals (England and Wales),
93 Ebury Bridge Road,
London SW1 8RE
Tel: 01-730 9161 and 730 6015

also
19-29 Woburn Place,
London WC1H 0LU
Tel: 01-632 4921

Ashford
The Assistant Secretary,
Regional Office of the Industrial Tribunals,
Tufton House,
Tufton Street,
Ashford,
Kent
Tel: Ashford (0233) 21346

Birmingham
The Assistant Secretary,
Regional Office of the Industrial Tribunals,
Phoenix House,
1–3 Newhall Street,
Birmingham B3 3NH
Tel: 021–236 6051

Bristol
Assistant Secretary,
Regional Office of the Industrial Tribunals,
2nd Floor, Prince House,
43–51 Prince Street,
Bristol BS1 4PE
Tel: Bristol (0272) 298261

Bury St Edmunds
Assistant Secretary,
Regional Office of the Industrial Tribunals,
118 Northgate Street,
Bury St Edmunds
Tel: Bury St Edmunds (0284) 62171

Cardiff
Assistant Secretary,
Regional Office of the Industrial Tribunals,
Caradog House,
St. Andrews Place,
Cardiff
Tel: Cardiff (0222) 372693

Exeter
Assistant Secretary,
Regional Office of the Industrial Tribunals,
Renslade House (10th Floor),
Bonhay Road,
Exeter
Tel: Exeter (0392) 79665

Liverpool
Assistant Secretary,
Regional Office of the Industrial Tribunals,
4th Floor,
No. 1, Union Court,
Cook Street,
Liverpool L2 4UJ
Tel: 051–236 9397

Manchester
The Assistant Secretary,
Regional Office of the Industrial Tribunals,
Alexandra House,
14–22, The Parsonage,
Manchester M3 2JA
Tel: 061–833 0581

Newcastle upon Tyne
Assistant Secretary,
Regional Office of the Industrial Tribunals,
Watson House (3rd Floor),
Pilgrim Street,
Newcastle upon Tyne 1
Tel: Newcastle upon Tyne (0632) 28865–7

Nottingham
Assistant Secretary,
Regional Office of the Industrial Tribunals,
7th Floor,
Birkbeck House,
Trinity Square,
Nottingham
Tel: Nottingham (0602) 45701

Sheffield
Assistant Secretary,
Regional Office of the Industrial Tribunals,
Fargate Court (1st Floor),
Fargate,
Sheffield S1 2HD
Tel: Sheffield (0742) 70348

Southampton
Assistant Secretary,
Regional Office of the Industrial Tribunals,
Dukes Keep,
Marsh Lane,
Southampton
Tel: Southampton (0703) 3955

Scotland
Central Office of the Industrial Tribunals (Scotland),
St Andrew House,
141 West Nile Street,
Glasgow C1 2RU
Tel: 041-331 1601

Central Arbitration Committee
1 The Abbey Garden,
Great College Street,
London SW1P 3SE
Tel: 01-222 8571-4

Employment Appeal Tribunal
4 St James Square,
London SW1
Tel: 01-214 6000

Equal Opportunities Commission
Overseas House,
Quay Street,
Manchester M3 3HN
Tel: 061-833 9244

Health and Safety Executive
Inspectorate Addresses
Headquarters: Regina House, 259/269 Old Marylebone Road,
London NW1 5RR Tel.: 01-723 1262
1 South West
Inter City House, Victoria Street,
Bristol BS1 6AN
Tel: 0272 290681

2 South
Priestley House, Priestley Road,
Basingstoke RG24 9NW
Tel: 0256 3181

3 South East
Paymaster General's Building,
Russell Way, Crawley,
West Sussex RH10 1UH
Tel: 0293 511671

4 London NW
Chancel House, Neasden Lane,
London NW10 2UD
Tel: 01-459 8844

5 London NE
Maritime House,
1 Linton Road,
Barking, Essex IG11 8HF
Tel: 01-594 5522

6 London
1 Long Lane,
London SE1 4PG
Tel: 01-407 8911

7 East Anglia
39 Baddow Road, Chelmsford,
Essex CM2 0HL
Tel: 0245 84661

8 Northern Home Counties
King House, George Street West,
Luton LU1 2DD
Tel: 0582 34121

9 East Midlands
Belgrave House, 1 Greyfriars,
Northampton
Tel: 0604 21233

10 West Midlands
McLaren Building, 2 Masshouse Circus,
Queensway, Birmingham B4 7NP
Tel: 021-236 5080

11 Wales
Brunel House, 2 Fitzalan Road,
Cardiff CF2 1SH
Tel: 0222 497777

12 The Marches
2 Hassell Street,
Newcastle under Lyme,
Staffs ST5 1DT
Tel: 0782 625324

13 North Midlands
Birkbeck House, Trinity Square,
Nottingham NG1 4AU
Tel: 0602 40712

14 South Yorkshire
Sovereign House, 40 Silver Street,
Sheffield S1 2ES
Tel: 0742 739081

15 N & W Yorks
8 St Paul's Street,
Leeds LS1 2LE
Tel: 0532 446191

16 Greater Manchester
Quay House, Quay Street,
Manchester M3 3JB
Tel: 061–831 7111

17 Merseyside
The Triad, Stanley Road,
Bootle L20 3PG
Tel: 051–922 7211

18 North West
Victoria House, Ormskirk Road,
Preston PR1 1HH
Tel: 0772 59321

19 North East
Government Buildings, Kenton Bar,
Newcastle upon Tyne NE1 2YX
Tel: 0632 869811

20 Scotland East
Meadowbank House,
153 London Road,
Edinburgh EH8 7AU
Tel: 031–661 6171

21 Scotland West
Royal Exchange Assurance House,
314 St. Vincent Street,
Glasgow G2 8XG
Tel: 041-204 2646

Employment Medical Advisory Service
Baynards House,
1 Chepstow Place,
Westbourne Grove,
London W2 4JY
Tel: 01-229 3456

Manpower Services Commission
Selkirk House,
166 High Holborn,
London WC1V 6PB
Tel: 01-836 1213

Training Services Division
162-168 Regent Street,
London W1R 6DE
Tel: 01-214 6000

Employment Service Division
7-8 St Martin's Place,
London WC2N 4JH
Tel: 01-930 7833

Commission for Racial Equality
Head Office
Elliot House,
10-12 Allington Street,
London SW1E 5EH
Tel: 01-828 7022

Regional Offices
Daimler House,
Paradise Street,
Birmingham B1 2BJ
Tel: 021-643 8281

Maybrook House,
40 Blackfriars Street,
Manchester M3 2EG
Tel: 061-831 7782-8

133 The Headrow,
Leeds LS1 5QX
Tel: Leeds (0532) 34413/4

Haymarket House, 4th Floor,
Haymarket Shopping Centre,
Leicester LE1 3YG
Tel: 0533 57852

Certification Officer for Trade Unions and Employers' Associations
Head Office
Vincent House Annexe,
Hide Place,
London SW1P 4NG
Tel: 01-821 6144

Scotland
19 Heriot Row,
Edinburgh EH3 6HT
Tel: 031-556 4371

Department of Employment

General Enquiries
England and Wales   Caxton House,
                                 Tothill Street,
                                 London SW1H 9NA
                                 Tel: 01-213 3000

Scotland   43 Jeffrey Street,
                                 Edinburgh EH1 1UU
                                 Tel: 031-556 8433

Regional Offices
Northern   93a Grey Street,
                                 Newcastle NE1 6HE
                                 Tel: Newcastle (0632) 26011

Yorkshire and Humberside   City House,
                                 New Station Street,
                                 Leeds LS1 4JH
                                 Tel: Leeds (0532) 38232

London and   Hanway House,
South Eastern   27 Red Lion Square,
                                 London WC1R 4NH
                                 Tel: 01-405 8454

South Western	The Pithay, Bristol BS1 2NQ Tel: Bristol (0272) 291071
Midlands	2 Duchess Place, Hagley Road, Birmingham B16 8NS Tel: 021–455 7111
North Western	Sunley Buildings, Piccadilly Plaza, Manchester M60 7JS Tel: 061–832 9111
Wales	4th Floor, Companies House, Crown Way, Maindy, Cardiff CF4 3UW Tel: Cardiff (0222) 388588